LIBRARY OF NEW TESTAMENT STUDIES

324

Formerly The Journal For The Study Of The New Testament Supplement Series

Editor
Mark Goodacre

Editorial Board
John M.G. Barclay, Craig Blomberg, Kathleen E. Corley,
R. Alan Culpepper, James D.G. Dunn, Craig A. Evans, Stephen Fowl,
Robert Fowler, Simon J. Gathercole, John S. Kloppenborg, Michael Labahn,
Robert Wall, Steve Walton, Robert L. Webb, Catrin H. Williams

TAKING AWAY THE POUND

WOMEN, THEOLOGY AND THE PARABLE OF THE POUNDS
IN THE GOSPEL OF LUKE

ELIZABETH V. DOWLING

t&t clark

Published by T&T Clark International
A Continuum imprint
The Tower Building, 11 York Road, London SE1 7NX
80 Maiden Lane, Suite 704, New York, NY 10038

www.tandtclark.com

British Library Cataloguing-in-Publication Data
A catalogue record for this book is available from the British Library

ISBN-10: 0-567-04364-9 (hardback)
ISBN-13: 978-0-567-04364-1 (hardback)

Typeset by Data Standards Limited, Frome, Somerset, UK
Printed on acid-free paper in Great Britain by Biddles Ltd, King's Lynn,
Norfolk

To my parents, Bill and Kath Dowling,
with thanks for their love and constant support

Contents

ACKNOWLEDGMENTS

The writing of this book has been a long journey, yet one that I have thoroughly enjoyed. It has been a privilege to be able to undertake this research. Many people have assisted me in various ways throughout my journey. First of all, I wish to express my profound appreciation to Dorothy Lee and Veronica Lawson who have supported and mentored me throughout my research. I thank them for their inspiration, enthusiasm, generosity, depth of knowledge, wisdom and guidance. Both of these women have contributed enormously to Australian biblical scholarship by their own work and by their encouragement of other scholars.

Two academic institutions have been associated with the production of this book. The Melbourne College of Divinity was my research center from 2002 until April 2005. I thank all those associated with the College for their assistance and intellectual stimulation over this time. Since April 2005, I have been lecturing at Australian Catholic University. I am grateful to my colleagues in the School of Theology and the staff at the Aquinas Campus for their ongoing encouragement and support.

In 2003, I presented papers at the Australian Catholic Biblical Association conference in Sydney and a Fellowship for Biblical Studies meeting in Melbourne. The feedback and suggestions I received from both presentations provided significant insights. The staff at the Joint Theological Library in Melbourne have assisted me greatly in obtaining references. I thank them for their knowledge, support, willingness and patience.

My thanks to Anne Elvey, Elaine Wainwright, Barbara Reid, Catherine McCahill and Carmel Powell for their interest in my work and for their helpful comments on my work at different stages of its development. I am grateful to T&T Clark International for publishing my work and to Rebecca Vaughan-Williams for her editorial assistance in preparing the work for publication.

My family kindled my love of learning and ideas, and I am deeply grateful for their constant love. Thanks to my friends whose support and encouragement have helped sustain me over this time. My Mercy sisters have likewise sustained me in many ways and given unfailing support to my engagement with biblical wisdom. I am profoundly grateful to them for the opportunity to pursue my call and to discover new steps in the dance of Mercy.

To all who have contributed in some way to this undertaking, I express my heartfelt appreciation.

ABBREVIATIONS

AB	Anchor Bible
AusBR	*Australian Biblical Review*
BAGD	Walter Bauer, William F. Arndt, F. Wilbur Gingrich and Frederick W. Danker, *A Greek-English Lexicon of the New Testament and Other Early Christian Literature*, 2nd ed. (Chicago: University of Chicago Press, 1979)
BDB	Francis Brown, S. R. Driver and Charles A. Briggs, *A Hebrew and English Lexicon of the Old Testament* (Oxford: Clarendon Press, 1907)
Bib	*Biblica*
BibInt	*Biblical Interpretation: A Journal of Contemporary Approaches*
BJS	Brown Judaic Studies
BT	*The Bible Translator*
BTB	*Biblical Theology Bulletin*
CBQ	*Catholic Biblical Quarterly*
ExpTim	*Expository Times*
FCB	Feminist Companion to the Bible
FCNT	Feminist Companion to the New Testament and Early Christian Writings
GCS	Die griechische christliche Schriftsteller
HeyJ	*Heythrop Journal*
Int	*Interpretation*
JBL	*Journal of Biblical Literature*
JR	*Journal of Religion*
JSNT	*Journal for the Study of the New Testament*
JSNTSup	Journal for the Study of the New Testament, Supplement Series
JSOT	*Journal for the Study of the Old Testament*
JTS	*Journal of Theological Studies*
LCL	Loeb Classical Library
LD	Lectio divina
LXX	Septuagint
NovT	*Novum Testamentum*
NRSV	New Revised Standard Version
NTS	*New Testament Studies*

RevScRel	*Revue des sciences religieuses*
SBL	Society of Biblical Literature
SBLDS	SBL Dissertation Series
SBLSP	SBL Seminar Papers
SNTSMS	Society for New Testament Studies Monograph Series
TDNT	Gerhard Kittel and Gerhard Friedrich (eds.), *Theological Dictionary of the New Testament*, trans. Geoffrey W. Bromiley, 10 vols. (Grand Rapids: Eerdmans, 1964–76)
TTod	*Theology Today*
TynBul	*Tyndale Bulletin*
ZNW	*Zeitschrift für die neutestamentliche Wissenschaft*

Babylonian Talmudic Literature

B. Mez.	*Baba Mezi'a*
Ber.	*Berakoth*
Kid.	*Kiddushin*
Ned.	*Nedarim*

Josephus

Ant.	*Jewish Antiquities*
Apion	*Against Apion*
War	*The Jewish War*

INTRODUCTION

While many have written about the characterizations of women in the Gospel of Luke, fewer scholars have focused on the Parable of the Pounds (Lk. 19.11-28) for detailed examination. As yet, however, no study has had a dual focus on both the Parable of the Pounds and Lukan women. This study will have such a focus, using the parable as a lens through which to view the Lukan women's characterizations.

At first glance it may appear that the Parable of the Pounds has little connection with the characterizations of women in the Lukan Gospel. No woman is identified as playing a role in the parable. Rather, the parable is concerned with a nobleman, his fellow-citizens and his slaves.[1] It is not, however, the similarity (or lack thereof) in content between the parable and the women's stories that is the interest of this study. Instead, the focus is on the power dynamics operating within the stories. I will investigate whether the power dynamic evident in the Parable of the Pounds can shed any light on the dynamic operating in the Lukan women's stories. Can a reading of the Parable of the Pounds which focuses on power dynamics give insight into the characterizations of women in this Gospel?

While the Lukan Parable of the Pounds (Lk. 19.11-28) has obvious similarities with the Matthean Parable of the Talents (Mt. 25.14-30), it also contains another storyline that colors the reading of the entire parable. Against the majority opinion, I will argue that the Lukan parable is a story about the use and abuse of power. The parable is also the story of those who suffer adverse consequences when they oppose unjust power structures.

In this reading of the Parable of the Pounds, a class difference between the characters creates an inequity in power. A further inequity is established by the imperialist structure whereby a foreign country has control over another country. As a result, the nobleman has power over

---

1. It is possible that women could be included in the group of bystanders (19.24-25) but there is no explicit identification that this is the case. The citizens who send a delegation to oppose the nobleman are assumed male since women, according to Roman law, could be of citizen status but were excluded from 'citizen functions.' See Jane F. Gardner, *Women in Roman Law and Society* (Bloomington, IN: Indiana University Press, 1991), 262.

his slaves and the citizens of his country, and the resistance of the third slave and the citizens is the resistance of those who challenge the dominating power structure. In my reading of the parable, I will argue that the actions of the nobleman are exploitative and oppressive, and that those who oppose this oppressive use of power have acted honorably. The opposition and resistance come at a cost, however, as the parable makes clear. The nobleman is threatened by the challenge and seeks to eliminate the opposition, resulting in the less powerful losing what they have. At the same time, those who do not threaten the power structure have the opportunity to benefit under the system. The parable does not explicitly commend the actions of the less powerful nor condemn the oppressive actions of the more powerful. From the wider context of the Gospel of Luke, however, it will be argued that the reader is able to critique such abuse of power.[2]

This suppression of challenge to oppressive power structures evidenced in the Parable of the Pounds fits a pattern that operates in other parts of the Lukan Gospel. We see the pattern, in particular, in the arrest and crucifixion of Jesus. At several points in the Gospel Jesus challenges the religious authorities and it is these who conspire to have Jesus killed (5.29-32; 6.6-11; 11.37-54; 13.10-17; 14.1-6; 20.9-26, 45-47; 22.1-2, 66-71).[3] The Parable of the Pounds holds a strategic position within the Lukan narrative. It comes at the end of Jesus' journey to Jerusalem (9.51–19.28), and leads into his entry into that city (19.29-48). The reader has been told that Jerusalem is the place where Jesus will be killed (18.31-33) but the twelve are yet to understand this (18.34). The dynamics of the parable give insight into the fate awaiting Jesus in Jerusalem. The position of the parable within the Lukan narrative encourages this link with Jesus' story. Earlier in the Gospel we also meet the suppression of challenge to oppressive power structures in the arrest and killing of John the Baptist by Herod. When John the Baptist challenges the actions of the powerful Herod, he is eliminated (3.19-20; 9.9).

The Parable of the Pounds can be seen as a paradigm for the stories of those characters in the Lukan Gospel who 'lose their pound' when they challenge an oppressive power structure, where 'pound' becomes a metaphor for what one has that can be potentially taken away by those in a position of power. For John the Baptist, Jesus and the citizens in the Parable of the Pounds, the 'pound' which each loses for challenging the oppressive power is his life. The taking away of his 'pound' has different

2. In the first century, more people would have *heard* the Gospel of Luke rather than *read* it themselves. Hence, the term 'hearer/reader' may be more appropriate here. For convenience, however, the term 'reader' is used to cover both situations.

3. The religious authorities operate within a context of Roman imperial rule and it is Pilate who ultimately condemns Jesus to death (23.1-25).

consequences for the third slave in the parable. As we will see, the third slave loses the possibility of attaining power or status, and also loses the possibility of freedom.

Given the patriarchal context for the Gospel of Luke, can a dynamic of suppression of challenge to oppressive structures also illuminate the characterization of women in this Gospel? In the following chapter, I will outline diverse scholarly views on the characterization of the Lukan women. While some see this Gospel as portraying women favorably, others argue that women's roles are limited. Can the power dynamic of the Parable of the Pounds help to explain how such a range of positions have emerged? That the Parable of the Pounds describes different outcomes for different slaves, suggests that it may be particularly apposite to providing insight into the different Lukan women's characterizations. In this study I will investigate whether the pattern of taking away the 'pound' is seen within stories of women characters who resist patriarchal ideals and expectations. Do the women who engage in autonomous public actions or speech 'lose out' in some way? If so, what do the women 'lose'? Do any women 'gain' without 'losing out'? Does the dynamic of the Parable of the Pounds give any insight into which women 'lose' and which women 'gain'? The characterizations of the women in the Lukan Gospel will be viewed through the lens of the Parable of the Pounds. New lenses provide new opportunities for perception. I will explore what is opened up by this way of viewing the text.

1. *Hermeneutical Framework and Methodology*

The study will utilize a feminist hermeneutical framework. Since feminism is not a monolithic concept and incorporates a variety of strands, the designation of this study as a 'feminist reading' requires clarification.[4] Robyn Warhol argues that the term 'feminist reading' has two senses based on whether 'reading' focuses on texts or receivers of texts. In the first sense, a 'feminist reading' presumes that gender is a key element in the meaning of a text, influencing the representations within the text or the experience of the author or reader.[5] In the second sense, a 'feminist reading' is concerned with countering patriarchal oppression. It is 'the

---

4. Elisabeth Schüssler Fiorenza identifies a range of different feminist approaches including equal rights/liberal feminism, ecofeminism, postcolonial feminism, and critical liberationist feminism. She adopts the last of these approaches in her own work. For an outline of each approach, see Elisabeth Schüssler Fiorenza, *Wisdom Ways: Introducing Feminist Biblical Interpretation* (Maryknoll, NY: Orbis, 2001), 60–64.

5. Robyn R. Warhol, 'Reading,' in *Feminisms: An Anthology of Literary Theory and Criticism*, (eds.) Robyn R. Warhol and Diane Price Herndl (New Brunswick, NJ: Rutgers University Press, 1991), 489.

reception and processing of texts by a reader who is conceived of not only as possibly female, but also as conscious of the tradition of women's oppression in patriarchal culture. The feminist reader–whether in fact male or female–is committed to breaking the pattern of that oppression by calling attention to the ways some texts can perpetuate it.'[6] Both nuances of 'feminist reading' are appropriate here. In particular, I align myself in this study with the second sense in that I will explore patterns of oppression and attempt to call attention to the way these patterns can be reinforced by a text or by an interpretation.

Since an understanding of 'patriarchy' is integral to this discussion of feminist reading, some discussion of the term is necessary at this point. Patriarchy literally means 'the rule of the father.' According to Gerda Lerner, patriarchy commenced for Western civilization in the Ancient Near East during the third millennium BCE, with the process taking nearly 1500 years to develop.[7] 'Gender – the different roles and behavior deemed appropriate to each of the sexes – was expressed in values, customs, and social roles. During the long period that led to the establishment of patriarchally organized archaic states, gender definitions became institutionalized in laws, the organization of hierarchies and in religion.'[8] The Gospel of Luke was written within the context of the Greco-Roman patriarchal society.

Patriarchy is a system whose sphere of influence extends not just within the family but more broadly to the whole of society. Though women are not powerless within such a system, it is men who occupy the positions of power in the society's key structures. Lerner defines patriarchy as

> the manifestation and institutionalization of male dominance over women and children in the family and the extension of male dominance over women in society in general. It implies that men hold power in all the important institutions of society and that women are deprived of access to such power. It does *not* imply that women are either totally powerless or totally deprived of rights, influence, and resources.[9]

It is important to recognize that women cannot be considered a homogeneous group. Women differ with regard to any number of

6. Warhol, 'Reading,' 489.
7. Gerder Lerner, *Why History Matters: Life and Thought* (New York, NY: Oxford University Press, 1997), 105, 154. Tikva Frymer-Kensky writes, 'The world by the end of the second millennium was a male's world.' However, she questions the usefulness of the term 'patriarchy' in describing gender relationships in the Ancient Near East, due to the 'imprecision' and 'political resonances' of the term. Tikva Frymer-Kensky, *In the Wake of the Goddesses: Women, Culture, and the Biblical Transformation of Pagan Myth* (New York, NY: Free Press, 1992), 80, 120.
8. Lerner, *Why History Matters*, 155.
9. Gerder Lerner, *The Creation of Patriarchy* (New York, NY: Oxford University Press, 1986), 239.

categories, including race, class and religion. Lerner issues an essential caveat: 'If one ignores "differences" one distorts reality. If one ignores the power relations built on differences one reinforces them in the interest of those holding power.'[10]

Differences can be and have been exploited to justify domination: 'There seems to be an implicit understanding that difference must result in hierarchy.'[11] Groups that are different from the hegemonic group are labeled as 'Other' and this is then seen as justification that they should be ruled by the hegemonic group. For Lerner, '[o]nce the system of dominance and hierarchy is institutionalized in custom, law, and practice, it is seen as natural and just and people no longer question it, unless historical circumstances change very dramatically.'[12] Marilyn Frye, likewise, argues that subordination is particularly effective when the structure is perceived to be 'natural' rather than kept in place by human structures. The subordinated group may even accept the domination since it appears inevitable.[13]

It can also be seen that those who are disadvantaged by the society because of 'difference' in one category may dominate those who are 'different' in another category. In this way different disadvantaged groups can be set against each other. Forms of oppression based on gender, class, race, and any other category of difference are interconnected and inseparable. Lerner explains that the multifaceted forms of oppression are all features of the one system of domination and that this system is sustained by the reality which it constructs.[14] Elisabeth Schüssler Fiorenza uses the term 'kyriarchy,' literally the rule of the master or lord (or lady), to refer to such a system: 'Kyriarchy is best theorized as a complex pyramidal system of intersecting multiplicative social structures of superordination and subordination, of ruling and oppression. Kyriarchal relations of domination are built on elite male property rights as well as on the exploitation, dependency, inferiority, and obedience of wo/men.'[15] Like Lerner, Schüssler Fiorenza recognizes the multifaceted forms of oppression and their interrelatedness.

---

10. Lerner, *Why History Matters*, 133.
11. Ranjini Rebera, 'Power and Equality,' *Voices from the Third World* 21, no. 2 (1998): 91.
12. Lerner, *Why History Matters*, 135.
13. Marilyn Frye, *The Politics of Reality: Essays in Feminist Theory* (New York, NY: Crossing Press, 1983), 33–34. See also Mary Ann Tolbert, 'The Politics and Poetics of Location,' in *Reading from this Place: Volume 1, Social Location and Biblical Interpretation in the United States*, (eds.) Fernando F. Segovia and Mary Ann Tolbert (Minneapolis, MN: Fortress Press, 1995), 308.
14. Lerner, *Why History Matters*, 138.
15. Schüssler Fiorenza, *Wisdom Ways*, 118. Schüssler Fiorenza uses the term 'wo/men' to highlight the differences between women and indicate that women do not constitute a

One of the consequences of the interconnectedness of various forms of oppression is that not all women have access to the same level of power and some women reinforce the kyriarchal structure because they benefit from elements of that structure. Thus, for instance, women of color are oppressed by white women, non-elite women by elite women, colonized women by women of the colonizing culture.[16] The differences among women mean that it is not possible to generalize one woman's experience to that of all women. Experience is contingent upon particular social location.[17]

Women from different social locations bring different insights to the study of a text. Musa Dube challenges feminist biblical practitioners to integrate postcolonial insights into their liberationist approach. She defines a postcolonial approach as 'a complex myriad of methods and theories which study a wide range of texts and their participation in the making or subversion of imperialism.'[18] Since 'Two-Thirds World women suffer more from imperialist intrusion ... they are more conscious of it.' Western women who 'benefit from their social location' can overlook such analysis and, as a result, contribute to the maintenance of imperialist structures.[19]

Influences across a range of differences affect both the way a text is constructed and the way in which it is interpreted. In this study, particular attention will be given to difference. The term 'difference' is used here in regard to categories which can be used to oppress, where one in a particular category has power over one in another category. In particular,

---

homogeneous group (p. 216). For a detailed description of patriarchy/kyriarchy in the classical Greco-Roman world, see Elisabeth Schüssler Fiorenza, *But She Said: Feminist Practices of Biblical Interpretation* (Boston, MA: Beacon Press, 1992), 114–20.

16.   For a critique of oppressive practices of Australian women theologians, see Anne Pattel-Gray, 'Not Yet Tiddas: An Aboriginal Womanist Critique of Australian Church Feminism,' in *Freedom and Entrapment: Women Thinking Theology*, (eds.) Maryanne Confoy, Dorothy A. Lee, and Joan Nowotny (Blackburn, Vic: Dove, 1995), 165–92.

17.   My particular social location is that of a white, middle-class Australian woman who is a member of a Catholic religious order. As such I recognize that I have opportunities that are not available to all women and that in some ways I have benefited from the patri/kyriarchal system at the same time as I have been disadvantaged by some elements.

18.   Musa W. Dube, 'Toward A Post-Colonial Feminist Interpretation of the Bible,' *Semeia* 78 (1997): 14. The effects of colonization and neo-colonization on the African story are told in Musa W. Dube, 'Fifty Years of Bleeding: A Storytelling Feminist Reading of Mark 5:24-43,' in *Other Ways of Reading: African Women and the Bible*, (ed.) Musa W. Dube (Atlanta, GA: SBL, 2001), 50–60. For a discussion of the use of postcolonial theory in biblical studies, see Richard A. Horsley, 'Subverting Disciplines: The Possibilities and Limitations of Postcolonial Theory for New Testament Studies,' in *Toward a New Heaven and a New Earth: Essays in Honor of Elisabeth Schüssler Fiorenza*, (ed.) Fernando F. Segovia (Maryknoll, NY: Orbis Books, 2003), 90–105.

19.   Dube, 'Post-Colonial Feminist Interpretation,' 20. My work is informed by postcolonial insights derived from my personal reflection on the so-called 'war on terror.'

power inequities caused by differences in gender, class and imperial strategies will be explored in the text. An attempt will be made in this study to be aware of those who are oppressed by dominant power structures and to listen to voices of resistance to these power structures.

The methodological approach for this study, therefore, must facilitate the exposition of oppressive practices within the text and the exploration of its effects. Consistent with developments in literary theory, biblical criticism has witnessed the rise of a variety of methods of biblical interpretation. In an overview of changes in models of interpretation over the last century, Fernando Segovia describes three different paradigms, though he argues that these 'need not be seen as mutually exclusive but rather as subject to creative interaction.'[20]

The first of these paradigms is historical criticism which was the dominant model of biblical interpretation until the 1970s. Historical criticism is primarily concerned with the world behind the text, 'the author(s) and her or his historical, theological, and ideological agenda as well as the community to which the text was originally addressed and the ancient world in which that community lived.'[21] In this model, the text is perceived as a means to access the original message and intention of the author.[22]

As literary theory began to challenge the focus on the author and the centrality of the author's intention to a reader's interpretation, a new focus emerged – the text itself.[23] This led to the emergence of literary criticism (the second paradigm identified by Segovia) as a model for biblical interpretation. Literary criticism began to focus on the world generated by the text. The text is viewed as a communication between the author and the reader, and the literary and rhetorical nature of the text is explored.[24] As literary criticism developed further, the focus began to swing towards the reader of the text. With the reader's role in the production of meaning highlighted, the concept of the plurality of meanings grew, challenging the concept of a single meaning which was the

20.   Fernando F. Segovia, '"And They Began to Speak in Other Tongues": Competing Modes of Discourse in Contemporary Biblical Criticism,' in *Reading from This Place: Volume 1, Social Location and Biblical Interpretation in the United States,* (eds.) Fernando F. Segovia and Mary Ann Tolbert (Minneapolis, MN: Fortress Press, 1995), 5.

21.   Sandra M. Schneiders, *The Revelatory Text: Interpreting the New Testament as Sacred Scripture* (San Francisco, CA: Harper, 1991), 113.

22.   For a discussion of the principles and shortcomings of historical criticism, see Segovia, 'And They Began,' 9–14.

23.   For a helpful overview of this shift in thinking, see Roger Webster, *Studying Literary Theory: An Introduction,* 2nd edn. (London: Arnold, 1996), 17–24.

24.   Segovia, 'And They Began,' 15. See also Elizabeth Struthers Malbon and Janice Capel Anderson, 'Literary-Critical Methods,' in *Searching the Scriptures. Volume One: A Feminist Introduction,* (ed.) Elisabeth Schüssler Fiorenza (North Blackburn, Vic: Collins-Dove, 1993), 241.

quest of historical criticism.[25] As Teresa Okure explains, 'people whose socio-cultural locations differ from ours will see the same text differently. No reading in any age or context exhausts the possibilities of meaning of a given text.'[26]

The third paradigm which Segovia identifies as developing alongside literary criticism is cultural criticism.[27] Using theory obtained from the social sciences, cultural criticism explores the social and cultural dimensions of the text. The emphasis in this method of interpretation is 'on the text as a product and reflection of its context or world, with specific social and cultural codes inscribed, and hence as a means for reconstructing the sociocultural situation presupposed, reflected, and addressed.'[28] While this model has links with historical criticism in looking at the world behind the text, the concern is with the social and cultural dimensions of the text and its ideological nature.

In addition to the three paradigms for biblical interpretation outlined above, Segovia identifies the seeds of a further paradigm which has emerged from the increasing awareness of the significance of the real reader in an act of interpretation. The concept of the objective and impartial reader to which historical criticism aspired is 'a praiseworthy goal but also quite naive and dangerous.'[29] Instead, the real reader is understood to be 'always positioned and interested; socially and historically conditioned and unable to transcend such conditions.'[30] Segovia describes the seeds of the new paradigm in terms of 'cultural studies' – 'a joint critical study of texts and readers, perspectives and ideologies.'[31]

Elaine Wainwright also sees the interaction of text, readers and context as important to biblical interpretation. Working within a feminist hermeneutical framework, Wainwright names the combination of methods which she employs an 'engendered reading.' Her reading incorporates three foci: The *poetics of engendered reading* focuses on the text, the *rhetorics of engendered reading* focuses on the reader, and the *politics of engendered reading* focuses on the context.[32] Wainwright,

25. See Segovia, 'And They Began,' 15–20, for a detailed outline of the rise of literary criticism and its principles.
26. Teresa Okure, ' "I Will Open My Mouth in Parables" (Matt 13.35): A Case for a Gospel-Based Biblical Hermeneutics,' *NTS* 46 (2000): 461.
27. Segovia, 'And They Began,' 21.
28. Segovia, 'And They Began,' 22.
29. Segovia, 'And They Began,' 29. See also Kerry M. Craig and Margret A. Kristjansson, 'Women Reading as Men/Women Reading as Women: A Structural Analysis for the Historical Project,' *Semeia* 51 (1990): 121–22.
30. Segovia, 'And They Began,' 28–29. As Teresa Okure notes, 'No scholarship is context free, value free or purpose free.' Okure, 'Gospel-Based Biblical Hermeneutics,' 455.
31. Segovia, 'And They Began,' 29.
32. See Elaine M. Wainwright, *Shall We Look For Another? A Feminist Rereading of the Matthean Jesus* (Maryknoll, NY: Orbis, 1998), 19–32.

however, highlights the interconnectedness of text, reader and context: 'Within the feminist paradigm as interactive, the gospel *text* is not seen as a fixed object in dualistic opposition to reader/interpreter or to social context. Rather, it is "actor and agent" in acts of meaning construction that constitute a dialogical process. It encodes a network of connections that link it to an entire socio-symbolic system.'[33]

I aim in this study to use the Parable of the Pounds as a lens through which to view stories of women in the Lukan Gospel. Consequently, I am concerned with such features of the text as structure, characterization and plot. I also explore how the reader shapes and is shaped by the text. Further, I will draw on social and cultural contexts which influence and are influenced by the text and, finally, I will consider some implications for a present reading of the text. In the study, therefore, I will focus on text, reader and context, and their interconnectedness.[34] These foci suggest that a combination of methods drawn from literary criticism, cultural criticism and cultural studies be employed.

Since the term 'reader' can incorporate a variety of understandings, some clarification is required here. Tremper Longman argues that '[i]t is appropriate to make some distinctions when referring to the reader of the text. One may speak of the original reader, the later reader, and the implied reader.' The first readers of the text comprise the original audience, while '[t]he later reader refers to the history of interpretation and contemporary interpretations.'[35] The implied reader can be defined as the 'image of "the reader in the text": the reader presupposed or produced by the text as (in some theories) its ideal interpreter.'[36]

In this study, the term 'reader' will refer to real readers – of the first century and of the present day – rather than an ideal reader. As Wainwright explains, '[r]eaders from both these socio-cultural contexts did not and do not perfectly fulfil the task of being ideal readers according to the constructions within the text. Hence multiple factors in the reader's social context shape the reading and its rhetorical and persuasive

---

33. Wainwright, *Shall We Look?*, 21. Gale A. Yee also offers a critical framework for biblical criticism in Gale A. Yee, 'The Author/Text/Reader and Power: Suggestions for a Critical Framework for Biblical Studies,' in *Reading from this Place: Volume 1, Social Location and Biblical Interpretation in the United States*, (eds.) Fernando F. Segovia and Mary Ann Tolbert (Minneapolis, MN: Fortress Press, 1995), 109–18. Yee claims that privileging any of the three elements – author/text/reader – over the other two is problematic. She argues that the focus should be on the way in which power influences the author, text and reader.

34. As such, I am influenced by Wainwright's methodological approach.

35. Tremper Longman, *Literary Approaches to Biblical Interpretation* (Grand Rapids, MI/Leicester: Academie Books/Apollos, 1987), 67.

36. Stephen D. Moore, *Literary Criticism and the Gospels: The Theoretical Challenge* (New Haven, CT: Yale University Press, 1989), 46.

effects.'[37] At the same time, I recognize that the image of these real readers is influenced by my own assumptions, hermeneutical stance and context. That is, the readers assumed in a study are '*heuristic constructs* imaged by the interpreters themselves.'[38]

As previously noted, the study will pay attention to difference. The theoretical work of Mikhail Bakhtin, which explores the dialogic process associated with language, can be of assistance in this endeavor.[39] Of particular interest to this study is Bakhtin's consideration that different languages or voices can be identified within a text,[40] and that such 'heteroglossia' produces multiplicity and contradiction within the text. Furthermore, different voices emerge from different social locations.[41]

While 'centripetal' forces of language emphasize one language and strive for unity, they are opposing 'the realities of heteroglossia' promoted by 'centrifugal' forces: 'Alongside the centripetal forces, the centrifugal forces of language carry on their uninterrupted work; alongside verbal-ideological centralization and unification, the uninterrupted processes of decentralization and disunification go forward.'[42] Thus, while dominant voices may give the appearance on the surface of unity within a text, different voices can create ambiguities and fissures in the text. In Chapter 6 of this study, some consideration will be given to dominant voices and resistant voices within the Gospel of Luke.

The presence of multiple voices in the Gospel of Luke is observed by Gary Phillips who adds that the Lukan text 'is itself the intersecting space of many texts and discourses (both implicit and explicit) drawn from a variety of sources and traditions.'[43] The heteroglossia of the Lukan text

---

37. Wainwright, *Shall We Look?*, 28. Wainwright is focusing here on the Matthean text but her argument applies equally to the Lukan text. Frances Young claims that an ethical reading must take account of the gap that exists between the actual reader and the reader implied by the text. See Frances Young, 'Allegory and the Ethics of Reading,' in *The Open Text: New Directions for Biblical Studies*, (ed.) Frances Watson (London: SCM Press, 1993), 109.

38. John A. Darr, *On Character Building: The Reader and the Rhetoric of Characterization in Luke-Acts* (Louisville, KY: Westminster/John Knox Press, 1992), 21. See also Wainwright, *Shall We Look?*, 28.

39. See M. M. Bakhtin, *The Dialogic Imagination: Four Essays*, (ed.) Michael Holquist, trans. Caryl Emerson and Michael Holquist (Austin, TX: University of Texas Press, 1981).

40. Though Bakhtin focuses on the different voices in a novel, his theory is also applicable to the Gospel of Luke. Cf. Wainwright, *Shall We Look?*, 36, who applies Bakhtin's theory to the Gospel of Matthew.

41. Bakhtin, *Dialogic Imagination*, 271–72.

42. Bakhtin, *Dialogic Imagination*, 272.

43. Gary A. Phillips, '"What is Written? How Are You Reading?" Gospel, Intertextuality and Doing Lukewise: A Writerly Reading of Lk 10:25-37 (and 38-42),' in *SBL 1992 Seminar Papers*, (ed.) Eugene H. Lovering Jr., SBLSP 31 (Atlanta, GA: Scholars Press, 1992), 272.

reflects the 'variety of sources and traditions' with a multiplicity of voices speaking from a multiplicity of social locations. While this variety of traditions is shaped by an author, different voices which reflect this variety can be heard within the text. '[T]he voices from the margins are still present and can be heard by the attentive ear.'[44] Attention to different voices can give insight, not only into resistance to dominant ideologies, but also into attempts to silence these voices.

In highlighting oppressive practices and their suppression of resisting voices, it is important to be aware of who is given voice and who is not given voice. A key element of this study, therefore, will be the category of speech and/or silence and the power dynamics it reinforces. Within this category, a distinction will be made between speech in public and private settings. This will assist in identifying the rhetoric surrounding women's voices in the Gospel of Luke. As we will see, different dynamics are evident for women's speech in different settings. Linking elements of the characterizations of slaves in the Parable of the Pounds and the characterizations of Lukan women is another key feature of the study. While several scholars have undertaken studies of the women's characterizations in the Gospel of Luke, using the Parable of the Pounds as a lens through which to view the women's portrayal is a unique contribution of this investigation.

For this study, then, issues of slavery, different forms of oppression, speech/silence and public/private space become central. These issues inform the study, giving insight into the social and cultural context which shapes and is shaped by the text. In the remainder of this introductory chapter, these issues will be explored. Furthermore, the ongoing influence of the rhetoric shaping and shaped by the text will be highlighted.

2. *Women and Slaves in the Greco-Roman World*

The first area of the socio-cultural context for investigation will be the relationships between the portrayals of women and slaves in the ancient Greco-Roman world, since to link the Parable of the Pounds with Lukan stories about women is to link stories about slaves and women. It must be made clear that this study is in no way attempting to equate the lived experiences of all first-century women and slaves, although slave-women are in both categories. Clearly, different social locations lead to different experiences. Moreover, in the ancient Greco-Roman world the status and power of women varied considerably, being influenced by such

---

44. Suzanne Kehde, 'Voices from the Margin: Bag Ladies and Others,' in *Feminism, Bakhtin, and the Dialogic*, (eds.) Dale M. Bauer and Susan Jaret McKinstry (Albany, NY: State University of New York Press, 1991), 28. Kehde's comment here on the heteroglossia of the novel applies also to the Gospel of Luke.

factors as class and location. So too did the situation and opportunities of slaves vary, depending on the positions and dispositions of their masters. Thus, in practice, there was no unified status for either women or slaves. While this was the case in practice, however, some of the literature of the Greco-Roman world reflects a particular understanding of free women and slaves in relation to free men. The pervasive writings of the fourth-century BCE Greek philosopher Aristotle, for instance, discuss the natures of women and slaves and can provide a link between an elite male perception of women and slaves in the ancient world.

In Aristotle's understanding, a woman is a 'deformed male':

> Just as it sometimes happens that deformed offspring are produced by deformed parents, and sometimes not, so the offspring produced by a female are sometimes female, sometimes not, but male. The reason is that the female is as it were a deformed male; and the menstrual discharge is semen, though in an impure condition; *i.e.*, it lacks one constituent, and one only, the principle of Soul.[45]

The woman is described not in terms of what she is but rather of what she is lacking.[46] That which she is lacking and which the man possesses makes the woman inferior to the man: '[T]he male is by nature superior and the female inferior, the male ruler and the female subject.'[47] In the words of Christine M. Senack: 'specifically woman is privation of man, and that which she lacks is important and vital to being treated as an equal on the sociological level.'[48]

Slaves also can be perceived in Aristotelian thought to be of a different nature from free men: 'It is manifest therefore that there are cases of people of whom some are freemen and the others slaves by nature, and for these slavery is an institution both expedient and just.'[49] While Aristotle argues that slaves by their nature are ruled by free men, as are women, he identifies a distinct difference between the natures of women and slaves:

> [T]here are by nature various classes of rulers and ruled. For the free rules the slave, the male the female, and the man the child in a different way. And all possess the various parts of the soul, but possess them in different ways; for the slave has not got the deliberative part at all, and

---

45. Aristotle, *Generation of Animals* 737a25–30. See also Aristotle, *Generation of Animals* 775a10–20. In this study, the classical texts used are from the Loeb Classical Library.

46. Christine M. Senack, 'Aristotle on the Woman's Soul,' in *Engendering Origins: Critical Feminist Readings in Plato and Aristotle*, (ed.) Bat-Ami Bar On (Albany, NY: State University of New York Press, 1994), 228.

47. Aristotle, *Politics* 1254b14–15.

48. Senack, 'Aristotle,' 229.

49. Aristotle, *Politics* 1255a1–3.

the female has it, but without full authority, while the child has it, but in an undeveloped form.[50]

Thus, according to Aristotle, those who are slaves by nature are lesser than women because they have no deliberative ability at all. Woman is described as 'an inferior class' whereas the slave is described as 'wholly paltry.'[51] In using the term 'woman' here, Aristotle cannot be referring to a slave woman since, according to his definition, a woman, unlike a slave, has a deliberative ability. Therefore, in his use of the term 'woman,' Aristotle is referring to a free woman and gender issues and class issues are intertwined.[52]

The writings of Aristotle propose that free women differ from slaves (male and female) in 'function, virtue, and nature.'[53] Yet these writings also suggest that free women and slaves are connected by their inferiority to free men. While Aristotle argues for differences between the manners of rule, the free man rules both the slave and the free woman.[54] As Spelman understands it: '[t]o twist a phrase from Nietzsche, Aristotle holds that women and slaves are human, but not too human.'[55]

Aristotle's writing establishes a link between free women and slaves in that both are to be ruled by free men. Women and slaves are thus linked in their deemed inferiority to free men. As Lerner explains, Aristotle's fourth-century BCE ideas were influential in the ongoing development of Western thought:

> In the democratic polis based on slavery, about which Aristotle was writing, the very definition of citizenship had to exclude all those deemed inferior—helots, slaves, women. Thus, Aristotle's political science institutionalizes and rationalizes the exclusion of women from political citizenship as the very foundation of the democratic polity. It is

50. Aristotle, *Politics* 1260a8–14.

51. Aristotle, *Poetics* 1454a20. See also Elizabeth V. Spelman, 'Who's Who in the Polis,' in *Engendering Origins: Critical Feminist Readings in Plato and Aristotle*, (ed.) Bat-Ami Bar On (Albany, NY: State University of New York Press, 1994), 102.

52. For further discussion on Aristotle's use of the term 'woman,' see Spelman, 'Who's Who,' 103–5; also Carolyn Osiek, 'Female Slaves, *Porneia*, and the Limits of Obedience,' in *Early Christian Families in Context: An Interdisciplinary Dialogue*, (eds.) David L. Balch and Carolyn Osiek (Grand Rapids, MI: Eerdmans, 2003), 255–56; and Mary Ann Tolbert, 'Social, Sociological, and Anthropological Methods,' in *Searching the Scriptures: A Feminist Introduction*, (ed.) Elisabeth Schüssler Fiorenza (North Blackburn, Vic: Collins Dove, 1993), 265.

53. Spelman, 'Who's Who,' 102.

54. For a discussion of the natural inferiority of women and slaves in Aristotle's view, see Page duBois, *Centaurs and Amazons: Women and the Pre-History of the Great Chain of Being* (Ann Arbor, MI: University of Michigan Press, 1991), 141–45.

55. Spelman, 'Who's Who,' 107.

this heritage ... which Western civilization would use for centuries in its
science, its philosophy, and its gender doctrine.[56]

In fact, Lerner describes Aristotelian philosophy's assumption of women's
inferiority as a 'founding metaphor' of Western civilization.[57]

The Parable of the Pounds and the stories of women in the Gospel of
Luke, then, are not as disconnected as may have appeared at first glance.
Both the parable and the women stories deal with 'inferior beings'
according to Aristotle's philosophy which had an ongoing influence. A
link between free women and slaves is also found in the first-century CE
writings of Josephus, who asserts that both women and slaves are
unacceptable witnesses: 'From women let no evidence be accepted,
because of the levity and temerity of their sex; neither let slaves bear
witness because of the baseness of their soul, since whether from cupidity
or fear it is like that they will not attest the truth.'[58] Unlike the ontological
difference between men and women pronounced by Aristotle, Josephus'
perception of women here presumes more of a moral difference.
Nevertheless, once again in the writings of an elite male, women and
slaves are linked by their perceived deficiency in comparison with free
men. Sheila Briggs also finds a link between the status of women and that
of slaves in Galatians: 'The juxtaposition of gender and slavery in
Galatians 3–4 should make it difficult to separate the question of the
status of women in early Christian communities from that of slaves.'[59]

Thus, I am not alone in making connections between the status of
women and slaves in the Greco-Roman world: 'Women and slaves were
similarly distinguished from free men by their social subordination and
their imagined otherness. Both were excluded from full participation in
political life; both occupied an ambiguous position in the patrilocal family
as indispensable outsiders; and both were viewed as morally deficient and

---

56.   Lerner, *Creation of Patriarchy*, 211. duBois, *Centaurs and Amazons*, 9, also notes the
ongoing influence of Aristotle's (and Plato's) thoughts: 'Hierarchical ideas of difference
formulated by Plato and Aristotle continue to define relations of dominance and submission
in Western culture and in philosophical discourse today.' Sarah B. Pomeroy, *Goddesses,
Whores, Wives, and Slaves: Women in Classical Antiquity* (New York, NY: Schocken, 1975),
180, notes the presence of Aristotelian views in a speech represented by Livy centuries later.

57.   Lerner, *Creation of Patriarchy*, 10.

58.   Josephus, *Ant.* 4.219. Josephus accords women an inferior status to men: 'The
woman, says the Law, is in all things inferior to the man.' Josephus, *Apion* 2.201. For further
discussion of Josephus' perceptions and portrayals of women, see Cheryl Anne Brown, *No
Longer Be Silent: First Century Jewish Portraits of Biblical Women* (Louisville, KY:
Westminster/John Knox Press, 1992).

59.   Sheila Briggs, 'Slavery and Gender,' in *On the Cutting Edge: The Study of Women in
Biblical Worlds*, (eds.) Jane Schaberg, Alice Bach, and Esther Fuchs (New York, NY:
Continuum, 2003), 174–75.

potentially dangerous.'[60] Within the patriarchal and slave societies of this ancient world, however, being a woman and being a slave were 'very different kinds of liability,' though female slaves were in both categories. While there was a possibility of slaves becoming free at some stage of their life, gender did not change. Moreover, free women did not have the property status attached to slaves and so had an honor not available to slaves.[61] Thus, while there were some similarities in the subordinate status of women and slaves, there were also differences.

Some further exploration of slavery in the ancient world will help to inform our discussion of the Parable of the Pounds. In discussing slavery in the ancient Greco-Roman world, M. I. Finley highlights three components – the slave's property status, the totality of the power over the slave, and the denial of legal kinship bonds for slaves.[62] As property, slaves not only lose control over their labor but also lose control over their very persons.[63]

It is important to recognize, though, that varied contexts resulted in quite different situations for slaves in the Greco-Roman world. Carolyn Osiek notes, for instance, that while agricultural slaves provided labor for large agricultural estates, urban slaves were often 'trusted agents and administrators in business affairs' and their status was dependent on the class and status of their owners.[64] Slaves, therefore, did not have a fixed social location. Moreover, from a purely material perspective, some slaves would have been better off than some of the free poor, and those slaves of the Roman emperor had the possibility of attaining 'political influence and relatively high social esteem.'[65]

The manumission of slaves was not uncommon in the ancient Greco-Roman world,[66] and manumission can be described as a slave's 'most precious of hopes.'[67] One of the motives for manumission was to reward slaves for faithful service and obedience over time. The possibility of future manumission acted as an incentive and reward for slaves and so

60. Sandra R. Joshel and Sheila Murnaghan, 'Introduction: Differential Equations,' in *Women and Slaves in Greco-Roman Culture: Differential Equations*, (eds.) Sandra R. Joshel and Sheila Murnaghan (London: Routledge, 1998), 3.

61. Joshel and Murnaghan, 'Differential Equations,' 3.

62. M. I. Finley, *Ancient Slavery and Modern Ideology* (London: Chatto and Windus, 1980), 75, 77.

63. Finley, *Ancient Slavery*, 73–74.

64. Carolyn Osiek, 'Slavery in the Second Testament World,' *BTB* 22 (1992): 175.

65. K. R. Bradley, *Slaves and Masters in the Roman Empire: A Study in Social Control* (Bruxelles: Latomus, 1984), 15. See also Osiek, 'Slavery,' 176; and Jennifer A. Glancy, *Slavery in Early Christianity* (Oxford: Oxford University Press, 2002), 111.

66. Glancy argues, however, that while many slaves received manumission, most did not and therefore died as slaves. See Glancy, *Slavery*, 94.

67. Glancy, *Slavery*, 93.

served to control slave behavior.[68] Slaves could also pay their own manumission price if they were able to accumulate a considerable amount of money themselves. This was a possibility for slaves in some occupations but was not possible for the majority of slaves.[69]

Despite the variation in situations of slaves and the possibility for some slaves to achieve influence, K. R. Bradley makes an important qualification:

> The distinction between slavery and freedom was not meaningless, and no matter how relatively privileged some slaves may have been they nonetheless remained the juridical peers of those less fortunate. Indeed, Cicero gives important expression to the idea that whereas slaves themselves may have been conscious of their own distinct statuses, from the master's point of view they were all servile regardless.[70]

Furthermore, as commodities, slaves were often used for the maximum benefit of their slave-owners and so were the constant subjects of social and economic exploitation.[71]

An important difference in situation between a slave and a free person was that a slave's body was often the subject of punishment or abuse.[72] Greco-Roman slaves were regularly subjected to brutality and acts of violence, either as punishment or as a result of the capriciousness of their owner. Punishments and acts of cruelty included flogging, shackling, torture, sexual abuse and execution.[73] A slave who offended the slave-owner could expect severe punishment.[74] Additionally, a slave was considered to be sexually available to the owner. Thus, the bodies of slaves were constantly vulnerable to both corporal punishment and sexual use and abuse.[75] In theory, under Roman law a slave's complaints of cruel treatment could be heard by a city prefect or governor, but in practice it is questionable how frequently a slave would have been successful in such a procedure.[76]

Several parables within the New Testament feature interactions

---

68. See Osiek, 'Slavery,' 176; Bradley, *Slaves and Masters*, 83; and Mary Ann Beavis, 'Ancient Slavery as an Interpretive Context for the New Testament Servant Parables with Special Reference to the Unjust Steward (Luke 16:1-8),' *JBL* 111 (1992): 43.

69. Bradley, *Slaves and Masters*, 106–8.

70. Bradley, *Slaves and Masters*, 17–18.

71. Bradley, *Slaves and Masters*, 18.

72. See Demosthenes, *Orations* 22.55.

73. See Bradley, *Slaves and Masters*, 118–22; Beavis, 'Ancient Slavery,' 42–43; and Finley, *Ancient Slavery*, 95.

74. Bradley, *Slaves and Masters*, 122.

75. The vulnerability of a slave's body is highlighted in Glancy, *Slavery*. Glancy argues that the bodies of female and young male slaves were particularly vulnerable to being used for their master's sexual pleasure (pp. 21–23).

76. Bradley, *Slaves and Masters*, 123–24.

between slaves and their masters,[77] and advice to slaves and masters also features among household codes within some New Testament letters. These household codes reinforce a hierarchical structure in describing the relationships between husbands and wives, masters and slaves, and parents and children (Col. 3.18–4.1; Eph. 5.21–6.9; 1 Tim. 2.8-15, 3.4, 6.1-2; Tit. 2.2-10; 1 Pet. 2.18–3.6). Wives are instructed to be obedient to their husbands, slaves obedient to their masters, and children to their parents. Women and slaves are therefore instructed to be submissive to those who have authority over them, with obedience and submission portrayed as virtues. Free men are portrayed in a position of authority over both women and slaves. Hence, the ethic evidenced in Aristotelian writing of privileging free men over free women and slaves (male and female) can also be seen to be evident in these household codes written several centuries later.[78]

Osiek notes that, within the New Testament period, slavery was taken for granted and not challenged, although she claims that 'Christian teaching attempted to humanize the relationships.'[79] We find in some of the household codes, for instance, injunctions to masters to treat their slaves justly and fairly and not to threaten them (Col. 4.1; Eph. 6.9). Nevertheless, the basic patriarchal structure remains.[80]

Points of connection between lives of slaves and women in the ancient world are considered by Osiek. She points out that 'women and slaves of the ancient Greco-Roman world shared much in common within the male perspective of the patriarchal household' and that both groups by their nature, according to Aristotle, were fit to be ruled rather than to rule.[81] At the same time, Osiek emphasizes Aristotle's distinction between free women and slave women. A female slave is at 'the bottom of the dominated heap' and 'doubly images body that is to be conquered and dominated, both as female in sex and as slave in class,'[82] highlighting the vulnerability of the body of a female slave.

We can conclude that the experiences of slaves varied in the ancient world, some having the possibility to obtain influence and status, but that all slaves were subject to exploitation and were vulnerable to corporal

77. Slavery in the Lukan Jesus' parables and teachings is discussed further in Chapter 3.
78. While Aristotle's writing may have had an indirect influence on the household codes, Aristotle's image of woman as a 'deformed male' does not feature in the codes. This ancient Greek concept differs from the Hebrew tradition of woman and man both created in the image of God (Gen. 1.27).
79. Osiek, 'Slavery,' 178.
80. Glancy, *Slavery*, 144, queries what Roman slave holders would have understood by just and fair treatment, and asks whether corporal punishment would be considered within these parameters.
81. Osiek, 'Female Slaves,' 255.
82. Osiek, 'Female Slaves,' 256.

punishment and sexual abuse. Slaves were property to be used for the benefit of the owner and had no legal kinship bonds. Freedom in later life for faithful service was an incentive which served to control slave behavior.

An informed reader brings this material on slavery in the ancient world to the discussion in later chapters of the power dynamics and oppression evident in the Parable of the Pounds. As we have seen, a slave who resists following the master's orders risks corporal punishment, as well as losing opportunities for advancement and future manumission. Such a slave knows well the consequences of resistance. Bringing this context to a reading of the Parable of the Pounds influences the way the reader perceives the third slave and the risk involved in his course of action.

The violence evidenced in the Parable of the Pounds is overt. The nobleman commands that the pound of the third slave be taken away from him despite the protestations of bystanders (19.24-26). Further, the nobleman orders that those citizens who had opposed his rule be brought before him and slaughtered (19.27). While such physical violence is not present in the women's stories, the stories will be explored in order to discover whether other forms of violence and oppression are evidenced in the text nonetheless. The following examination of different forms of oppression will inform this investigation of the Lukan women's characterizations. Silencing, as a particular aspect of oppression, will be a prime focus since the dynamics of speech and silence are integral to this study.

3. *The Oppression of Silencing*

Oppression can be manifested in a variety of ways. In a study of oppression of contemporary social groups, political scientist Iris Marion Young observes that not all oppressed groups experience oppression to the same extent nor in the same ways. She develops five faces of oppression – exploitation, marginalization, powerlessness, cultural imperialism and violence.[83] Young claims that being subject to any of these categories is sufficient for a group to be considered oppressed. Different oppressed groups may experience different combinations of these categories, as may different individuals within each group.[84] The extent and form of oppression experienced is determined by the particular combination of criteria that are applicable. While oppression can result from the intentions of a tyrant, Young explains that oppression can also

---

83. Iris Marion Young, *Justice and the Politics of Difference* (Princeton: Princeton University Press, 1990), 40. See also Elisabeth Schüssler Fiorenza, *Sharing Her Word: Feminist Biblical Intepretation in Context* (Boston, MA: Beacon Press, 1998), 29–31.

84. Young, *Justice*, 64.

be structural involving systemic constraints on groups. The causes of structural oppression 'are embedded in unquestioned norms, habits, and symbols, in the assumptions underlying institutional rules and the collective consequence of following those rules.'[85]

Within Young's study the categories of exploitation, marginalization and powerlessness relate to the social division of labor. Exploitation involves the labor of one group being used to benefit another group. Marginalized people are those whom the labor system either cannot use or chooses not to use. Among other injustices, powerlessness is associated with being restricted in developing one's capabilities and being treated contemptuously because of one's status.[86] Young clarifies what she classes as cultural imperialism: 'To experience cultural imperialism means to experience how the dominant meanings of a society render the particular perspective of one's own group invisible at the same time as they stereotype one's group and mark it out as the Other.'[87] Although the category of violence focuses on physical violence, she also includes harassment, intimidation or ridicule used to degrade, humiliate or stigmatize.[88] Thus, Young also takes psychological elements of violence into account.

While Young's study centers on contemporary groups and definitions, her categories of oppression can inform this exploration of the women's characterizations in the Gospel of Luke since categories of marginalization, cultural imperialism and violence, in particular, are relevant to this study. It will be the Lukan text, however, rather than the system of labor which will be under particular focus.

To Young's list of criteria, Schüssler Fiorenza adds two more which she claims to be particularly applicable to women in theology and religion. The added criteria are 'Silencing' and 'Vilification and Trivialization.'[89] It is not necessary, however, to make silencing and vilification and trivialization into additional criteria. They can be incorporated into Young's criteria, becoming particular aspects of marginalization, cultural imperialism and violence, for example. The violence generated by silencing and vilification and trivialization is not necessarily a physical violence. It may rather incorporate psychological abuse which can be equally debilitating. Schüssler Fiorenza's comments are significant, however, since they draw attention to silencing, vilification and trivialization as important aspects of oppression. As such, they will be given detailed consideration.

---

85. Young, *Justice*, 41.
86. Young, *Justice*, 49–58.
87. Young, *Justice*, 58–59.
88. Young, *Justice*, 61.
89. Schüssler Fiorenza, *Sharing Her Word*, 31.

In this study I will explore the Lukan Gospel and assess whether any of Young's criteria (which incorporate Schüssler Fiorenza's criteria) apply to the social group of women within the text. Such an exploration will enable a judgment to be made as to whether or not the Lukan Gospel's women characters are an oppressed group i.e. whether or not they are subject to marginalization, cultural imperialism, violence or any other of Young's categories of oppression. As an important part of this exploration, patterns of speech and silence will be investigated to highlight the rhetoric of the text in regard to the portrayal of women. For each woman character in the Lukan Gospel narrative, the following will be considered among the woman's overall portrayal:

- Does the woman speak or does she remain silent?
- If she does speak, are her words directly reported?
- To whom and in the presence of whom does the woman speak, if at all?
- How are the woman's words received? What is the response to her words?

Of course, the actions of the women characters are also important and will therefore also be considered in the exploration of the Gospel rhetoric. In some cases it may be argued that 'actions speak louder than words' as the adage informs us. The Hebrew word דבר usually carries the meaning 'speech' or 'word,' but in the plural it can also mean 'acts.'[90] Thus דבר connects word and action. The two are further linked by the consideration of symbol. Both word and action are capable of expressing the symbolic. Within the prophetic tradition of the Hebrew Scriptures this can be seen, for example, in the image of Israel as the unfruitful vineyard in Isa. 5.1-8, and in the marriage of Hosea to a prostitute in Hos. 1.2-9. A prophet's message can be expressed symbolically in both word and deed. Both speech and actions, therefore, have significance in characterization. As we will see, however, speech creates its own dynamic.[91]

From his study of Hebrew biblical narrative, Robert Alter concludes that biblical writers prefer direct speech to indirect speech, and he notes that thought is often rendered as direct speech. Comparing direct discourse to indirect, he claims that '[t]he difference between the two forms of presentation is not trivial' and that direct speech 'has the effect of bringing the speech-act into the foreground.'[92] Hence, Alter is aware of the power of direct speech. I will explore in this study whether the preference for direct speech is evident in the women's stories in the Lukan

90. See BDB, 182–83.

91. I recognize that there are cultural differences in the value attributed to speech and that my interest in direct speech is influenced by my particular social location.

92. Robert Alter, *The Art of Biblical Narrative* (New York, NY: Basic Books, 1981), 67. Alter draws out the significance of direct speech on pp. 63–87.

Gospel, and will consider the effect on characterization when direct speech is not included.

Alter describes various ways in which narratives can influence a reader's concept of a character:

> Now, in reliable third-person narrations, such as in the Bible, there is a scale of means, in ascending order of explicitness and certainty, for conveying information about the motives, the attitudes, the moral nature of characters. Character can be revealed through the report of actions; through appearance, gestures, posture, costume; through one character's comments on another; through direct speech by the character; through inward speech, either summarized or quoted as interior monologue; or through statements by the narrator about the attitudes and intentions of the personages, which may come either as flat assertions or motivated explanations.[93]

Thus, according to Alter, direct or inward speech gives a more reliable insight into character than the report of actions, though he acknowledges that 'speech may reflect the occasion more than the speaker.' Alter accords the greatest certainty, however, to 'the reliable narrator's explicit statement of what the characters feel, intend, desire.'[94]

Within a literary work, the narrator is a rhetorical device used by the author and has significant influence on the reader:[95] 'The narrator plays a pivotal role in shaping the reaction of the reader to the passage he or she is reading. The narrator achieves this response in a variety of ways, from presenting and withholding information from the reader to explicit commentary.'[96] The actions of a character who remains silent are represented and interpreted by another – either another character who has voice within the narrative or the narrator – in conjunction with the reader. The representation and interpretation of the one who has voice influences the process of interpretation of the actions of the silent one. For those characters who do speak in the narrative, the narrator can present or withhold the direct speech. When direct speech is recorded, the voice of the character is heard but when speech is indirect or merely implied, the reader hears the voice of the narrator rather than the speaker. The power of the narrator in the process of meaning-making, therefore, should not be ignored.

Since this study focuses on the Gospel of Luke, the role of the Lukan narrator cannot be ignored. Darr describes the narrator of Luke-Acts as 'omniscient, omnipresent, retrospective, and fully reliable.' He considers

93. Alter, *Biblical Narrative*, 116–17; see also Darr, *On Character Building*, 43–44.
94. Alter, *Biblical Narrative*, 117.
95. R. Alan Culpepper, *Anatomy of the Fourth Gospel: A Study in Literary Design* (Philadelphia, PA: Fortress Press, 1983), 16; and Longman, *Literary Approaches*, 85.
96. Longman, *Literary Approaches*, 85.

the narrator's point of view in the Gospel of Luke as 'god-like' since it is authenticated by a ' "*divine*" frame of reference.'[97] As such, Darr claims that 'the reader's evaluation of and identification with (or sympathy for) various characters is largely controlled by the narrator.'[98] The reliability of the Lukan narrator, though, needs to be examined more closely. In what sense is the narrator reliable? Darr argues that 'the narrator is reliable in that his perspective is always borne out in the text and he always speaks in accord with its norms. In other words, he fully represents the implied author.'[99] Whether the narrator is reliable in portraying men's and women's speech in a similar fashion, however, will be investigated in this study.

Examining patterns within a text of who has voice, who remains silent, and who is effectively silenced can give insight into power dynamics operating in a text, and can highlight aspects of oppression. Silence can be understood differently in varied situations. Sometimes silence has a distinctive quality which surpasses all words. Silence may be the appropriate response when experiencing wonder or revelation. At other times, one may choose to be silent to portray a symbolic message, to emphasize a particular point or to exercise power.[100] In these situations the power dynamic is very different from one in which silence results from fear or from force, when silence results from silencing. Silence, then, is ambiguous and complex. It can represent a positive response or choice or a way of exerting influence. It can also result from abuse of power. It is in the latter case that silencing becomes an aspect of various forms of oppression.

The power of voice, then, should not be underestimated. In *The Origins of Greek Thought*, Jean-Pierre Vernant describes the importance of public speech within the ancient Greek world: 'The system of the *polis* implied, first of all, the extraordinary preeminence of speech over all other instruments of power. Speech became the political tool par excellence, the key to all authority in the state, the means of commanding and dominating others.'[101] In such a system where public speech is a means of power, lack of public speech coincides with a diminishment of power.

Speech was not only a means of power in the ancient world, however.

97. Darr, *On Character Building*, 50–51.
98. Darr, *On Character Building*, 51.
99. Darr, *On Character Building*, 181.
100. Barbara E. Reid, *Choosing the Better Part? Women in the Gospel of Luke* (Collegeville, MN: Liturgical Press, 1996), 106, gives the Madres de la Plaza de Mayo as an example of a group of women who use their silent marches as a form of protest.
101. Jean-Pierre Vernant, *The Origins of Greek Thought* (London: Methuen, 1982), 49. See also Karen Jo Torjesen, *When Women Were Priests: Women's Leadership in the Early Church and the Scandal of Their Subordination in the Rise of Christianity* (San Francisco, CA: Harper, 1993), 120.

Over the past thirty years in particular, attention has been focused on the ways in which language operates in modern society and the relative silence of women in patriarchal societies. Dale Spender, for example, believes that it is through language that we make sense of our world, and that language enables us to order, classify and manipulate our world.[102] Spender, therefore, considers the consequences for those who are silent in language and in the use of language: 'Research should begin to concern itself with the relative silence of over half the population. Language is a powerful tool and we must begin to ask what role it plays in maintaining and perpetuating existing social structures, what contribution it makes to our hierarchically ordered classist, racist and sexist world view.'[103] Spender argues that the group which controls the structure of language and thought has the power to shape the world so that the members of the group become the central figures and non-members are on the periphery, leaving them open to exploitation.[104]

Furthermore, it is not only in Western cultures that the power of language is evident. For instance, Mercy Amba Oduyoye considers that language is also a powerful tool used against women in African culture: 'The daily language about women prevalent in proverbs and sayings is a source not only of socialisation but "the scripture" that encourages and inscribes into African culture the subjugation and brutalisation of women.'[105] Oduyoye believes that the negative sayings about women that are passed down from generation to generation reinforce the practice of violence against women. She argues that for many women in African countries, the most effective weapon against this is the female tongue, 'hence the silencing of women by patriarchal caveats.'[106]

A text can thus be a powerful tool of control. For literary theorist, Pierre Macherey, a text's ideology is revealed more by what it does not say than by what it says, by the implicit more than the explicit: 'Either all around or in its wake the explicit requires the implicit: for in order to say anything, there are other things *which must not be said*.'[107] Therefore, the silences and absences in a text must be investigated to show the ideology underlying the text. Macherey directs the critic to make the silence speak,

102. Dale Spender, *Man Made Language*, 2nd edn. (London: Routledge & Kegan Paul, 1985), 3.

103. Spender, *Man Made Language*, 51.

104. Spender, *Man Made Language*, 143.

105. Mercy Amba Oduyoye, 'Violence Against Women: Window on Africa,' *Voices from the Third World* 18, no. 1 (1995): 171.

106. Oduyoye, 'Violence Against Women,' 172.

107. Pierre Macherey, *A Theory of Literary Production*, trans. Geoffrey Wall (London: Routledge & Kegan Paul, 1978), 85.

and to learn what the unspoken is saying. He questions whether what the text is really saying is what it is not saying.[108]

In this study the text of the Gospel of Luke is put under the microscope. Who is it that controls the language and speech within the Lukan Gospel? What power dynamic can be evidenced from studying the speech or silence of the women characters in the text? The silences of women characters within the Lukan Gospel will be made to 'speak' in order to discover whether forms of oppression are evidenced.

According to the *Collins English Dictionary*, silence may be defined as 'the absence of sound or noise' and also 'oblivion or obscurity.'[109] In considering women's silence in this study, then, it is necessary to recognize that silence is not simply the absence of speech but also the rendering of women's voice and activity to obscurity. With this in mind, strategies which result in the silencing of women need to be explored.

The work of Michelle Boulous Walker can inform an exploration of strategies of silencing.[110] Investigating women's silence within the realm of philosophy, Walker argues:

> Silencing, then, is no simple matter. Not speaking, or not being permitted to speak are only two possible prohibitions that constitute women as mute. The effective silencing of women ... also involves the refusal of philosophy to listen, i.e. a blank denial of their claim to subjectivity. This is important because if we are able to understand silencing as a complex series of strategies aimed at denying women their role as philosophical subjects, then we are better equipped to counteract these ...[111]

For Walker, these complex strategies of silencing include exclusion, denial and repression.[112] She argues that a spatial logic which considers women

---

108.   Macherey, *Literary Production*, 86. See also Terry Eagleton, *Criticism and Ideology: A Study in Marxist Literary Theory* (London: NLB, 1976), 89–90; and Timothy K. Beal, 'Ideology and Intertextuality: Surplus of Meaning and Controlling the Means of Production,' in *Reading Between Texts: Intertextuality and the Hebrew Bible*, (ed.) Danna Nolan Fewell (Louisville, KY: Westminster/John Knox Press, 1992), 36. Beal underscores the importance of recognizing the relationship 'between writing and ideology, and thus between interpretation and power.'

109.   *Collins English Dictionary*, Fourth Australian edn (Glasgow: HarperCollins, 1998), 1429. While other definitions are also provided, these two are the most appropriate to this study.

110.   Michelle Boulous Walker, *Philosophy and the Maternal Body: Reading Silence* (London: Routledge, 1998). Bernadette Kiley, 'Silence as Repression and Denial: Insights from Mark's Stories of Women,' (paper presented at the Women Scholars of Religion and Theology Conference, Melbourne, 2004), first drew my attention to the work of Walker.

111.   Walker, *Reading Silence*, 11.

112.   Walker, *Reading Silence*, 103.

as 'outside' the philosophical realm is too simplistic. Drawing on the work of Michèle Le Doeuff, she claims that 'woman simultaneously inhabits philosophy's (empty) interiority while remaining exterior to the practices that would confer subjectivity and voice upon her.'[113] As such, philosophical practices 'assign women to silence while simultaneously placing them at the very heart of its domain.'[114]

Therefore, it is not only women's presence or absence within a particular domain that is significant, but also the range of practices in which women are able to participate and exhibit subjectivity. A more subtle method of silencing is to allow women to be physically present while restricting their subjectivity and hence their voice. This is relevant to the present study in relation to the characterization of women in the Gospel of Luke. It will not be sufficient to consider whether women characters are present in the narrative. Whether the women are depicted as taking the initiative in actions and speech will be important for determining their subjectivity, as will the range of practices in which they are involved.

A further consideration is that sometimes women are given access to a domain but in such a way that, rather than extending their subjectivity, it reinforces men's significance. As Walker observes: 'It is perhaps philosophy's master stroke to silence and exclude women most effectively by allowing them entry to the inner sanctum of the classical texts as sacred guardians and dutiful daughters of their fathers' and lovers' truth.'[115] Hence, the women's actions reinforce women's ultimate exclusion from significance within the domain. Similarly, when women speak, it is necessary to consider whose voice is really being heard: 'So women may well speak from inside philosophy, and may well be heard, but yet remain effectively silenced if all they mouth is determined by the ventriloquist's art.'[116] In terms of the present study, once again this raises the question of whether the characterizations of women in the Gospel of Luke portray the subjectivity of women or their marginalization.

Another issue with regard to the silence of women is raised by Gail Ashton in her investigations of female hagiography by male hagiographers. She indicates that these texts are typically 'marked by control, suppression, and closure. Any potential transgressions conflicting with a cultural ideal of womanliness – such as moments of autonomous action or speech – are glossed, and a potentially subversive subject is brought back

113. Walker, *Reading Silence*, 20.
114. Walker, *Reading Silence*, 2.
115. Walker, *Reading Silence*, 22.
116. Walker, *Reading Silence*, 11. For more on the question of whether woman speaks with her own voice, see Diane Price Herndl, 'The Dilemmas of a Feminine Dialogic,' in *Feminism, Bakhtin, and the Dialogic*, (eds.) Dale M. Bauer and Susan Jaret McKinstry (Albany, NY: State University of New York Press, 1991), 16.

into the safe confines of hagiographical genre and the Church.'[117] Ashton's insights demonstrate that male ideals for women's behavior can influence the way that women are portrayed in male writing. Often the fate of the potentially subversive woman in such texts is to be brought in line with patriarchal expectations. Once again, this has relevance for the present study. How are the women in the Gospel of Luke who engage in autonomous action or speech portrayed? What is the response to their demonstration of autonomy? Are women's voices suppressed? Do women inhabit the domain of the Lukan Gospel as disciples but remain outside the dominant logic of the Gospel narrative?

Women's 'otherness' can be perceived as a threat. French psychoanalyst, Hélène Cixous, relates a Chinese story of a general, Sun Tse, training a group of women to be soldiers. The one hundred and eighty women were all wives of the king and it was the king's suggestion that they should be made into soldiers. Rather than follow the beat of the military drum, however, the women laughed and talked and paid no attention to their teacher. Deeming the women's actions mutinous, Sun Tse beheaded the two women leaders and then sounded the drum again. This time, the women practised the art of war in silence with no mistakes.[118] Cixous argues that the story is a perfect example of a relationship between a masculine economy and a feminine economy, in which the masculine order educates the feminine by force. She describes the force as effectively decapitation, with women having no other choice than to be decapitated:[119] '[I]f they don't actually lose their heads by the sword, *they only keep them on condition that they lose them*—lose them, that is, to complete silence, turned into automatons.'[120] According to Cixous, the feminine order (or rather disorder) is threatened by decapitation. She suggests that the male castration anxiety, as proposed by Freud, results in the decapitation of women: 'If man operates under the threat of castration, if masculinity is culturally ordered by the castration complex, it might be said that the backlash, the return, on women of this castration anxiety is

---

117. Gail Ashton, *The Generation of Identity in Late Medieval Hagiography: Speaking the Saint* (London: Routledge, 2000), 12. See also the discussion in Kathleen McPhillips, 'Postmodern Sainthood: "Hearing the Voice of the Saint" and the Uses of Feminist Hagiography,' *Seachanges* 3 (2003): 10–13, http://www.wsrt.com.au/seachanges/volume3/doc/mcphillips.doc. Accessed June 4th, 2006.

118. Hélène Cixous, 'Castration or Decapitation,' *Signs: Journal of Women in Culture and Society* 7 (1981): 42.

119. Cixous, 'Castration or Decapitation,' 42.

120. Cixous, 'Castration or Decapitation,' 43.

its displacement as decapitation, execution, of woman, as loss of her head.'[121]

The 'decapitation' which Cixous describes is symbolic rather than literal. Nevertheless, the symbolism of decapitation which Cixous uses to describe the power exerted over women appears somewhat extreme. In her story of the women being forced to follow the beat of the military drum, the women lose their outer voice but they can still see and hear. Decapitation suggests that the functions of sight and hearing are no longer possible. Rather, it is the women's capacity to use their voices which is taken away from them. Therefore, the image of a woman with a taped mouth may be more appropriate than decapitation to symbolize the silencing to which Cixous refers.[122]

As we have noted, silencing involves complex strategies. Two areas which will be explored further here are the reinforcement of silence as the appropriate state for women, and the vilification and trivialization of women's voice and words so that even when women are not silent they are effectively silenced. For, as Kathleen Corley notes, 'One way to control human behavior is through criticism. Labeling and the setting up of categories of ideal and proscribed behaviors is a powerful form of social control.'[123]

In the fifth-century BCE play *Ajax*, the Greek dramatist, Sophocles, portrays Tecmessa recounting words that Ajax has spoken to her: 'Woman, silence makes a woman beautiful.'[124] While Tecmessa's speaking role continues, Ajax's admonitions to Tecmessa's speech also appear at other stages of the play: 'Speak to those who will listen to you!' and 'Already you have said too much!'[125] Such words portray an image of silence as the desired state for women.[126]

A similar image is reinforced in the Book of Sirach: 'A silent wife is a gift from the Lord' (Sir. 26.14), and also in the New Testament in 1 Tim.

---

121. Cixous, 'Castration or Decapitation,' 43. See also Howard Eilberg-Schwartz, 'Introduction: The Spectacle of the Female Head,' in *Off With Her Head!: The Denial of Women's Identity in Myth, Religion, and Culture*, (eds.) Howard Eilberg-Schwartz and Wendy Doniger (Berkeley, CA: University of California Press, 1995), 6.

122. Within a contemporary Australian context, another image can powerfully symbolize silencing. Some asylum seekers have sewn their lips together to highlight their lack of voice.

123. Kathleeen E. Corley, *Women and the Historical Jesus: Feminist Myths of Christian Origins* (Santa Rosa, CA: Polebridge Press, 2002), 119.

124. Sophocles, *Ajax* 293.

125. Sophocles, *Ajax* 591–92.

126. In *Antigone*, another of his plays, Sophocles portrays Antigone as courageously speaking out and acting against the edict of her uncle Creon, the ruler, by burying her brother. As a result she is sentenced to death and entombed alive, but commits suicide within the tomb. Though Antigone captures the support and sympathy of the audience, she is permanently silenced.

2.11-12 and 1 Cor. 14.34-35.[127] Even when it is considered that a woman speaks truthfully and has something important about which to speak, there is pressure exerted not to listen to the woman. As Origen writes in his commentary on 1 Cor. 14.34-35 in the third century CE: '[I]t is improper for a woman to speak in an assembly, no matter what she says, even if she says admirable things or even saintly things; that is of little consequence since they come from the mouth of a woman.'[128] The concern reflected in this quote is not with the content of the woman's speech but with the very nature of who is doing the speaking. Origen deems the combination of woman and voice as inappropriate in a public setting.

In other instances, women's speech is given sexual overtones. In the Babylonian Talmud, the following examples of this are evident: 'A woman's voice is a sexual incitement' (*b. Ber.* 24a); also 'and do not converse much with women, as this will ultimately lead you to unchastity' (*b. Ned.* 20a).[129] The first of these statements is part of a discussion on what is considered indecent exposure in a woman. The statement and discussion suggest that if a woman's voice is heard by a man reciting the Shema, then this constitutes indecent exposure.[130] Both statements demonstrate that by eroticizing the female voice, women are denied the power of speech.[131]

Rather than advocating silence for women as appropriate behavior, an alternative means of effectively 'silencing' women is by the vilification and trivialization of women's speech. This is done by suggesting either that women talk too much or that what women talk about is not worth serious

127.   These two New Testament passages will be discussed later in this chapter.

128.   Greek text in Claude Jenkins, 'Documents: Origen on 1 Corinthians. IV,' *JTS* 10 (1909): 42, translated in Karen Jo Torjesen, 'Reconstruction of Women's Early Christian History,' in *Searching the Scriptures: A Feminist Introduction*, (ed.) Elisabeth Schüssler Fiorenza (North Blackburn, Vic: Collins Dove, 1993), 306.

129.   See Howard Eilberg-Schwartz, 'The Nakedness of a Woman's Voice, the Pleasure in a Man's Mouth: An Oral History of Ancient Judaism,' in *Off With Her Head!: The Denial of Women's Identity in Myth, Religion, and Culture*, (eds.) Howard Eilberg-Schwartz and Wendy Doniger (Berkeley, CA: University of California Press, 1995), 167–68. Since the rabbinic literature reflects a diversity of opinions, it is wrong to assume that these statements are typical of Jewish thought. Kraemer points out that 'rabbinic literature intentionally transmits multiple voices, whose weight in the tradition is not necessarily equal. Some opinions may be preserved in the tradition precisely in order to be contradicted. The mere presence of an opinion cannot be taken as evidence that it reflects normative views or social practice, let alone both.' Ross S. Kraemer, 'Jewish Women and Christian Origins: Some Caveats,' in *Women and Christian Origins*, (ed.) Ross Shepard Kraemer and Mary Rose D'Angelo (New York, NY: Oxford University Press, 1999), 37. While these statements from the Babylonian Talmud are not representative of Jewish opinion, they are further examples evidenced through history of men arguing that it is inappropriate for women to speak.

130.   Eilberg-Schwartz, 'Nakedness of a Woman's Voice,' 167–68.

131.   Eilberg-Schwartz, 'Female Head,' 9.

consideration. Significantly, in Luke 24.10-11 we read of the situation where women announce the resurrection to male apostles. The men, however, deem the women's words to be 'an idle tale' and do not believe them. When women's words are considered nonsense, then they are easily dismissed. A tendency of women to gossip is also suggested in 1 Tim. 5.13.

Different dynamics can result in silencing. The imposition of restrictions and 'the more genteel tyrannies of custom and practice' can specifically block someone from speaking or being heard. Silencing can also result from silencing oneself due to 'fear of being ridiculed, attacked, or ignored.'[132] Cultural dynamics, therefore, impact on a person's ability and willingness to speak.

Various studies have explored gender differences in regard to speech. In a 1977 study, for example, Cheris Kramer explored perceptions of female and male speech held by white women and men in the United States. The results of the study identify perceived stereotypes of male and female speech characteristics. Traits which were thought to be characteristic of male speakers include: demanding voice; dominating speech; authoritarian speech; and aggressive speech. Traits which were perceived to be characteristic of female speakers include: gossip; talk about trivial topics; talk a lot; emotional speech; and gibberish.[133] Hence the study indicates that, for white U.S. men and women, women's speech is perceived to be idle, incoherent and excessive, unlike men's speech. Kramer notes that such stereotypes influence and are influenced by the mass media presentations: 'The stereotypes of male and female speech play a large part in determining how the speech behaviour of women and men is represented in the mass media, and this representation in turn strengthens the pervasiveness and stability of the stereotypes.'[134]

While it is a common assumption in Western culture that women talk more than men, the research into gender differences in amount of conversation does not support this. Many studies actually conclude that men talk more than women in mixed-sex interactions, but the overall research does show inconsistencies in results.[135] In a detailed review of this research, Deborah James and Janice Drakich argue that the type of interaction, combined with the perceived status and cultural expectations of participants, impacts on conversational behavior.[136] In formal, task-

---

132. Deborah Cameron, 'Introduction: Why is Language a Feminist Issue?,' in *The Feminist Critique of Language*, (ed.) Deborah Cameron (London: Routledge, 1990), 4.

133. Cheris Kramer, 'Perceptions of Female and Male Speech,' *Language and Speech* 20 (1977): 155–57. See also Spender, *Man Made Language*, 41.

134. Kramer, 'Female and Male Speech,' 159.

135. Deborah James and Janice Drakich, 'Understanding Gender Differences in Amount of Talk: A Critical Review of Research,' in *Gender and Conversational Interaction*, (ed.) Deborah Tannen (New York, NY: Oxford University Press, 1993), 281–84.

136. James and Drakich, 'Understanding Gender Differences,' 281–312.

oriented interactions, cultural expectations result in those of a perceived higher status talking more than those of a lower status. While these expectations assign a lower status to women than men, factors such as expert knowledge or a leadership role may serve to nullify the gender expectations. Furthermore, women talk more in single-sex interactions than they do in mixed-sex interactions within these settings.[137]

Querying why the stereotype of women talking more than men continues to flourish without supportive research, James and Drakich suggest that it may be influenced by the different uses of language by men and women. Men who do not appreciate the social value of women's talk may perceive it to be excessive.[138] Spender claims that this misconception is derived from patriarchal expectations: 'When silence is the desired state for women (and I suggest that it is in a patriarchal order ...), then any talk in which a woman engages can be too much.'[139] Therefore, according to Spender, a woman who speaks at all in a patriarchal world is perceived to have talked excessively.

Thus, what we find reflected in the perceptions about women's speech in the Western world in more recent times remains in line with the way women's speech has frequently been portrayed in literature for over two thousand years. Women's speech is often perceived as idle chatter or gossip, suitable for talk with other women. In a public situation, when males are present, however, women should be silent or silenced if they dare to speak. In this way, women are cut off from decision-making and influence in the *polis*. This is in line with the argument of Simone de Beauvoir who asserts that throughout history woman has been established as man's 'Other' and kept in a state of dependence.[140] She claims further that women tend to act out the roles that civilization as a whole ascribes to them.[141] In effect, women's behavior has been controlled by the beating of the drum of the patriarchal society. Women have learnt to be silent or be silenced.

Within the Hebrew Scriptures there are several examples of the poor and oppressed crying out to God for help, with God hearing their cries and saving them. The pivotal Exodus experience is described in this way. The Israelites, oppressed by slavery, cry out and their cry is heard. Having heard their cry, God delivers them from their slavery (Exod. 2.23-24, 3.7-8). In Deut. 26.6-8, God is described as hearing the voice of the oppressed and coming to their rescue. This linking of hearing and saving also

137. James and Drakich, 'Understanding Gender Differences,' 289–94.
138. James and Drakich, 'Understanding Gender Differences,' 302–3.
139. Spender, *Man Made Language*, 42.
140. Simone de Beauvoir, *The Second Sex*, trans. H. M. Parshley (London: Jonathan Cape, 1953), 159–61, 273.
141. de Beauvoir, *Second Sex*, 273.

appears in the psalms. When the righteous or oppressed cry out, they are heard and saved (Pss. 34.17; 145.19). That God hears the cry of the poor and acts in response is a common theme in the Hebrew Scriptures. But what if the oppressed do not cry out? What if the afflicted have no voice? If hearing signifies saving, then what does not being heard signify? When silence is imposed rather than chosen it is oppressive.

Imposed silence, vilification and trivialization are forms of marginalization, powerlessness, cultural imperialism and violence. A group which is subjected to any of these categories is an oppressed group, according to Young's criteria. As we have seen, portrayals of women in ancient literature often promote the image of silent women. This literature both reinforces and is reinforced by cultural codes operating in the ancient world. Of particular interest to this study are the private and public roles ascribed to women and men respectively within these codes and the literature. This public and private distinction will be explored below. As we will see, however, the actual situation of women in the ancient world was not as clear-cut as the literature and cultural codes might suggest. Some women did have influence in the public sphere and some had a public voice. In reality, not all women of the ancient world were silent in the public arena.

4. *Public and Private Space*

Much has now been written about the genderization of public and private space in New Testament times.[142] Perceived public and private roles are influenced by the cultural codes of honor–shame within the ancient Mediterranean world. Honor is 'a claim to positive worth along with the social acknowledgment of that worth by others.'[143] Bruce J. Malina and Jerome H. Neyrey describe honor as having a male and female component, the male aspect being called 'honor' and the female aspect called 'shame,' where shame refers to a woman's sensitivity to how others regard her worth.[144] For males, honor is concerned with exhibiting virility and loss of honor produces negative shame. In contrast, female honor is concerned with sexual exclusiveness and positive shame. The honorable woman tries to avoid situations that would make her vulnerable to

142. See, for instance, Bruce J. Malina and Jerome H. Neyrey, 'Honor and Shame in Luke-Acts: Pivotal Values of the Mediterranean World,' in *The Social World of Luke-Acts: Models for Interpretation*, (ed.) Jerome H. Neyrey (Peabody, MA: Hendrickson, 1991), 41–44; Torjesen, 'Reconstruction,' 290–310; and Kathleen E. Corley, *Private Women, Public Meals: Social Conflict in the Synoptic Tradition* (Peabody, MA: Hendrickson, 1993), 15–17.

143. Malina and Neyrey, 'Honor and Shame,' 26.

144. Malina and Neyrey, 'Honor and Shame,' 41.

shamelessness. Male honor is also involved with maintaining the sexual
purity of female family members.[145]

The gender division of honor is replicated in a particular understanding
of space in which public space is considered the male domain and
domestic or private space is considered the female domain. 'Male honor
looks outward to the public sphere, whereas female honor looks inward to
the domestic.'[146] The words of the philosopher Philo reflect this gender
ideology in the first century:

> A woman, then, should not be a busybody, meddling with matters
> outside her household concerns, but should seek a life of seclusion. She
> should not shew herself off like a vagrant in the streets before the eyes of
> other men, except when she has to go to the temple, and even then she
> should take pains to go, not when the market is full, but when most
> people have gone home ...[147]

In this understanding, the honorable woman restricts herself to the
household and does not go out in public unless for purposes of religious
worship. Even within the house, it is suggested that women's quarters
were separate from men's quarters.[148] For Philo, a public setting appears
to be a setting in which a woman would encounter or be seen by 'other
men,' presumably men other than her own relatives.[149] Usually such a
public setting would be outside a woman's home. Public meals were also
held in private homes, however, so that a public setting could also be
within the home. Formal Greek-style public banquets consisted of a meal
followed by a symposium (drinking party). At the symposium it was
customary for entertainers and courtesans to be present with the male
guests.[150] While 'private' Greek women were expected not to attend public

145. Malina and Neyrey, 'Honor and Shame,' 43–44. For a discussion of honor and
shame as pivotal values within the Mediterranean world of the first century, see Bruce J.
Malina, *The New Testament World: Insights from Cultural Anthropology*, Third, revised and
expanded edn (Louisville, KY: Westminster John Knox Press, 2001), 27–57.

146. Malina and Neyrey, 'Honor and Shame,' 42.

147. Philo, *The Special Laws* 3.171. While Philo's descriptions are often presumed to be
descriptive of Jewish social practice, Kraemer argues that this is unlikely. See Ross S.
Kraemer, 'Jewish Women and Women's Judaism(s) at the Beginning of Christianity,' in
Women and Christian Origins, (eds.) Ross Shepard Kraemer and Mary Rose D'Angelo (New
York, NY: Oxford University Press, 1999), 60.

148. See Jerome H. Neyrey, 'What's Wrong With This Picture? John 4, Cultural
Stereotypes of Women, and Public and Private Space,' *BTB* 24 (1994): 79–80. But see the
qualifications of this in Ian Morris, 'Remaining Invisible: The Archaeology of the Excluded
in Classical Athens,' in *Women and Slaves in Greco-Roman Culture: Differential Equations*,
(eds.) Sandra R. Joshel and Sheila Murnaghan (London: Routledge, 1998), 211–18.

149. Neyrey describes the 'private' world as 'the house and spaces related to household
duties.' See Neyrey, 'What's Wrong?,' 79.

150. Satoko Yamaguchi, *Mary and Martha: Women in the World of Jesus* (Maryknoll,
NY: Orbis Books, 2002), 24.

meals, it would seem that elite Roman women had more freedom in this regard and did attend public meals.[151]

Female honor is symbolized by 'the female virtues of silence, chastity, and obedience.'[152] The virtue of silence does not mean that an honorable woman would never speak; rather she would not speak in a public setting. Such an ideal served to control women's behavior: 'The virtue of silence for women created another protective barrier against women's intrusion in the public sphere.'[153] While such a gender division of space excluded women from the public and political domain, they could hold considerable power within their household.

While the distinction of public–private spheres as male and female is frequently reinscribed in literature,[154] the question which needs to be asked is how well this gender distinction reflects the actual lives of the people within the ancient Mediterranean world. Dorothy Sly comments that Philo's instruction on how a woman should act presumes that a woman has household help so that she does not have to run household errands herself. Thus, it is only relevant to the wealthy class and may not reflect the lives of ordinary people.[155] As such, Philo's words can be seen as a prescription rather than a description. They reflect an elite male ideology, outlining the perceived 'ideal' behavior for women rather than describing the actual situation for many women. Satoko Yamaguchi also notes that many women in the first century worked outside their home for economic survival. She argues that 'the elite male ideology of public/male versus private/female seems to have been irrelevant for the daily life practices of the majority of women.'[156]

A further challenge to the public–private dichotomy is presented by Eric M. Meyers. From an archaeological study of domestic space in

---

151. See Corley, *Private Women*, 28–30; and Neyrey, 'What's Wrong?,' 80.

152. Torjesen, *When Women Were Priests*, 118.

153. Torjesen, *When Women Were Priests*, 120.

154. In his fifth-century BCE play, *Trojan Women*, Euripides has a female character describe her ideal behavior. Andromache says that what causes a bad reputation for a woman is not remaining inside. She claims to have done all that has been found proper for a woman – remaining within the house, being silent and calm. Euripides, *Trojan Women* 645–655. See also Mary R. Lefkowitz and Maureen B. Fant, *Women's Life in Greece and Rome: A Source Book in Translation*, 2nd edn (Baltimore, MD: Johns Hopkins University Press, 1992), 11.

155. Dorothy Sly, *Philo's Perception of Women* (Atlanta, GA: Scholars Press, 1990), 197. See also Kraemer, 'Women's Judaism(s),' 61. Against this, Corley claims that many peasant households in the ancient world had at least one slave. See Corley, *Women and the Historical Jesus*, 37.

156. Yamaguchi, *Mary and Martha*, 20. Glancy, *Slavery*, 41, too, claims that the public–private division for women was influenced by issues of status and class. On the dangers of not distinguishing between ideology and real life in ancient Athens, see David Cohen, 'Seclusion, Separation, and the Status of Women in Classical Athens,' *Greece and Rome* 36 (1989): 4–7.

Jewish Galilee, he concludes that 'Jewish households cannot be considered areas of confinement or concealment for women.'[157] He argues that women participated more fully than might be suggested by literary sources in a range of social and professional activities in ancient Jewish society, and that archaeological evidence assists in identifying women's 'true' role.[158]

Further support for countering the suggestion that women had no influence in the public sphere comes from epigraphical evidence. In the second century CE, Aufria of Delphi is described as delivering 'many excellent and enjoyable lectures at the assembly of Greeks at the Pythian games.'[159] Thus, not all women were silent in public, and Aufria was acclaimed for her public speech. Many inscriptions describe women as benefactors, an indication of the economic power of these women.[160] Epigraphical evidence also suggests that wealthy women were able to hold a variety of public offices, being described, for example, as ruler, wreath-bearer, civic officer, sponsor of contests, and gymnasiarch – ruler of the cultural and educational center.[161] In considering the question of whether these offices were derived from the status of the women's husbands, James Malcolm Arlandson concludes that 'the evidence points toward independence more often than scholarship has so far acknowledged.'[162] Moreover, he claims that not all women's offices were honorary; some were positions of real power, particularly in terms of public finances and policies. He notes, too, that men's offices were often honorary so that 'the emphasis should not be placed on how the men or women might have carried out their duties.'[163]

An inscription dating from the first century BCE honors a benefactor

---

157. Eric M. Meyers, 'The Problems of Gendered Space in Syro-Palestinian Domestic Architecture: The Case of Roman-Period Galilee,' in *Early Christian Families in Context: An Interdisciplinary Dialogue*, (eds.) David L. Balch and Carolyn Osiek (Grand Rapids, MI: Eerdmans, 2003), 68.

158. Meyers, 'Problems of Gendered Space,' 68–69.

159. Lefkowitz and Fant, *Women's Life*, 158.

160. Lefkowitz and Fant, *Women's Life*, 158–60. These inscriptions of female benefactors mainly range from the first century BCE to the second century CE. See also Gardner, *Women*, 264.

161. James Malcolm Arlandson, *Women, Class, and Society in Early Christianity: Models from Luke-Acts* (Peabody, MA: Hendrickson, 1997), 31–32. For each of these offices, the period of dating includes the first century CE. See also Pomeroy, *Goddesses, Whores*, 126, for information on female magistrates from the second and first centuries BCE.

162. Arlandson, *Women, Class, and Society*, 34.

163. Arlandson, *Women, Class, and Society*, 34. For a discussion on honorific titles, see Bernadette J. Brooten, *Women Leaders in the Ancient Synagogues: Inscriptional Evidence and Background Issues*, BJS 36 (Chico, CA: Scholars Press, 1982), 7–10. Brooten concludes that 'there is no indication in the ancient sources that any of the titles of synagogue leadership were honorific at any period' (p. 10).

named Phile: 'Phile, daughter of Apollonius wife of Thessalus son of Polydeuces; as the first woman *stephanephorus* she dedicated at her own expense a cistern and the water pipes in the city.'[164] Apart from her benefaction, the inscription gives information about her family and her office. Her father's name and husband's name are provided but neither has a title or office mentioned after his name. Phile, on the other hand, is described as 'the first woman *stephanephorus*,' a magistrate with the right to wear a wreath or crown (στέφανος).[165] There is nothing to suggest that this title is derived from her husband or father. Further, her benefaction draws on her own finances. The inscription therefore emphasizes Phile's office as independent of her husband's position, affirming that women could hold public offices and have influence in their own right.

Jane F. Gardner comments from epigraphical attestations that, particularly from the late Republic onwards, wealthy Roman women 'give the appearance ... of playing a role in the public sphere.'[166] Similarly, Natalie Boymel Kampen draws attention to 'the ability of wealthy women to exercise power in public despite the dominant ideology of female incapacity and domesticity.' Kampen notes, however, that women rarely feature in Roman historical reliefs, despite other evidence revealing that women were often 'active public historical subjects.'[167] When women do appear in the public framework of historical reliefs, gender symbolism 'places them firmly in the private realm of family and reproduction.' This leads Kampen to describe Roman historical reliefs as a 'propagandistic form that presents idealizing narratives of power and kinship' and thus reinforcing a private role for women.[168]

Inscriptions provide evidence that some women held public offices. While the greater number of inscriptions with men's names suggests that far more men held these offices than women, the fact remains that some women could and did exert significant influence in the public sphere in the ancient Mediterranean world, including in the first and second centuries CE. The public–private gender dichotomy was in reality not as clear as literature or historical reliefs might suggest. Mary Taliaferro Boatwright notes 'the public visibility of women in the Roman empire, so clear in the epigraphic and numismatic evidence and yet so much at odds with the

164. Lefkowitz and Fant, *Women's Life*, 158.

165. See Lefkowitz and Fant, *Women's Life*, 346, n. 50; and Arlandson, *Women, Class, and Society*, 32.

166. Gardner, *Women*, 264. Gardner suggests, however, that the women's 'highly visible activities' were 'more formal than real.'

167. Natalie Boymel Kampen, 'Between Public and Private: Women as Historical Subjects in Roman Art,' in *Women's History and Ancient History*, (ed.) Sarah B. Pomeroy (Chapel Hill: University of North Carolina Press, 1991), 218.

168. Kampen, 'Between Public and Private,' 243.

picture presented by the literature.'[169] Karen Jo Torjesen explains this discrepancy by distinguishing between the 'generic woman' and the 'individual woman.' She argues that literary sources depict the 'generic woman' which in patriarchal societies is 'a reified notion of woman expressive of male interests in controlling them.'[170] The image of 'generic woman' is generally used to limit woman's influence and power.[171] In contrast, documentary sources, such as inscriptions, epitaphs, statues and portraits, present the achievements of an 'individual woman' within a context in which her activities are being honored rather than controlled.[172]

In a volume devoted to women's voices in ancient Greek society and literature, aptly titled *Making Silence Speak*, the agency of women and their speech are evidenced:

> This volume seeks to show that the voices and speech of women played a much more important role in Greek literature and society than previously recognized. Rather than confirming the old model of binary oppositions, in which women's speech was viewed as insignificant and subordinate to male discourse, the sources examined in this volume reveal a dynamic and potentially explosive interrelation between women's speech and the realm of literary production and public discourse.[173]

The volume focuses on women's voices from the archaic period, classical period and late classical period and beyond, incorporating letters found in Greco-Roman Egypt in the early second century CE. Thus, women's voices in the ancient world can be heard by those who have the ears to hear.

The presence of women in leadership positions within religious contexts in the ancient Mediterranean world is increasingly being recognized. Using inscriptional evidence, Bernadette Brooten demonstrates that Jewish women held a variety of offices including head of the synagogue, leader, elder, priestess and mother of the synagogue. Such widespread inscriptions span the period from the first century BCE to the sixth century CE and cover a diverse region around the Mediterranean.[174] One of the inscriptions that refer to a woman as an elder is dated between the

169. Mary Taliaferro Boatwright, 'Plancia Magna of Perge: Women's Roles and Status in Roman Asia Minor,' in *Women's History and Ancient History*, (ed.) Sarah B. Pomeroy (Chapel Hill, NC: University of North Carolina Press, 1991), 260.

170. Torjesen, 'Reconstruction,' 292.

171. Torjesen, 'Reconstruction,' 292.

172. Torjesen, 'Reconstruction,' 293.

173. Laura McClure, 'Introduction,' in *Making Silence Speak: Women's Voices in Greek Literature and Society*, (eds.) André Lardinois and Laura McClure (Princeton, NJ: Princeton University Press, 2001), 16.

174. Brooten, *Women Leaders*, 5–99.

first century BCE and third century CE. A reference to a woman as priestess dates from the first century BCE. Of the three Greek inscriptions referring to a woman as head of the synagogue, one probably dates from the second century CE.[175] Furthermore, Brooten argues against the assumption that these titles were honorary.[176] On the other hand, Judith Romney Wegner claims that many mishnaic laws were designed to keep women out of the public arena.[177] This suggests that once again an inscriptional investigation can present a different picture from that which is reflected in the literature. Corley notes that some women were present among a variety of groups, including 'the Cynics, Epicureans, Pythagoreans, Stoics, Therapeutae, the Zealot group led by Simon son of Gioras, the disciples of John the Baptist and the sectarians at Qumran,' as well as the Jesus movement.[178]

A range of epigraphical evidence supports women's presence in a variety of roles within early Christianity – prophets, theological teachers, presbyters, enrolled widows, deacons, bishops and stewards – though this evidence is dated later than the first century CE.[179] Combining this epigraphical evidence with early literary evidence, however, Ute E. Eisen concludes: 'It is clear that women were active in the expansion and shaping of the Church in the first centuries.'[180]

Evidence from the New Testament and early Christian writings support Eisen's statement. Junia, a woman apostle, is referred to in Romans 16.7.[181] Moreover, the Samaritan woman of Jn 4.1-42 is referred to as an

175. See Brooten, *Women Leaders*, 5–14.

176. Brooten, *Women Leaders*, 10.

177. Judith Romney Wegner, *Chattel or Person? The Status of Women in the Mishnah* (New York, NY: Oxford University Press, 1988), 173–74. Judith M. Lieu, however, warns it is a 'misuse of the Jewish sources' to take 'as descriptive of the first century the prescriptive construction of a world by the second-century male scholarly elite we know as the rabbis.' See Judith M. Lieu, 'The "Attraction of Women" in/to Early Judaism and Christianity: Gender and the Politics of Conversion,' *JSNT* 72 (1998): 6.

178. Corley, *Women and the Historical Jesus*, 78. For an argument for equitable functions for men and women among the Therapeutae, see Joan E. Taylor, 'The Women "Priests" of Philo's *De Vita Contemplativa*: Reconstructing the Therapeutae,' in *On the Cutting Edge: The Study of Women in Biblical Worlds*, (eds.) Jane Schaberg, Alice Bach, and Esther Fuchs (New York, NY: Continuum, 2003), 102–22.

179. Ute Eisen, *Women Officeholders in Early Christianity: Epigraphical and Literary Studies*, trans. Linda M. Maloney (Collegeville, MN: Liturgical Press, 2000). Many of the inscriptions date between the fourth and sixth centuries CE.

180. Eisen, *Women Officeholders*, 224.

181. Some translate the name here as referring to a man, Junias, though there is no attestation of this name in antiquity. See, for instance, Ernst Käsemann, *Commentary on Romans*, trans. Geoffrey W. Bromiley (Grand Rapids, MI: Eerdmans, 1980), 411; and Matthew Black, *Romans* (London: Marshall, Morgan & Scott, 1973), 181. However, most modern scholars translate the name as Junia, referring to a woman. See, for instance, Bernadette Brooten, '"Junia ... Outstanding Among the Apostles" (Romans 16:7),' in

apostle by Origen in the third century,[182] and Mary Magdalene is given the title, 'Apostle to the Apostles,'[183] though neither woman is specifically named as an apostle in the Gospels. Anna (Lk. 2.36) and the daughters of Philip (Acts 21.9) are identified as prophets, while Phoebe is described as a διάκονος of the church at Cenchreae (Rom. 16.1),[184] and women deacons are found in 1 Tim. 3.11. The reference to διάκονοι in Philippians 1.1 suggests that the role of deacon was a recognized office at an early stage of the Church.

Priscilla (Prisca) is well attested in New Testament literature. Along with her husband, Aquila, she is described as a co-worker of Paul and the host of a house church (Acts 18.2, 18; Rom. 16.3-5; 1 Cor. 16.19; 2 Tim. 4.19). In Acts 18.26, Priscilla and Aquila are portrayed as explaining God's way to Apollos. It should be noted, however, that Codex Bezae (D) reverses the order of the names to list Aquila first. Hence, D lessens the prominence of Priscilla and promotes the importance of Aquila.[185]

Women Priests: A Catholic Commentary on the Vatican Declaration, (eds.) Leonard Swidler and Arlene Swidler (New York, NY: Paulist Press, 1977), 141–44. For a discussion of the history of the name's translation, see Joseph A. Fitzmyer, *Romans: A New Translation with Introduction and Commentary* (New York, NY: Doubleday, 1993), 737–38. For a recent detailed investigation of whether the name refers to a woman and whether this person is considered an apostle, see Richard Bauckham, *Gospel Women: Studies of the Named Women in the Gospels* (Grand Rapids, MI: Eerdmans, 2002), 165–86.

182. Origen, *Commentary on the Gospel according to John*, trans. Ronald E. Heine, 2 vols., The Fathers of the Church 80, 89 (Washington, DC: Catholic University of America Press, 1989–93), 13.169.

183. Hippolytus includes Mary Magdalene as an apostle in Hippolytus, 'ΕΙΣ ΤΟ ΑΣΜΑ,' in *Hippolytus Werke: Exegetische und Homiletische Schriften*, (ed.) G. N. Bonwetsch and H. Achelis, GCS 1 (Leipzig: J. C. Hinrichs'sche Buchhandlung, 1897), XV. 353. See also Esther de Boer, *Mary Magdalene: Beyond the Myth*, trans. John Bowden (Harrisburg, PA: Trinity Press International, 1997), 61; Eisen, *Women Officeholders*, 51; and Dorothy Lee, *Flesh and Glory: Symbolism, Gender and Theology in the Gospel of John* (New York, NY: Crossroad, 2002), 230. For a thorough discussion of the tradition of Mary Magdalene as apostle, see Ann Graham Brock, *Mary Magdalene, The First Apostle: The Struggle For Authority* (Cambridge, MA: Harvard University Press, 2003).

184. Brendan Byrne writes, 'While it is probably anachronistic to read into the term "deacon" all the features attaching to the office of the "diaconate" in the later church, the description implies that Phoebe exercised the ministry of "service" ... in a continuing and officially recognized capacity.' Brendan Byrne, *Romans*, Sacra Pagina 6 (Collegeville, MN: Liturgical Press, 1996), 447. Considering Paul's uses of the term διάκονος, Gillman argues that Phoebe should be viewed as a teacher and missionary in the Church of Cenchreae. See Florence M. Gillman, *Women Who Knew Paul* (Collegeville, MN: Liturgical Press, 1992), 63.

185. This is in line with the tendency in D to reduce the significance of women. See Bruce M. Metzger, *A Textual Commentary on the Greek New Testament*, 2nd edn (Stuttgart: Deutsche Bibelgesellschaft, 1994), 402–3, 413–14; Elisabeth Schüssler Fiorenza, *In Memory of Her: A Feminist Theological Reconstruction of Christian Origins*, 2nd edn (London: SCM Press, 1995), 52; and Susanne Heine, *Women and Early Christianity: Are the Feminist Scholars Right?*, trans. John Bowden (London: SCM Press, 1987), 43–44.

Several other women are also mentioned in the New Testament as actively engaged in the Christian mission – Euodia and Syntyche (Phil. 4.2); Nympha (Col. 4.15); Mary, Tryphaena, Tryphosa and Persis (Rom. 16.3-16). Further, in the second-century extracanonical *Acts of Paul and Thecla*, Thecla is portrayed as a preacher and teacher who is inspired to continue the mission of Paul.[186]

Evidence of women's activities can also be found in written instructions against women pursuing particular activities. In 1 Tim. 2.12 we read: 'I permit no woman to teach or to have authority over a man; she is to keep silent.' This prohibition against women teaching suggests that, at the time the Pastoral Epistles were written,[187] women must have been exercising teaching roles in the community and at worship.[188] In the third-century church order, the *Didascalia*, we read a further injunction against women teaching: 'Therefore it is not required nor necessary that women should be teachers, especially about the name of the Christ, and about salvation by His Passion, for women were not appointed to teach, especially not a widow, but that they should make prayer and supplication to the Lord God.'[189] Also in the *Didascalia* we find a similar injunction against women baptizing – '*It is not permitted to a woman to baptize.*'[190] This suggests that women were participating in this activity.[191] As Margaret Y. MacDonald reminds us, 'the presence of traditional ideologies in early Christian documents should not lead to the immediate conclusion that women were

186.   'The Acts of Paul and Thecla,' in *The New Testament and Other Early Christian Writings: A Reader*, (ed.) Bart D. Ehrman (New York, NY: Oxford University Press, 1998). 177–82. While Margaret Y. MacDonald questions the historicity of the accounts of Thecla. she claims that 'in this early Christian text, women's influence is exaggerated because women's influence was real and perceived as dangerous.' Margaret Y. MacDonald, 'Was Celsus Right? The Role of Women in the Expansion of Early Christianity,' in *Early Christian Families in Context: An Interdisciplinary Dialogue*, (eds.) David L. Balch and Carolyn Osiek (Grand Rapids, MI: Eerdmans, 2003), 182.

187.   The majority of contemporary scholars locate the writing of the Pastoral Epistles at either late first century or early second century. See, for instance, Joanna Dewey, '1 Timothy,' in *The Women's Bible Commentary*, Expanded edition, (eds.) Carol A. Newsom and Sharon H. Ringe (Louisville, KY: Westminster John Knox Press, 1998), 444; and Raymond F. Collins, *Letters That Paul Did Not Write: The Epistle to the Hebrews and the Pauline Pseudepigrapha* (Wilmington, DE: Michael Glazier, 1988), 92.

188.   Eisen, *Women Officeholders*, 102. See also Dewey, '1 Timothy,' 445; and Robert M. Price, *The Widow Traditions in Luke-Acts: A Feminist-Critical Scrutiny*, SBLDS 155 (Atlanta, GA: Scholars Press, 1997), xxxii.

189.   *Didascalia Apostolorum in English*, trans. Margaret Dunlop Gibson (London: Clay and Sons, 1903), f. 50b, p. 72.

190.   *Didascalia*, f. 53a, p. 75.

191.   See Torjesen, 'Reconstruction,' 292; and Francine Cardman, 'Women, Ministry, and Church Order in Early Christianity,' in *Women and Christian Origins*, (eds.) Ross Shepard Kraemer and Mary Rose D'Angelo (New York, NY: Oxford University Press, 1999), 308–11.

without influence and power.'[192] Even the first-century prescription of Philo against women being seen in public, referred to earlier, indicates that women must have moved beyond the private sphere. Each of these instructions is further evidence that women were involved in various public activities in the ancient Mediterranean world.

Hence, the public/private distinction does not give the whole story of women's activities. If the restriction of women to the private sphere reflects the ideal behavior of women according to elite males, it is clear that not all women abided by the restriction. Whether from economic necessity, an interest in religious and public affairs or fidelity to their call to serve in public domains, some women resisted attempts to confine them to the domestic sphere and participated in the public arena. Further, some women wielded significant power in the public world, over and above the power they had within their household. It is important, therefore, to recognize the diversity of women's experiences rather than stereotype women of the ancient world.[193]

As has been noted above, both literary and epigraphical evidence demonstrate that women held a variety of positions of leadership within Christianity in the early centuries. Early Christian communities gathered for worship in private homes, creating the concept of 'household church' (1 Cor. 16.19; Rom. 16.3-5; Col. 4.15; Phlm. 2). Women as well as men acted as heads of these households. Torjesen claims that the duties exercised by those who hosted house-churches have much in common with the duties of early 'bishops' and 'presbyters.'[194] Since these house-churches were located in the private sphere, she argues: '[T]he public-private gender ideology did not constitute a cultural barrier to women's leadership. First- and second-century Christians, familiar with the authority and leadership role of the female head of household, would have perceived women's leadership within the church as not only acceptable but natural.'[195] Torjesen argues further that Christian worship was not distinctly characterized as taking place in public space until the fourth century when basilicas were built.[196]

Torjesen considers that as long as women's leadership was considered

192. Margaret Y. MacDonald, 'Rereading Paul: Early Interpreters of Paul on Women and Gender,' in *Women and Christian Origins*, (eds.) Ross Shepard Kraemer and Mary Rose D'Angelo (New York, NY: Oxford University Press, 1999), 251. Amy-Jill Levine's observation – 'Texts must be sifted to distinguish description of what is from prescription for what should be' – is particularly appropriate here. See Amy-Jill Levine, 'Gender, Judaism, and Literature: Unwelcome Guests in Household Configurations,' *BibInt* 11 (2003): 241.

193. Corley, *Women and the Historical Jesus*, 78.

194. Torjesen, 'Reconstruction,' 305.

195. Torjesen, 'Reconstruction,' 305.

196. Torjesen, 'Reconstruction,' 305.

to be undertaken in a 'quasi-private sphere,' it did not challenge the gender ideology. With the development from private to public space for Christian worship, however, women's leadership became 'controversial and problematic.' The church was no longer linked with the household. From the third century, Christian ministries were perceived as public duties and hence suitable for men only and Christian writers invoked the public–private ideology to oppose women's leadership among men.[197]

While Torjesen's discussion of the private and public understandings of Christian worship is helpful, it can be argued that women's leadership in the churches became controversial well before the third century. Francine Cardman claims that while the process of institutionalization of the churches was complete by the end of the fourth century, it was under way by the end of the first century.[198] As already noted, we see evidence of attempts to restrict women's leadership in the Pastoral Epistles, written in the late first or early second century. The prohibition against women teaching in 1 Tim. 2.12 has similarities to the pronouncement in 1 Cor. 14.34-35: '[W]omen should be silent in the churches. For they are not permitted to speak, but should be subordinate, as the law also says. If there is anything they desire to know, let them ask their husbands at home. For it is shameful for a woman to speak in church.'[199]

The silencing of women is demonstrated by these texts. Since women are encouraged to ask their husbands at home whatever they desire to know, however, private speech is obviously considered acceptable. It is public speech, in this case speech in the assemblies/churches, which is proscribed.[200] It would seem that the real concern evidenced here is with women's leadership among men in a formal setting, particularly the leadership of married women. The instruction to women to ask their husbands what they want to know is clearly not applicable to those women without husbands – widows, unmarried and divorced women – who therefore acquire a more independent status. That the situation of

197. Torjesen, 'Reconstruction,' 305–6.

198. Cardman, 'Women, Ministry, and Church Order,' 300.

199. There is debate about the authenticity of 1 Cor. 14.34-35. That women are assumed to prophesy in 1 Cor. 11.5 fuels the debate. A detailed discussion of the issue is provided in Gordon D. Fee, *The First Epistle to the Corinthians* (Grand Rapids, MI: Eerdmans, 1987), 699–705. Fee concludes that these verses should be seen as an interpolation. Dewey suggests that 1 Cor. 14.34-35 may be a later addition into 1 Corinthians, possibly made by the author of the Pastoral Epistles to strengthen the case against women's leadership. See Dewey, '1 Timothy,' 446–47.

200. For a different view, see Ben Witherington, *Women and the Genesis of Christianity* (Cambridge: Cambridge University Press, 1990), 172–78. In discussing 1 Cor. 14.33b-36, Witherington argues that Paul is not banning all of women's speech in worship, but rather addressing a particular abuse of speech. He asks why women are singled out in vv. 34-35 and concludes that '[t]he answer is that they were the cause of the problem, the ones needing correction' (p. 178).

widows was a cause of controversy in the early Church can be seen from 1 Tim. 5.3-16.[201]

Given the above statements in 1 Corinthians and 1 Timothy, it is difficult to accept Torjesen's view that the public–private gender ideology was not invoked by Christian writers until the third century. From the first century, distinctions between the church setting and the private house sphere are made. This raises the question of whether Christian worship is perceived within the private or public sphere. Following Torjesen, the architectural space for Christian worship is clearly defined as public from the third and fourth centuries onwards.[202] But what about the first two centuries when worship took place within private houses? Was the Christian house-church perceived as part of the private realm or did some perceive it as more in the public realm and therefore, invoking a public–private gender ideology, not the place for women to teach or even speak?

While Torjesen insists that Christian worship took place in private space, Kathleen Corley presents a contrasting view, claiming that 'the primary setting of early Christian dialogue and worship was a formal, public meal.'[203] Hence, different views are expressed on the perceived public or private nature of Christian meals in the early centuries. As Judith M. Lieu comments, 'The question of where early Christianity was seen and saw itself as located in the rhetorical division between public and private is a complex one although it undoubtedly is strongly gendered.'[204] This question is key, however, in considering the gender expectations and prescriptions invoked in some Christian writings. The pronouncements in 1 Tim. 2.12 and 1 Cor. 14.34-35 would suggest that at least some in the churches in the early centuries perceive themselves more in the public than private spheres. A gender ideology of public–private, incorporating the code of honor–shame, shapes the pronouncements.[205]

Such pronouncements are in line with first-century laws and literature which sought to limit women's public activity. In the early Empire, Roman women experienced a certain amount of freedom and privilege though their 'emancipation' was limited and was mainly relevant to the upper classes.[206] While women's public activity at this time changed, however, the ideology which sought to limit women's behavior continued: 'This change in women's activities in the public sphere generated by

---

201.   See Price, *Widow Traditions*, 1–13.
202.   Torjesen, 'Reconstruction,' 305–6.
203.   Corley, *Private Women*, 24.
204.   Lieu, 'Attraction of Women,' 8.
205.   For more on the effects of fusing the private and public spheres, see Margaret Y. MacDonald, 'Reading Real Women Through the Undisputed Letters of Paul,' in *Women and Christian Origins*, (eds.) Ross Shepard Kraemer and Mary Rose D'Angelo (New York, NY: Oxford University Press, 1999), 205.
206.   Corley, *Private Women*, 54.

economic and social currents does not necessarily indicate a change in the social ideology about women's proper behavior or their social status. Once the political ramifications of women's changing behavior were recognized, Roman men sought to restrict women's liberties ...'[207]

Legislation and literature sought to influence women's behavior. Augustan legislation on marriage particularly impacted on upper-class women. The unmarried were penalized, and advantages were given to women who bore three (or in some cases four) legitimate children.[208] Adultery was declared a criminal offence but the law did not apply equally to women and men.[209] Along with this legislation, literature contrasted 'the ideal wife and the immoral assertive woman.'[210] The pronouncement in 1 Cor. 14.34-35 is an example of literature which promotes such a contrast.

The above discussion promotes an awareness of both the ideology and the incomplete picture of women's roles which literature can reinforce. The dichotomy of public–male/private–female was not all encompassing in the ancient Mediterranean world. Some women did take part in the public sphere and had considerable influence. Women in early Christianity had a variety of leadership roles including apostle, prophet and teacher, all of which would have required women's speech to be authoritative (cf. 1 Cor. 11.10).[211] The New Testament pronouncements which silence women's authority do not reflect the historical situation so much as reflect an elite male gender ideology. The Gospel of Luke is addressed to the most excellent Theophilus (1.3), offering the reader the position of 'an elite, male Christian – elite within Roman imperial society and informed as a Christian.'[212] An exploration of women's characterizations in the Lukan Gospel will help determine whether the Lukan text also invokes an elite gender ideology of public–private in regard to speech in the Lukan Gospel. If this is the case, then the Lukan characterization of women may contribute to marginalization, powerlessness, cultural imperialism and violence against women – faces of oppression in Young's list of criteria of oppression.

---

207. Corley, *Private Women*, 54–55.

208. Gardner, *Women*, 77–78.

209. See Gardner, *Women*, 127–31; also Pomeroy, *Goddesses, Whores*, 159.

210. Corley, *Private Women*, 55.

211. For a discussion of 1 Cor. 11.10, see Morna D. Hooker, 'Authority on her Head: An Examination of 1 Cor. XI. 10,' *NTS* 10 (1964): 410–16. Hooker argues that the head covering is a sign of the authority which is given to the woman from God (pp. 415–16).

212. Mary Rose D'Angelo, 'The ANHP Question in Luke-Acts: Imperial Masculinity and the Deployment of Women in the Early Second Century,' in *A Feminist Companion to Luke*, (eds.) Amy-Jill Levine and Marianne Blickenstaff (London: Sheffield Academic Press, 2002), 54.

5. *Outline of Chapters*

In this study, the power dynamics within the Parable of the Pounds will be the lens used to focus the characterizations of women in the Lukan Gospel. As previously explained, I will focus on context, text and reader, and their interconnectedness. I will also operate within a feminist hermeneutical framework, highlighting differences that are used as grounds for oppression. The discussion in this opening chapter has introduced the social and cultural context which informs and is informed by the text, setting the scene for the exploration in the chapters ahead.

Chapter 1 will present a discussion of the current state of scholarship on both the Parable of the Pounds and the characterization of women in the Lukan Gospel. As will be seen, in each case scholarly opinion is divided. With the Parable of the Pounds, different opinions are expressed on whether the third slave in the parable has failed or, indeed, acted honorably. With the characterization of women, views range from understanding the Lukan text as promoting the equality of women to seeing it as subordinating women to men. Yet other views suggest that both of these elements can be found in the Lukan presentation of women.

Chapter 2 provides some insight into the nature of 'parable' and the multiple interpretations which a parable encourages. Then a reading of the Parable of the Pounds, which aligns itself with those readings that perceive the third slave as honorable and the master as a tyrant, is presented. This reading focuses on the power dynamics which operate in the parable.

Chapter 3 is divided into two sections. First it explores aspects of the Lukan theology that permit the parable to be set within its wider Lukan theological context. Second, it explores how a metaphorical reading of the Parable of the Pounds can provide insight into the consequences that other Lukan characters face when they oppose oppressive power structures.

Chapters 4 and 5 explore the Lukan Gospel's characterizations of women within their narrative context, and begin to demonstrate how the women's characterizations can be described metaphorically using the language of the Parable of the Pounds. In particular, the portrayal of women's speech and silence is investigated. The characterization of several women as demon-possessed is also highlighted. A distinction is made between those women who appear as characters within the narrative and those women who appear in parables (characters in a story within a story).

Drawing on the work of the previous two chapters, Chapter 6 presents a thematic reading of the women characters of the Lukan Gospel in order to explicitly focus these women's characterizations through the lens of the Parable of the Pounds. Like the slaves in the Parable of the Pounds, some women are shown to 'gain' and some are shown to have their 'pound taken away' within their portrayals in the Lukan Gospel. It will be argued that this dynamic occurs in a variety of ways, and that often it is the issue of women's public speech which triggers the taking away of their 'pound.' Moreover, the power dynamic operating in the parables with women characters is shown to be different from that operating in the other women's stories within the Lukan Gospel. This suggests that different voices may be heard within the text. It will also be argued that using the Parable of the Pounds as a lens enables the taking away of the women's 'pound' to be critiqued from within the Lukan Gospel itself.

The final chapter, draws conclusions on what has been found in this study. It also considers some implications of the study for contemporary times and makes suggestions for a present-day reading of the Gospel of Luke.

Chapter 1

THE PARABLE OF THE POUNDS AND LUKAN WOMEN: THE CURRENT STATE OF SCHOLARSHIP

Since I am concerned in this study with the insight which the Parable of the Pounds can give to the characterization of women in the Gospel of Luke, it will be important to first establish the current state of scholarship on both these issues. As will be seen, both areas generate a wide range of opinions, some of which are conflicting.

1. *Scholarship on the Parable of the Pounds*

Given the vast amount of literature written on the Gospel of Luke, the Parable of the Pounds (Lk. 19.11-28) has attracted relatively minor attention. It is discussed in commentaries, of course, along with the rest of the Gospel but few scholars have chosen to concentrate on this Lukan parable in a monograph or journal article. Often articles focus more on the Parable of the Talents (Mt. 25.14-30) than on the Lukan Parable of the Pounds. Though these two parables have obvious similarities there are also significant differences between them. In particular, the Lukan parable has a theme of a nobleman seeking a βασιλεία amid opposition which is not included in the Matthean parable.[1] Therefore it is important that the Lukan parable is studied in its own right and not merely given a cursory glance while focusing on the Matthean story. For the purposes of this study, a thorough re-reading is essential.

a. *The Failure of the Third Slave*
The narrator's comment in Lk. 19.11 suggests that the Lukan parable is told to address the expectations of the imminent appearance of the βασιλεία. Many scholars interpret the parable as explaining the delay in the appearance of the parousia and as instructing the early Church in the appropriate way to live in the 'in-between time' until the full arrival of the βασιλεία.[2] Several scholars read the parable allegorically. Joseph A.

---

1. A discussion of the Matthean Parable of the Talents is provided in Chapter 2.
2. That the delay in the parousia is the main point of the parable is stated by Hans Conzelmann, *The Theology of St. Luke*, trans. Geoffrey Buswell (London: Faber & Faber,

Fitzmyer, for instance, states: '[T]he man of noble birth who goes off to obtain a kingly title becomes Jesus the Son of God, who is about to begin his "ascent" to the Father from the city of destiny. In that ascent he will be recognized as king (i.e. as the glorified Messiah ...) and will return in judgment ...'[3] Fitzmyer argues that, according to the Lukan 'allegorized parable,' on his return Jesus will do two things. He will call his servants[4] to account to see what they have done with 'the blessings of his kingdom-preaching' with which they have been entrusted, and 'he will take vengeance on his Palestinian compatriots who have not wanted him to be king over them.'[5]

Within this interpretation Fitzmyer sees the parable as indicating the different responses that a Christian disciple can make. A disciple can respond to the blessings of the kingdom with obedience (like the first two servants in the parable) or with disobedience (like the third servant). Fitzmyer perceives the third servant as not having done his duty. On the other hand, the first two servants are rewarded far beyond all expectation.[6] Darrell Bock extends the allegory by considering the identity of the servants in the parable, claiming that they 'represent all those who tie

---

1960), 74, 113. See also Armand Puig i Tàrrech, 'La Parabole des Talents (Mt 25, 14–30) ou des Mines (Lc 19, 11–28),' in *À Cause de l' Évangile: Études sur les Synoptiques et les Actes*, (ed.) François Refoulé (Paris: Publications de Saint-André, 1985), 172; C. H. Dodd, *The Parables of the Kingdom*, revised edn (London: Collins, 1961), 109; M. Zerwick, 'Die Parabel vom Thronanwärter,' *Bib* 40 (1959): 672–74; and Joachim Jeremias, *The Parables of Jesus*, third revised edn (London: SCM Press, 1972), 59. Eduard Schweizer suggests that the Lukan concern is not with the delay of God's kingdom but with what the community does in the interim period. See Eduard Schweizer, *The Good News According to Luke*, trans. David E. Green (London: SPCK, 1984), 293; and Joel B. Green, *The Gospel of Luke* (Grand Rapids, MI: Eerdmans, 1997), 674–75.

3. Joseph A. Fitzmyer, *The Gospel According to Luke*, 2 vols., AB 28, 28a (New York, NY: Doubleday, 1981–85), 2.1233. See also Eugene La Verdiere, *Luke* (Dublin: Veritas, 1980), 227–28; David Gooding, *According to Luke: A New Exposition of the Third Gospel* (Leicester: Inter-Varsity Press, 1987), 300–1; Roland Meynet, *L'Évangile Selon Saint Luc: Analyse Rhétorique Commentaire* (Paris: Les Éditions du Cerf, 1988), 187; Francis D. Weinert, 'The Parable of the Throne Claimant (Luke 19:12, 14-15a, 27) Reconsidered,' *CBQ* 39 (1977): 506; Jan Lambrecht, *Once More Astonished: The Parables of Jesus* (New York, NY: Crossroad, 1983), 188; and *idem*, 'The Parable of the Throne Claimant (Luke 19,11–27),' in *Understanding What One Reads: New Testament Essays* (Leuven: Peeters, 2003), 113.

4. In this literature review, both terminologies of 'slaves' and 'servants' will be used, reflecting the varied terminology within the scholarship. My own reading of the parable will refer to slaves. The distinction will be explained further in Chapter 2.

5. Fitzmyer, *Luke*, 2.1233. For an allegorical interpretation similar to that of Fitzmyer, see Charles H. Talbert, *Reading Luke: A Literary and Theological Commentary on the Third Gospel* (New York, NY: Crossroad, 1982), 178; and Sharon H. Ringe, *Luke* (Louisville, KY: Westminster John Knox Press, 1995), 234–35.

6. Fitzmyer, *Luke*, 2.1232–33.

themselves to Jesus.'[7] He argues that the third servant displays a lack of trust and faith in his master which indicates that, while he serves his master, he is not allied with him. This leads Bock to suggest that the third servant perhaps represents Judas.[8]

I. Howard Marshall also understands the Lukan parable as told to counter the expectation that the consummation of the βασιλεία will follow Jesus' arrival in Jerusalem. According to Marshall the parable presents the idea that Jesus is departing and will not be designated as king until his return. On his return, the Jewish people who have rejected him will experience judgment. The parable calls the servants of Jesus to profitable service in the period of Jesus' absence and warns that judgment and deprivation will be experienced by the servant who is unprofitable.[9] While Marshall notes the difficulty in using the imagery of revenge and massacre in relation to the judgment of Jesus on those who have rejected him (19.27), his explanation for its use is that the language, though strange to modern readers, 'would make sense to Jesus' hearers and convey to them the seriousness of their positions.'[10]

The work of Francis D. Weinert concentrates on the strand of the parable concerned with a nobleman seeking a βασιλεία amid opposition (vv. 12, 14-15a, 27). Weinert argues that a Jewish audience would sympathize with the citizens who oppose the ruler,[11] and therefore the harsh ending of the parable would confront the hearers. He concludes that the story serves as a harsh warning to those who oppose Jesus' ministry. With the arrival of the βασιλεία, opponents will be held accountable for their actions.[12]

A creative suggestion for these verses is made by Wilhelm Resenhöfft who argues that Lk. 19.11-12, 14-15a, 27 form part of a separate parable that is completed by Mt. 22.6-7. He argues that these Matthean verses are an insertion into the Parable of the Wedding Feast (Mt. 22.1-10), just as these Lukan verses are an insertion into the Parable of the Pounds.[13] Presenting a combined version of the Matthean and Lukan versions of the

---

7.   Darrell L. Bock, *Luke* (Downers Grove, IL: InterVarsity Press, 1994), 309.

8.   Bock, *Luke*, 309–10.

9.   I. Howard Marshall, *The Gospel of Luke: A Commentary on the Greek Text* (Exeter: The Paternoster Press, 1978), 700–1. Ringe, too, argues that the message for the disciples and church is the need for profitable management of what has been entrusted to them rather than simply preservation. See Ringe, *Luke*, 235.

10.   Marshall, *Luke*, 709.

11.   Weinert explains that the story would remind Jewish hearers of Jewish groups who had opposed hated rulers such as Archelaus and Demetrius. See Weinert, 'Throne Claimant,' 512–13.

12.   Weinert, 'Throne Claimant,' 514.

13.   Wilhelm Resenhöfft, 'Jesu Gleichnis von den Talenten, ergänzt durch die Lukas-Fassung,' *NTS* 26 (1980): 318, 327–28.

Parable of the Talents, Resenhöfft criticizes the third servant for failing to provide responsible service.[14] His interpretation is thus aligned in this regard with the majority reading.

Against those who argue that the parable is told to explain the delayed parousia, Luke Timothy Johnson claims that the parable is used to confirm the expectation that the βασιλεία is to appear immediately (19.11).[15] Johnson interprets the Matthean Parable of the Talents as one of 'eschatological judgment' but notes that there is no time delay in the Lukan parable. He suggests that the Matthean story has influenced the interpretation of the Lukan story.[16] Johnson argues that the Lukan text 'associates the Kingdom explicitly with the words and works of Jesus' and 'pictures the Kingdom as imminent, indeed immanent.'[17] This is supported by the proclamation of Jesus as king when he arrives in Jerusalem (19.38). While Johnson has a different understanding from the majority of scholars on the function of the parable in the Lukan narrative, he nevertheless envisages the nobleman as an image of Jesus.[18]

A more complex view of the Lukan representation of the βασιλεία is presented by Laurie Guy who argues that both the delay in the appearance of the βασιλεία and its present coming are indicated in Luke 19. For Guy, while the parable amends eschatological expectations, it also links with the following pericopae which suggest a present coming of the βασιλεία: 'There is tension within the parable, and within the larger Lukan passages under study, expressing tension within Lukan theology as a whole: the kingdom is future, but it is also present.'[19]

The characterization of the ruler in the Parable of the Pounds is important for the parable's interpretation. David Tiede notes that the ruler is portrayed as harsh and exacting and that his servants are aware of their master's character. According to Tiede, '[t]he master is not a direct picture of God or the Messiah, but he is a worldly wise businessperson who puts his servants to their tasks and expects performance.'[20] Tiede argues that the parable shows that Jesus understands the way the 'real

14. Resenhöfft, 'Gleichnis von den Talenten,' 318–24.

15. Luke Timothy Johnson, 'The Lukan Kingship Parable (Lk. 19:11-27),' *NovT* 24 (1982): 139–59.

16. Johnson, 'Lukan Kingship Parable,' 143.

17. Johnson, 'Lukan Kingship Parable,' 150–51, 154.

18. See Johnson, 'Lukan Kingship Parable,' 158. For another view which differs from the majority reading yet still understands the nobleman as imaging Jesus, see Ignace de la Potterie, 'La Parabole du Prétendant à la Royauté,' in *À Cause de l' Évangile: Études sur les Synoptiques et les Actes*, (ed.) François Refoulé (Paris: Publications de Saint-André, 1985), 638–41.

19. Laurie Guy, 'The Interplay of the Present and Future in the Kingdom of God (Luke 19:11-44),' *TynBul* 48 (1997): 137.

20. David L. Tiede, *Luke* (Minneapolis, MN: Augsburg, 1988), 325.

world' operates. When they can, kings execute those opposed to them.[21]
While Tiede considers that the actions of the ruler on his return are not a
direct picture of what Jesus will do on his return, he nevertheless asks,
'And would not the Lord and Messiah have the same right simply to **slay**
his enemies if he chose to exercise it?'[22]

Some interpret the master in the parable as a God figure. John Nolland
claims that it is unclear how the historical Jesus used the original parable
but he suggests that it is more likely that 'the returning master was an
image of God, rather than of Jesus himself.'[23] Nolland proposes that, in
the character of the third servant who does not want to take responsibility, the historical Jesus was addressing those who were 'unwilling to
make themselves answerable to God's expectations in any committed
sense.'[24] The parable not only challenges the logic of 'opting out' but also
challenges assumptions of God as tyrant. God is shown to be prepared to
accept any attempt to carry out the directive.[25]

J. D. M. Derrett likewise describes the master as a God figure. In the
manner of Achan (Josh. 7.1-26), the third servant is understood to be a
traitor who denies the master's (God's) sovereignty. Similarly, the citizens
who oppose the master are traitors who must be eliminated. Therefore,
according to Derrett, the slaughter of the citizens is appropriate since
those who resist God's rule must be exterminated.[26]

Once the nobleman/master is interpreted as being an image of Jesus or
God, then it follows that the third slave who disobeys his master has done
the wrong thing and acted dishonorably. If, however, the master is not
automatically assumed to be an image of Jesus or God, then it is possible
to assess the characters of the master and the third slave according to their
merits as portrayed in the parable.[27]

Though Joachim Jeremias claims that the Lukan interpretation of the
parable announces the delay of the parousia, he is critical of the Lukan
author for interpreting the nobleman as representing Jesus:

> Luke, then, would seem to have interpreted the nobleman who received
> a kingdom and demanded a reckoning from his servants on his return,
> as the Son of Man departing to heaven and returning to judgement. But
> Luke is certainly wrong. For it is hardly conceivable that Jesus would
> have compared himself, either with a man 'who drew out where he had

---

21. Tiede, *Luke*, 325–26.
22. Tiede, *Luke*, 326.
23. John Nolland, *Luke*, 3 vols. (Dallas, TX: Word Books, 1989–93), 3.911–12.
24. Nolland, *Luke*, 3.912.
25. Nolland, *Luke*, 3.912. Puig i Tàrrech, too, considers that the behavior of the master
reminds us of the magnanimity of God. See Puig i Tàrrech, 'Parabole des Talents,' 189.
26. J. D. M. Derrett, 'A Horrid Passage in Luke Explained,' *ExpTim* 97 (1986): 137–38.
27. See Denis McBride, *The Parables of Jesus* (Hampshire: Redemptorist Publications,
1999), 79–80.

not paid in, and reaped where he had not sown' (Luke 19.21), that is, a rapacious man, heedlessly intent on his own profit: or with a brutal oriental despot, gloating over the sight of his enemies slaughtered before his eyes . . .[28]

Jeremias assumes that Jesus originally directed the parable to the scribes who had been given the Word of God and who would soon be called to account for their use of this gift. '[I]t would be seen whether they had used it in accordance with the will of God, or whether, like the third servant, they had frustrated the operation of the divine word by self-seeking and careless neglect of God's gift.'[29] Thus, even though Jeremias perceives the ruler in despotic terms, he is critical of the third servant who does not follow the ruler's directions.

Not all scholars believe that the parable is allegorical and several scholars argue that the ruler acts like a tyrant. Frederick W. Danker suggests that the parable has allegorical elements but claims that 'there is no strict correspondence between characteristic features of earthly kings and those of Jesus as a royal figure.'[30] While noting that the ruler bears the marks of a tyrant, Danker labels the third slave as faithless and as an example of total failure.[31] C. F. Evans also argues: '[T]he parable is another of the risqué parables, like those of the Unrighteous Steward and the Unrighteous Judge, in which the central figure is a reprehensible character, and the lesson conveyed, even by a dangerous example, is "be profitable at all costs and by all means." '[32] Danker and Evans, then, both see the third slave as having done the wrong thing by not making a profit as his master expected. Hence, despite not identifying the ruler as Jesus, both Danker and Evans still perceive the third slave's actions as dishonorable. The honorable course of action in their view is to do just as the master would have wished.

An alternative interpretation is proffered by Brendan Byrne who argues that the two storylines of the parable address different issues. The storyline of the throne-claimant speaks to the rejection awaiting Jesus in Jerusalem. According to Byrne, '[t]he king's brutal revenge is not commended. Even less should it be seen as a paradigm for the action of God. It is simply the sort of thing that happened in the world of Jesus and his audience (cf. 13:1-5).'[33] The punishment of those who oppose the king

28. Jeremias, *Parables of Jesus*, 59–60.

29. Jeremias, *Parables of Jesus*, 62.

30. Frederick W. Danker, *Jesus and the New Age: A Commentary on St Luke's Gospel*, completely revised and expanded edn (Philadelphia, PA: Fortress Press, 1988), 307.

31. Danker, *New Age*, 308–9.

32. C. F. Evans, *Saint Luke* (London/Philadelphia, PA: SCM Press/Trinity Press International, 1990), 667. See also Danker, *New Age*, 307.

33. Brendan Byrne, *The Hospitality of God: A Reading of Luke's Gospel* (Collegeville, MN: Liturgical Press, 2000), 153.

is prophetic of the destruction of Jerusalem in 70CE.[34] Byrne claims the
main storyline speaks to the circumstances of the early Christian
communities living in the time between the resurrection and Jesus' return:
'The parable makes the simple point that the time before the arrival of the
Son of Man is a time of opportunity for creative service, for which those
who have been particularly gifted will be required to give an account (cf.
12:35-48).'[35] Byrne interprets the third servant as having failed to take the
opportunity for this service.

While there are differences in interpretation of the parable, the majority
view reflected in scholarly opinion is that the third slave has failed while
the first two slaves model the appropriate response to their master. In
contrast, I will argue that the actions of the third slave are to be
commended and that it is the master, the one who has the power, who is
the 'villain' in the story. Some scholars have presented this minority view
and it is to these scholars that we now turn.

b. *Honoring the Third Slave*
Several early patristic interpretations of the Parable of the Talents see the
money entrusted as representing the word of God which is to be preached
by the Church in the absence of Jesus.[36] The non-canonical *Gospel of the
Nazoreans* appears to present a different interpretation, however. While
no extant copy of the *Gospel of the Nazoreans* is available, an outline of
this story can be found in the writings of Eusebius:

> But since the Gospel [*written*] in Hebrew characters which has come into
> our hands enters the threat not against the man who had hid [*the talent*],
> but against him who had lived dissolutely – for he [*the master*] had three
> servants: one who squandered his master's substance with harlots and
> flute-girls, one who multiplied the gain, and one who hid the talent; and
> accordingly one was accepted (with joy), another merely rebuked, but
> the other cast into prison – I wonder whether in Matthew the threat
> which is uttered after the word against the man who did nothing may

34. Byrne, *Hospitality of God*, 153. See also Lambrecht, 'Throne Claimant,' 120. At the
same time, Lambrecht notes the difficulty in identifying the violent action of the king with the
destruction of Jerusalem: 'Can such an intramundane catastrophe be seen as God's
punishment because Israel – part of it! – rejected her Messiah? Nowadays, most
commentators will hesitate to answer this question positively, and it would seem rightly
so' (p. 124).

35. Byrne, *Hospitality of God*, 153. Byrne understands the ruler as giving different sums
of money to his servants. This is the situation in the Matthean version of the parable (Matt.
25.14-15) but in the Lukan version each is given the same amount. This suggests that Byrne's
interpretation of the Lukan parable is influenced by the Matthean version.

36. For a summary of patristic interpretations of the Parable of the Talents and some
references to the Parable of the Pounds, see Frédéric Manns, 'La Parabole des Talents
Wirkungsgeschichte et Racines Juives,' *RevScRel* 65 (1991): 343–62.

refer not to him, but by epanalepsis to the first who had feasted and drunk with the drunken.[37]

Such an interpretation sees the slave who multiplies the gain as being rebuked by the master rather than the slave who protects what he has been given.[38]

Some scholars use insights from the social sciences, particularly the notion of 'limited good,' to assist them in their interpretation of the Parable of the Pounds. As anthropologist George M. Foster explains, members of a society have a common understanding of the 'rules' for living: 'The members of every society share a common cognitive orientation which is, in effect, an unverbalized, implicit expression of their understanding of the "rules of the game" of living imposed upon them by their social, natural and supernatural universes.'[39] Foster proposes that the 'Image of Limited Good' gives the best justification for the behavior of people in a peasant society. This model suggests that peasants view 'good' things, such as land, wealth, status and power, as finite entities.[40] Within this view an increase for an individual or a family can only come at the expense of others. 'Hence an apparent relative improvement in someone's position with respect to any "Good" is viewed as a threat to the entire community.'[41]

In a society operating within the cultural code of 'limited good,' Malina argues that the one who seeks to accumulate wealth is dishonorable. He quotes from a fourth-century Mediterranean proverb: 'Every rich person is a thief or the heir of a thief.' Malina proposes that this was also the outlook in the first-century Mediterranean world.[42] As he explains: 'If all

37. Original Greek text in Erich Klostermann, (ed.), *Apocrypha*, 3rd edn, vol. 2 (Berlin: De Gruyter, 1929), 9, n. 15, and translated in Wilhelm Schneemelcher and R. McL. Wilson, (eds.), *New Testament Apocrypha Vol One: Gospels and Related Writings*, revised edn (Cambridge: James Clarke and Co, 1991), 161–62. The Greek text with an alternative translation is provided in William D. Stroker, *Extracanonical Sayings of Jesus* (Atlanta, GA: Scholars Press, 1989), 45.

38. Merrill Kitchen, 'Rereading the Parable of the Pounds: A Social and Narrative Analysis of Luke 19:11-28,' in *Prophecy and Passion: Essays in Honour of Athol Gill*, (ed.) David Neville (Adelaide: Australian Theological Forum, 2002), 238–39, argues that *2 Clement* and Irenaeus also promote an understanding whereby the third slave is the protagonist of the parable and the compliant slaves are antagonists.

39. George M. Foster, 'Peasant Society and the Image of Limited Good,' *American Anthropologist* 67 (1965): 293.

40. Foster, 'Peasant Society,' 296. For an alternative understanding to the concept of 'limited good' see James R. Gregory, 'Image of Limited Good, or Expectation of Reciprocity?,' *Current Anthropology* 16 (1975): 73–92.

41. Foster, 'Peasant Society,' 297. For a summary of peasant understanding of 'limited good,' see Halvor Moxnes, *The Economy of the Kingdom: Social Conflict and Economic Relations in Luke's Gospel* (Philadelphia, PA: Fortress Press, 1988), 76–79.

42. Malina, *New Testament World*, 97–98.

Taking Away the Pound

goods are limited, and all human beings were created more or less on equal footing, then those who have more, or their ancestors, must have taken it from those who now have less, or from their ancestors.'[43]

Using the notion of 'limited good,' Malina and Richard L. Rohrbaugh claim that peasant hearers of the Parable of the Pounds would perceive the first two servants as robbers cooperating with their master in extortion. The peasant expectation would be to maintain honorably what one has without seeking more, as the third servant does.[44] That the third servant is condemned for his actions and the 'robbers' are rewarded by their master would fit peasants' experience of the real world.[45] Malina and Rohrbaugh argue that the Lukan parable indicates that the βασιλεία of God was not as imminent as some might expect, by indicating that extortion was still being practised. Given that the story of Zacchaeus (19.1-10) precedes the Parable of the Pounds, they claim:

> Having just told a story of a rich man who surprisingly shared his goods with the poor, Luke fears his readers might mistakenly think the theocracy Jesus proclaimed had arrived. Being near Jerusalem and the end of Luke's travel narrative might suggest the same. To prevent that conclusion Luke now records a parable of Jesus featuring a rich man who is anything but a model of the kingdom. The good example of Zacchaeus is paralleled with the bad example of the nobleman ... Jesus tells the story lest anyone prematurely think that extortion had been eradicated by the forthcoming arrival of the kingdom.[46]

This suggests that Malina and Rohrbaugh here perceive the Lukan author as deliberately contrasting the actions of the nobleman in the parable with the actions of Zacchaeus in 19.1-10, and that the nobleman is portrayed as an extortionist.

In a separate article Rohrbaugh explores the Parable of the Talents/ Pounds in more detail, though he focuses on the dealings of the master with his servants and does not pay attention to the additional Lukan

43. Bruce J. Malina, 'Wealth and Poverty in the New Testament and its World,' *Int* 41 (1987): 363. For more detatil on the code of 'limited good,' see Malina, *New Testament World*, 81–107.
44. Bruce J. Malina and Richard L. Rohrbaugh, *Social-Science Commentary on the Synoptic Gospels*, 2nd edn (Minneapolis: Fortress Press, 2003), 385. While the audience of the historical Jesus' parables may have included a significant peasant population, the Lukan community is likely to have a smaller percentage of peasants, and to include a significant wealthier population. Michael Trainor suggests that the Lukan community consisted of peasants, social elite and artisans. See Michael Trainor, '"And on Earth, Peace…" (Luke 2.14): Luke's Perspective on the Earth,' in *Readings from the Perspective of Earth*, (ed.) Norman C. Habel (Sheffield: Sheffield Academic Press, 2000), 176–77.
45. Malina and Rohrbaugh, *Social-Science Commentary*, 385.
46. Malina and Rohrbaugh, *Social-Science Commentary*, 304.

theme of the opposition of the citizens.[47] He suggests that the parable acts as a 'text of terror' for peasants since 'the strong trample the weak and are rewarded for doing so.'[48] Rohrbaugh argues that those who have 'imaginations socialized in the capitalized West' have difficulty in picturing 'the agrarian social dynamics to which the parable once appealed.'[49] He claims further that modern readers tend to assume that the historical Jesus condemns the third servant, but it is just as possible that Jesus instead condemns the master's viewpoint, as his peasant hearers would have done. 'The parable is a warning. But to whom? Jesus' peasant hearers would almost certainly have assumed it was a warning to the rich about their exploitation of the weak!'[50] Thus the social location of the hearer/reader impacts on the way the parable is understood.[51]

According to Rohrbaugh, the Matthean and Lukan additions to the original parable of Jesus transform the story into an allegory about diligence in the time before the arrival of the parousia. He claims, however, that Jesus' story was a parable rather than an allegory.[52] Rohrbaugh suggests, therefore, that the Lukan author, along with the Matthean author, has not understood Jesus' condemnation of the master's attitude whereas Eusebius and the writer of the *Gospel of the Nazoreans* have.[53] By stating that the Lukan author has not understood the condemnation of the master implied in the parable, Rohrbaugh is arguing from a different standpoint from the understanding outlined in his work with Malina mentioned above. Rohrbaugh is proposing here that the Lukan understanding of the parable does not conform to Jesus' purposes in telling the parable.

Focusing on oppressive practices, William Herzog understands the historical Jesus' parables as being told to increase awareness of the ways in which exploitation and oppression operated in the world of his hearers.

47. See Richard L. Rohrbaugh, 'A Peasant Reading of the Parable of the Talents/Pounds: A Text of Terror?,' *BTB* 23 (1993): 32–39.

48. Rohrbaugh, 'Peasant Reading,' 33, 35. Rohrbaugh uses the term 'text of terror' which was coined by Phyllis Trible. See Phyllis Trible, *Texts of Terror: Literary-Feminist Readings of Biblical Narrative* (London: SCM Press, 2002). This understanding of the parable is also outlined in Barbara E. Reid, *Parables for Preachers: The Gospel of Luke Year C* (Collegeville, MN: Liturgical Press, 2000), 324–26.

49. Rohrbaugh, 'Peasant Reading,' 32.

50. Rohrbaugh, 'Peasant Reading,' 38.

51. John Dominic Crossan argues that the diversity among Jesus' audience would have led to debate about the interpetation of parables. See John Dominic Crossan, 'The Parables of Jesus,' *Int* 56 (2002): 252–53.

52. Rohrbaugh, 'Peasant Reading,' 33.

53. Rohrbaugh, 'Peasant Reading,' 38. For a critique of Rohrbaugh's use of material and argument concerning the *Gospel of the Nazoreans*, see Joel R. Wohlgemut, 'Entrusted Money (Matthew 25:14-28),' in *Jesus and his Parables: Interpreting the Parable of Jesus Today*, (ed.) V. George Shillington (Edinburgh: T&T Clark, 1997), 113–14.

He draws on the work of Paolo Freire and compares the parables to the conscientization process which Freire undertook in working with oppressed peoples, designed to raise the awareness of the nature of their oppression and what contributes to it.[54] Herzog sees Freire's work as helpful in understanding the role of Jesus' parables. He argues that the parables of Jesus were designed to challenge hearers to see the reality of their social situation, to be able to identify and name oppressive structures in order that new ways of understanding could be developed. By exploring how the spiral of violence and poverty created by oppression could be broken, the parables were subversive of the operating power structures. It is not surprising then, Herzog argues, that Jesus was executed by those whom he was challenging, those who benefited from those power structures. Herzog outlines that Freire's conscientization process also brought him into conflict with the authorities who were challenged by his actions.[55] In Herzog's opinion, 'the parables were not earthly stories with heavenly meanings but earthy stories with heavy meanings, weighted down by an awareness of the workings of exploitation in the world of their hearers. The focus of the parables was not on a vision of the glory of the reign of God, but on the gory details of how oppression served the interests of a ruling class.'[56] While it is not necessary to form a dichotomy between a focus on the glory of the reign of God and a focus on political interests, Herzog's point is clear.[57]

He argues that the praise which the master gives to the first servant masks 'the ugly realities suppressed beneath the profit margin.'[58] Against this, the words of the third servant are critical. 'They expose the sham of what has happened and place it under the unobstructed light of clear analysis and prophetic judgment.'[59] In this sense, the third servant is uncovering the secret and bringing it into the light (cf. 12.2-3). As Herzog notes, the parable makes clear that acting alone against the power structures makes one vulnerable. Herzog sees the third servant as a retainer who has probably benefited from the system in the past but who now challenges it.[60] Hearers of the parable who may have suffered at the hands of retainers are challenged to consider their response to the retainer

54. For a detailed explanation of Freire's conscientization process and how Herzog analyzes the parables of Jesus, see William R. Herzog, *Parables as Subversive Speech: Jesus as Pedagogue of the Oppressed* (Louisville, KY: Westminster/John Knox Press, 1994), 9–29.

55. Herzog, *Parables*, 25–8.

56. Herzog, *Parables*, 3.

57. Similarly understanding the actions of the master and first two slaves as exploitative, writer Ngugi wa Thiong'o employs the parable in his critique of practices in Kenya. See Ngugi wa Thiong'o, *Devil on the Cross* (Oxford: Heinemann, 1987), 82–86, 104–8.

58. Herzog, *Parables*, 163. See also McBride, *Parables of Jesus*, 85.

59. Herzog, *Parables*, 165.

60. Herzog, *Parables*, 167.

turned whistle-blower in the story. Do they welcome him or do they reject one who has cooperated with the system, making it more difficult for others to challenge the system in the future? For Herzog, the parable confronts hearers to explore the ways in which they contribute to the oppression and its perpetuation even as they are victims of that oppression.[61] Herzog concentrates on the historical Jesus rather than the Lukan Jesus in his discussion. There is insufficient evidence in the Lukan text, however, to support his reading that the third servant has been one of the oppressors in the past.[62]

Like Herzog, Robert T. Fortna draws upon the perspectives of the oppressed, the 'underclass,' to argue that Jesus' original parable was likely to have been 'a declaration ... of the liberating and political empowerment afforded by the Reign of God to those who previously believed themselves powerless.'[63] Fortna uses Rohrbaugh's understanding of the *Gospel of the Nazoreans*, which welcomes the action of the third slave, to support his case. In discussing the versions in the canonical Gospels, Fortna's interest is mainly in the Matthean story, with only a few references to the Lukan story. He does claim, however, that the 'Throne-Claimant' strand, which he believes to be a Lukan insertion, turns the story into a denouncement of the non-Christian Jews of the Lukan author's time.[64] Thus he reads the Lukan story allegorically. No discussion of the 'Throne-Claimant' strand is given in the article, however.

Similar to Malina and Rohrbaugh in their commentary, James M. Dawsey contrasts Zacchaeus in 19.1-10 with the nobleman of the Parable of the Pounds. Whereas Zacchaeus gives to the poor, the nobleman is intent on taking away from the one who has little. Dawsey argues that Jesus told the parable to contrast the βασιλεία of God, which 'brings salvation but means giving,' with the worldly βασιλεία, which is 'unjust, built upon taking, and leads to death.'[65]

The most detailed study of the Parable of the Pounds has been undertaken by Merrill Kitchen. Kitchen, too, argues that the conflict in the parable mirrors the conflict in the Gospel narrative between the βασιλεία of God and the βασιλεία of this world: 'Jesus, as embodiment of the kingdom of God, is consistently presented confronting the many

---

61. Herzog, *Parables*, 167–68.

62. For a discussion and critique of the interpretations of Rohrbaugh and Herzog, see Wohlgemut, 'Entrusted Money,' 109–16.

63. Robert T. Fortna, 'Reading Jesus' Parable of the Talents Through Underclass Eyes: Matt 25:14-30,' *Forum (Foundations and Facets)* 8 (1992): 226.

64. Fortna, 'Reading Jesus' Parable,' 219, n. 22.

65. James M. Dawsey, *The Lukan Voice: Confusion and Irony in the Gospel of Luke* (Macon, GA: Mercer University Press, 1986), 98.

agents of the ruling secular and religious kingdoms.'[66] Furthermore, she argues that the third servant exhibits characteristics which mirror the character of Jesus. Both refuse the opportunity of worldly power and suffer the consequences.[67] Kitchen also compares the nobleman in the parable (19.11-28) with the devil in the temptation scene (4.1-13). Both demand obedience, claim control over kingdoms and promise rewards.[68] Thus Kitchen understands the third servant to be honorable and the nobleman to be antagonistic. She asserts that the nobleman who claims control and exploits others cannot be likened to Jesus who proclaims and embodies the jubilee ethics of Lk. 4.18-19.[69]

Through her study, Kitchen attempts to identify the literary intentions of the Lukan author. She understands the conflict in the Parable of the Pounds as a deliberate literary device used by the author to depict the struggle between two kingdoms.[70] She notes that the parable occurs in the narrative towards the end of Jesus' journey to Jerusalem and claims that '[i]t signifies the purpose of that journey and highlights the conflict existing about that purpose.'[71]

Bringing his background as a clinical psychologist to his study of the parables of Jesus, Richard Q. Ford identifies three levels in the Parable of the Talents/Pounds: the 'exploiting slave-master,' the 'well-positioned slaves who are called upon to exploit' and the 'poorly positioned laborers who are exploited,' though he notes that only two of these are explicit in the parable. The laborers whom the first two slaves have robbed in order to present 'obscene profits' to their master are not identified.[72] In a subsequent article, Ford describes the courage of the third slave as his refusal to participate in the exploitation which produces 'obscene profits.' Ford also claims it would have been obvious to Jesus' original audience that such profits were criminal.[73]

Ched Myers argues that the parable reads more coherently when it is not interpreted allegorically with the master representing God, but is rather 'read as a cautionary tale of realism about the mercenary selfishness

66. Merrill A. Kitchen, 'The Parable of the Pounds' (unpublished TheolM thesis, Melbourne College of Divinity, 1993), 136.

67. The comparison between the third servant and Jesus is outlined in more detail in Kitchen, 'Parable of the Pounds,' 134, and is further explained in Chapter 3 below.

68. See Kitchen, 'Parable of the Pounds,' 138. This is explained in more detail in Chapter 3 below.

69. Kitchen, 'Parable of the Pounds,' 68.

70. Kitchen, 'Parable of the Pounds,' 13.

71. Kitchen, 'Parable of the Pounds,' 123.

72. Richard Q. Ford, *The Parables of Jesus: Recovering the Art of Listening* (Minneapolis, MN: Fortress Press, 1997), 36.

73. Richard Q. Ford, 'Body Language: Jesus' Parables of the Woman With the Yeast, the Woman With the Jar, and the Man with the Sword,' *Int* 56 (2002): 302.

of the debt system.'[74] This reading recognizes the third servant as 'the hero who pays a high price for speaking truth to power (Matthew 25:24-30)—just as Jesus himself did.'[75] Thus Myers, too, recognizes links between the actions of the third servant and Jesus. Warren Carter displays a similar understanding of the Matthean Parable of the Talents (Mt. 25.14-30). Carter points out that the master behaves in a tyrannical manner which contradicts Jesus' previous teaching. The third slave, being more faithful to Jesus' teaching, should be commended for not depriving others in order to increase the master's wealth.[76] Carter also parallels the third slave with Jesus. '[I]n his resistance to the imperial scheme he reflects both Jesus' actions and Jesus' fate as one who will also be expelled from this society.'[77] Carter, however, reads the Matthean parable as reinforcing dominant cultural values in which the wealthy and powerful become even more so at the expense of others. He, therefore, argues that the 'audience must ... supply the critique of the parable's content from the larger gospel context.'[78]

c. *Conclusions from the Literature Review of the Parable of the Pounds*
As can be seen from the literature review, the current scholarly literature on the Lukan Parable of the Pounds can be divided into two groups: that which sees the third slave as worthy of condemnation and that which perceives this slave as worthy of honor. Those scholars who read the parable allegorically are a subset of the first group. If the nobleman is understood to represent Jesus or God then the slave who opposes the nobleman is automatically perceived in a poor light. Also included in the first group are those scholars who note the problems associated with interpreting the parable allegorically, but still interpret the third slave as having failed in contrast with the first two slaves. I will argue in this study that any reading of the Parable of the Pounds which justifies the actions of the nobleman and/or values the actions of the first two slaves as opposed to the third slave can be critiqued from within the Lukan context itself. Thus, I align myself with the minority reading which reads the third slave as the hero of the narrative. This reading will be used as a lens through which to focus the characterizations of women in the Lukan Gospel.

74. Ched Myers, 'Jesus' New Economy of Grace,' *Sojourners* 27, no. 4 (1998): 39.
75. Myers, 'Economy of Grace,' 39.
76. Warren Carter, *Matthew and the Margins: A Socio-Political and Religious Reading*, JSNTSup 204 (Sheffield: Sheffield Academic Press, 2000), 487–88.
77. Carter, *Matthew*, 488. See also McBride, *Parables of Jesus*, 88.
78. Carter, *Matthew*, 488.

2. *Scholarship on Women in the Gospel of Luke*

The Gospel of Luke has attracted more attention than the other Synoptics regarding the issue of the portrayal of women. As is the case with the Parable of the Pounds, a range of views on Lukan presentation of women can be found. At one end of the spectrum, some argue that the Lukan Gospel depicts inclusiveness and equality and presents perhaps the most favorable image of women in the New Testament. At the other end of the spectrum, it is argued that this presentation deliberately and systematic-ally portrays women in subordinate roles, reinforcing the silence of women. Prior to 1980, the general consensus amongst scholars was that the Lukan Gospel presents a positive view of women. In the 1980s, however, this view began to be challenged.[79] As critical feminist biblical hermeneutics developed, a more critical exploration of the texts was undertaken, raising awareness of how texts can serve patriarchal and androcentric interests.[80] From that time on, a more negative view of the Lukan portrayal of women rubbed shoulders with the positive view that had predominated. This situation led Robert J. Karris in 1994 to label the issue of the Lukan view of women as the new 'storm-center' of Luke-Acts.[81] Thus the scholarly literature on this issue offers a range of differing views.[82] Not all views lie at one or other extreme, however, with some views being more nuanced. Elements of this debate will now be explored.

a. *The Gospel for Women*

One aspect of the Lukan Gospel which leads many to consider this Gospel as being favorable to women is that there are significantly more stories concerning women in the Gospel of Luke than in any of the other Gospels. Thus women have a higher profile in this Gospel than in the other Gospels. Furthermore, many of these passages about women are unique to the Lukan Gospel.[83] Alfred Plummer claims accordingly that women are given a prominent place throughout the Third Gospel and that

---

79. See Elisabeth M. Tetlow, *Women and Ministry in the New Testament* (New York, NY: Paulist, 1980), 101–9, for an early example of this challenge.

80. A ground-breaking work in critical feminist biblical hermeneutics was Schüssler Fiorenza, *In Memory of Her*, first published in 1983.

81. Robert J. Karris, 'Women and Discipleship in Luke,' *CBQ* 56 (1994): 5.

82. Such a range of views on the Lukan women is reflected within the articles presented in Amy-Jill Levine and Marianne Blickenstaff, (eds.), *A Feminist Companion to Luke*, FCNT 3 (London: Sheffield Academic Press, 2002). Several of these articles will be incorporated into the discussion in this and later chapters.

83. Passages which are unique to the Lukan Gospel and contain women characters or parables with women include: Lk. 1–2; 7.11-17, 36-50; 8.1-3; 10.38-42; 11.27-28; 13.10-17;

this Gospel 'is in an especial sense the Gospel for *women*.'[84] In an early assessment, Bonnie Bowman Thurston agrees with Plummer's view and she considers that the Lukan Gospel has a 'more emancipated attitude toward women.'[85]

The existence in the Lukan Gospel of parallel stories concerning men and women has also been influential in forming the views of many scholars.[86] Since most of the pairings are not in the other Synoptic Gospels and such pairs also exist in Acts, Helmut Flender argues that this parallelism of stories about men and women reflects a deliberate intention: 'Luke expresses by this arrangement that man and woman stand together and side by side before God. They are equal in honour and grace, they are endowed with the same gifts and have the same responsibilities (cf. Gen. 1:27; Gal. 3:28).'[87] Several other scholars have drawn on this understanding of gender pairing. Jane Kopas, for instance, comments on the sensitivity of the Lukan Gospel to women and claims that the pairings suggest a measure of equality which was unexpected in Jesus' time.[88]

For Constance Parvey, the pairings reflect an awareness that the Third

---

15.8-10; 18.1-8; 23.27-31. Leonard Swidler, *Biblical Affirmations of Women* (Philadelphia, PA: Westminster Press, 1979), 254–55, enumerates forty-two passages dealing with women in the Gospel of Luke with twenty-three of these being unique to this Gospel.

84. Alfred Plummer, *The Gospel According to S. Luke*, 5th edn (Edinburgh: T. & T. Clark, 1922), xlii.

85. Bonnie Bowman Thurston, *The Widows: A Women's Ministry in the Early Church* (Minneapolis, MN: Fortress Press, 1989), 23. In a later work, however, Thurston discusses the mixed messages of liberation and subordination within the Lukan Gospel. See Bonnie Thurston, *Women in the New Testament: Questions and Commentary* (New York, NY: Crossroad, 1998), 127.

86. See, for example, the lists of pairs in Helmut Flender, *St. Luke: Theologian of Redemptive History*, trans. Ilse and Reginald Fuller (Philadelphia, PA: Fortress Press, 1967), 9–10, n. 2; Mary Rose D'Angelo, 'Women in Luke-Acts: A Redactional View,' *JBL* 109 (1990): 444–46; Mary Rose D'Angelo, '(Re)Presentations of Women in the Gospel of Matthew and Luke-Acts,' in *Women and Christian Origins*, (eds.) Ross Shepard Kraemer and Mary Rose D'Angelo (New York, NY: Oxford University Press, 1999), 182–84; and Turid Karlsen Seim, *The Double Message: Patterns of Gender in Luke-Acts* (Edinburgh: T. & T. Clark, 1994), 15.

87. Flender, *St. Luke*, 10. See also Eugene H. Maly, 'Women and the Gospel of Luke,' *BTB* 10 (1980): 101; Ben Witherington, *Women in the Earliest Churches* (Cambridge: Cambridge University Press, 1988), 129; Dennis M. Sweetland, 'Luke the Christian,' in *New Views on Luke and Acts*, (ed.) Earl Richard (Collegeville, MN: Liturgical Press, 1990), 60; Talbert, *Reading Luke*, 91–92; and Robert F. O'Toole, *The Unity of Luke's Theology: An Analysis of Luke-Acts* (Wilmington, DE: Michael Glazier, 1984), 118–20.

88. Jane Kopas, 'Jesus and Women: Luke's Gospel,' *TTod* 43 (1986): 192. See also Robert C. Tannehill, *The Narrative Unity of Luke-Acts: A Literary Interpretation. Volume 1: The Gospel According to Luke* (Philadelphia, PA: Fortress Press, 1986), 132–33. David L. Balch, 'Luke,' in *Eerdman's Commentary on the Bible*, (ed.) James D. G. Dunn and John W. Rogerson (Grand Rapids, MI: Eerdmans, 2003), 1117, notes the limits of the gender pairing, however, since only males preach and are leaders.

Gospel's listeners include men and women. Claiming that the elements within each pair carry the same message about the Kingdom, she argues that the only apparent reason for the repetition is to make the message clearly understandable to both female and male listeners. Thus the different accounts are designed to appeal to different audiences.[89] Parvey suggests that the Lukan Gospel setting included a significant number of women who were either students of the Scriptures or potential converts: 'Though the other gospels also include many references to women in relation to the life and teachings of Jesus, the Gospel of Luke gives the richest evidence of being shaped by a social context in which there were large numbers of women present who were schooled in the scriptures.'[90]

From an exploration of the function and roles of women in the Lukan Gospel, E. Jane Via argues for the theological significance of women and 'feminine imagery' in this Gospel. She considers that each of the women of the infancy narrative – Elizabeth, Mary and Anna – is a means of revelation and that the theological and prophetic voices of these women are important elements of Luke 1–2.[91] Further, she highlights the various examples of women benefiting from Jesus' ministry (4.38-39; 7.11-17, 36-50; 8.40-56; 13.10-17), suggesting that these indicate that women are included in the messianic blessings.[92] Because women accompany Jesus and he teaches them (8.1-3; 10.39; 24.6-8), Via claims that readers are led to recognize women as Jesus' disciples.[93] Moreover, she draws on the presence of 'female figures in Jesus' teaching' (4.25-26; 15.8-10; 18.1-8) and 'feminine imagery' to describe Jesus' self (13.34) to reinforce her position that women have significant roles in this Gospel.[94]

Studying the Lukan redaction of Markan and Q source material, Ben Witherington identifies an interest in women and their roles.[95] This interest is further highlighted in the material which is unique to the Lukan Gospel and is particularly evident in the infancy narratives in Luke 1–2. Witherington argues that the portrayal of Elizabeth, Mary and Anna in these opening chapters reinforces the Lukan theme of reversal: 'As part of

89.   Constance F. Parvey, 'The Theology and Leadership of Women in the New Testament,' in *Religion and Sexism: Images of Woman in the Jewish and Christian Traditions*, (ed.) Rosemary Radford Ruether (New York, NY: Simon & Schuster, 1974), 138–40. See also Stevan Davies, 'Women in the Third Gospel and the New Testament Apocrypha,' in *'Women Like This': New Perspectives on Jewish Women in the Greco-Roman World*, (ed.) Amy-Jill Levine (Atlanta, GA: Scholars Press, 1991), 190.

90.   Parvey, 'Theology and Leadership,' 140–41.

91.   E. Jane Via, 'Women in the Gospel of Luke,' in *Women in the World's Religions, Past and Present*, (ed.) Ursula King (New York, NY: Paragon House, 1987), 38–41.

92.   Via, 'Women,' 41–45.

93.   Via, 'Women,' 46. See also Rosalie Ryan, 'The Women from Galilee and Discipleship in Luke,' *BTB* 15 (1985): 56–59.

94.   Via, 'Women,' 48–49.

95.   Witherington, *Women in the Earliest Churches*, 129–30.

Luke's presentation of the reversal the Gospel brings about, Luke stresses the way women rejoice and are liberated as God acts.'[96] In the final chapter of the Gospel, Witherington notes another example of reversal when women announce the good news to the apostles 'whose future it would soon be to make such proclamations' (24.9-10).[97] While he points out that women are not featured as much in Acts as in the Gospel, he argues that the various roles which women perform in Acts show how the Lukan Gospel liberates women and creates new possibilities for them. According to Witherington, while the Lukan author does not totally reject the patriarchal framework of his culture, he presents a transformed vision of this framework which incorporates women in various ministerial roles.[98]

The number of stories pertaining to women in the unique Lukan material leads Leonard Swidler to hypothesize that the author of Lk. 1.1–2.52, 9.51–18.14 may have been a woman.[99] Via notes that the presence of women disciples throughout Luke-Acts supports the hypothesis of a woman author of the Third Gospel and argues that '[i]ntellectual honesty demands consideration of this hypothesis.'[100] While the author of the Gospel is unknown, however, the use of the masculine participle παρηκολουθηκότι in 1.3 presents a male narrator, which suggests that the real author is male.[101]

b. *The Need for Watchfulness*

The movement away from perceiving the Gospel of Luke as 'the Gospel for women' is creatively described by Robert M. Price:

> Recent studies of Luke-Acts have awakened an unwelcome realization that this New Testament work, long perceived as an important weapon in the arsenal of Christian feminism, might turn out instead to be a dangerous Trojan Horse smuggled into the camp by the enemy. If one dared look carefully, might one find the Lukan text harboring dangerous opponents?[102]

---

96. Witherington, *Women in the Earliest Churches*, 143. According to Francis J. Moloney, *Woman in the New Testament* (Homebush, NSW: St Paul Publications, 1981), 61, the Lukan women (in particular, Mary the mother of Jesus) 'are often presented as being both chronologically and qualitively "first" in the order of faith.'

97. Witherington, *Women in the Earliest Churches*, 131.

98. Witherington, *Women in the Earliest Churches*, 156–57.

99. See Swidler, *Biblical Affirmations*, 261–62.

100. Via, 'Women,' 50.

101. See D'Angelo, 'Women in Luke-Acts,' 443; and Jane Schaberg, 'Luke,' in *Women's Bible Commentary*, expanded edition, (eds.) Carol A. Newsom and Sharon H. Ringe (Louisville, KY: Westminster John Knox Press, 1998), 366.

102. Price, *Widow Traditions*, 247.

As previously noted, the work of Schüssler Fiorenza has been influential in the study of Lukan women. Her critical feminist interpretation of the Martha and Mary story (10.38-42), in particular, challenges the positive interpretation of the Lukan presentation of women.[103] Schüssler Fiorenza highlights the kyriocentric nature of the narrative and draws attention to the silent woman being approved while the independent and active woman is rebuffed:[104] 'The rhetorical interests of the Lukan text are to silence women leaders of house-churches who, like Martha, might have protested, and to simultaneously extol Mary's "silent" and subordinate behavior.'[105] Using a fourfold hermeneutical process – hermeneutics of suspicion, hermeneutics of remembrance, hermeneutics of proclamation and hermeneutics of creative actualization and celebration – she draws attention to the dynamics operating in the text and how they further patriarchal interests, as well as articulating an alternative interpretation which is liberating for women.[106]

While Luise Schottroff acknowledges that the language of the Gospel of Luke (and the other Synoptic Gospels) is androcentric,[107] she focuses her critique on the history of interpretation of various texts. Within interpretations, she identifies androcentric bias and structures which support patriarchal violence. Using women's experience as an important element in her social-historical feminist approach, Schottroff aims to use the biblical texts to determine a liberating praxis. Her work on Lukan texts therefore provides a significantly different approach to the inter-pretation of these texts.[108]

While many laud Lukan efforts to promote equality and inclusiveness, others identify another dimension in the Lukan Gospel.[109] Rather than focusing on the number of women in the Lukan narrative, these scholars examine the roles which the women play and do not play in this Gospel.

---

103. See Elisabeth Schüssler Fiorenza, 'A Feminist Critical Interpretation for Liberation: Martha and Mary: Luke 10:38-42,' *Religion and Intellectual Life* 3, no. 2 (1986): 21–36; and Schüssler Fiorenza, *But She Said*, 52–76.

104. Schüssler Fiorenza, *But She Said*, 57–62.

105. Schüssler Fiorenza, *But She Said*, 68.

106. The fourfold hermeneutical process for feminist critical biblical interpretation is proposed in Elisabeth Schüssler Fiorenza, *Bread Not Stone: The Challenge of Feminist Biblical Interpretation (With a New Afterword)* (Boston, MA: Beacon Press, 1995), and further developed in Schüssler Fiorenza, *But She Said*.

107. Luise Schottroff, *Let the Oppressed Go Free: Feminist Perspectives on the New Testament*, trans. Annemarie S. Kidder (Louisville, KY: Westminster/John Knox Press, 1993), 194.

108. See the interpretations of Lukan texts in Luise Schottroff, *Lydia's Impatient Sisters: A Feminist Social History of Early Christianity*, trans. Barbara and Martin Rumscheidt (London: SCM Press, 1995), and Schottroff, *Let the Oppressed*.

109. For an overview of different interpretations of some of the women's stories in the Lukan Gospel, see Thurston, *Women in the New Testament*, 100–16.

Jane Schaberg states, for instance, that women speak only fifteen times in the Gospel of Luke and their words are recorded only ten times. In contrast, men speak hundreds of times. Furthermore, she reports that in Acts women speak only five times and their words are recorded only three times.[110] These statistics of Schaberg require some clarification. Speech can be directly or indirectly reported or implied by the narrative. In the Lukan Gospel a woman's direct speech is, in fact, given on twelve occasions while on a further five occasions it is reported or implied that a woman uses her voice but her direct words are not given.[111] In Acts, a woman's direct speech is given on three occasions while it is indirectly reported or implied that a woman speaks in two other scenes.[112] Women are mentioned eighteen times in the teachings of Jesus, while men are mentioned 158 times. The apostles' teachings in Acts only mention women once.[113]

These statistics reveal two significant points. First, although the Lukan Gospel contains more women characters than the other Gospels, male presence and voice still predominate. Second, as the narrative progresses from the Gospel to Acts, Lukan attention to women decreases and women's voices are heard less and less. Schaberg contends that the Gospel of Luke attempts to control those women who seek to practise prophetic ministry by portraying women role models who are quiet, grateful, prayerful and supportive of male leadership.[114] 'Luke blurs traditional and historical traces of women's leadership and exaggerates the leadership by men.'[115] Schaberg goes so far as to label the Gospel of Luke as dangerous because it characterizes women as models of subordinate service and subtly seduces the reader to accept that gender roles are divinely ordained.[116] Another who considers that women's leadership

---

110. Schaberg, 'Luke,' 368.

111. A woman's direct speech is given in 1.25, 34, 38, 42-45, 46-55, 60; 2.48; 10.40; 11.27; 15.9; 18.3; 22.56. (Note that two of these instances involve the speech of women characters in parables.) Indirect or implied speech is attributed to women in 2.38; 8.47; 13.13 and 24.9. In 23.27, the women are described as mourning and wailing for Jesus but whether this involves speech is not specified.

112. Direct speech of a woman is given in Acts 5.8; 16.15, 17. (Notice, however, that the speech of the slave-girl in 16.17 is actually attributed to the voice of the spirit of the python within her.) See Veronica Mary Lawson, 'Gender and Genre: The Construction of Female Gender in the Acts of the Apostles' (Unpublished PhD Thesis, Trinity College, Dublin, 1997), 264. Indirect or implied speech is attributed to a woman in Acts 12.14-15 and 18.26.

113. These statistics are from Schaberg, 'Luke,' 368. While Schaberg does not identify the single reference to which she here refers, Pharaoh's daughter is mentioned in Stephen's speech in Acts 7.21. For details on the number of times men and women are named in Acts 2.1–8.3, see Lawson, 'Gender and Genre,' 163.

114. Schaberg, 'Luke,' 363.

115. Schaberg, 'Luke,' 367.

116. Schaberg, 'Luke,' 363.

roles are diminished in the Lukan Gospel is Ann Graham Brock. In particular, she argues that this Gospel diminishes the witness of Mary Magdalene while highlighting the status of Peter.[117]

Mary Rose D'Angelo, too, maintains that while the increased number of stories relating to women in the Lukan Gospel in comparison with the other Gospels reflects a definite intention by the author, the roles which are assigned to women are more limited.[118] Though Elizabeth and Mary speak prophetically (1.42-45, 46-55), D'Angelo argues that in the ministry of Jesus women are no longer presented as prophets. Rather, she notes that the women characters in 7.36-50 and 10.38-42 who do not speak are approved by Jesus. Those who do speak to Jesus are corrected (10.41-42: 11.27-28; 23.28).[119] Furthermore, no woman's prophetic voice is heard in Acts. D'Angelo asserts that in Luke-Acts 'the roles in which women appear are more restricted by what is acceptable to the convention of the imperial world than are the roles of women in Mark or John.' This reflects an anxiety that Christian women should not be seen undertaking 'un-Roman activities.'[120]

Similarly, Helga Melzer-Keller considers the Lukan author as concerned with maintaining propriety so as not to bring Christianity into discredit. She describes the author as conservative and in agreement with those of his contemporaries who seek to limit the freedom of women. For Melzer-Keller, the pairings of male–female pericopes reflects the number of women in the Lukan community rather than an attempt to promote equality of the sexes.[121]

Noting that the role of women lessens as the Lukan narrative progresses, Elisabeth M. Tetlow suggests that women had a significant and active role in the Lukan community and that the Lukan author's attitude to this situation influenced his writing: '[H]e could not ignore the importance of women altogether, but, reacting negatively to their present active role, he could, through the theology of his gospel, attempt to argue for the restriction of women's role in the Church of his day.'[122] Thus,

---

117. See Brock, *Mary Magdalene*, 19–40. I have argued that John 21 produces a similar outcome. See Elizabeth Dowling, 'Rise and Fall: The Changing Status of Peter and Women Disciples in John 21,' *AusBR* 52 (2004): 48–63.

118. D'Angelo, 'Women in Luke-Acts,' 442.

119. D'Angelo, 'Women in Luke-Acts,' 451–52; and D'Angelo, '(Re) Presentations of Women,' 186–87. See also Seim, *Double Message*, 253–55, for a summary of how women are brought to silence.

120. D'Angelo, 'Women in Luke-Acts,' 442–43. See also Thurston, *Women in the New Testament*, 96–128.

121. Helga Melzer-Keller, *Jesus und die Frauen: Eine Verhältnisbestimmung nach den synoptischen Überlieferungen* (Freiburg: Herder, 1997), 328.

122. Tetlow, *Women and Ministry*, 101.

Tetlow argues that the Lukan author shapes his narrative to restrict women to passive roles.

A comprehensive study of the roles of the women and men disciples in Luke-Acts has been undertaken by Barbara Reid.[123] While Reid maintains that Lukan women are patently portrayed as disciples, she concludes that the Lukan text presents different discipleship roles for women and men. Unlike male disciples, women disciples are not presented as being called or commissioned, and do not teach or heal.[124] Reid suggests that the Lukan author is probably aware of women who performed apostolic ministries (cf. Rom. 16.1-12; Phil. 4.2-4) and therefore claims that the Lukan author has deliberately omitted the stories of these women: 'We must conclude that Luke, like the author of the Pastoral letters, knowing of such women, is intent on restricting them to silent, passive, supporting roles. He is conveying the message that women and men have different ways of being disciples.'[125] Since the Lukan episodes depict separate gender roles, Reid contends that their patriarchal framework must be challenged and 'choosing the better part' involves reading against the Lukan author's purpose.[126] In this way, the 'liberating potential' of the Lukan women's stories can be released for contemporary times.[127]

Another to advocate a counter-reading of the Gospel of Luke is Brigitte Kahl,[128] who identifies a different dynamic in Luke 1 from that operating in the rest of the Gospel. She claims that the actions and speech of Elizabeth and Mary in Lk. 1.24-57, culminating in Mary's proclamation of the Magnificat, contrast with the largely silent role of women in the Third Gospel. Kahl proposes that Lk. 1.24-57 be used as the key to transposing the patriarchal Lukan text. In other words, she advocates 'reading Luke against Luke,' a subversive reading which is grounded in the text itself.[129]

---

123. Reid, *Choosing the Better Part?*, 21–54.

124. Reid, *Choosing the Better Part?*, 52. While women do announce the resurrection to the apostles and others, they are not believed (24.1-11).

125. Reid, *Choosing the Better Part?*, 53.

126. Reid, *Choosing the Better Part?*, 54.

127. Reid, *Choosing the Better Part?*, 205. For the liberating potential of Lukan narrative and parable, see also the articles Barbara E. Reid, ' "Do You See This Woman?" A Liberative Look at Luke 7.36-50 and Strategies for Reading Other Lukan Stories Against the Grain,' in *A Feminist Companion to Luke*, (eds.) Amy-Jill Levine and Marianne Blickenstaff (London: Sheffield Academic Press, 2002), 106–20; and Barbara E. Reid, 'Beyond Petty Pursuits and Wearisome Widows: Three Lukan Parables,' *Int* 56 (2002): 284–94.

128. Brigitte Kahl, 'Reading Luke Against Luke: Non-Uniformity of Text, Hermeneutics of Conspiracy and the "Scriptural Principle" of Luke 1,' in *A Feminist Companion to Luke*, (eds.) Amy-Jill Levine and Marianne Blickenstaff (London: Sheffield Academic Press, 2002), 70–88.

129. Kahl, 'Reading Luke Against Luke,' 85–88.

Across a range of scholarship, it can be seen that the Lukan text has been described both in terms of raising the status of women and of subordinating women. In her detailed study of gender-patterns in Luke-Acts, Turid Karlsen Seim argues that it is not surprising that such divergent views have emerged about the Lukan writings since these writings contain a 'double message': 'The tension in Luke's narrative has indeed shown itself to be its ambivalent evidence both of strong traditions about women on the one hand, and of the social and ideological controls that brought women to silence and promoted male dominance in positions of leadership on the other.'[130] While arguing that the Lukan narrative imposes structures which enforce silence, she claims that this is done in such a way that women's dignity is not denied. According to Seim, women in the Lukan story 'are brought to silence and at the same time they continue to be given the right to speak.'[131] Thus, Seim forges a path between the divergent views, highlighting the tension evident in the portrayal of the women in Luke-Acts.

c. *Conclusions from the Literature Review of the Lukan Women*
The above discussion identifies different ways of understanding the Lukan text and its approach to women. Issues of the status and silence of women feature in the various approaches. The words of Karris, given as an exhortation at the end of an address on women and discipleship in the Gospel of Luke, are appropriate here: 'Remember ... it is not the Lucan text which has changed over the years, but it is we, its interpreters, who have changed, who will change, and who should change as new times and new methods challenge us to "re-vision" our look at Luke's view of women.'[132] This study is engaged with such 're-visioning.' The Parable of the Pounds (19.11-28) will provide the new lens for this re-visioning. Such a lens will attempt to focus the stories of women in the Lukan Gospel and form an image, real rather than virtual. Since different lenses provide different possibilities for viewing, the Parable of the Pounds will provide its own opportunities for insight and transformation. It is to the Parable of the Pounds, therefore, that we now turn.

---

130. Seim, *Double Message*, 249. See also Turid Karlsen Seim, 'The Gospel of Luke,' in *Searching the Scriptures: A Feminist Commentary*, (ed.) Elisabeth Schüssler Fiorenza (New York: Crossroad, 1994), 761.

131. Seim, *Double Message*, 249.

132. Karris, 'Women and Discipleship,' 20. This exhortation comes at the end of an article in which Karris comes down in favor of the position which perceives the third Gospel as being favorable to women. The exhortation to re-vision is appropriate irrespective of Karris' own position.

Chapter 2

READING THE PARABLE OF THE POUNDS

As the literature review revealed, there have been various interpretations proffered for the Parable of the Pounds (Lk. 19.11-28), some of which reflect divergent understandings of the parable. Some investigation of the nature of parable will help to explain the emergence of these multiple interpretations. This chapter will begin, therefore, with a discussion on the nature of parable. Following this, elements of the Matthean Parable of the Talents will be outlined and then a reading of the Lukan Parable of the Pounds will be presented. This reading will pay attention to the power dynamics evidenced in the parable.

1. *The Nature of 'Parable'*

Parables have been the subject of several detailed studies. From C. H. Dodd we have a classic description of a parable: 'At its simplest the parable is a metaphor or simile drawn from nature or common life, arresting the hearer by its vividness or strangeness, and leaving the mind in sufficient doubt about its precise application to tease it into active thought.'[1] In Paul Ricoeur's work on parables, it is possible to see similarities between his understanding and that of Dodd. For Ricoeur, '[m]etaphor is nothing other than the application of a familiar label to a new object which first resists and then surrenders to its application.'[2] Ricoeur uses this understanding to produce a more refined connection between parable and metaphor, proposing that a parable combines a narrative form with a metaphoric process.[3] He argues that the narrative in a parable must be read metaphorically rather than literally.[4]

Like Dodd, Ricoeur notes that parables consist of stories about situations which are familiar to the hearers but which contain an 'element of extravagance,' mixing the extraordinary with the ordinary.[5] Comparing

1. Dodd, *Parables of the Kingdom*, 16.
2. Paul Ricoeur, 'Biblical Hermeneutics,' *Semeia* 4 (1975): 86.
3. Ricoeur, 'Biblical Hermeneutics,' 30.
4. Ricoeur, 'Biblical Hermeneutics,' 89.
5. Ricoeur, 'Biblical Hermeneutics,' 99.

parables with miracles, he notes that in both cases 'the course of ordinary life is broken, the surprise bursts out. The unexpected happens; the audience is questioned and brought to think about the unthinkable.'[6]

A parable cries out for interpretation since, as Dodd states, the mind is provoked into 'active thought' because of its doubt about the parable's 'precise application.' At the same time, however, Ricoeur describes the parable as open-ended and capable of being reinterpreted in ways appropriate to new situations. In this sense the parable has more potential than can be grasped by any one interpretation.[7] Mary Ann Tolbert also argues that the indeterminate nature of the parable enables the text to be polyvalent: 'Multiple interpretations of the parables ... are not aberrations in methodology or logic but rather the necessary consequence of the parable form itself.'[8] She maintains that the meaning of a parable is dependent on its context, so that every new context into which the parable is placed will result in a new interpretation. For this reason, the particular orientations of the interpreter profoundly affect the parable's meaning. Since the interpreter provides the lens through which the world of the story is viewed, the interpreter becomes the co-creator of the parable.[9] Because of a parable's dynamic indeterminacy, 'the interpreter must provide some material out of his or her own experience and concerns. Moreover this material, already shaped by the personal orientation of the critic, forms the context within which a parable is read, and the parable, much like the enigmatic chameleon, combines with this context to show back its particular coloring.'[10]

The unfinished state of the parable is argued further by Robert W. Funk. He understands a parable as inviting the reader/hearer to enter the narrative and to live out the story. Thus the interpretation is not imposed by the parable but depends on the reader/hearer adopting roles in the story and acting out the drama:[11] '[T]he parable opens onto an unfinished world because that world is in course of conception. This means that both narrator and auditor *risk* the parable; they both participate (*sic*) the narrative and venture its outcome.'[12] Funk is therefore in accord with Ricoeur and Tolbert in arguing that multiple interpretations emerge as

6. Ricoeur, 'Biblical Hermeneutics,' 102.

7. Ricoeur, 'Biblical Hermeneutics,' 134–35. See also John R. Donahue, *The Gospel in Parable: Metaphor, Narrative and Theology in the Synoptic Gospels* (Philadelphia, PA: Fortress Press, 1988), 25.

8. Mary Ann Tolbert, *Perspectives on the Parables: An Approach to Multiple Interpretations* (Philadelphia, PA: Fortress Press, 1979), 39.

9. Tolbert, *Perspectives on the Parables*, 48, 115.

10. Tolbert, *Perspectives on the Parables*, 50.

11. See Robert W. Funk, *Parables and Presence: Forms of the New Testament Tradition* (Philadelphia, PA: Fortress Press, 1982), 29–34.

12. Funk, *Parables and Presence*, 30.

different readers/hearers respond in different ways to different situations. Thus it is not surprising that the Parable of the Pounds should produce such divergent interpretations. In this study I will attempt to read through the eyes of the oppressed, producing a different interpretation from those who read from a position of power.

So that the recognition of polyvalency does not lead to anarchy in the interpretation of a parable, Tolbert proposes guidelines for interpretation. Her first axiom is that 'preservation of the integrity of the parable story should be the guiding principle of all interpretations.'[13] Not only does she argue that the interpretation must 'fit' the parable story, but it must consider the entire arrangement of the story and not just one section of it.

The second axiom that Tolbert asserts is that 'in a literary work form and content, though distinguishable, are inseparable.'[14] She proposes that an exploration of the surface structure of a parable is vital to its interpretation. Two methods for this analysis involve identifying the manner of discourse (either narrated or direct discourse) and exploring the rhetorical style evidenced by repetition of words and phrases, and parallel or chiastic designs.[15] Tolbert argues that a reading that is guided by consideration of surface structure is better able to preserve the integrity of the parable. In the reading of the Lukan Parable of the Pounds (19.11-28) which follows, these two axioms will guide the interpretation. Both strands of the parable will be explored. An examination of the structure of the story will highlight the link between the two strands and the repetition of words and phrases in the discourse will help to elucidate the rhetoric of the text.

The work of John Dominic Crossan has also made an important contribution to parable scholarship. He maintains that parables are 'stories which shatter the deep structure of our accepted world.'[16] Crossan identifies three types of parable – parables of advent, reversal and action. Parables of advent incorporate one or more of the strands: 'hiddenness and mystery,' 'gift and surprise,' and 'discovery and joy.' Included in this category are the Parable of the Fig Tree (Mk 13.28/pars.), the Parable of the Sower (Mk 4.3-8/pars.) and the Parable of the Lost Sheep (Lk. 15.4-6/par.).[17]

Parables of reversal intend to reverse the world of their hearers: 'When the north pole becomes the south pole, and the south the north, a world is reversed and overturned and we find ourselves standing firmly on utter

13. Tolbert, *Perspectives on the Parables*, 71.
14. Tolbert, *Perspectives on the Parables*, 71.
15. See Tolbert, *Perspectives on the Parables*, 73–83.
16. John Dominic Crossan, *The Dark Interval: Towards Theology of Story* (Niles, IL: Argus Communications, 1975), 121–22.
17. See John Dominic Crossan, *In Parables: The Challenge of the Historical Jesus* (Sonoma, CA: Polebridge Press, 1992), 38.

uncertainty.'[18] Crossan argues that the parables of reversal told by the historical Jesus have nearly all been turned into example stories, with the Lukan author in particular showing a liking for such alteration. The classic case of this phenomenon can be seen in the Parable of the Good Samaritan (Lk. 10.30-37). If this were told as an example story to demonstrate that one should come to the assistance of anyone in need, then Crossan believes it would have been more effective to portray the wounded man as a Samaritan and the one who helps as an ordinary Jewish man. Instead, the thrust of the story as Jesus tells it urges the hearer to name the Samaritan as 'good' which is a reversal of the world-view of Jesus' audience.[19]

In the Gospels there are more instances of parables of reversal than of advent, but the largest category, according to Crossan, is that of parables of action which portray a crisis situation: 'These parables portray crucial or critical situations which demand firm and resolute action, prompt and energetic decision.'[20] He classes all the servant parables in this category. These are parables that involve both a master–servant dynamic and a time of reckoning. Crossan sees Lk. 19.12-27 as consisting of two parables, the Parable of the Talents/Minas and the Parable of the Throne-claimant. Both of these he includes in the subsection of servant parables that he regards as having 'a certain *normalcy* about them' in that good servants are rewarded and bad servants are punished.[21] He identifies a second sub-section of servant parables, however, in which this expected normalcy is overturned. Good servants go unrewarded and bad servants fare well. Included in this strand are such parables as The Unjust Steward (Lk. 16.1-7). Crossan identifies this overturning within the servant parable theme as another example of the phenomenon evident in the parables of reversal that attempt to destroy the complacency of the hearer's/reader's world.[22]

For Crossan, the first two servants in Lk. 19.12-27 are considered the good servants whereas the third servant is the bad servant. Crossan notes that the terms 'good' and 'bad' refer to the master–servant relationship within the world of the parable.[23] I will challenge these categories and the normalcy which Crossan identifies in the narrative. In the following reading of the Parable of the Pounds, I will argue that the master/king becomes the 'bad' figure in the story and that the first two slaves[24] who

18.   Crossan, *In Parables*, 54.

19.   See Crossan, *In Parables*, 52–76.

20.   Crossan, *In Parables*, 82.

21.   See Crossan, *In Parables*, 94–101.

22.   See Crossan, *In Parables*, 101–17.

23.   Crossan, *In Parables*, 101.

24.   In this study, I will translate δοῦλος as 'slave' rather than 'servant' which Crossan uses. 'Slave' brings out more forcefully the dependence of the δοῦλος on the κύριος. For a detailed discussion on the meaning and use of δοῦλος, see K. H. Rengstorf, 'δοῦλος,' *TDNT*

cooperate with the master emerge from the story with the same label. On the other hand, the third slave who defies his master becomes the 'good' figure in the story. Thus, the parable can be classed as a parable of reversal in which the reader's world-view is overturned.

2. *The Matthean Parable of the Talents*

As indicated in the literature review in Chapter 1, more scholarly attention has been given to the Parable of the Talents in the Gospel of Matthew (Mt. 25.14-30) than to the Parable of the Pounds (Lk. 19.11-28). The two stories have obvious links. In both, a man entrusts money to his slaves before he goes away. On his return the slaves give an account of what they have done with the money. Two slaves have increased their money while a third returns only what he was given. The master rewards the first two slaves but criticizes the third slave for not investing the money so that the master could have received back his money with interest. The money of the third slave is taken from him and given to the slave with the most money. Both stories also contain the saying, 'To all those who have, more will be given; but from those who have nothing, even what they have will be taken away' (Mt. 25.29; Lk. 19.26).

As well as these elements that are included in both stories, however, the Matthean story contains significant differences from the Lukan version. In the Matthean Gospel, the disciples alone hear Jesus deliver the apocalyptic discourse (Mt. 24.3) including the Parable of the Talents. The audience for the telling of the Parable of the Pounds in the Lukan Gospel is not so clearly specified. As part of the apocalyptic discourse in the Matthean Gospel, the Parable of the Talents follows the Parable of the Ten Virgins (Mt. 25.1-13) and leads into the judgment of the nations (Mt. 25.14-46). Donald Senior argues that given this context, 'it is clear that the reader is to see the return of the master as signifying the *parousia* of the Son of Man.'[25] As with the rest of the apocalyptic discourse, Senior sees the Parable of the Talents as exhorting the community to be alert and ready for the Son of Man's return.[26]

2.261–80. See also Beavis, 'Ancient Slavery,' 40; Arland J. Hultgren, *The Parables of Jesus: A Commentary* (Grand Rapids, MI: Eerdmans, 2000), 473–76; and Ceslas Spicq, *Theological Lexicon of the New Testament*, trans. James D. Ernest, 3 vols. (Peabody, MA: Hendrickson Publishers, 1994), 1.380–86. Spicq claims that translating δοῦλος as 'servant' obscures its precise signification in first-century language (p. 380).

25. Donald Senior, *Matthew* (Nashville: Abingdon Press, 1998), 278. See also Daniel J. Harrington, *The Gospel of Matthew* (Collegeville, MN: Liturgical Press, 1991), 353.

26. Senior, *Matthew*, 279. See also Christoph Kahler, *Jesu Gleichnisse als Poesie und Therapie: Versuch eines integrativen Zugangs zum kommunikativen Aspekt von Gleichnissen Jesu* (Tübingen: J. C. B. Mohr, 1995), 187–88.

Some of the phrases in the Matthean parable, which are not in the Lukan story, are often interpreted as contributing to this understanding. In the Matthean version the man returns after a long time. This 'delay motif' and the settling of accounts when the master returns (Mt. 25.19) support a reading which sees the parable as being about the last judgment.[27] No such delay in return is indicated in the Lukan story. In Mt. 25.21, 23, the first two slaves are praised and told that they will be put in positions of authority. The future dimension of this reward and the injunction to 'enter into the joy of your master' are also used to support an eschatological element in the reading. In contrast, the first two slaves in the Lukan story are given authority over cities in the present rather than at some future time (Lk. 19.17, 19).[28] Further, the master in the Matthean story orders that the third slave be thrown 'into the outer darkness, where there will be weeping and gnashing of teeth' (Mt. 25.30; cf. Mt. 8.12; 13.42, 50; 22.13; and 24.51). Daniel J. Harrington asserts that the 'outer darkness' suggests condemnation at the last judgment. This contrasts with entering into the joy of the master which alludes to a positive verdict at the last judgment.[29] No corresponding punishment is given to the third slave in the Lukan version.

While in the Lukan version each slave is initially given the same amount (Lk. 19.13), the master in the Matthean story gives a different amount to each slave, giving to each according to his ability (Mt. 25.15). Further, the monetary unit used in each story is different. The Lukan story has each slave receive a μνᾶ, translated here as a pound. A μνᾶ is a Greek monetary unit equivalent to one hundred drachmas.[30] The monetary unit in the Matthean parable is the τάλαντον with the slaves receiving five, two and one talent respectively. While there are a variety of understandings of the talent's precise value, it is considerably more valuable than a pound.[31]

The first two slaves in the Matthean story double their money in the

---

27. Harrington, *Matthew*, 352.
28. Johnson, 'Lukan Kingship Parable,' 143–44.
29. Harrington, *Matthew*, 352–53.
30. See BAGD, 524; Raphael Sealey, *Women and Law in Classical Greece* (Chapel Hill, NC: University of North Carolina Press, 1990), 190; and James Hope Moulton and George Milligan, *The Vocabulary of the Greek Testament: Illustrated from the Papyri and Other Non-Literary Sources* (London: Hodder and Stoughton, 1930), 414. The drachma can be considered the same value as the denarius, the usual daily wage for a male laborer. See Moxnes, *Economy of the Kingdom*, 66–67. Schottroff argues, however, that this was the wage for a male laborer and that women workers earned half this rate. See Schottroff, *Lydia's Impatient Sisters*, 94.
31. In BAGD, 803, the value of a talent is described as varying considerably, depending on times and places. Sealey evaluates a talent as equivalent to sixty minai. See Sealey, *Women and Law*, 190; also Moxnes, *Economy of the Kingdom*, 67. Schweizer understands the talent as being one hundred times more valuable than the pound. See Eduard Schweizer, *The Good News According to Matthew*, trans. David E. Green (London: SPCK, 1975), 470.

master's absence (Mt. 25.20, 22), compared with the slaves in the Lukan story who make 1000 per cent and 500 per cent profits (Lk. 19.16, 18). The third slave in the Matthean parable hides his money in the ground (Mt. 25.18) while the third slave in the Lukan parable wraps his money in a piece of cloth (Lk. 19.20). In both stories, the third slave accuses the master of reaping what he does not sow (Mt. 25.24; Lk. 19.21). While the slave in the Matthean version also accuses his master of gathering where he did not scatter seed (Mt. 25.24), in the Lukan version the extra accusation concerns taking up what he does not deposit (Lk. 19.21). In both stories, the master repeats accusations of the slave against himself without denying them (Mt. 25.26; Lk. 19.22). It is only in the Lukan version, however, that the master repeats the description of himself as a harsh man. This qualification is not present in the Matthean version.[32]

These differences between the two stories are very significant for their respective interpretations. Along with the fact that the Lukan parable also includes a theme of opposition from citizens to one seeking a kingdom for himself (Lk. 19.12, 14-15a, 27), these differences paint a subtly distinct picture of the nature of the master and his practices in the Lukan story in comparison with the Matthean version. These elements will be explored further in the following discussion of the Parable of the Pounds. The common eschatological interpretation of the Matthean Parable of the Talents may have influenced scholarly interpretation of the Lukan Parable of the Pounds. Despite the different context in the Lukan Gospel and the absence of many of the eschatological features which are often ascribed to the Matthean story, most scholars assume a similar interpretation for the Lukan version to that commonly ascribed to the Matthean version. But if we listen more closely to the voice of resistance and read the parable with fresh eyes/ears without influence from the predominant interpretation, then an alternative reading of the parable is possible.[33] I will argue that in the Lukan parable the master is portrayed as exploitative and oppressive, while the third slave is portrayed as acting honorably. The characteristics of the parable which are unique to the Lukan Gospel will be shown to support this reading.

3. *Lukan Context for the Parable of the Pounds*

The Parable of the Pounds (Lk. 19.11-28) comes immediately before Jesus' entry into Jerusalem. Since 9.51, the Lukan Jesus has been journeying to Jerusalem. Hence for ten chapters the reader has been anticipating the

32. See Harrington, *Matthew*, 353.
33. Alternative readings of the Lukan parable are discussed in Chapter 1, above. Alternative readings of the Matthean version, which critique the actions of the master, are given in Herzog, *Parables*, 150–68; and Carter, *Matthew*, 487–88.

arrival of Jesus in that city. The parable, therefore, comes at a crucial stage within the Lukan narrative. Prior to the telling of the parable,

- Jesus converses with a rich ruler (18.18-30);
- Jesus makes his third passion prediction to the twelve (18.31-34);
- Jesus cures a blind beggar who then follows him (18.35-43); and
- Jesus encounters and is welcomed by the tax collector, Zacchaeus (19.1-10).

While on the journey to Jerusalem, Jesus unsuccessfully invites a rich man to distribute his wealth to the poor and he announces that it is difficult for the wealthy to enter the βασιλεία of God (18.22-25). Following this, Jesus speaks of his passion for the third time in Luke 18.31-33. Here Jesus states clearly that Jerusalem is the place where he will be killed (cf. 13.33) and the twelve's failure to understand this is highlighted (18.34). Jesus' concern for the poor is demonstrated once again in his healing of a blind beggar (18.35-43). That the beggar glorifies God and follows Jesus indicates his spiritual insight and openness to the workings of God.

The Zacchaeus pericope concerns a rich man who gives half of his possessions to the poor and who is intent on not defrauding anyone (19.8). Jesus announces that Zacchaeus is included in the community of salvation (19.9). The Zacchaeus narrative is linked to the following story, the Parable of the Pounds, by 19.11. The same audience which hears Jesus' pronouncement in 19.9-10 will hear the parable which Jesus tells.

The narrator's introduction to the Parable of the Pounds indicates that Jesus tells the parable 'because he was near Jerusalem' and because they thought the βασιλεία of God would 'appear immediately' (19.11).[34] The lack of understanding that Jerusalem is the place of conflict and death for Jesus is once again evident. The ensuing Parable of the Pounds can be read as describing the consequences for opposing the oppressive practices of those in power.[35] With such a reading, the fate of those in the parable who resist these practices is linked with the fate of Jesus in Jerusalem.[36] The oppressive practices portrayed in the parable also indicate that the βασιλεία of God is not yet being experienced in all its fullness, correcting the expectations of the arrival of the βασιλεία triggered by the proximity to Jerusalem.

After the parable the narrator tells us that Jesus continues his journey to Jerusalem (19.28). Roland Meynet sees v. 11 and v. 28 as forming an

---

34. The identity of the 'they' who are expecting the kingdom is not obvious. Dawsey argues that 'they' refers to the crowd who complain in 19.7. Dawsey, *Lukan Voice*, 95. Ringe identifies the audience as the disciples. Ringe, *Luke*, 234. Since it is unlikely that opponents of Jesus would be expecting the kingdom of God to appear once Jesus arrives in Jerusalem, it is more likely that 'they' refers to supporters, including the disciples.

35. Reid, *Parables for Preachers*, 325–26.

36. See Kitchen, 'Parable of the Pounds,' 161.

inclusio, with being near to Jerusalem (v. 11b) parallel to going up to Jerusalem (v. 28).[37] The narrator's introduction and conclusion to the parable, therefore, reinforce the focus on Jerusalem. Jesus is welcomed as king when he enters Jerusalem (19.38).[38] Hence we are reminded that the βασιλεία *is* present. The impending destruction described in 19.43-44 and the attempts by religious leaders to find a way to kill Jesus (19.47), however, indicate that there is also an aspect of the βασιλεία that has not yet fully arrived.

The pericopae following the Parable of the Pounds feature opposition and destruction. Guy links the opposition of the citizens in 19.14 with the opposition of the Pharisees in 19.39, and also links the slaughter of the citizens in 19.27 with the slaughter of 19.44. He describes these connections as 'a textual web of interrelationship' between the parable and the following pericopae.[39] While 19.44 warns of judgment for rejection (cf. 13.1-5), there are problems with linking this verse with 19.27, and 19.39 with 19.14. To do so presupposes that the nobleman/king of the Parable of the Pounds represents Jesus. As the following reading of the parable will show, the nobleman is portrayed as an oppressor and as such his actions are the antithesis to those of Jesus in this Gospel. Links between the Parable of the Pounds and the following pericopae can be established, however. The opposition of the citizens and the third slave to the nobleman can be linked with the opposition of Jesus to the religious leaders, and the consequences experienced by the citizens and third slave correspond with the consequences Jesus faces for this challenge. Both Jesus' challenge and the consequences of his challenge come to a climax when Jesus is in Jerusalem.

4. *Structure of the Parable of the Pounds*

A summary of the plot of the Lukan Parable of the Pounds (Lk. 19.11-28) is as follows:

- A nobleman goes to a distant country seeking a βασιλεία for himself.
- Before he leaves, he gives a pound to each of ten slaves and directs them to trade with them while he is away.
- Although his fellow-citizens send a delegation to protest, the man returns having obtained the βασιλεία.

37. Meynet, *Saint Luc*, 185. For a different view, see François Bovon, *Das Evangelium nach Lukas*, 3 vols. (Zürich; Neukirchen-Vluyn: Benziger; Neukirchener Verlag, 1989–2001), 3.283–4.

38. For a discussion of how Jesus' kingship is portrayed in 19.28-40, see Guy, 'Present and Future,' 128–35.

39. Guy, 'Present and Future,' 125.

- He summons his slaves to find out the results of their trading.
- The first slave has made ten more pounds. He is praised by his master and is given authority over ten cities.
- The second slave has made five more pounds and is given authority over five cities.
- The third slave, however, has not traded. Instead, he has wrapped his pound in a cloth, and he gives the pound back to his master whom he describes as an exacting man, taking up what he has not laid down and reaping where he has not sown.
- The nobleman criticizes this third slave for not putting the pound into the bank so that it could be collected with interest and he orders that the pound of this slave be taken from him and given to the slave who has ten pounds.
- To counter an objection from the bystanders to this command he declares that those who have will be given more, but those who have nothing will lose the little that they have.
- He then decrees that the citizens who had opposed him be slaughtered.

Given that the Matthean story does not contain the storyline of the nobleman receiving a βασιλεία amid opposition, it is debatable whether this strand is a Lukan addition to material in Q,[40] or whether the strands were already combined in the version which the Lukan author inherited.[41] Some argue that two of Jesus' parables have been combined in the Lukan version.[42] Regardless of the circumstances surrounding its construction, however, the reader approaches Lk. 19.11-28 as a single narrative unit, being told in 19.11 that Jesus goes on to tell a παραβολή – one parable, not two.

---

40. As with the majority viewpoint, I hold that the Gospel of Mark and Q were sources for the Lukan and Matthean Gospels. For a detailed discussion of this viewpoint and the debate over Lukan sources, see Fitzmyer, *Luke*, 1.63–97; and Luke Timothy Johnson, *The Gospel of Luke*, Sacra Pagina 3 (Collegeville, MN: Liturgical Press, 1991), 6. For an argument against this viewpoint, see William R. Farmer, 'Modern Developments of Griesbach's Hypothesis,' *NTS* 23 (1976–77): 275–95. Farmer maintains that the Gospel of Mark was written after the Gospels of Matthew and Luke. For another different view, see Michael Goulder, *Luke: A New Paradigm*, 2 vols. (Sheffield: JSOT Press, 1989), 1.3–128. Goulder argues for Markan priority but argues against the existence of Q. Instead, Goulder believes that the Lukan author used the Gospels of Mark and Matthew as sources.

41. Lambrecht claims that the throne claimant strand is a Lukan addition to the parable in Q. See Lambrecht, 'Throne Claimant,' 113. Guy favors the view that the Lukan version is an expansion of the main parable because the additions have links with the following Lukan pericopae in 19.28-44. See Guy, 'Present and Future,' 120. Joel R. Wohlgemut, on the other hand, considers that varieties in detail between the Matthean and Lukan versions cast the common source hypothesis into question. He argues that the Matthean simpler storyline is more original. See Wohlgemut, 'Entrusted Money,' 105–6.

42. See Jeremias, *Parables of Jesus*, 59. For a summary of the debate about sources, see Nolland, *Luke*, 3.910–11.

The Parable of the Pounds (19.11-28) can be seen to have the following structure:

> v. 11 Narrator's introduction
>> v. 12 Nobleman travels to obtain a βασιλεία
>>> v. 13 Slaves given pounds
>> vv. 14-15a Citizens unsuccessfully oppose rule
>>> vv. 15b-24 Accounting of slaves to nobleman
>>> (v. 25 Objection by bystanders)
>>> v. 26 Logion as explanation
>> v. 27 Slaughter of opponents
> v. 28 Narrator's conclusion

This presentation of the structure aims to facilitate the identification of the two storylines and to show how they are combined. After the narrator's introduction in 19.11, the story of the man who seeks a βασιλεία but is opposed by his fellow-citizens is given in 19.12, 14-15a, 27. The account of a man entrusting money to his slaves is given in 19.13, 15b-24, 26. The man described as a nobleman (ἄνθρωπος τις εὐγενὴς, 19.12) is common to both strands of the story though the story is also linked by 19.25. This objection voiced by the bystanders concerns one of the slaves, yet it also links with the opposition to the man's actions voiced by the citizens (19.14). The narrator's conclusion in 19.28 links with 19.11, drawing the reader's focus to Jerusalem.

The manner in which the two strands are presented in the parable is important for its interpretation.[43] We do not read one storyline presented and then, after its conclusion, commence the second storyline. Rather, the intertwining of the two indicates that they must be considered together. One will help our understanding of the other and vice versa. The opposition voiced by the citizens (19.14) and the command to slaughter these citizens (19.27) frame the accounting of the servants to their master. This frame is not included in the Matthean story of the Parable of the Talents (Mt. 25.14-30). In the Lukan story, however, the frame demands consideration from the reader. It cannot be ignored in establishing an interpretation of the parable.

Different motifs have been used to interpet the parable. Funk, for example, identifies the Parable of the Talents (both the Matthean and Lukan versions) as belonging to a group of parables which have three major characters. Characteristic of this group is that one of the principal characters acts as the 'determiner' while the other two characters display contrasting responses to the situation created by the determiner. He includes such examples as the Parable of the Laborers in the Vineyard

---

43. See Louis Panier, 'La Parabole des Mines: Lecture Sémiotique (Lc 19, 11–27),' in *Les Paraboles Évangéliques*, (ed.) J. Delorme (Paris: Éditions du Cerf, 1989), 337.

(Mt. 20.1-15) and the Parable of the Lost Son (Lk. 15.11-32) in this grouping. To fit the Parable of the Talents into this framework, Funk classes the first two slaves together as making a common response to their master's directive in contrast with the response of the third slave.[44]

The structure of the Lukan Parable of the Pounds is more clearly seen, however, when the response of each slave is considered separately, allowing a pattern to be established before the final slave's response is given. In that case, the accounting of the slaves to their master is an example of a motif of three. The reader is given a set of three responses to the same request. Three slaves come and declare what they have done with the entrusted money. In the Lukan Gospel, this motif has already been experienced in the Parable of the Good Samaritan (10.30-37). In that story the responses of a priest (10.31) and Levite (10.32) are given to the described situation, followed by the response of a Samaritan (10.33-35) to the same situation. The first two responses establish a pattern which is broken by the third response. The third response is described in far more detail than the previous two responses, and is further highlighted by the use of direct discourse (10.35).

That a similar motif of three also exists in the Parable of the Pounds indicates that an interpreter must consider carefully how the pattern is structured and focus on the third response as vital to the dynamic of the parable. In this parable, there is no clear contrast to be made from identifying narrated and direct discourse since the majority of the parable is in direct discourse. The narrated discourse is predominantly located in vv. 12-13a, 14a, and 15, while the direct discourse occurs in vv. 13b, 14b, and 16-27. This indicates that as the parable continues, more direct discourse is featured, bringing the story to a climax.

5. *Reading the Parable – The Opposition of the Citizens*

The first strand of the parable to be explored is that of the opposition of the citizens. The word βασιλεία appears in the narrator's introduction to the parable (19.11), in relation to the kingdom/reign of God. The word appears again in vv. 12 and 15, with its related verb form βασιλεύω in vv. 14 and 27. Thus it is the key word in the storyline of the nobleman obtaining a kingdom amidst opposition. The NRSV translates βασιλεία as 'kingdom' in 19.11, referring to the kingdom of God. Yet in vv. 12 and 15, the same word is translated as 'royal power.' While both are valid translations,[45] using *different* translations reduces the impact of the repetition of the same word. The same word has been used deliberately

---

44. See Funk, *Parables and Presence*, 35–39.
45. See BAGD, 134.

and should thus be translated identically throughout 19.11-28. The subtle change of wording reduces the grounds for comparison.

Within the Gospel of Luke, the βασιλεία of God has both a present and future dimension. Drawing on the Lukan theme of the 'hospitality of God,'[46] Anne Elvey understands the Lukan presentation of the βασιλεία as that of gift: 'For Luke *he basileia tou theou* ... is a divine gift. The *basileia* is a present reality, characteristic of the Lukan today and evident in the community around Jesus, but it is also the content of an expected future. In both present and future aspects it is marked by the hospitality of God.'[47] This understanding of βασιλεία as gift can be contrasted with the portrayal of the nobleman in the parable. Rather than receiving the βασιλεία as gift, he seeks to take a βασιλεία for himself.

A key phrase in 19.12 is λαβεῖν ἑαυτῷ βασιλείαν. While the phrase could be translated as 'receive a kingdom for himself,'[48] a stronger reading is possible. The verb λαμβάνω can be translated more actively as 'take hold of' or 'take (into one's possession).'[49] Thus, 19.12 can be understood as a nobleman traveling to a distant country 'to take a βασιλεία for himself.' From Josephus we learn that this situation has parallels in the ancient world. Herod the Great, for example, is said to have traveled to Rome and thus obtained his βασιλεία, though Josephus writes that Herod actually went to Rome to claim the βασιλεία for his wife's brother rather than for himself since he thought that the Romans would not offer him [Herod] the βασιλεία.[50]

More specifically, the citizens who send a delegation to object to the nobleman ruling over them (19.14) have links with the historical situation of 4BCE in which Archelaus traveled to Rome seeking to be named by Augustus as king over the territory which his father, Herod, had ruled.[51] According to Josephus, a delegation of fifty Jews arrived in Rome to protest the appointment and were joined by over eight thousand of the Jews in Rome.[52] Given permission to speak to Augustus, the delegation first described the tyranny which they had endured under Herod's reign and then proceeded to describe the cruelties of Archelaus' rule. They

---

46. This theme will be explored in Chapter 3.

47. Anne Elvey, 'Storing Up Death, Storing Up Life: An Earth Story in Luke 12.13–34,' in *The Earth Story in the New Testament*, (eds.) Norman C. Habel and Vicky Balabanski, Earth Bible 5 (London: Sheffield Academic Press, 2002), 103.

48. Johnson, *Luke*, 288.

49. BAGD, 464.

50. See Josephus, *Ant.* 14.370–89.

51. The link with Archelaus is commonly noted by scholars. See, for instance, Green, *Gospel of Luke*, 676; Johnson, *Luke*, 290; and Kyoung-Jin Kim, *Stewardship and Almsgiving in Luke's Theology*, JSNTSup 155 (Sheffield: Sheffield Academic Press, 1998), 163. A detailed discussion of the issue is presented in Zerwick, 'Thronanwärter,' 660–66.

52. See Josephus, *Ant.* 17.219–22, 299–303.

argued that Archelaus' intentions were clear when one of the first acts
which he performed before his fellow-citizens (πολῖται) and God was to
cause the slaughter (σφαγή) of three thousand of his countrymen in the
temple precinct.[53]

Josephus writes that after listening to the delegation and to a friend of
Archelaus who defended Herod and Archelaus from the allegations made
against them, Augustus appointed Archelaus as ethnarch (rather than
king) of Judea, Idumea and Samaria. On his return to Judea, Archelaus
continued his tyranny and cruelty until, in the tenth year of his rule,
Augustus responded to charges brought against Archelaus by leading
Jews and Samaritans and banished him to Gaul.[54]

Thus, the original reader of the Parable of the Pounds may not be
unfamiliar with such a situation of a man seeking a βασιλεία for himself
or with the brutality of such rulers. For this reason, an original reader
may be suspicious of a man described in such a light. A modern-day
reader, however, may also be uneasy. Postcolonial awareness leads to
suspicion and critique of a situation in which one obtains power from a
'distant country' to rule. Dube gives insight into the dynamics of
imperialist rule: 'The imperialist strategy of "control-at-a-distance" …
engages some local groups (usually the upper class) to become its ruling
representatives, and this conceals the face of the imperial oppressor
among the colonized.'[55] Thus, the nobleman can be seen as contributing
to imperialist domination. A reader attentive to the use and abuse of
power may well ask, 'What right does the man have to assume power over
others?' Such a reader also listens for the voice of resistance. This comes in
v. 14 when the citizens (πολῖται), who hate the man, officially protest,
stating that they do not want him to be king/rule (βασιλεῦσαι) over them.
It is obvious from v. 15a, however, that their protest is unsuccessful since
the man returns, having 'taken' or claimed the βασιλεία.

Friberg, Friberg and Miller note the differing rights of the πολίτης and
δοῦλος. They define the πολίτης as: '(1) one who shares in the political
organization and rights of a city or city-state *citizen* (AC 21.39), opposite
δοῦλος (*slave, servant*) and ξένος (*foreigner, alien*); (2) as an associate in a
particular civic group *fellow citizen, fellow countryman* (LU 19.14).'[56] This
indicates that the πολῖται of 19.14, unlike δοῦλοι, could expect to have a
say in the politics of their city/state.[57] Sending a delegation would be a

---

53. Josephus, *Ant.* 17.304–14.
54. Josephus, *Ant.* 17.315–18, 339–44. See also Josephus, *War* 2.111.
55. Dube, 'Post-Colonial Feminist Interpretation,' 15.
56. Timothy Friberg, Barbara Friberg, and Neva F. Miller, *Analytical Lexicon of the Greek New Testament* (Grand Rapids, MI: Baker Books, 2000), 321.
57. H. Strathmann, 'πόλις,' *TDNT* 6.534, states that, in the context of the Parable of the Pounds, 'the πολῖται as distinct from the δοῦλοι are economically and personally "independent inhabitants." In relation to the ἄνθρωπος εὐγενής they are in a sense

reasonable action, given such an expectation. Indeed, Josephus notes that the nation had permission from Varus, the Roman governor of Syria, to send to Rome the delegation of Jews who opposed Archelaus.[58] The citizens in the Lukan parable hate the man and oppose his intention to rule over them. While they have acted within their rights, a reader attentive to power structures within the narrative notes that their protests are shown to be futile. Since the nobleman is able to *take* his βασιλεία regardless (v. 15a), it appears that the resistant voices have not been heard. The ruler is hated and has been vigorously opposed, but he returns with the power. The citizens are powerless to stop him. This perception is confirmed in 19.27 when the ruler orders that those who had opposed him, and whom he now calls his enemies, be brought and slaughtered in front of him.

The verb κατασφάζω, to slaughter, is an interesting choice of word here. This is its only appearance in the New Testament. In the Gospel of Luke, the verb ἀποκτείνω occurs twelve times and the verb ἀπόλλυμι occurs twenty-seven times. Thus other options for words with the meaning 'to kill' or 'to destroy' were readily available. The related word σφάζω appears ten times in the New Testament – twice in 1 John and eight times in Revelation. No instances occur in the Gospels. The word σφάζω appears eighty-four times in the LXX in relation to ritual slaying or profane slaying. With regard to people, σφάζω can mean 'violently and pitilessly to slaughter' or it 'can be used for a massacre in war or civil strife.'[59] The noun form σφαγή occurs twenty-four times in the LXX and three times in the New Testament, though again no instances occur in the Gospels.

The verb κατασφάζω, which is used in the Parable of the Pounds, occurs eleven times in the LXX. Of these eleven occurrences of κατασφάζω, eight are in 2 Maccabees.[60] In 2 Macc. 5.11-14, Antiochus who is king, βασιλεύς (2 Macc. 5.11), returns from Egypt, thinking that Judea is in revolt, and commands his soldiers to cut down all they meet and to slaughter (κατασφάζω) those who go into their houses (2 Macc. 5.12). Eighty thousand are destroyed in three days (2 Macc. 5.14). Following this, Antiochus enters and profanes the temple and removes its riches (2 Macc. 5.15-20). He leaves governors to oppress the people and Menelaus is described as worse than the others in lording it over the

---

fellow-citizens. But they are not citizens in the Greek sense, since, being under a king, they do not have any share in κρίσις and ἀρχή.' However, the historical situation of sending a delegation to oppose rulers shows that such is not unreasonable behavior of citizens.

58. Josephus, *Ant.* 17.299–300. Weinert notes that a Jewish delegation also undermined the authority of Demetrius, a hated ruler (1 Macc. 8.17-32). See Weinert, 'Throne Claimant,' 512.

59. O. Michel, 'σφάζω,' *TDNT* 7.930–32.

60. 2 Macc 5.12, 24; 6.9; 8.24; 10.17, 31, 37; 12.26.

citizens (πολῖται). Out of malice to the Jewish citizens (πολῖται) an army is commanded to slaughter (κατασφάζω) the men and sell the women and young ones. As a result, great numbers of people are killed in Jerusalem (2 Macc. 5.23-24).[61] Thus, in 2 Macc. 5.11-26 we have a story of a king who slaughters citizens whom he believes to be opposing him. The character of Antiochus is made abundantly clear when he is described as a murderer and blasphemer at his death (2 Macc. 9.28). Antiochus' cruelty and actions of contempt were so extreme as to provoke the Maccabean revolt. The Jewish feast of Dedication commemorates the rededication of the temple after the defilement by Antiochus. Thus, first-century readers would be well aware of the character and exploits of Antiochus.

While the word πολίτης occurs twenty-one times in the LXX, the only times it occurs in the same context as κατασφάζω are in 2 Macc. 5. It does occur in the same context as the noun σφαγή earlier in the same chapter, 2 Macc. 5. In this instance, Jason slaughters his fellow-citizens (πολῖται). The hatred and abhorrence for Jason as a result of his actions are emphasized and he finally dies a miserable death after being sent into exile (2 Macc. 5.6-10). Hence, in the only instances that κατασφάζω or its cognates are used in relation to πολίτης, it is clear that the action is deserving of hatred and is the action of a tyrant or corrupt operator. The language of the Lukan Parable of the Pounds echoes the language of 2 Macc. 5 in relation to the slaughter of citizens.[62] Bringing the context of 2 Macc. 5 to a reading of the Parable of the Pounds suggests that the actions of the nobleman in the parable are also to be abhorred and implies that he too is corrupt and tyrannical.[63]

61. There is ambiguity about whether the malice toward the Jewish citizens is the reason for Menelaus lording it over the citizens (v. 23) or whether it is the reason for the command to slaughter the people (v. 24). Either way it is clear that vv. 22-26 link the oppression of citizens with the slaughter.

62. In *The Roman Missal – Lectionary, Readings for Weekdays*, 33rd Week in Ordinary Time, Wednesday of Year I, the Gospel reading of the day is Lk. 19.11–28. The first reading which precedes this is from 2 Macc. 7.1, 20-31 – the story of Antiochus torturing a mother and her seven sons, with the focus on the seventh son who refuses the promises of wealth made by the tyrant and pays for his resistance with his life. The combination of readings leads the hearer to connect the actions of the tyrant, Antiochus, with the actions of the king in the Parable of the Pounds. See *Lectionary*, 3 vols. (London: Collins Liturgical Publications, 1983), 2.398–401.

63. This presumes that the readers and hearers are familiar with the LXX so that the allusion is picked up. The composition of the Lukan community is debatable. The majority of scholars support a predominantly Gentile audience. See, for example, Johnson, *Luke*, 9–10; Fitzmyer, *Luke*, 1.57–9; and Schaberg, 'Luke,' 365. William S. Kurz argues that the implied readers have a familiarity with the Greek scriptures which enables them to recognize the many biblical allusions. See William S. Kurz, *Reading Luke-Acts: Dynamics of Biblical Narrative* (Louisville, KY: Westminster/John Knox Press, 1993), 13. In a detailed discussion of the composition of the Lukan community, Philip Francis Esler argues for an audience comprising Jewish and Gentile Christians and that a significant proportion of the Gentile

The language and context of 2 Macc. 4 provides a further echo to the Parable of the Pounds. Here, charges are brought against Menelaus (2 Macc. 4.43-44). Though guilty, Menelaus uses bribery to obtain an acquittal, while those who had brought the case against Menelaus are sentenced to death (2 Macc. 4.45-47). The injustice of this penalty is highlighted (2 Macc. 4.48). Menelaus remains in office, growing in wickedness, and plotting against his fellow-citizens, πολῖται (2 Macc. 4.50).

As previously noted, the opposition voiced by the citizens (19.14) and the subsequent command to slaughter these citizens (19.27) frames the interaction between the nobleman and his slaves. Therefore, it must shed light on the story within. We have seen that the nobleman has returned with power (19.15a) and then abused that power. The citizens who had dared to voice their protest are the victims of this abuse. Their powerlessness increases over the course of the parable.[64] With this knowledge, we approach the second strand of the parable.

6. *Reading the Parable – Calling the Slaves to Account*

It is in 19.13 that we are introduced to the storyline of slaves (δοῦλοι) entrusted with money in the absence of their master. Ten slaves are summoned and given ten pounds, though it becomes clear at an ensuing stage that these slaves are given a pound each (vv. 16, 18, 20). The instruction given to each is to 'Do business with these until I come back' (v. 13). The verb, πραγματεύομαι, can be translated as 'do business, trade.'[65] Joel B. Green claims, however, that the text assumes exploitative practices.[66] Green relies here on the explanation for πραγματεύομαι of Ceslas Spicq who argues that the meaning is not 'do business' but 'administrate, manage profitably the capital at your disposal.' Spicq believes '[t]he emphasis is on this exploiting, this turning to good account.'[67] The related verb διαπραγματεύομαι occurs in 19.15.[68]

After returning, the nobleman summons the slaves in order to find out what they have gained from their trading. While ten slaves were given a

members were 'God-fearers' who attended the synagogue prior to becoming Christians. Esler suggests that both the Lukan author and his readers were familiar with the LXX from their association with the synagogue. See Philip Francis Esler, *Community and Gospel in Luke-Acts: The Social and Political Motivations of Lucan Theology* (Cambridge: Cambridge University Press, 1987), 30–45.

64. Kitchen, 'Parable of the Pounds,' 135.
65. BAGD, 697.
66. See Green, *Gospel of Luke*, 678.
67. Spicq, *Theological Lexicon*, 3.151.
68. The reading τί διεπραγματεύσαντο (witnessed, for example, in ℵ B D) is preferred to either of the textual variants τίς τί διεπραγματεύσατο (witnessed in A Θ) or τίς τί

pound each, only three reappear in the narrative. Though this creates some awkwardness in reading the parable, it matches the three responses in the Matthean version (Mt. 25.14-30). As previously noted, a threefold response has its own dynamic that needs to be carefully considered.

A pattern is established by the first two responses. The first two slaves address the man as κύριε, refer to ἡ μνᾶ σου and state the profit they have made (19.16, 18). The first has made ten more pounds and the second five pounds. The first two slaves therefore achieve profits of 1000 per cent and 500 per cent respectively.[69] This is an extraordinary rate of profit, far exceeding the profit of 100 per cent found in the Matthean version (Mt. 25.20, 22).[70]

The Lukan profit margins seem to be examples of what Tolbert describes as 'exaggerated details' in the parables. She argues that 'these elements within the stories themselves evidence the presence of the "extraordinary within the ordinary," the clearly symbolic within the realistic.'[71] The Lukan profits are designed to cause astonishment and outrage at the extraordinary result. They are symbolic of enormous and outrageous profits. Rohrbaugh states that in Roman sources, the legal interest rate was 12 per cent. Hence, he argues that 1000 per cent interest is an 'hyperbole calculated to draw an astonished gasp from the listening audience.'[72] The exaggerated interest rates have been used to indicate the nature of the transactions. That such incredible rates are produced by the first and second slaves strongly suggests that the means used to procure them were more foul than fair (cf. Sir. 26.29). The symbolic interest rates point beyond themselves to the activities which have produced such profits. It would seem that these slaves have been involved in extortion.

ἐπραγματεύσατο (witnessed in W Δ) in which the verb is third person singular, giving a more precise reading. It is more likely that the plural verb was changed to the singular, than vice versa.

69. Judith M. Lieu, *The Gospel of Luke* (London: Epworth Press, 1997), 149, lists the rates as 100 per cent and 50 per cent respectively, following her understanding that each slave is given ten pounds. While this understanding is possible from v. 13, later verses indicate that each slave receives one pound (see vv. 16, 18, 20).

70. See Bernard B. Scott, *Hear Then the Parable: A Commentary on the Parables of Jesus* (Minneapolis, MN: Fortress, 1989), 226. Scott claims that the Matthean rate of interest is not unusual by the standards of the day but that a tenfold profit is very high. For a discussion on the charging of interest in New Testament times, see Kahler, *Jesu Gleichnisse*, 174–79.

71. Tolbert, *Perspectives on the Parables*, 90. Tolbert here uses the terminology of Ricoeur who writes of the extravagant elements of the parables, the presence of the extraordinary alongside the ordinary. See Ricoeur, 'Biblical Hermeneutics,' 99.

72. Rohrbaugh, 'Peasant Reading,' 35. Fortna also claims that the profits are greatly exaggerated. Fortna, 'Reading Jesus' Parable,' 217, n. 16. On the other hand, while Wohlgemut insists that the gains are designed to cause amazement, he claims that they would not lead the listeners to outrage but to laughter directed at the third slave 'for missing out on such an apparently glorious opportunity.' Wohlgemut, 'Entrusted Money,' 119.

The title κύριε is used by each slave. To emphasize the dynamic between κύριος and δοῦλος, κύριε is best translated here as 'master.' The word κύριος occurs 104 times in the Gospel of Luke and approximately forty of these occurrences refer to Jesus.[73] On a slightly fewer number of occasions the word refers to God.[74] Dawsey notes that many of the uses of κύριος to refer to Jesus occur in material unique to the Lukan Gospel and he suggests that the author thought it 'singularly appropriate' for his narrator to refer to Jesus in this way.[75]

It is interesting to ponder, therefore, whether those who read the Parable of the Pounds allegorically, and see the nobleman as representing Jesus or God,[76] have been influenced by the fact that the slaves refer to the nobleman as κύριε. In Funk's opinion, 'the Lord is a synonym for God. In the New Testament the term [κύριος] is also used of Jesus, and it is very likely that the modern reader assigns the meaning "divinity" to it whenever it occurs in the text.'[77] If the vocative, δέσποτα, had been used in the parable instead, as it is in 2.29, the connection may not have been made so automatically.[78]

While κύριος is often used to refer to Jesus or God in the Gospel of Luke, there are several occasions on which the term refers more generally to a master of slaves or an owner of property.[79] In 14.22, for instance, the vocative κύριε is used by a slave to address his master, as it is used by the slaves of the Parable of the Pounds to address their master (19.16, 18, 20). The use of κύριος cannot be assumed to refer to Jesus or God in every context in this Gospel. Hence, the use of the word κύριος in the Parable of the Pounds does not automatically make the nobleman a representative of Jesus or God. Rather, the word may be used here to contrast the nobleman with Jesus who is often referred to as κύριος. Kitchen argues that the use of the title in Lk. 19.11-28 contrasts the 'lordship' of the

---

73. While the referent on some occasions is ambiguous, it is likely that the following uses refer to Jesus – 1.43, 76; 2.11; 5.8, 12; 6.5, 46 (x2); 7.6, 13, 19; 9.54, 59, 61; 10.1, 17, 39, 40, 41; 11.1, 39; 12.41, 42; 13.15, 23; 17.5, 6, 37; 18.6, 41; 19.8 (x2), 31, 34; 22.33, 38, 49, 61; 24.3, 34. Dawsey also includes 3.4; 13.25; 19.25; 20.42, 44; but excludes 6.5 from his list. See Dawsey, *Lukan Voice*, 9–10. Also see Kitchen, 'Parable of the Pounds,' 126.

74. Likely references to God occur in – 1.6, 9, 11, 15, 16, 17, 25, 28, 32, 38, 45, 46, 58, 66, 68; 2.9 (x2), 15, 22, 23 (x2), 24, 26, 39; 3.4; 4.8, 12, 18, 19; 5.17; 10.2, 21, 27; 13.35; 19.38; 20.37, 42.

75. Dawsey, *Lukan Voice*, 10. Kim notes that, among the narrators in the Synoptic Gospels, only the Lukan narrator refers to Jesus as κύριος. See Kim, *Stewardship*, 115.

76. See, for instance, Fitzmyer, *Luke*, 2.1233; Talbert, *Reading Luke*, 178; and La Verdiere, *Luke*, 227.

77. Funk, *Parables and Presence*, 14. For more on the use of κύριος in the Lukan Gospel, see Dawsey, *Lukan Voice*, 9–13.

78. While δεσπότης is synonymous with κύριος, it is used less frequently to refer to God.

79. E.g. 12.36, 37, 42, 43, 45, 46, 47; 13.8, 25; 14.21, 22, 23; 16.3, 5 (x2), 8, 13; 19.16, 18, 20, 25, 33; 20.13, 15.

nobleman with that of Jesus, evidenced through the gospel: 'It is only Jesus who can be rightly called "Lord" in the midst of many who claim the title.'[80]

The responses of the nobleman to each of the first two slaves (19.17, 19) indicate that the actions of the slaves have fulfilled the expectations of their master. The first slave is commended and is described as being faithful (19.17). It is clear that his master approves of the business he has conducted. The nobleman rewards the first two slaves by granting them authority over a number of cities, corresponding to the number of pounds which they have made from their trading (19.17, 19).

In the Matthean version, the master tells the first two slaves, 'I will put you in charge of many things; enter into the joy of your master' (Mt. 25.21, 23). In contrast to the future aspect of this reward and the eschatological slant which the master's words are given in the Matthean text, the Lukan reward is political: 'The reward to those who have handled their charge well does not consist in some future overseeing of possessions, but is present (ἴσθι, γίνου), and consists in power (ἐξουσία) over cities within the King's realm (Lk. 19:17, 19).'[81]

It is fascinating to note how different perspectives influence the interpretation of different features of the passage. Since a pound (μνᾶ) is no more than one sixtieth of the value of a talent (the currency used in the Matthean version), some scholars refer to it as a paltry sum. Danker, for instance, states 'the contrast between the trifling amount and the responsibility now entrusted to the slave points to the surpassing generosity of the king.'[82] Michael Goulder is caustic in his assessment of the Lukan parable, believing it to be 'an unhappy blend of inconsequence and absurdity.'[83] He argues further that since the Lukan author has 'an aversion from big business, ... he reduces the investments to a μνᾶ apiece, 100 denarii, three months wages' and that this gives 'a stingy feel to the story.'[84] Yet to a laborer who must work for three months to receive this amount in wages, a pound is not a 'trifling amount' and the parable does not have a 'stingy feel.'[85] One's perspective influences the response to this detail. From the perspective of the less powerful this is a significant amount, while to those who stand in the position of the wealthy and powerful, it can appear trivial.

The Greek historian, Xenophon, relates a discussion between the poet, Simonides, and the tyrant (τύραννος), Hiero. Hiero bemoans the fact that

---

80. Kitchen, 'Parable of the Pounds,' 129.
81. Johnson, 'Lukan Kingship Parable,' 144.
82. Danker, *New Age*, 308.
83. Goulder, *Luke*, 2.680.
84. Goulder, *Luke*, 2.681.
85. Moreover, if Schottroff, *Lydia's Impatient Sisters*, 94, is correct, women workers would need to work for twice this time to earn the amount.

it is risky for tyrants to travel abroad since their property is too insecure to be entrusted to others.[86] This reflection by a tyrant may assist in the interpretation of our parable. The rewards which are given to the first two slaves, rather than reflecting 'the surpassing generosity of the king,' may reflect the fact that he has found two slaves whom he can trust to further his extortive practices in his absence. In this case it would be no surprise that these slaves are given the authority to extend these practices. The first two slaves have become oppressors themselves. Those who cooperate with the oppressive system have the opportunity to benefit from the system.[87]

It is at this point that the third slave comes to center stage in the story.[88] His first words, κύριε, ἰδοὺ ἡ μνᾶ σου (19.20), continue the pattern established by the first two slaves. From here, however, the expected format undergoes a dramatic rupture (19.20-21). Rather than stating how many pounds he has made, the third slave produces the pound that he had put away in a cloth. He has not traded with the pound. The slave describes his master as harsh (αὐστηρός). According to Jean-Nöel Aletti, αὐστηρός is a technical word but its use is equally metaphoric with negative connotations.[89] As in the Matthean version (Mt. 25.24), the slave also describes the master as reaping what he does not sow. Where this is associated with gathering where he does not scatter seed in the Matthean version, however, in the Lukan story the master is said to take up or withdraw (αἴρω) what he does not deposit (τίθημι) (19.21).[90] Thus, in the Matthean parable the agricultural image is continued whereas in the Lukan parable the image changes to a commercial one.[91]

The rule, 'Do not take up what you do not deposit,' has similar forms in several ancient writings.[92] Josephus, for instance, lists the breach of this law among crimes with severe penalties.[93] Evans concludes that the master is identified as an extortionist: '[C]ontravention of this law was to be guilty of some kind of fraud or expropriation, and this is what the slave accuses

---

86. See Xenophon, *Hiero* 1.11–12. See also Danker, *New Age*, 307–8.

87. See McBride, *Parables of Jesus*, 84.

88. In 19.20 it is literally 'the other' who comes to the master at this point. This raises an awkward feature of the narrative. If ten slaves were given money and two have come forward, there should be eight rather than one still to come.

89. Jean-Nöel Aletti, 'Parabole des Mines et/ou Parabole du Roi. Lc 19, 11–28: Remarques sur l'Écriture Parabolique de Luc,' in *Les Paraboles Évangéliques: Perspectives Nouvelles*, (ed.) J. Delorme, LD 135 (Paris: Éditions du Cerf, 1989), 317.

90. For this translation, see BAGD, 816.

91. See Johnson, *Luke*, 291. Puig i Tàrrech notes that the Lukan version includes six technical expressions from the world of finance. See Puig i Tàrrech, 'Parabole des Talents,' 173.

92. For a summary of references to this law in ancient times, see Evans, *Saint Luke*, 671–72.

93. Josephus, *Apion* 2.216.

his master of, and what the master admits to be the case.'[94] With his words therefore, the third slave is exposing his master's exploitative practices.[95]

The wording of the third slave's accusations against his master (19.21) is repeated by the master himself in 19.22. The repeated phrases, concerning reaping without sowing and taking without depositing, serve to emphasize these words and as such form a key to the story's interpretation. The character and practices of the master are clearly exposed to view. The master repeats, but does not deny any of the allegations. Labeling the slave as πονηρός, the master argues that the slave should have given the money to a bank so that he could have obtained interest on it (19.23).[96] Since collecting interest on a loan to an Israelite is forbidden according to Deut. 23.19-20 (cf. Exod. 22.25 and Lev. 25.36-37), Fitzmyer suggests that the master is implying that the slave could have lent the money to Gentiles.[97] The master's words in 19.23 also serve to highlight his character as one who seeks a profit at any cost. This fits the third servant's description of him as an exacting man (19.21). While the NRSV translates πονηρὲ δοῦλε (19.22) as 'wicked slave,' in this context the translation 'worthless slave' may be more appropriate since it reinforces that the slave has not increased the master's profits. Whatever the translation, by labeling him as πονηρὲ δοῦλε, the master seeks to discredit the criticism that the slave has addressed to the master.[98]

The vast majority of scholars see the third slave as having failed. Tannehill, for instance, argues that the fear of the third slave has paralyzed him.[99] Similarly, Sharon H. Ringe argues that 'for fear of losing the coin and angering the noble, he has simply stashed it away.'[100] For Danker, the third slave's actions represent 'total failure.' In Danker's eyes, the slave takes no chances and risks nothing.[101] Another reading, however, is possible.

94. Evans, *Saint Luke*, 672.

95. Both Green and Herzog describe the third slave as blowing the whistle on his master's business practices. See Green, *Gospel of Luke*, 677; and Herzog, *Parables*, 167. For the exploitative practices of actual rulers in New Testament times, see Martin Hengel, *Property and Riches in the Early Church: Aspects of a Social History of Early Christianity* (London: SCM Press, 1974), 15–16. Hengel argues that the Romans and the rulers they appointed, such as Herod and his successors, continued the form of intensive exploitation practised by the Greco-Macedonian colonizers during the Hellenistic period.

96. The word τράπεζα (19.23) can be understood as a money-changer's table. See BAGD, 824.

97. Fitzmyer, *Luke*, 2.1237.

98. See Kitchen, 'Parable of the Pounds,' 106–7, for the labeling within this parable.

99. Robert C. Tannehill, *Luke*, (Nashville, TN: Abingdon Press, 1996), 281. See, also, Gooding, *According to Luke*, 301.

100. Ringe, *Luke*, 235.

101. Danker, *New Age*, 308.

To say that the slave has been paralyzed suggests that he has not acted in any way. In fact, he *has* acted.[102] He has put the money away in a cloth (19.20). In the Matthean version, the slave hides the money in the ground (Mt. 25.18). A view expressed in Rabbinic literature is that the safest protection for money is to bury it in the ground. If a person entrusted with money does not bury it and the money is stolen, then the person is considered negligent (*b. B. Mez.* 42a). Furthermore, if money is deposited with a person and that person bundles it up without keeping it in the hand then that person is liable if the money is lost or stolen (*b. B. Mez.* 42a). Since the third slave in the Lukan parable wraps the money in a cloth rather than hiding it in the ground, Herzog claims that this indicates his irresponsibility.[103] Yet the fact that he does not lose the money and is able to return the pound to his master would suggest that his care has not been inadequate. Rather, it would seem that the slave has been vigilant to protect the money.

From a peasant viewpoint, governed by an understanding of 'limited good,' Malina and Rohrbaugh claim that an honorable person is one who maintains what one has without seeking more. From this perspective, then, it is the third slave who has acted honorably. He has protected what he has been given, but not attempted to obtain a profit from trading.[104] This interpretation fits Eusebius' explanation of the version in the *Gospel of the Nazoreans*.[105] Since the third slave in the Lukan story did not bury the entrusted money in the ground, he was responsible for protecting it from theft. That he was successful suggests an ongoing commitment on his part to preserving the money. He has not simply 'stashed it away' as has been suggested.

By not trading with the pound, the third slave has refused to continue the extortion practised and endorsed by his master. Given that he knows the character and expectations of his master, the slave knows that his action will have repercussions. Some claim that the slave takes no risks. Yet the slave takes an enormous risk by resisting his master and the oppressive practices. As discussed in the introductory chapter, a slave who offends the master could expect severe corporal punishment and even

---

102. Rohrbaugh, 'Peasant Reading,' 38.
103. Herzog, *Parables*, 151; also Resenhöfft, 'Gleichnis von den Talenten,' 324.
104. Malina and Rohrbaugh, *Social-Science Commentary*, 385.
105. This is outlined in Chapter 1, above. As Rohrbaugh notes, Jeremias changes the order of the slaves in his discussion of the version in the *Gospel of the Nazoreans*. Therefore, according to Rohrbaugh, Jeremias incorrectly argues that the one who multiplies the gain is commended. This does not fit the chiastic pattern which Rohrbaugh identifies in the *Gospel of the Nazoreans* story. See Rohrbaugh, 'Peasant Reading,' 36–37, and Jeremias, *Parables of Jesus*, 58.

execution. Therefore, in acting honorably and not exploiting others, he risks no less than his life.[106]

Evans interprets the argument of 19.21 as 'I feared you as one who does not live honestly by his own labours, but by fraud and misappropriation, ... and is prepared to make profit at all costs and by all means. I was unwilling to behave like you; I return your pound to you.'[107] Evans then interprets the master's response to mean, 'since you knew me to be such a person it was your duty to behave as I do, and at all costs to have got interest.'[108] This interpretation fits with the understanding that a slave should always follow the instructions of the master (cf. Lk. 12.47 and Col. 3.22). Evans sees the message of the parable as being to 'be profitable at all costs and by all means.'[109] This implies that the third slave should have followed the master's instructions, despite knowing that he would be involved in the practice of extortion.

Several scholars question the third slave's perception of his master. Tannehill sees it as a 'one-sided description' since, while the master is harsh with the slave who disobeyed him, he is generous with the first two slaves.[110] Bernard B. Scott notes the dilemma of the audience, confronted with the slave's description of his master and the master's label of the third slave as wicked or worthless (19.21-22). Scott suggests that the audience is forced into retrospection, to consider the master's treatment of the first two slaves. 'Nothing in the narration indicates that the master was hard and ruthless with them or that they were in fear of him. At the story's end, a hearer is left with a dilemma. Whom do I trust? Where does the truth lie?'[111]

It is at this point that the structure of the parable needs to be considered once again. The story of the slaves accounting to their master is framed by the storyline of the opposition of the citizens. As such, the frame should be considered in interpreting the story held within. As we have seen, the frame gives us a picture of a nobleman who grasps power and abuses that power, slaughtering those who oppose him. This reinforces the characterization of the man presented by the third slave. In effect, the frame vindicates the words and actions of the third slave. The dilemma

---

106. Kitchen, 'Parable of the Pounds,' 70, states that the slave 'risks all by confronting the trade practices of his master.' She understands the risk in terms of condemnation and financial insecurity (pp. 70–71).

107. Evans, *Saint Luke*, 667.

108. Evans, *Saint Luke*, 667. See, also, Kim, *Stewardship*, 162–63. Since the third slave has disobeyed his master, Kim sees nothing wrong with the master's punishment of the slave (p. 163).

109. Evans, *Saint Luke*, 667.

110. Tannehill, *Luke*, 281. See also Nolland, *Luke*, 3.916.

111. Scott, *Hear Then the Parable*, 232.

Scott posed for the audience is solved by the frame. The truth lies in the slave's description of the master.

Taking the structure of the whole parable into account, then, the reader is led to perceive the master as an oppressive and violent ruler. The hatred of the citizens is therefore understandable. Their voice of resistance is finally silenced by their slaughter. The slaves know well the character of their master and the extortive practices which he expects. Those who obey the master are seen to be generously rewarded, thus ensuring that the extortive practices will not only continue but be expanded. The slave who chooses to act honorably and, therefore, resists the instructions of the master, knows that he will have to suffer the consequences of his actions.[112] The master violently opposes all who challenge the power structure which gives him authority.

The master orders those standing by to take the pound away from the third slave and to give it to the slave who has ten pounds (19.24). Their response expresses surprise and perhaps outrage (19.25).[113] The slave who only has one pound has it taken away from him, while the slave who has ten pounds is given another.[114] The master replies with a saying – 'I tell you, to all those who have, more will be given; but from those who have nothing, even what they have will be taken away' (19.26). A similar saying appears earlier in the Gospel in 8.18 (cf. Mk 4.25; Mt. 13.12). That occurrence, along with its parallels in the Gospels of Mark and Matthew, comes in the context of Jesus speaking to his disciples after the Parable of the Sower. As Dawsey points out, however, the saying in 8.18 is not referring to material possessions but rather 'understanding the good news of the kingdom.'[115] Thus, in the context of the Parable of the Pounds, the meaning of the saying has shifted.[116]

Dodd argues that a saying of Jesus has been turned into a general maxim and given a new context in the parable: 'That the maxim is an original saying of Jesus is fairly certain, in view of its multiple attestation, but its original application is lost beyond recall.'[117] Further, Dodd believes that the situation of the parable is not a perfect example of the saying since the third slave does not lose his pound because he only has a little, but because he does not increase what he has, which is a different

---

112. Kitchen, 'Parable of the Pounds,' 137.

113. Though some texts (e.g. D W) omit 19.25, perhaps to bring it in line with the Matthean story, the strongest attestation is for the inclusion of the verse. Among those witnesses which include the verse are ℵ and A, while B includes the verse but omits κύριε.

114. Puig i Tàrrech argues that the master does no wrong to the slave here, since the slave has already offered his money. See Puig i Tàrrech, 'Parabole des Talents,' 179.

115. Dawsey, *Lukan Voice*, 96.

116. Kitchen, 'Parable of the Pounds,' 148, argues that placing a saying in a new context can serve to 'defamiliarise the reader.'

117. Dodd, *Parables of the Kingdom*, 110.

situation.[118] In the different context of the parable, the saying reinforces
the concept of the rich getting richer and the poor getting poorer, or more
particularly, the powerful becoming more powerful and the powerless
losing what little opportunities they have. '[T]he terms *rich* and *poor* are
political before they are economic. That is, to be rich is to have the power
to maintain what one has, or even to increase it, while to be poor is to be
unable to defend even what one has.'[119]

Meeting the saying for the second time in 19.26, the observant reader
remembers that it is Jesus who pronounces the saying in 8.18. This
establishes a connection in the reader's mind between Jesus and the
nobleman of the parable, which may contribute to the assumption made
by many scholars that the nobleman is an image of Jesus. Some go so far
as to argue that these words are to be interpreted in 19.26 as spoken by
Jesus rather than the master.[120] The different context of the saying in the
Parable of the Pounds, the shift in meaning and the extortive actions of
the nobleman, however, should rather be interpreted as providing a
contrast with Jesus' actions and his use of the words. Dawsey sees the
difficulty in identifying the speaker of 19.26 with Jesus: 'How can the
harsh saying in Lk 19:26 ... be reconciled with the Parable of the Rich
Man and Lazarus? And how can the vengeful king of the parable (Lk
19:27) be the same Jesus who prays from the cross "Father, forgive them
for they know not what they do" (Lk 23:34)?'[121] The use of the similar
sayings in 8.18 and 19.26 enable a contrast to be made about the concerns
of the two proclaimers of the sayings. Where Jesus is concerned with
proclaiming the βασιλεία (8.1, 10), the nobleman is concerned with
financial gain at any cost.

In the Matthean story, the third slave is thrown into the outer darkness
(Mt. 25.30). This aspect is not included in the Lukan version. In Danker's
estimation, the third slave does not receive any special punishment: 'He is
simply not entrusted with the program of the future.'[122] Similarly, for
Johnson, 'this man is simply deprived of his pound (and his potential

---

118.   Dodd, *Parables of the Kingdom*, 110–11. See also Crossan, *In Parables*, 99–100. In
contrast, David Flusser believes that the logion fits the Parable of the Talents/Pounds and
that the parallel sayings in Mk 4.25/pars. are taken from the context of the Parable of the
Talents/Pounds. See David Flusser, 'Aesop's Miser and the Parable of the Talents,' in
Parable and Story in Judaism and Christianity, (eds.) Clemens Thoma and Michael
Wyschogrod (Mahwah, NJ: Paulist Press, 1989), 23, n. 15. Lambrecht suggests that the
logion was originally a wisdom saying which was added to the Parable of the Pounds by the
early church. See Lambrecht, *Once More Astonished*, 181.
119.   Rohrbaugh, 'Peasant Reading,' 35.
120.   See, for example, Goulder, *Luke*, 2.681–2; also Schweizer, *Luke*, 295.
121.   Dawsey, *Lukan Voice*, 96.
122.   Danker, *New Age*, 309.

leadership).'[123] The consequences for the third slave, however, should not be dismissed so quickly; for the one who is oppressed, these consequences are dire. Though the resistance of the third slave links him with the resistance of the citizens, there is no explicit claim that the slave will be among those slaughtered. While the slave has risked his life by offending his master, no corporal punishment is described. Rather, what he has been given and carefully protected is taken away from him by the one who has power over him.

As explained in the introductory chapter, a loyal imperial slave in the ancient world had a good chance of advancement in power and status and ultimately of being freed. By resisting his master, the third slave in the Parable of the Pounds compromises his opportunity for advancement and, in particular, his opportunity for manumission. Danker's description of being 'not entrusted with the program of the future' could be interpreted as implying that the slave will not have any power to influence his future. Because he has challenged the power structure which is operating, he must lose any power that he has so that he will not be in a position to continue his challenge. Thus, what the third slave loses is political, social and economic in consequence.

As discussed previously, some interpretations of the Parable of the Pounds connect the slaughter of the citizens who oppose the nobleman (19.27) with the judgment of those who reject Jesus, linking this to the destruction of Jerusalem in 70 CE (cf. 19.41-44; 21.6, 20-24). Some passages within the Lukan Gospel do refer to a time of judgment for those who do not repent (e.g. 10.13-15; 11.29-32; 13.1-5). Furthermore, interpretations of the Parable of the Tenants (20.9-19) often incorporate an element of destruction for those who reject Jesus.[124] Thus, there is a theme of violence and judgment in the Gospel of Luke which is used to support this interpretation of the Parable of the Pounds. This theme violently condemns those who reject Jesus and his teaching.

Such a theme is appropriate to an interpretation of the Parable of the Pounds, however, only if the nobleman is presumed to represent Jesus or live according to the values of the βασιλεία which Jesus proclaims and embodies. If this is the case, then those citizens who reject the nobleman represent those who reject Jesus and his teaching (cf. 19.44), but if the nobleman is not perceived as aligned with Jesus' teaching, then this comparison breaks down.[125] If, as I will argue in the following chapter, it

---

123. Johnson, 'Lukan Kingship Parable,' 144.

124. See for instance, Johnson, *Luke*, 308–9; Byrne, *Hospitality of God*, 158; and Marshall, *Luke*, 726, 731–32. For a contrasting interpretation, see Herzog, *Parables*, 98–113.

125. See the comparison of Luke 19.11-28 and Luke 20.9-19 in Kitchen, 'Parable of the Pounds,' 169. Kitchen parallels the nobleman of the first parable with the tenants in the other parable.

is the third slave who can be linked with Jesus, then the nobleman can be perceived rather as one who needs to repent.

There is also a theme of cunning and worldly wisdom evidenced in the Gospel of Luke which is sometimes used to account for the depiction of the nobleman. The Parable of the Steward in 16.1-9, where the master commends the steward for his shrewdness, provides an example of this motif. There is an important difference, however, between the portrayal of this steward and the nobleman of the Parable of the Pounds. The steward reduces the debts of his master's debtors.[126] Therefore, he relieves the burdens of those in debt which aligns him with Jesus' pronouncement of release to captives (4.18). In contrast, the nobleman of the Parable of the Pounds practises extortion and expects his slaves to do the same. It is the third slave who refuses to continue this oppression.

A reading of the parable which affirms the actions of the nobleman can be seen to maintain and justify imperialist strategies since the man cooperates with foreign powers and thus obtains power for himself over others. On the other hand, a reading which critiques the nobleman's actions challenges imperialist and classist domination and exploitation of one by another. The parable does not explicitly commend the actions of the less powerful ones nor condemn the oppressive actions of the more powerful. From the wider context of the Lukan Gospel, however, the reader is implicitly invited to critique such abuse of power. An exploration in the following chapter of elements of the theology of the Lukan Gospel will lay the grounds for this critique. As we will see, a reading of the Parable of the Pounds which justifies the actions of the nobleman and/or values the actions of the first two slaves as opposed to the third slave can be critiqued by using the Lukan text itself. Within the Lukan Gospel, therefore, it can be argued that the Parable of the Pounds functions to critique abuse of power and the desire for wealth at the expense of others,[127] and to explain that the βασιλεία of God has not yet arrived in its fullness. It also points to the fate of those who resist oppressive power, leading into Jesus' entrance into Jerusalem which Jesus has repeatedly announced to be the place where he will be killed.

126.   Byrne suggests that the steward cuts his own commission and thus models the right response by giving away his wealth. See Byrne, *Hospitality of God*, 134. For a more detailed reading of Luke 16, see Brendan Byrne, 'Forceful Stewardship and Neglectful Wealth: A Contemporary Reading of Luke 16,' *Pacifica* 1 (1988): 1–14.

127.   Reid, *Parables for Preachers*, 327.

Chapter 3

LUKAN THEOLOGY AND THE PARABLE OF THE POUNDS AS METAPHOR

The Parable of the Pounds (19.11-28) contributes to the Lukan rhetoric: it highlights the abuse of power by an oppressive ruler and the contrasting honorable actions of a slave, as well as illustrating the consequences of resisting an oppressive power. The parable leads into the arrival of Jesus in Jerusalem where he will be greeted as king but soon face death. By pointing to the fate awaiting Jesus, the parable serves both a narrative and a theological function within the Gospel. In this study I argue that the parable also serves as a metaphor for the challenge to oppressive structures evidenced in the wider Lukan Gospel narrative.

I have claimed in the previous chapter that the ruler of the Parable of the Pounds does not live according to the values of the βασιλεία which Jesus proclaims and embodies. Rather, it is the third slave who is aligned with Jesus' values. At this point, then, it is necessary to investigate further just what it is that Jesus does proclaim and embody in the Lukan Gospel. This chapter, therefore, will explore aspects of Lukan theology which are particularly pertinent to this, enabling the Parable of the Pounds to be set within the wider context of the Gospel of Luke. This will form the groundwork for a critique of the actions of the ruler in the Parable of the Pounds and an honoring of the actions of the third slave. Thus the text itself will be used to show that the third slave, rather than the ruler, adheres to the values proclaimed and embodied by the Lukan Jesus. Following this, the chapter will explore how the parable can be seen to function as a metaphor within the Lukan Gospel.

1. *Lukan Theology*

A number of Lukan themes are especially significant for this investigation. As will be seen, themes of visitation and hospitality, release and social justice set the context within which the portrayal of the Lukan Jesus and the salvation which he embodies can be understood. These themes are developed more explicitly in the Lukan Gospel than in the other Gospels. The focus on salvation continues in the portrayal of Jesus' death, and God's raising of Jesus authenticates this salvation.

Though the Lukan author has used sources and traditions in writing his narrative, the final result reflects his individual style for he uses his material to further his own designs: ' "[T]he world of Luke" signifies the world as Luke wants it to be, the world which, according to his theological perspective, God purposes. Thus, Luke is not concerned to present the world "as it really is," but purposefully shapes the story in such a way that some of its facets are undermined, others legitimated.'[1] Of particular interest in this study is to explore what the Lukan narrative undermines and what it legitimates in regard to the women's characterizations. This will be the focus of the following chapters. In the present chapter. however, the focus will be on what elements are legitimated and emphasized in Lukan theology.

It is not only the content of the narrative, but also the way in which the story evolves which is important for understanding Lukan theology. In an important early study of Lukan theology, Hans Conzelmann argues for the distinctive nature of the Lukan portrayal of salvation history: 'What distinguishes him [the Lukan author] is not that he thinks in the categories of promise and fulfilment, for this he has in common with others, but the way in which he builds up from these categories a picture of the course of saving history, and the way in which he employs the traditional material for this purpose.'[2]

Many recognize that the infancy narrative is an integral element in establishing this theology (Lk. 1–2).[3] Rather than being a sideshow to the main event, the first two chapters of the Lukan Gospel set the scene for what is to follow in the narrative. Several characters in these chapters recognize that in the birth of Jesus the promise of salvation is being fulfilled. Canticles interspersed through the infancy narrative especially capture the reader's attention and give insight into important Lukan themes (*Magnificat* 1.46-55; *Benedictus* 1.67-79; *Gloria* 2.13-14; and *Nunc Dimittis* 2.28-32).[4] In particular, the *Benedictus*, which introduces the theme of visitation, has been described as offering 'the best summary of the theology of the Gospel.'[5]

---

1.   Joel B. Green, *The Theology of the Gospel of Luke* (Cambridge: Cambridge University Press, 1995), 5.

2.   Conzelmann, *Theology of St. Luke*, 13.

3.   See, for example, Mark Coleridge, *The Birth of the Lukan Narrative: Narrative as Christology in Luke 1–2*, JSNTSup 88 (Sheffield: JSOT Press, 1993), 22–24; Tannehill, *Narrative Unity*, 20–21; Raymond E. Brown, *The Birth of the Messiah: A Commentary on the Infancy Narratives of Matthew and Luke* (New York, NY: Doubleday, 1979), 38, 242–43.

4.   The canticles are commonly called by the Latin names attributed to them.

5.   Byrne, *Hospitality of God*, 27.

a. *Visitation and Hospitality*

The *Benedictus* is placed at the end of the first chapter of the infancy narrative (1.67-79). In Luke 1.67 Zechariah is portrayed as receiving insight from the Holy Spirit and prophesying. He is empowered to interpret and proclaim the significance of the events. It is ironic that Zechariah, whose earlier lack of discernment of the signs culminated in his loss of speech (1.18-20), is now able to discern God's action and proclaim. At the beginning and end of the *Benedictus* there are references to a visitation (1.68, 78). The verb ἐπισκέπτομαι appears in both verses.[6] Such a framework for the canticle suggests that the theme of 'divine visitation' describes God's action and presence in Jesus. This theme continues in 7.16 and 19.44. Hence, integral to the Gospel of Luke is the understanding that, in the coming of Jesus and his ministry, God is visiting God's people.[7] The Lukan Gospel focuses on both the nature of this visitation and the response to it.

The theme of fulfilment of promise is a significant element of the *Benedictus*, and indeed of the whole infancy narrative. Given insight from the Holy Spirit, Zechariah can discern that this visitation is the fulfilment of what God has spoken through the prophets (1.70), and the fulfilment of the covenant which God has made with the ancestors (1.72-73). As the canticle progresses, the understanding of salvation moves from the political overtones in 1.71-75 to being concerned with forgiveness (ἄφεσις) of sins in 1.77. The meaning of ἄφεσις is literally 'release,' suggesting that salvation in this sense is the release from the barriers in relating to God. Such an understanding of salvation develops over the course of the Lukan narrative. At the beginning of his ministry, Jesus proclaims a time of 'release' (4.18-19), and his entire ministry enacts this release.

Zechariah's son, John, as prophet of the Most High (1.76), will announce this salvation which the divine visitation brings about. He will give 'knowledge of salvation' (γνῶσιν σωτηρίας) to the people (1.77). Mark Coleridge notes that γνῶσις 'here moves beyond a sense of factual knowledge to an experience of what is known (in this case, forgiveness).'[8] The ministries of both John and Jesus will bring people to an experience of release.

6. A textual difficulty arises in 1.78, with the manuscript evidence divided over the form of the verb – either the future tense, ἐπισκέψεται, or the aorist tense, ἐπεσκέψατο. Brown opts for the aorist form, arguing that it is the more difficult reading. See Brown, *Birth of the Messiah*, 373. However, it is likely that the future form was changed to the aorist to conform with 1.68. See Metzger, *Textual Commentary*, 110. Since the movement of the canticle is from the past to the future, the future tense appears more appropriate here.

7. See Coleridge, *Birth of the Lukan Narrative*, 22–23; Green, *Theology*, 31; and Byrne, *Hospitality of God*, 4, 28.

8. Coleridge, *Birth of the Lukan Narrative*, 121, n. 1. See also Byrne, *Hospitality of God*, 28.

Using the theme of divine visitation to portray the life and ministry of Jesus attunes the reader to observe the responses to this visitor throughout the rest of the Gospel. Byrne expands the theme of visitation and the theme of hospitality, showing how those who welcome Jesus are drawn into God's extravagant love or the 'hospitality of God,' as Byrne names it:

> The crucial point is that those who do receive him [Jesus] find that he brings them into a much wider sphere of hospitality: the 'hospitality of God.' The one who comes as visitor and guest in fact becomes *host* and offers a hospitality in which human beings and, potentially, the entire world, can become truly human, be at home, can *know* salvation in the depths of their hearts.[9]

It is possible to see the story of Zacchaeus as a paradigm for this understanding of the hospitality of God in the Lukan Gospel (Luke 19.1-10). Zacchaeus, who is marginalized as a tax-collector and labeled a sinner (19.7), provides hospitality to Jesus and as a result discovers the hospitality of God. Jesus announces that Zacchaeus is included in the community of salvation (19.9). In so doing, Jesus upholds the dignity of Zacchaeus, the dignity of the marginalized.[10] Zacchaeus is brought to knowledge of his salvation (cf. 1.77).

b. *Proclaiming and Embodying Release*

Release (ἄφεσις) is a key feature of Lukan salvation. The word ἄφεσις occurs five times in the Lukan Gospel. As we have seen, it is included in the *Benedictus* in Lk. 1.77 relating to the forgiveness (ἄφεσις) of sins – that is, release from the barriers in relating to God. In Lk. 3.3 John the Baptist proclaims a baptism of repentance for the release (ἄφεσις) of sins, and in Lk. 24.47 proclaiming repentance and release (ἄφεσις) of sins is part of the mission given to the disciples by the risen Jesus. The use of ἄφεσις in relation to the forgiveness of sins occurs too in Acts 2.38; 5.31; 10.43; 13.38; and 26.18. The word ἄφεσις also appears twice in Jesus' proclamation in the synagogue at the beginning of his public ministry (Lk. 4.18-19).

As Green defines it, a sinner is one whose behavior places them outside the boundaries established by a group.[11] Within the context of Israel's covenantal relationship, sinners are those whose behavior puts them outside the dictates of the Torah. It is from within this context that the knowledge of salvation by the release from sins must be understood (Lk. 1.77). Jesus deliberately welcomes those not known for their faithfulness

---

9. Byrne, *Hospitality of God*, 4.

10. See Byrne, *Hospitality of God*, 152. Byrne also sees the story of the woman who anoints Jesus (7.36-50) as a paradigm here.

11. Green, *Theology*, 85.

to the law.[12] God, to whom the Torah belongs, can welcome these 'sinners.' Jesus, as the agent of the divine visitation, embodies God's welcome to all thought to be 'outside' the law. Jesus gathers in those considered lost or 'dead' according to the law. Thus an aspect of salvation in the Gospel of Luke is inclusion in the community of God. While all are welcome in this community, the inclusion of 'sinners' is particularly emphasized.

The Parables of the Lost in Luke 15 are told in response to the grumbling of the Pharisees and scribes that Jesus welcomes and eats with sinners (15.2). All three parables speak to the human condition of being lost and describe the joy when the lost is found (15.7, 10, 32). The third of these parables, the Parable of the Two Sons, gives the most detailed description of the implications of being lost and the welcome back of the lost one (15.11-32). By claiming his share of the inheritance and then squandering it (15.12-13), the younger son in the parable 'has effectively disinherited himself from his own family' and 'essentially forfeited the right of sonship.'[13] The portrayal of this younger son feeding pigs highlights the alienation from his Jewish heritage which he experiences as a result of his actions (15.15),[14] and puts him outside the dictates of the Torah, thus including him in the category of 'sinner.' Yet, on the younger son's return, his father welcomes him. Marianne Meye Thompson points out that the words of the father in 15.24 indicate that the father considers him once again as a son and heir (15.24).[15] A lost one has been welcomed back into the family and receives the accompanying privileges.

The words of the father to the older son, 'this brother of yours was dead and has come to life; he was lost and has been found' (15.32), call the older son to also welcome a lost one back into the family.[16] The irony in the parable is that the older son's actions and words to his father reveal that he also is alienated in a sense from the family (15.28-30). While he has been physically present, a sense of relationship with his father is absent. He states that he works for his father 'like a slave' rather than like a son (15.29). Hence there are actually two lost sons in the story. Whether the older son chooses to be part of the family celebration is left open at the end of the parable.

While the Gospel of Luke highlights the journey to Jerusalem (9.51–19.27), in Acts the focus moves outward to the incorporation of the Gentiles into the promises of salvation (cf. Acts 11.18). Thompson claims

12. See Marianne Meye Thompson, *The Promise of the Father: Jesus and God in the New Testament* (Louisville, KY: Westminster John Knox Press, 2000), 100.
13. Thompson, *Promise of the Father*, 101.
14. Johnson, *Luke*, 237. See also Thompson, *Promise of the Father*, 101.
15. Thompson, *Promise of the Father*, 102.
16. Thompson, *Promise of the Father*, 102.

that this inclusion of the Gentiles is the acting out of the implications of the three Parables of the Lost.[17] Gentiles, considered 'outside' the law, are sought and welcomed. Both Jews and Gentiles are welcome in the community of God.

It can be seen then that an important element of salvation in the Gospel of Luke is release from sin and the welcoming of those who are thought to be 'outside' the law. The two appearances of the word ἄφεσις in Jesus' proclamation in the synagogue at the beginning of his public ministry, however, incorporate a further dimension apart from the release from sin (Lk. 4.18-19). The context is that of social justice, with ἄφεσις encompassing release from the structures which serve to oppress. This aspect of the ἄφεσις which Jesus proclaims and embodies will now be explored.

c. *Social Justice Ethos*

The mission of the Lukan Jesus is clearly announced at the beginning of his ministry, and ἄφεσις is an essential element of that mission. Emerging from his encounter with the Devil in the wilderness (4.1-13) and filled with the power of the Spirit (4.14), Jesus begins his public ministry in Galilee. In 4.15 Jesus begins to teach in the synagogues, though we are not given any detail as to the content of his teaching. It is the next story of Jesus in his hometown of Nazareth which provides more information for the reader and which proves crucial to understanding Jesus' mission according to the Gospel of Luke (4.16-30). Unlike the Markan version (Mk 6.1-6), the ministry in Nazareth occurs at the start of Jesus' public ministry in the Lukan narrative. This change in the order of the Markan presentation is not by chance. The location of the story in a place of prominence highlights the significance of this event for interpreting the entire mission of Jesus. Further, unlike the Markan version, the Lukan text provides the content of Jesus' teaching in this scenario. On other occasions in Luke 4 we read that Jesus teaches in the synagogue but we are not given the content of that teaching (4.15, 31-37, 44). That Jesus' words are given in Luke 4.16-30 suggests again the importance of this event for understanding what is to follow.

The words that Jesus reads from the scroll of the prophet Isaiah in Lk. 4.18-19 are from the LXX version of Isa. 61.1-2, with a few significant changes. Much of the wording in Lk. 4.18-19 is identical with the LXX version of the corresponding section of Isa. 61.1-2. Two phrases in Isaiah concerned with binding up the broken-hearted and the day of divine judgment, however, are not in the Lukan text while a phrase from Isa. 58.6 concerned with letting the oppressed go free is included. This

---

17. Thompson, *Promise of the Father*, 104.

addition can perhaps be explained by the word ἄφεσις which occurs in the included phrase as well as Isa. 61.1.[18]

The effect of the addition is to emphasize the concept of ἄφεσις. As Tannehill notes, 'repetitions indicate that something which has already been said is being picked up and repeated but also enriched and expanded through new expression.'[19] The added phrase from Isa. 58.6 is part of a social justice statement in Isa. 58.6-7 which announces what is acceptable to God. The use of the phrase from Isa. 58.6 in the Lukan text brings the whole context of Isa. 58.6-7 into the reading of Jesus in Lk. 4.18. 'It fills out the sense of releasing the oppressed with the wider program of social justice and hospitality to the poor announced in v. 7 [Isa. 58.7].'[20] Thus the inclusion of the extra phrase has a significant impact.

After reading from Isaiah, Jesus announces 'Today this scripture has been fulfilled in your hearing' (Lk. 4.21). The reader already knows that the Spirit is upon Jesus from Lk. 4.14, and now learns what the 'day' of Jesus is all about. Jesus' ministry will fulfil the words of the prophet and bring good news to the poor (4.18). Philip Francis Esler argues that a more appropriate translation for πτωχοί is 'beggars,'[21] and that in Hellenistic cities of the Roman East in the first century CE there would have been people who struggled daily to get sufficient food to live.[22] Esler maintains that the situation of the destitute among the Lukan community has influenced Lukan theology. The release promised in Lk. 4.18 incorporates salvation at a physical as well as spiritual level, involving relief from destitution and healing of disabilities.[23]

The ministry of Jesus to the wealthy Zacchaeus (19.1-10), however, suggests that 'the poor' are not only those with meagre economic resources. The understanding of the term can be expanded to refer to those with little or no honor, power or privilege, and those who are excluded.[24] While the financially destitute comprise a significant proportion, the term 'the poor' is more an indication of social location as an outsider than an economic indicator. Just as the poor are linked with captives, the blind and the oppressed in Lk. 4.18, they are linked with those with diseases, impurities or the excluded in several places in the Gospel (e.g. 6.20-21; 7.22 and 14.13). Green argues that these lists of 'the

18.   See Byrne, *Hospitality of God*, 49; and Peter Doble, *The Paradox of Salvation: Luke's Theology of the Cross*, SNTSMS 87 (Cambridge: Cambridge University Press, 1996), 49.

19.   Tannehill, *Narrative Unity*, 62.

20.   Byrne, *Hospitality of God*, 49.

21.   Esler, *Community and Gospel*, 180. For support of this translation see BAGD, 728.

22.   Esler, *Community and Gospel*, 175.

23.   Esler, *Community and Gospel*, 181. Kim, *Stewardship*, 49–50, also claims that the Lukan community contained both the wealthy and the destitute.

24.   See John O. York, *The Last Shall Be First: The Rhetoric of Reversal in Luke*, JSNTSup 46 (Sheffield: JSOT Press, 1991), 101–2.

poor' indicate who ought to be included.[25] Bringing good news to the
poor, then, implies that Jesus announces and embodies God's extravagant
love by welcoming the poor, and including the excluded (4.18). Already
the scripture is being fulfilled as those who hear Jesus' announcement hear
the good news (4.21). The day of divine judgment mentioned in Isa. 61.2 is
omitted from the Lukan account. At this point, the Lukan text stresses the
divine acceptance rather than divine judgment (4.18).

As the Gospel narrative progresses, the reader observes that Jesus'
ministry fulfils the commission of Lk. 4.18-19. He restores sight to the
blind (7.21; 18.35) and releases people from the burdens which capture
and oppress them. This release takes a variety of forms ranging from
healing physical disabilities and infirmities (e.g. 5.12-13) and forgiveness
of sins (e.g. 5.17-26), to restoration of social status (e.g. 19.1-10). In 4.43-
44 three pivotal verbs of 4.18-19 are repeated – εὐαγγελίζομαι,
ἀποστέλλω and κηρύσσω. By means of the repetition, the Lukan
narrator reinforces that the commission of 4.18-19 provides the key to
understanding Jesus' ministry and, further, that Jesus is carrying out that
mission.[26] Again, in 7.22 a summary of Jesus' ministry provides evidence
that the commission is being fulfilled. That Jesus continues to proclaim
the good news is made explicit in Lk. 8.1 and Lk. 20.1, with the twelve
proclaiming good news and healing in Lk. 9.6. Thus, the Lukan narrative
portrays Jesus as fulfilling the commission of Lk. 4.18-19 throughout his
ministry.

Given this portrayal of the Lukan Jesus, it is clear that the ruler of the
Parable of the Pounds who engages in oppressive practices cannot be
aligned with Jesus who proclaims good news to the poor and releases the
oppressed from their burdens (4.18). The third slave in the parable, who
refuses to continue the oppression, is the one who displays the values
which are aligned with Jesus' commission.

Throughout the Lukan Gospel the poor embrace the teachings of Jesus
while many of those with power and privilege fail to understand. Many
times in the Gospel of Luke we read about the dangers of wealth and the
need to share possessions.[27] While the poor receive good news, there are
indications that the news may not be so good for the rich. Following the
Beatitudes which announce the poor to be blessed (6.20-23) are the 'woes'
addressed to the rich (6.24-26). There will be a time of reversal when the
hungry will be filled and those who are full now will be hungry, when
those who weep will laugh and those who are laughing now will weep

25. Green, *Theology*, 81. Green provides an excellent discussion on the use of the term
'the poor' and the significance of 'preaching good news to the poor' on pp. 79–84.
26. See Tannehill, *Narrative Unity*, 77–78.
27. See, for example, 12.15, 16-21, 32-34; 14.33; 16.13; 18.22.

(6.21, 25). Jesus announces that 'some are last who will be first, and some are first who will be last' (13.30).

This theme of reversal, of the lowly being raised and the exalted being humbled, is expounded also in several parables (14.7-11, 16-24; 18.9-14) with the parable of the rich man and Lazarus providing the classic example of reversal for the rich and the poor (16.19-30). Jesus is critical of those in power who lord it over others (22.24) and declares himself instead as one who serves (22.27). In the *Magnificat* (1.46-55), Mary proclaims that God works in surprising ways, raising the lowly and bringing down the powerful, filling the hungry and sending the rich away empty (1.52-53). Further, Simeon announces that Jesus 'is destined for the falling and the rising of many in Israel' (2.34). Thus, from the infancy narrative it is possible to see the seeds of the theme of reversal which will feature so prominently in the rest of the Gospel.[28]

The hearers of Jesus' proclamation in the synagogue in Nazareth are amazed (θαυμάζω, 4.22). The word θαυμάζω is used thirteen times in the Gospel of Luke and reflects a range of responses.[29] In 1.63-65 and 8.25, for instance, the verb θαυμάζω is linked with fear while in 24.41 it is associated with disbelief. In 11.38 and 20.26 it is opponents of Jesus who are amazed by him. Hence θαυμάζω does not always indicate a favorable response, but in 7.9 it is Jesus who is amazed by the faith of the centurion. The use of θαυμάζω in 4.22 then does not clarify the response of the hearers, but another verb in 4.22, μαρτυρέω, may give more of an indication. The word can mean 'bear witness' but in the context of 4.22 a more appropriate meaning is 'speak well (of), approve (of).'[30] It would therefore seem that the hearers initially respond favorably to the proclamation of Jesus. As their expectations are reversed, however, those in the synagogue who hear Jesus' words turn against him, driving him out of town and aiming to throw him off a cliff (4.28-30). Thus a situation of conflict develops by the end of the pericope.

d. *Death and Resurrection*

From the beginning, Jesus' words and actions bring him into conflict with those who consider themselves 'on the inside' and who seek to maintain the exclusion of those 'on the outside.' The escalation of conflict that develops over the Gospel narrative ultimately leads to Jesus' death by crucifixion (Luke 22–23). 'In Luke-Acts Jesus' death is not an isolated

---

28. For more on the theme of reversal, see York, *Last Shall Be First*; and Tannehill, *Narrative Unity*, 28–31.

29. Θαυμάζω appears in 1.21, 63; 2.18, 33; 4.22; 7.9; 8.25; 9.43; 11.14, 38; 20.26; 24.12 and 24.41.

30. These meanings are from BAGD, 492–93.

event, but is a part of Jesus' entire life of revealing a faithful God.'[31] In
Lk. 23.35-39 the verb σῴζω appears four times as Jesus on the cross is
taunted about saving himself by leaders, soldiers and one of the criminals
put to death with him. Repetition of the word brings salvation into the
forefront of the reader's mind. The request of the other criminal − 'Jesus,
remember me when you come into your kingdom' (23.42) − reflects, in
contrast to these taunts, faith and trust. Jesus replies with words of
salvation − 'Truly I tell you, today you will be with me in Paradise'
(23.43).[32] Thus, as he has throughout his ministry, Jesus draws this
outcast into experience of his salvation. The criminal's faith has saved him
(cf. 7.50; 8.48; 17.19; 18.42).

Jesus' last words on the cross, the prayer of trust derived from Ps. 31.5,
underlie Jesus' own faith in God (23.46). The words of the centurion who
witnesses Jesus' death (23.47) also shape the Lukan portrayal. Jesus dies
as a δίκαιος one who trusts in God. Peter Doble uses these Lukan features
in his argument that the Lukan passion story has been influenced by the
portrayal of the δίκαιος one (or ones) in Wisdom 2–5.[33] The δίκαιος one
opposes the actions of oppressors and this brings him into conflict with
them. These oppressors test his faith and commitment and condemn him
to a shameful death (Wis. 2.10-20). Those who condemn him, however, do
not know the secret purposes of God (Wis. 2.22). The δίκαιος one trusts
in God (Wis. 3.1-9) and is finally vindicated by God (Wis. 5.1-8).
According to Doble, the use of Wisdom's δίκαιος model anchors Jesus'
'shameful death' both in scripture and the plan of God.[34]

The plan of God as portrayed in the Lukan narrative is also illuminated
by the use of epiphanies (e.g. 1.11, 26; 3.22; 9.35; 24), fulfilment of
prophecy (e.g. 4.21; 24.27), and verbs such as δεῖ and μέλλω (e.g. 2.49;
4.43; 9.22, 44; 13.33; 17.25; 24.7) which indicate a divine necessity.[35] John
T. Squires concludes, 'Luke presents the passion of Jesus, from the very
beginning, as part of God's plan.'[36] This Lukan identification is clearly
seen in two of Peter's speeches in Acts, where the death of Jesus is
associated with the plan of God (Acts 2.23; 4.28). The freedom of the

31. Robert J. Karris, *Luke: Artist and Theologian* (New York, NY: Paulist, 1985), 80.

32. See Joseph A. Fitzmyer, *Luke the Theologian: Aspects of his Teaching* (New York,
NY: Paulist Press, 1989), 212–13.

33. Doble, *Paradox of Salvation*, 25–225.

34. Doble, *Paradox of Salvation*, 229.

35. John T. Squires, *The Plan of God in Luke-Acts* (Cambridge: Cambridge University
Press, 1993), 2, 103–73.

36. Squires, *Plan of God*, 187. Several feminist scholars have critiqued this understanding
of Jesus' death. For an outline of feminist discussion and critique of some of the images and
language used to proclaim the Jesus story, see Wainwright, *Shall We Look?*, 12–14.

human will, however, is not overridden by this plan (cf. 7.30; 23.50-51), and 'there is a real freedom to choose for or against it.'[37]

As we have seen, the death of Jesus is by no means the final word in the story. In Lk. 24.6, it is announced to the women who have come to the tomb that Jesus has been raised (ἠγέρθη). The use of the divine passive here indicates that God has raised Jesus.[38] Passive forms of ἐγείρω also appear in Lk. 9.22 and 24.34. The theme of God raising Jesus is emphasized in Acts with active forms of the verbs ἐγείρω and ἀνίστημι being used with God as subject (Acts 2.24, 32; 3.15; 4.10; 5.30; 10.40; 13.30, 33-34, 37; 17.31).[39] God's raising of Jesus not only vindicates the faith of Jesus but also authenticates Jesus' entire ministry and the salvation which Jesus has embodied. God overcomes the powers of darkness (Lk. 22.53; 23.44). With the resurrection and the ascension, the Gospel of Luke finishes with the supreme reversal. Thus, 'in a profoundly ironic way, the passion of Jesus is joined by his exaltation, and these together embody in an ultimate way the salvation-as-reversal theme that threads its way throughout the Gospel of Luke.'[40]

The ascension of Jesus ends the Lukan Gospel (24.50-53). Jesus blesses his disciples and is taken up into heaven, with the use of the divine passive here again signifying God's action (24.51). The ascension is described also in the opening chapter of Acts (Acts 1.6-11), and thus forms a bridge between the two volumes. In Acts, after Jesus has been lifted up, two men in white clothing announce that Jesus has been taken up into heaven and speak also of a future coming of Jesus (Acts 1.11; cf. divine agents seen in the Lukan Gospel – 1.11-20, 26-38; 2.9-15; 9.30-32; 22.43; 24.4-7).[41]

This departure of Jesus has been referred to earlier in the Gospel (9.30-31, 51). The ascension forms the end of the disciples experiencing Jesus in bodily form, but also heralds new modes of experiencing Jesus' presence, hence its position at both the end of the Gospel and the beginning of the story of the Church. The disciples will continue to experience Jesus' presence in the breaking of the bread (24.35).[42] Before his ascension, Jesus tells his disciples that they will be empowered when the Holy Spirit comes upon them (Acts 1.8) and this coming of the Spirit on the day of Pentecost is described in Acts 2.1-4. Peter is empowered to speak and gives the first of several kerygmatic speeches which include an account of Jesus' life, death and resurrection (Acts 2.14-36; 3.12-26; 4.8-12; 5.29-32; 10.34-43).

---

37. Squires, *Plan of God*, 181.
38. Fitzmyer, *Luke*, 2.1545.
39. See Fitzmyer, *Luke the Theologian*, 215; and Charles H. Talbert, *Reading Luke-Acts in its Mediterranean Milieu* (Leiden: Brill, 2003), 122.
40. Green, *Theology*, 68. This idea is also in Talbert, *Reading Luke-Acts*, 124–26.
41. For an examination of epiphanies in Luke-Acts and how they show God at work in Jesus' life, see Squires, *Plan of God*, 103–20.
42. See Fitzmyer, *Luke the Theologian*, 221–22; and Johnson, *Luke*, 406.

Paul's speech in Acts 13.16-41 continues the prominence of these speeches in the first half of Acts.[43] Under the influence of the Spirit, the life, death and resurrection of Jesus continue to be proclaimed to all the nations, drawing them into a knowledge and experience of the salvation which Jesus embodies.[44]

e. *Salvation*

There are several facets to the Lukan portrayal of salvation. Esler describes salvation as having both an 'other-worldly' dimension and a 'this-worldly' dimension. The Lukan narrative at times presumes a belief in an afterlife in which the rich would be stripped of the benefits which they had enjoyed in this life while the poor would be given all that they had lacked. Esler cites the parable of the rich man and Lazarus (16.19-31) as the clearest example of this understanding.[45] He demonstrates, however, that salvation in the Lukan Gospel does not only incorporate an eschatological reality but also involves the elimination of injustice and the release from burdens in this world.[46]

Luke 4.18 announces that Jesus will bring salvation by proclaiming good news to the poor and liberating the oppressed. As we have seen, this describes the ministry of Jesus throughout the rest of the Gospel. The liberation or 'release' which Jesus enacts incorporates physical as well as spiritual release. Sins are forgiven, disabilities and diseases are healed, dignity is restored. Those considered excluded from God's presence and socially excluded are released from their burdens and welcomed to the table. Green describes the Lukan Gospel's presentation of Jesus' ministry in terms of Lukan theology:

> Jesus' teaching is ... presented as undercutting the authority and social positions of those who dominate his world. Jesus is doing nothing less than *redefining* the way the world 'works.' What is more, by grounding his attitudes and behavior in his message of the in-breaking kingdom of God he asserts the divine legitimation of this alternative view of the world.[47]

Thus, the Lukan narrative presents Jesus as embodying the hospitality of God and drawing people into that hospitality where they experience

---

43. Earl Richard, 'Pentecost as a Recurrent Theme in Luke-Acts,' in *New Views on Luke and Acts*, (ed.) Earl Richard (Collegeville, MN: Liturgical Press, 1990), 145.

44. That women disciples are not portrayed as proclaiming in Acts, though, will be discussed in the following chapters.

45. Esler, *Community and Gospel*, 192.

46. Esler, *Community and Gospel*, 193–94.

47. Green, *Theology*, 66.

salvation in both a spiritual and physical sense, a 'release' (ἄφεσις) from all the barriers in relating to God and from all that dehumanizes.

At this point another connotation of ἄφεσις has importance. The word appears four times in Deut. 15.1-3 and again in Deut. 15.9 in relation to a time of 'release.' Every seventh year, there was to be remission of debts (Deut. 15.1-3) and release from slavery (Deut. 15.12-18) for Israelites. The word ἄφεσις also occurs fifteen times in Leviticus 25 in relation to every fiftieth year which was to be a year of jubilee, a year of 'release.' In this year, no crops were to be sown (Lev. 25.11-12) giving a year of rest for the land. Furthermore, land which had been sold because of financial necessity was to be returned to its original owners (Lev. 25.25-28) and Israelites were to be released from slavery (Lev. 25.39-43).[48] Byrne claims that Isa. 61.1-2 alludes to these practices of release and that 'there are good grounds for finding this sense of "release" included in the program of liberation that Luke has Jesus inaugurate here [Lk. 4.16–21].'[49] The jubilee laws were designed to counter the accumulation of wealth and allow people who had experienced hardship to make a new start. By liberating the oppressed, Jesus too is giving people a new start, allowing them to experience fullness of life and the knowledge of salvation.

Since an important feature of the jubilee laws was the release from slavery, it is significant to note that slaves feature in many of Jesus' parables and teachings in the Lukan Gospel.[50] The Lukan Jesus takes for granted the presence of slavery and the master–slave dynamic and uses this imagery in his teaching. A present-day reader who is aware of oppressive structures can critique this power dynamic in which one person has complete control over another. In none of the parables or teachings is slavery explicitly challenged, nor is there the call for release for slaves. Moreover, some passages reinforce the master–slave dynamic (e.g. 12.47). In some ways, it would appear from the portrayal of slaves in the Lukan Gospel that they have not benefited from Jesus' proclamation of good news.[51] Yet some elements of Jesus' words do suggest a reversal in position for slaves and servants. In 12.37, the situation described is one of slaves sitting down to eat while their master serves them. Further, Jesus tells the apostles that the greatest among them must be like the youngest

---

48. For more on the year of jubilee, see Ringe, *Luke*, 68–71.

49. Byrne, *Hospitality of God*, 49.

50. The word δοῦλος appears in the following parables and teachings of Jesus: 12.35-40, 42-48; 14.15-24; 15.11-32; 17.7-10; 19.11-28; 20.9-19. Other terms are also used – e.g. οἰκονόμος (12.42; 16.1, 3, 8); οἰκέτης (16.13); παῖς or παιδίσκη (12.45; 15.26). See Kim, *Stewardship*, 111–15, for an analysis of terms in the Gospel of Luke which reflect a slave–master motif.

51. Ringe, *Luke*, 8–9, notes that the celebration to welcome back the younger son in the Parable of the Two Sons may not represent good news for the slaves who have to work hard to enable the family's celebration to proceed (15.22-23).

and the leader like one who serves and Jesus identifies himself as one who serves (22.26-27).[52] 'The disciples are thus called to imitate the one whose leadership style reversed the ways of worldly rulers in accordance with God's divine principle – the humble servant will be exalted (1.47–55).'[53]

The reading of the Parable of the Pounds (19.11-28) which is presented in Chapter 2 of this study also suggests a reversal. The third slave is portrayed as the honorable one while the master is the oppressor, the dishonorable one. There is no explicit statement of this reversal in the parable but the actions of the characters clearly demonstrate their alignment or otherwise with the Lukan Gospel's message of liberation and salvation. The nobleman is the epitome of those kings who lord it over others (22.25), while the third slave refuses to oppress others and thus aligns himself with Jesus' proclamation of good news to the poor. Like the tax collector who goes home justified as opposed to the Pharisee (18.9-14), it is the third slave rather than his master who is shown to be righteous in the Parable of the Pounds.

To summarize, then, the theological context of the Lukan Gospel is illuminating for an interpretation of the Parable of the Pounds. Visitation and hospitality, release and social justice are important themes within the Lukan Gospel. Jesus embodies salvation, and God's raising of Jesus authenticates his entire ministry. The actions of the nobleman and the third slave in the Parable of the Pounds must be considered within this theological context. In this light, the nobleman's actions can be seen to constitute the antithesis of Jesus' proclamation of release. In contrast, like Jesus, the third slave stands on the side of the oppressed.

2. *The Parable as Metaphor*

I argue in this study that the power dynamics evident in the Parable of the Pounds are also present elsewhere in the Lukan Gospel and that, like the third slave, other characters who oppose oppressive practices also suffer the consequences. The parable can thus be interpreted metaphorically within the wider Lukan Gospel as a reading strategy that helps elucidate the text. The remainder of this chapter will explore similar power dynamics in the stories of John the Baptist and Jesus, and will then consider how the parable can be read metaphorically. Finally, the idea that a similar power dynamic is evident in the characterizations of women in the Lukan Gospel will be raised as a preliminary to detailed exploration of this idea in the following chapters.

The third slave in the Parable of the Pounds refuses to continue the

---

52. These different presentations of the slave–master dynamic which can be found in the Lukan Gospel may reflect the presence of different voices within the text.
53. York, *Last Shall Be First*, 171.

oppressive practices of his master and has his pound taken away from him. What the slave loses, however, is far more than money. By resisting and challenging his master, he loses the possibility for future manumission for faithful service. Since he loses the money he has, his future ability to pay a manumission price is also adversely affected. Moreover, he loses as well the opportunity to attain power and status which are granted to the first two slaves. He loses the opportunity to influence his future, reinforcing his vulnerability and powerlessness. The consequences for this slave, therefore, are more than economic. They are also political – determining the power (or lack of power) of the slave – and social – consigning him to continued slavery. Furthermore, the citizens in the parable who oppose the nobleman's rule over them are slaughtered. Thus the one with power over others controls the destinies of those who challenge, ensuring that their capacity to maintain their resistance is taken away from them. Suppression of those who speak the truth and resist oppressive structures does not only feature in this parable, however. John the Baptist and Jesus also suffer the consequences for challenging oppressive practices. Resistance and suppression is a thread that weaves through the Lukan Gospel.

According to John A. Darr, a confrontation between a philosopher and a tyrant formed a prevalent 'type-scene' in ancient Greco-Roman literature and was 'a popular means of expressing opposition to tyranny throughout the Greco-Roman world.'[54] In such scenes, the philosopher plays the protagonist who confronts the powerful tyrant, the antagonist: 'Sometimes the tyrant is won over by the philosopher; more often, the wise man becomes a martyr. In either case, the ideal of resistance to tyranny is upheld and the tyrant fails to get what he seeks – ultimate control over the sage.'[55] In addition, Darr discusses the 'prophet versus king' type-scene of the LXX which also depicts a charismatic figure confronting a wicked ruler – for example, Moses and Pharoah; Samuel and Saul; Nathan and David; Elijah and Ahab.[56] Darr considers that a first-century Greco-Roman reader would have expected the wise one to confront the tyrant. Further, he suggests that these conventions and expectations have shaped the Lukan depiction of the interactions between Herod and both John and Jesus.[57]

The portrayal of John the Baptist and Jesus as characters who confront oppressive rulers and leaders will be discussed below. I have argued in this

54. Darr, *On Character Building*, 151–52. Darr gives examples of Diogenes censuring Philip of Macedon and Perdiccas, and suggests that the Jewish story of Eleazar and the seven sons who resist and are killed by Antiochus (*4 Maccabees*) 'is testimony to the widespread influence of this Hellenistic convention.'
55. Darr, *On Character Building*, 151.
56. Darr, *On Character Building*, 155–58.
57. Darr, *On Character Building*, 155.

study that the third slave in the Parable of the Pounds also fits the pattern of one who confronts a tyrant. A first-century Greco-Roman audience might have expected such behavior from a wisdom figure or prophet, but not a slave. The parable would thus confront their expectations as a parable is wont to do.

a. *John the Baptist*

John's proclamation of the good news to the people brings him into conflict with the tetrarch, Herod. John challenges Herod because of his brother's wife, Herodias, and 'because of all the evil things that Herod had done' (3.19). The use of the verb ἐλέγχω to describe John's action suggests that John reproves or corrects Herod, but it also carries the connotation that John exposes Herod.[58] John brings the evil deeds of Herod to the light of day, just as the third slave exposes the oppressive practices of his master in the Parable of the Pounds. In both the Markan and Matthean narratives, Herod arrests John because John has been challenging him about Herodias (Mk 6.17-18; Mt. 14.3-4), but only in the Lukan narrative do we find the additional comment about Herod's evil deeds.[59] Thus, the oppressive practices of Herod are highlighted in the Lukan Gospel. The nature of these evil deeds is not made explicit in the text, but Darr suggests that John's speech (3.7-14) leads to a definition of evil as 'the selfish abuse of power, position, privilege, or possession.'[60]

Like the third slave in the parable, John suffers the consequences for challenging the oppression. Herod shuts John in prison (3.20). Later in the narrative we learn that Herod has beheaded John (9.9), though John's death is not narrated, unlike the Markan and Matthean versions (Mk 6.14-29; Mt. 14.1-12). John is beheaded by one who is in a position of power over him. He loses his life, just as the third slave loses his opportunity for freedom, power and status, and just as the citizens are slaughtered when they oppose one with power over them. In the Parable of the Pounds, class difference and imperialist strategies result in the ruler having power over his slaves and the citizens. Similarly Herod, as an elite ruler who cooperates with the Roman imperialist structure, has power over and dominates others.

No response to the death of John is narrated in the Lukan Gospel. Herod's act is not directly critiqued within the text. The reader, however, knows of John's significance within the narrative right from the start. The angel Gabriel announces his important role and that he will be filled with the Holy Spirit even before his birth (1.13-17). His significance in

---

58. See BAGD, 249.
59. Kitchen, 'Parable of the Pounds,' 140–41.
60. Darr, *On Character Building*, 137.

preparing the way of Jesus is further prophesied by Zechariah (1.76-77), and he is portrayed as leaping for joy, while still in the womb, in response to Mary's greeting (1.41-44). Moreover, the reader knows of Jesus' approval of John. Jesus has previously described John as more than a prophet, the messenger foretold in Scripture and that, of 'those born of women no one is greater than John' (7.26-28). As the agent of the divine visitation, Jesus speaks with authority. Hence, the reader understands that John's actions are vindicated. In the conflict between Herod and John, John has acted honorably while Herod has acted oppressively.

b. *Jesus*

Like the third slave in the Parable of the Pounds and John the Baptist, Jesus also confronts oppressive practices. While Jesus encounters conflict with a variety of characters, the main antagonists in the Lukan narrative are the religious authorities. Characters within this category include Pharisees, scribes, lawyers, chief priests, elders, rulers of synagogues and Sadducees.[61] While in reality these groups were diverse, within the Lukan narrative they become linked in their opposition to Jesus: 'Historically, these groups were not homogeneous but highly diverse, and the lines dividing them were hereditary, political, economic, religious, or professional in nature. Still, within Luke's story world these several groups … also stand out as a group character.'[62] These religious authorities become stereotyped in the narrative as the opponents of Jesus, ultimately conspiring to put him to death.[63] Regarding the characterization of the Pharisees, Darr notes that 'the negative values of the text are demonstrated in their actions and thoughts: pride, love of money, injustice, hypocrisy, lack of repentance, murmuring and so forth.'[64]

Jesus announces and embodies God's love and, in so doing, challenges

---

61. Jesus' critique of the religious authorities comes from his position within Judaism.

62. Jack Dean Kingsbury, *Conflict in Luke: Jesus, Authorities, Disciples* (Minneapolis, MN: Fortress Press, 1991), 21–22.

63. As Kingsbury notes, three individuals – Zechariah, a priest (1.5); Jairus, a leader of a synagogue (8.41); and Joseph of Arimathea, a member of the Sanhedrin (23.50-51) – are righteous and faithful and therefore function as foils for the other stereotyped religious authorities. See Kingsbury, *Conflict in Luke*, 25. Furthermore, some Pharisees warn Jesus that Herod wants to kill him (13.31). In Acts, the characterization of the Pharisee Gamaliel also provides a positive portrayal (Acts 5.34-39).

64. Darr, *On Character Building*, 126. The stereotyped presentation of the religious leaders, especially the Pharisees, has contributed to the development of anti-Jewish attitudes. Excellent guidelines for the interpretation of the New Testament which promote sensitivity to Jews and Judaism are presented in Council of Christians and Jews, (Victoria), *Rightly Explaining the Word of Truth: Guidelines for Christian Clergy and Teachers in their Use of the New Testament with Reference to the New Testament Presentation of Jews and Judaism* (Kew, Vic: Council of Christians and Jews Victoria Inc., 1994).

the practices of the religious authorities (cf. Wis. 2.10-12). Jesus chides a Pharisee for his lack of hospitality (7.44-46), denounces Pharisees for neglecting justice (11.42-44) and lawyers for imposing oppressive burdens on people (11.46). Jesus identifies a leader of the synagogue as acting hypocritically (13.14-16), and accuses the scribes of acting unjustly towards widows (20.45-47). Warning about the hypocrisy of the Pharisees, Jesus explains that nothing which is hidden will not be exposed (12.1-3). Jesus brings to light the oppressive actions of these authorities, just as John the Baptist exposes Herod's actions and the third slave in the Parable of the Pounds exposes his master's activities.

Jesus challenges the religious authorities with his actions as well as his words. He disturbs Pharisees and scribes by eating and drinking with tax collectors and sinners (5.29-32), and a Pharisee by not washing before a meal (11.37-41). He also comes into conflict with scribes, Pharisees and a leader of the synagogue for healing on the Sabbath (6.6-11; 13.10-17; 14.1-6). The complaint of the Pharisees regarding Jesus eating and drinking with tax collectors and sinners may partly reflect purity concerns but it is Jesus mixing with sinners which is the focus of the accusation in this instance (5.30). The consequence of Jesus challenging those in power and his exposition of their oppressive practices is that they conspire to kill him and successfully implement their scheme (19.47; 20.19; 22.2; 22.47–23.46).

From a narrative perspective there are clear links between the character of the Lukan Jesus and the third slave in the Parable of the Pounds. Both resist the oppressive practices of those in power, bringing the oppression out into the open, uncovering what is hidden (cf. 12.1-3). Both suffer the consequences for this resistance and challenge. The third slave loses his pound, power, status and the opportunity to influence his future. He also loses the possibility of future manumission. Jesus loses his life (as do the citizens in the parable and John the Baptist when they challenge).

Drawing on the interaction between Jesus and the Devil in the temptation scene (Lk. 4.1-13), Kitchen highlights several links between the characterization of Jesus and the portrayal of the third slave in the Parable of the Pounds. In particular, both reject worldly power and privilege and confront those who oppress. She makes another link between the two by noting that the third slave wraps his pound in a cloth and Jesus' body is wrapped in cloth after his death (23.53).[65]

Kitchen further strengthens this link between Jesus and the third slave in the Parable of the Pounds by demonstrating the connections between antagonists in the parable and some of the antagonists in Jesus' story within the Lukan Gospel. Both the nobleman and the Devil claim power over kingdoms and reward obedience (4.5-7; 19.11-27), and the first two slaves and Judas both gain financially by supporting the oppressive system

---

65. Kitchen, 'Rereading the Parable of the Pounds,' 235.

(19.16-19; 22.4-5).[66] The nobleman is thus aligned with the Devil and the first two slaves with Judas. Kitchen's insights reinforce that the third slave rather than the nobleman in the Parable of the Pounds is aligned with Jesus and βασιλεία values as proclaimed by Jesus.

c. *Reading Metaphorically*

The third slave in the parable literally has his pound taken away from him when he challenges his oppressive master. In this study I also use 'pound' in a metaphorical sense for what a character has that can potentially be taken away by an oppressive other, not only in the context of this parable, but within a wider context in the Lukan narrative. Metaphor can be defined as 'that figure of speech whereby we speak about one thing in terms which are seen to be suggestive of another.'[67] A metaphor encourages 'new categories of interpretation,'[68] and enlarges the understanding of the reader or hearer.[69] While the third slave in the Parable of the Pounds literally has his pound taken away, there is a sense in which he also metaphorically 'loses his pound' in that he loses his opportunity for status and power to influence his future and the possibility of manumission. Reading metaphorically, the citizens who oppose the nobleman can also be said to 'lose their pounds.' For these citizens, the 'pounds' they lose are their lives.

That a parable may express the dynamic of a Gospel narrative metaphorically has been previously argued by Mary Ann Tolbert. Using the Parable of the Sower and its interpretation in the Gospel of Mark metaphorically (Mk 4.3-8, 14-20), Tolbert demonstrates that various characters in the Markan Gospel illustrate the four possible responses to the word of Jesus as outlined in the parable – hardened path, rocky ground, choked by thorns, and the good earth. Some characters exemplify 'the good earth,' others the 'rocky ground,' and so forth.[70] Not only does the Parable of the Sower expound the role of Jesus in the Markan narrative, it also orients the reader to the responses of the characters within the narrative.[71]

Similarly, within the Lukan Gospel narrative, a metaphorical reading of the Parable of the Pounds can function to orient the reader to the fate awaiting Jesus in Jerusalem, and to describe both the actions of characters

---

66. Kitchen, 'Rereading the Parable of the Pounds,' 237.

67. Janet Martin Soskice, *Metaphor and Religious Language* (Oxford: Clarendon Press, 1985), 15.

68. Soskice, *Metaphor*, 62.

69. Lee, *Flesh and Glory*, 17.

70. Mary Ann Tolbert, *Sowing the Gospel: Mark's World in Literary-Historical Perspective* (Minneapolis, MN: Fortress Press, 1989), 121–230.

71. Tolbert, *Sowing the Gospel*, 123.

who oppress others and the fate of characters who challenge that oppression. In this sense, the Parable of the Pounds can be seen to function metaphorically, honoring those characters in the Gospel of Luke who challenge oppressive power structures and condemning those who oppress. The fate of the third slave and the citizens in the parable is also the fate of John the Baptist and Jesus in the wider Lukan narrative. Metaphorically all have their 'pounds' taken away by those in power, when they challenge oppressive practices. Reading metaphorically, therefore, encourages a link to be made between all those Lukan characters who 'lose their pounds' when they challenge oppression. Like the citizens in the parable, the 'pounds' that John the Baptist and Jesus lose are their lives.

As we have seen earlier, however, the Gospel of Luke also portrays another dimension to the death of Jesus. The Lukan narrator intertwines the story of the death of Jesus with the theme of salvation (23.39-43). For the Lukan narrative, in God's providence, the violence inflicted on Jesus becomes a means of salvation.[72] Moreover, while Jesus loses his life, this is not the end of the story. God raises Jesus (24.5). God vindicates the δίκαιος one (cf. Wis. 2–5). In the supreme reversal, God triumphs over the powers of darkness (Lk. 22.53; 23.44), authenticating Jesus' entire ministry and the salvation which Jesus has embodied. Thus the one who challenges the oppressive practices ultimately triumphs over those who impose violence on others.

This culminating reversal, this final vindication, also brings another dimension to the story of others who have stood on the side of Jesus, challenging oppressive practices and 'losing their pounds.' The third slave in the parable is aligned with Jesus, as the links between the characters reveal. The third slave and the citizens who oppose the ruler/master are vindicated against him. John the Baptist is vindicated against Herod. Jesus' resurrection vindicates the actions of the third slave and the citizens of the Parable of the Pounds and John the Baptist against their oppressors. While the third slave, the citizens and John the Baptist are not explicitly 'raised up' within the narrative as is Jesus, it can be understood that they have done the honorable thing by opposing the oppressive powers. Their actions are in line with the βασιλεία of God and they stand finally vindicated.

---

72. For a note of caution on the double-edged nature of the way the imagery regarding suffering in Christian literature has functioned, see Wainwright, *Shall We Look?*, 13. Wainwright highlights that this suffering imagery has been used to oppress women and to maintain oppressive structures.

d. *The Characterization of Women*

We have seen the fate of the third slave in the Parable of the Pounds who resists his master's oppressive practices and that the parable metaphorically describes the fate of Jesus and John the Baptist who resist oppressive practices. Each metaphorically 'loses his pound,' where 'pound' refers to what one has that can potentially be taken away by an oppressive other. In this study I argue that the parable can also shed light on the characterization of women in the Gospel of Luke.

The introductory chapter has demonstrated that speech is a powerful tool and that silencing is a particular manifestation of oppression. Furthermore, the effect of silencing can be achieved in a variety of ways. Strategies that serve to silence are oppressive. We have seen, too, that household codes in some letters in the New Testament instruct wives and slaves to be obedient to their husbands and masters respectively. Thus, women and slaves are instructed to be submissive to those who have authority over them. Furthermore, some texts in the New Testament proscribe public speech or teaching for women, reinforcing patriarchal ideals. It would seem that these texts reflect tension in the early Church around women's activities and speech. This raises the question of how the rhetoric of the Lukan Gospel addresses the issue. From the discussion in Chapter 1 it is clear that scholarly opinion is divided on the Lukan rhetoric concerning women.

The following chapters will explore how the fate of women characters in the Lukan Gospel can be metaphorically described by the Parable of the Pounds. Within the parable some slaves are rewarded for fulfilling expectations and another loses his pound for challenging these oppressive expectations. Thus, different slaves receive different treatment depending on whether they challenge the oppression or reinforce it. Questions which arise regarding Lukan women are:

- Do the women characters of the Gospel of Luke receive different 'treatment' depending on whether they challenge oppressive ideals?
- What is the fate of those women characters who engage in autonomous public actions or speech and thus depart from or resist patriarchal ideals for the behavior of women?
- Is there a sense in which those who resist patriarchal ideals have their 'pound' taken away?
- If so, to what does their 'pound' refer?
- What is the fate of those women characters who do not challenge patriarchal ideals?
- What insights do we get by using the Parable of the Pounds as a lens through which to view the characterization of women in the Gospel of Luke?

In the following chapters, the women's characterizations will be explored within their narrative context (Chapters 4 and 5), and the findings drawn together in a thematic treatment of insights derived from using the Parable of the Pounds as a lens (Chapter 6). As detailed in the introductory chapter, in exploring the women's characterizations, particular attention will be given to patterns of speech and silence. This will help to identify whether any strategies for the silencing of women are evident and thus highlight the rhetoric of the text in regard to the women's portrayals. Women's speech or silence is not the only feature of the women's characterizations which will be explored but it will be a common focus. Other elements of the women's portrayal will also provide insights into the rhetoric of the text. Viewing the characterization of women through the lens of the parable will focus the material in a particular way.

Chapter 4

THE CHARACTERIZATION OF WOMEN IN THE NARRATIVE
OF LUKE 1–2

Using the Parable of the Pounds to focus the portrayal of women
characters in the Lukan Gospel ensures that, in reading the women's
stories, attention is paid to oppressive practices, the voice of resistance.
and the consequences of this resistance. Our exploration of the women
characters begins, in this chapter, with a reading of women within the
context of the Lukan infancy narrative (1.5–2.52).[1] How are these women
portrayed and how does the rhetoric of the text affect their characterization? Do any of these women have their 'pound' taken away? The
implications for a metaphorical reading of these women characters using
the Parable of the Pounds will be spelt out thematically in Chapter 6.

The differences between this infancy narrative and that of the Matthean
Gospel give the Lukan Gospel a distinctive opening which introduces
important themes to be expanded in the rest of the Gospel. Mary, the
mother of Jesus, features in both infancy narratives but she has a far more
prominent role in the Lukan story than in the Matthean version. In the
Matthean story the action revolves around the character of Joseph, and
Mary is without voice.[2] In the Lukan story, it is Mary rather than Joseph
who receives a visit from an angel and Mary's voice is heard several
times.[3] Two other women, Elizabeth and Anna, unique to the Gospel of
Luke, also feature. Thus, in the Lukan infancy narrative, women have
prominent positions and roles.[4] The whole of the infancy narrative is
focused toward the birth of Jesus and its significance. Nevertheless, along
with important male characters, Zechariah, Simeon and John, women
take center stage at particular points in the story.

---

1. While the term 'infancy narrative' is commonly used for this section, Jesus is twelve
years of age by the end of Luke 2 and no longer an infant.

2. Joseph is not given speech in the Matthean infancy narrative either, though he is
central to much of the action.

3. For a discussion of the different mimetic emphasis evident in the Matthean and Lukan
infancy narratives, see Joanna Dewey, 'Women in the Synoptic Gospels: Seen but not
Heard?,' *BTB* 27 (1997): 53–54.

4. The prominent role of women in the Lukan infancy narrative is often noted. See for
instance, Schaberg, 'Luke,' 370–71.

1. *Elizabeth Introduced*

At the beginning of the Lukan infancy narrative, the narrator introduces Zechariah and Elizabeth to the reader. Zechariah is described as a priest belonging to the priestly order of Abijah. Elizabeth is identified as the wife of Zechariah and a descendant of Aaron (1.5). This introduction to the two characters identifies both Zechariah and Elizabeth as being 'of priestly stock.'[5] Both are also described as righteous (δίκαιοι), abiding by all God's commandments and ordinances, having no children and being advanced in their days (1.6-7). Thus their characterizations are paralleled here.

The only aspect of the characterizations of Elizabeth and Zechariah which differs in 1.6-7 is that Elizabeth is described as barren (στεῖρα). The narrator informs the reader that despite Elizabeth's and Zechariah's righteousness and blameless living, they have no children because (καθότι) Elizabeth is barren. The use of the conjunction καθότι attributes the childlessness directly to Elizabeth. She carries the burden of their childlessness.[6] 'The story assumes, ... that to be childless is a *disgrace* felt by the woman alone.'[7]

The description of Elizabeth as barren also has the function of linking with women from the Hebrew Scriptures who are similarly described. Sarah, Rebekah, Rachel and Samson's mother are each identified as being barren (στεῖρα, LXX Gen. 11.30; 25.21; 29.31; Judg. 13.2-3), while Hannah is portrayed as childless because God had 'closed her womb' (1 Sam. 1.5). The description of Sarah and Abraham as being advanced in their days is a further link with the situation of Elizabeth and Zechariah (Gen. 18.11). These women of the Hebrew Scriptures, though described as barren, all eventually conceive. The conception is understood to be God's blessing (Gen. 17.16), as God's granting of prayer (Gen. 25.21), as God remembering the woman and opening her womb (Gen. 30.22; 1 Sam. 1.19), and as the result of direct intervention by God (Judg. 13.2-23). It can be seen then that in the Hebrew Scriptures the situation of a barren woman finally conceiving is not uncommon. In each case, the conception is understood to be the result of God's action in the life of the woman and

---

5. Fitzmyer, *Luke*, 1.322.

6. While Loretta Dornisch's interpretation is that Zechariah is sterile and Elizabeth is barren, this is not supported by the text which only refers to the barrenness of Elizabeth. See Loretta Dornisch, *A Woman Reads the Gospel of Luke* (Collegeville, MN: Liturgical Press, 1996), 16.

7. Lieu, *Luke*, 6. For a present-day exploration of the stigma of childlessness in Africa, see Mary Lou Cummings, *Surviving Without Romance: African Women Tell Their Stories* (Scottdale, PA: Herald Press, 1991), 93-95. Cummings writes, 'Childlessness is a major theme in Africa, as it was in the Old Testament. The barren girl is a pariah. Her husband regards her as a false promise, a dead end' (p. 93).

man. In each case, too, it is a male child (or children) that is born to the woman and the child is prominent in Israel's story of salvation. Hannah specifically asks God to grant her a male child (1 Sam.1.11).[8] Bearing sons brings honor to the mother.[9]

The known outcomes of the barrenness of these women suggest to the reader of the Lukan Gospel that the righteous Elizabeth and Zechariah may also experience God's action in their life and that Elizabeth may conceive and bear a son who will have a significant role in the narrative. It is no great surprise to the reader then when an angel (later identified as Gabriel, 1.19) appears to Zechariah and announces that Elizabeth will bear a son (1.11-13). As Coleridge rightly observes, however, the characters in the narrative do not have the same knowledge base as the reader. Therefore, 'a sense of what is to come in the narrative will stir in the readers in a way denied to the characters.'[10] In contrast to the reader's expectations, Zechariah's response to the angel reflects scepticism. Despite having prayed for the precise scenario which the angel announces (1.13a), he questions the angel as to how he will know that this is so.[11] His questioning results in the angel silencing him for his disbelief until the events come to pass (1.18-20). From a narrative perspective, Coleridge argues that the silencing ensures that Zechariah does not take the initiative away from heaven, and that Zechariah retains 'his proper place' in the narrative.[12] Thus Coleridge is aware of the power of speech and that the one with speech has the potential to seize the initiative.

That what is announced by the angel comes to fulfilment is revealed in 1.24. The dynamic of promise–fulfilment is integral to the Lukan narrative. God's word is fulfilled in God's action.[13] In line with the pattern in the Hebrew Scriptures, Elizabeth recognizes her conception as the action of God in her life. God has 'looked favourably' on her and taken away her 'disgrace' (1.25; cf. Gen. 30.23).[14]

Elizabeth is thus portrayed as recognizing God's grace in a way that Zechariah does not at first. While Zechariah is silenced, Elizabeth is given

---

8.   The term used in the LXX is σπέρμα ἀνδρῶν, literally 'a seed of men.' Rachel, too, asks for another son (Gen. 30.24).

9.   After the birth of each of her sons, Leah is accorded direct speech (Gen. 29.31-35; 30.17-20) and she states that her husband will honor her because she has borne six sons (Gen. 30.20). No such speech, however, follows the birth of her daughter (Gen. 30.21).

10.   Coleridge, *Birth of the Lukan Narrative*, 31–32.

11.   The question of Zechariah is similar to the question of Abraham to God in Gen. 15.8. Zechariah's response to the divine announcement of a son is also in line with the response of Abraham to the announcement that Sarah will bear a son (Gen. 17.17). For an outline of the typical stages in a biblical annunciation of birth, see Brown, *Birth of the Messiah*, 156; and Fitzmyer, *Luke*, 1.318.

12.   Coleridge, *Birth of the Lukan Narrative*, 44.

13.   See Coleridge, *Birth of the Lukan Narrative*, 35.

14.   Elizabeth refers to God here as κύριος (1.25).

voice.[15] She speaks and her words are recorded, giving her interpretation of all that has happened to her (1.25). Since Elizabeth is in seclusion (1.24), no one within the narrative world is described as hearing her words.[16] The reader alone hears and ponders on her words.[17] While Coleridge acknowledges that Elizabeth interprets the sign of her pregnancy correctly, recognizing this as God's work, he claims that both the words which the narrator attributes to her and her concealment convey a sense of self-absorption: 'Locked by choice in a private world, Elizabeth gives no indication of having any comprehension of the wider, more public implications of her pregnancy, that is, that her child will prepare the way of the Lord.'[18]

Rather than self-absorption, however, Elizabeth's response may reflect her awareness and experience of the compassionate and liberating God of Israel's history.[19] These words reflect Elizabeth's enduring openness to God that will culminate in her prophetic statement in 1.42-44. That she has endured disgrace for being childless reveals the patriarchal nature of the Lukan narrative world in which a woman's perceived worth is influenced by her ability to bear children, particularly sons.[20] Seim goes so far as to label the slant of the narrative as 'explicitly patriarchal from the start' since the angel makes the announcement to Zechariah in response to his prayer and the promised son is depicted as his.[21]

This introduction of Elizabeth in the Lukan infancy narrative, therefore, may provide elements of ambiguity for the reader. Elizabeth is portrayed as faithful and righteous, able to recognize God's action in her life and to understand her pregnancy as the result of God's grace. She is given voice to express her insight – the first words spoken by a woman in the Lukan Gospel – though no one in the narrative world hears her

---

15. With the silencing of Zechariah, Brigitte Kahl claims that the patriarchal domination and ordering of the household is transformed. See Kahl, 'Reading Luke Against Luke,' 79–80.

16. Brown sees the seclusion as a literary device preparing for Gabriel's revelation to Mary of Elizabeth's conception in 1.36. The seclusion of Elizabeth means that her conception is not known, increasing the sign value of Gabriel's words. See Brown, *Birth of the Messiah*, 282. Green suggests instead that the seclusion is so that Elizabeth will not continue to experience disgrace as a barren woman. See Green, *Gospel of Luke*, 81.

17. See Joseph Vlcek Kozar, 'Reading the Opening Chapter of Luke from a Feminist Perspective,' in *Escaping Eden: New Feminist Perspectives on the Bible*, (eds.) Harold C. Washington, Susan Lochrie Graham, and Pamela Thimmes (Sheffield: Sheffield Academic Press, 1998), 63.

18. Coleridge, *Birth of the Lukan Narrative*, 48.

19. Reid, *Choosing the Better Part?*, 62.

20. See Schaberg, 'Luke,' 371. cf. Rachel's words in the Hebrew Scriptures: 'Give me children, or I shall die!' (Gen. 30.1).

21. Seim, *Double Message*, 199. Against this view, Anderson argues that the appearance to Zechariah does not marginalize Elizabeth. See Janice Capel Anderson, 'Mary's Difference: Gender and Patriarchy in the Birth Narratives,' *JR* 67 (1987): 194.

words.[22] In a sense, it is the reader who is addressed by her speech. The contemporary reader also becomes aware of the patriarchal context which underlies the narrative and which shapes Elizabeth's words, though Zechariah's silence counters patriarchal expectation.

2. Mary Introduced

Gabriel, the divine messenger who was earlier sent to Zechariah, appears again in the narrative in 1.26-38.[23] While the announcement of John's birth is made to Zechariah, in the case of Jesus' birth the annunciation is made to the mother. We discover the name of the town (Nazareth) to which Gabriel was sent by God and then the status of the message's recipient – a virgin engaged to Joseph of the house of David – before we discover her name (1.26-27). Thus the name and male lineage of the one to whom she is engaged are given before the woman's name. The name Μαριάμ brings to mind a woman of the LXX with the same name. Miriam, the sister of Moses and Aaron, is a prophet (προφῆτις) who sings a victory song after the crossing of the Red Sea with the words of her song recorded (LXX Exod. 15.20-21). Miriam is also the one stricken with leprosy by God when she and Aaron challenge the pre-eminent position of Moses (Num. 12.1-16).[24] Thus, when she performs the woman's role of victory celebration (cf. Judg. 11.34; 1 Sam 18.6-7),[25] Miriam's action and voice are affirmed, but when she speaks out to challenge the role of the male hero she is effectively silenced. She is banished for seven days, and does not speak again.[26] The next time she appears in the biblical narrative is when it is reported that she has died (Num. 20.1).

The angel's greeting begins with χαῖρε (1.28), enabling a link to be made between the virgin, Mary, and the Daughter of Zion (Zeph. 3.14-20).[27] Witherington suggests that Mary should rejoice because 'she is to be

22. If, in the Lukan narrative, God is the primary character of the narrative (as Doble, *Paradox of Salvation*, 2, suggests), then God can be considered to hear Elizabeth's words. None of the 'on-stage' characters in the Lukan narrative, however, hears her words.

23. For a list of parallels between the two annunciations, see Brown, *Birth of the Messiah*, 297.

24. Though both Aaron and Miriam challenge, only Miriam is punished with leprosy and exclusion from the camp.

25. See Drorah O'Donnel Setel, 'Exodus,' in *Women's Bible Commentary*, expanded edition, (eds.) Carol A. Newsom and Sharon H. Ringe (Louisville, KY: Westminster John Knox Press, 1998), 36.

26. The number seven represents totality and completeness. See K. H. Rengstorf, 'ἑπτά,' *TDNT* 2.628.

27. See Witherington, *Women in the Earliest Churches*, 134; and Lawson, 'Gender and Genre,' 144. For a critical discussion of this link, see Brown, *Birth of the Messiah*, 321–27.

graced with the privilege of giving birth to the Messiah.'[28] Mary's virginal status, however, indicates that, socially, her pregnancy 'provides neither happiness nor blessing, but an unseemly moral and legal offence.'[29] Gabriel's greeting indicates that Mary is favored and that God is with her (1.28).[30] As in 1.25, the metaphor κύριος is used to refer to God. The imagery evoked by the metaphor is multifaceted: 'The symbolic divine-human relationship encoded in the imagery is that of patriarch-subject, father-child, and master-slave. The Lukan Mary hears the title in terms of the master-slave refraction of the image and accepts this relationship, as reflected in her response in Lk 1.38.'[31] As with Zechariah, Gabriel enjoins Mary not to be afraid (1.30; cf. 1.13) and repeats that Mary has found favor (χάρις) with God.[32] The only other character in the Lukan Gospel to be so described is Jesus (2.40, 52).[33] The divine favor on Mary prefigures the divine favor on her son.

The announcement that Mary will conceive and bear a son and the description of the child's destiny (1.31-33) provoke Mary's question: 'How can this be, since I am a virgin?' (1.34). While Zechariah's questioning of the angel results in his silencing, Mary's question enables the angel to pronounce the coming of the Holy Spirit upon her (cf. 24.49; Acts 1.8), the significance of the child and the sign of Elizabeth's conception (1.35-37).[34] Mary, the favored one, does not suffer the same fate as Zechariah for questioning Gabriel. Some distinguish between the natures of Zechariah's and Mary's questions, arguing that Mary's question does not reflect the lack of faith which is evident in Zechariah's question.[35] Yet both are in the form of an objection to the angel's announcement and both are followed by a sign revealing the efficacy of Gabriel's words (1.20, 36-37).[36] At the same time, the different response of Gabriel in each case suggests that the reader is encouraged to interpret the two questions differently.

While Mary's initial response to Gabriel's words is one of perplexity (1.29) and she questions the angel over what is revealed to her (1.34), her

28. Witherington, *Women in the Earliest Churches*, 134.

29. Seim, *Double Message*, 203.

30. Additions to this verse found in some texts are likely to have been inserted as a result of 1.42.

31. Lawson, 'Gender and Genre,' 144. Mary's response in 1.38 will be explored below.

32. The enjoinder not to be afraid is a common element in appearance narratives. See Bovon, *Lukas*, 1.74.

33. Reid, *Choosing the Better Part?*, 67.

34. Seim notes the similarity between the angel's words about the Holy Spirit coming upon Mary and the words of Jesus to the disciples in Lk. 24.49 and Acts 1.8. See Seim, *Double Message*, 175.

35. See, for instance, Bovon, *Lukas*, 1.75; Kopas, 'Jesus and Women,' 193; and Coleridge, *Birth of the Lukan Narrative*, 64–65.

36. An objection and granting of a sign are common features in biblical narratives which announce a birth. See Brown, *Birth of the Messiah*, 156.

final words to Gabriel reflect acceptance of these revelations (1.38). These final words to the angel are in two parts. The NRSV translation of the first part is 'Here am I, the servant of the Lord' (1.38a). An alternative translation of the Greek, however, yields an interpretation in terms of 'the female slave (δούλη) of the lord/master (κύριος),' evoking master–slave imagery. The self-designation of Mary as the female slave of the κύριος occurs again in 1.48 and is reminiscent of the words of Hannah in 1 Sam. 1.11. Hannah, too, identifies herself as the female slave (δούλη) of the κύριος. The imagery of being a slave (δοῦλος) of God is also evident in Luke 2.29 in reference to Simeon.[37]

Elsewhere in the New Testament, the imagery of being a slave of God is used in Tit. 1.1 in reference to Paul, in Jas 1.1 in reference to James, and in Rev. 15.3 referring to Moses (cf. also Acts 2.18, 4.29, 16.17; Rev. 7.3).[38] These references suggest the imagery is used in the New Testament to refer to those who are faithful to God's purposes. Thus, the use of the metaphor ἡ δούλη κυρίου by Mary reflects her faithfulness to and acceptance of the word of God.

At the same time, however, the κύριος–slave imagery is refracted through a patriarchal (or kyriarchal) context: 'In terms of the socio-cultural context in the Greco-Roman world, ... the resonances of the kyriarchal imagery ... could be expected to inform the reception of the text.'[39] While the pericope focuses on Mary's faithfulness, the kyriarchal imagery should be recognized and critiqued.[40]

That Gabriel earlier announces what will happen to Mary rather than seeking her consent (1.35) would seem to correlate with the slave metaphor used by Mary in her response.[41] The second part of Mary's words, however, is important in determining the nature of her response. The optative mood of γένοιτο in this second part – 'let it be with me [γένοιτό μοι] according to your word' (1.38b) – suggests far more than passive resignation on the part of Mary. The optative mood is 'used to

37. In this case, however, δεσπότης rather than κύριος is used to refer to God.

38. Also in the New Testament, Paul, Timothy, James, Peter, Jude and John are described as slaves of Christ (Gal. 1.10; Phil. 1.1; Jas 1.1; 2 Pet. 1.1; Jude 1.1; and Rev. 1.1).

39. Lawson, 'Gender and Genre,' 146. See also Osiek, 'Female Slaves,' 267. Lives of female slaves in the ancient Greco-Roman world are described by Osiek in pp. 259–68.

40. Lawson, 'Gender and Genre,' 146.

41. For a discussion of Gabriel's words in terms of the divine necessity in the Gospel of Luke, see Anne Elvey, 'The Birth of the Mother: A Reading of Luke 2:1-20 in Conversation with Some Recent Feminist Theory on Pregnancy and Birth,' *Pacifica* 15, no. 1 (2002): 4–6. See also Vernon K. Robbins, 'Socio-Rhetorical Criticism: Mary, Elizabeth and the Magnificat as a Test Case,' in *The New Literary Criticism and the New Testament*, (eds.) Edgar V. McKnight and Elizabeth Struthers Malbon (Valley Forge, PA: Trinity Press International, 1994), 198–99.

denote an attainable wish.'[42] The use of the optative here suggests, therefore, a vibrant acceptance by Mary, portraying her as an active participant in salvation. Mary hears the word (ῥῆμα) of God and accepts it, modeling Lukan faithfulness to God's word (cf. 11.28).[43]

Thus, Mary is introduced to the narrative as one favored by God, one who hears and accepts the divine word and who models faithful response to God's purpose. Moreover, she is granted direct speech and is not silenced like Zechariah. At the same time the patriarchal (or kyriarchal) context of the narrative world influences the reception of the woman's words.

3. *The Meeting of Elizabeth and Mary*

The two women who have featured in the narrative to date are brought together in the next scene when Mary journeys to meet with Elizabeth (1.39-40). The journey is Mary's response to the sign of Elizabeth's pregnancy revealed by Gabriel (1.36). Mary travels with haste (μετὰ σπουδῆς), suggesting an eagerness to respond (1.39; cf. the shepherds' response in 2.16).[44] Mary is not described as having traveling companions and the meeting is confined in the narrative to the two women. Mary enters the house of Zechariah but Zechariah does not appear in the pericope. It is Elizabeth alone whom Mary greets (1.41). While the description of the house as belonging to Zechariah reflects again a patriarchal context,[45] in this meeting of Mary and Elizabeth, the reader is drawn into the insights and proclamations of two women. Indeed, developing a chiastic structure for 1.5-80 which has this pericope at its center, Richard Bauckham argues for the gynocentricity of the opening chapter since the meeting constitutes a rare biblical scene in which only women converse and it leads into Mary's song as an agent of God's salvation.[46] While the portrayal of these women is focused on their role as mothers of important sons, nevertheless Mary and Elizabeth take center stage at this point of the infancy narrative.

---

42. F. Blass and A. Debrunner, *A Greek Grammar of the New Testament and Other Early Christian Literature*, trans. Robert Funk (Chicago, IL: University of Chicago Press, 1961), §384.

43. See Elvey, 'Birth of the Mother,' 4; and Green, *Gospel of Luke*, 92. Schaberg describes her consent as 'an expression of her freedom and courage.' See Jane Schaberg, *The Illegitimacy of Jesus: A Feminist Theological Interpretation of the Infancy Narratives* (Sheffield: Sheffield Academic Press, 1995), 138.

44. Schaberg suggests that μετὰ σπουδῆς could alternatively indicate overtones of terror and anxiety. See Schaberg, *Illegitimacy of Jesus*, 89–90.

45. In contrast, Mary returns to her house after her visit (1.56). Her house is not linked with a man's name.

46. Bauckham, *Gospel Women*, 48–55.

The significance of Mary's greeting to Elizabeth is indicated by its threefold reference (1.40, 41, 44).[47] The first response to the greeting is that the child leaps in Elizabeth's womb (1.41a). The leaping of the child can be interpreted as John recognizing Jesus' significance and thus acting as a prophet even before his birth.[48] The second response to Mary's greeting is that Elizabeth, and hence also the child within her, is filled (ἐπλήσθη) with the Holy Spirit (1.41b), fulfilling Gabriel's prophecy of 1.15. Later in the infancy narrative, Zechariah also is filled (ἐπλήσθη) with the Holy Spirit and he prophesies (1.67).[49] Jesus is described as full (πλήρης) of the Holy Spirit in 4.1.[50]

Filled with the Holy Spirit, Elizabeth is given the insight to interpret the events. While the verb προφητεύω is not used to describe Elizabeth's speech, the presence of the Spirit indicates that Elizabeth's words are prophetic and she speaks with authority (cf. Num. 11.25; 1 Sam. 10.6). Elizabeth proclaims a blessing first upon Mary and then upon the fruit of her womb (1.42).[51] In pronouncing Mary as 'the mother of my Lord [κυρίος]' (1.43), Elizabeth becomes the first in the Lukan Gospel to use the title κυρίος as a reference to Jesus. To this point, κυρίος has been used only in reference to God.[52]

Elizabeth's speech moves to the third person in 1.45 as she announces that Mary is blessed for believing that God's word would be fulfilled: 'Elizabeth turns from addressing Mary directly to address a wider audience (including the readers) to whom she speaks about Mary and to

---

47. Coleridge, *Birth of the Lukan Narrative*, 80.

48. See, for example, Brown, *Birth of the Messiah*, 341, 365; Green, *Gospel of Luke*, 95; and Johnson, *Luke*, 40, n. 41. Such an interpretation reinforces the superiority of Jesus over John, a common theme in the Infancy Narrative. See Darr, *On Character Building*, 66–69. Against this view, Coleridge argues that there is no narrated evidence that Mary is pregnant at this stage. Coleridge, therefore, suggests that it is the presence of Mary, rather than that of Jesus, which triggers this response. See Coleridge, *Birth of the Lukan Narrative*, 78. Elizabeth's later words of blessing on the fruit of Mary's womb would seem to suggest, however, that Mary *is* pregnant when she visits Elizabeth (1.42).

49. In Acts, the same verb is used in reference to Peter, a group of believers and Paul being filled with the Holy Spirit (Acts 4.8, 31; 13.9).

50. While a different word is used in this instance from that used in relation to Elizabeth and Zechariah, the meanings can be considered synonymous. See G. Delling, 'πλήρης,' *TDNT* 6.283.

51. Reid, *Choosing the Better Part?*, 72. This is the first blessing of the Lukan Gospel. The description of Mary as blessed among women links her with Jael and Judith from the Hebrew Scriptures and Apocrypha (Judg. 5.24; Jdt. 13.18). See, for instance, Brown, *Birth of the Messiah*, 342; and Arie Troost, 'Elizabeth and Mary – Naomi and Ruth: Gender-Response Criticism in Luke 1–2,' in *A Feminist Companion to the Hebrew Bible in the New Testament*, (ed.) Athalya Brenner (Sheffield: Sheffield Academic Press, 1996), 174. Elizabeth's words of blessing also link with the words of the woman in the crowd in 11.28.

52. See 1.6, 9, 11, 15, 16, 17, 25, 28, 32, 38.

whom she holds Mary up as a paradigm of faith in the divine promise.'[53] While there is no wider audience described in the narrative as hearing Elizabeth's words, the reader is especially addressed by the use of the third person in her speech at this point. Apart from Mary, the reader is the only witness to Elizabeth's prophetic speech. The reader is the privileged insider to this private meeting of two women, one of whom acts as a prophet while the other is the model of faith in God's word. There is no sense of rivalry between these two mothers.[54] Instead, Elizabeth and Mary 'mediate the divine to one another.'[55]

Mary responds to the prophetic speech of Elizabeth with her own prophetic song (1.46-55).[56] Though the Holy Spirit is not specifically mentioned as inspiring Mary's words, it can be inferred that the Holy Spirit has come upon Mary, as announced by Gabriel in 1.35, since Mary is pregnant. Thus Mary's words can also be seen to be prophetic.[57] With this canticle, the theme of reversal which is important throughout the Lukan Gospel is expounded.[58] From the lips of a woman, the reader is given insight into the workings of the Lukan narrative to come. Once again kyriarchal imagery is present in Mary's words, referring to God as κύριος and herself as δούλη (1.47-48; cf. 1.38). Mary's canticle is modeled on Hannah's canticle in 1 Sam. 2.1-10, although it evokes a range of Old Testament imagery.[59] Just as Elizabeth's barrenness had earlier linked her with Hannah, now Mary's words link her to the same woman of the

53. Coleridge, *Birth of the Lukan Narrative*, 85.

54. In this sense, Elizabeth and Mary can be compared with Naomi and Ruth (Ruth 1–4). This is in contrast to the motif of rivalry evident in some stories of women, usually mothers, in the Hebrew Scriptures – for example, Sarah and Hagar (Gen. 16.4-6), Leah and Rachel (Gen. 29–30) and Peninnah and Hannah (1 Sam. 1.6-7). See Troost, 'Elizabeth and Mary,' 159–96; Reid, *Choosing the Better Part?*, 73–74; and Robbins, 'Socio-Rhetorical Criticism,' 197–98.

55. Elvey, 'Birth of the Mother,' 6.

56. A few later texts attribute the *Magnificat* to Elizabeth, but the overwhelming evidence of witnesses (including ℵ A B D W) attributes the canticle to Mary. For a thorough discussion of the internal and external evidence, see Paul Bemile, *The Magnificat Within the Context and Framework of Lukan Theology* (Frankfurt am Main: Verlag Peter Lang, 1986), 5–19; and René Laurentin, *The Truth of Christmas: Beyond the Myths: The Gospels of the Infancy of Christ*, trans. Michael J. Wren and associates (Petersham, MA: St. Bede's Publications, 1986), 3–11.

57. For a different position, see Coleridge, *Birth of the Lukan Narrative*, 87.

58. See Tannehill, *Narrative Unity*, 29–30. For a detailed discussion of the theme of reversal in the Gospel of Luke, see York, *Last Shall Be First*.

59. For links between the *Magnificat* and Old Testament passages, see Bemile, *Magnificat*, 116–33; Brown, *Birth of the Messiah*, 358–60; and York, *Last Shall Be First*, 46.

Hebrew Scriptures. Mary's song of deliverance also links with the song of
Miriam, her namesake, in Exod. 15.21.[60]

Mary's song of praise celebrates the reversal which she sees God to be
enacting. The synonymous parallelism of the first two verses (1.46-47)
establishes 'the celebrative character of the song.'[61] While 1.46-49a focus
on the effect of God's actions on Mary personally, the focus broadens in
the following verses to God's actions for all those who fear God. As such,
God's action in the life of Mary reflects God's action in the life of God's
people.[62] Her individual song of praise becomes a communal song.
Referring to her lowliness or humiliation (ταπείνωσις, 1.48),[63] she praises
the God who brings down the powerful and raises the lowly (ταπεινός,
1.52), who fills the hungry and sends the rich away empty (1.53).[64] God's
reversal of fortunes for the lowly is seen to be the fulfillment of God's
promises made to the ancestors (1.54-55). The canticle announces that
God's concern is for the powerless, the hungry. God's actions also bring
judgment on the proud, the powerful, and the rich. The reversal is brought
about by the actions of God rather than humans.[65]

Whether the lowly and hungry of the canticle indicate spiritual or
physical conditions has produced debate. Links have been made between
the lowly and hungry of the *Magnificat* and the *anawim*, the pious poor of
Judaism.[66] This leads Raymond E. Brown to suggest: '[t]he poverty and
hunger of the oppressed in the Magnificat are primarily spiritual, but we
should not forget the physical realities faced by early Christians.'[67] York,
however, rightly claims that it is not evident that the reference is to

60. Phyllis Trible, 'Miriam 1,' in *Women in Scripture: A Dictionary of Named and
Unnamed Women in the Hebrew Bible, the Apocryphal/Deuterocanonical Books, and the New
Testament*, (ed.) Carol Meyers (Boston, MA: Houghton Mifflin Company, 2000), 54. See also
Bauckham, *Gospel Women*, 54.

61. York, *Last Shall Be First*, 47. York notes the change in tense from present to aorist in
these two verses and suggests its effect is to link the past with the present.

62. Johnson, *Luke*, 43.

63. From the use of the verb ταπεινόω in the LXX to refer to the sexual humiliation of
women (Deut. 22.24; Gen. 34.2; Judg. 19.24; 20.5; Lam. 5.11), Schaberg argues that Mary's
words refer to her state of sexual humiliation but that God reverses her humiliation.
Schaberg, *Illegitimacy of Jesus*, 99–100. See also Robbins, 'Socio-Rhetorical Criticism,' 182–
84.

64. For a discussion of the structure of 1.52-53 and their parallelism, see York, *Last Shall
Be First*, 50–51. That the sense of these verses is a reversal of positions is supported by 6.20-
26 and particularly the parable of 16.19-31. With a different view, Ringe claims that the
opposites 'move toward a common middle ground.' See Ringe, *Luke*, 35. This fits with the
Isaiah reference in Lk. 3.4-5, which describes a leveling. It would seem that the reversal theme
is stronger in the Lukan narrative, however.

65. York, *Last Shall Be First*, 53–54.

66. York, *Last Shall Be First*, 54. See also Brown, *Birth of the Messiah*, 350–55, 361–62;
and Schaberg, 'Luke,' 373.

67. Brown, *Birth of the Messiah*, 363.

spiritual rather than physical circumstances. Instead, he states that it 'seems better to allow the Lukan text to establish its own meaning for the terms as the narrative proceeds.'[68] York argues that πτωχός is to be understood primarily in terms of physical rather than spiritual poverty in 4.16-18, 7.22, and 14.13. His conclusion elucidates the connection between economic, social and religious factors: 'Luke's use of πλούσιος and πτωχός is therefore rooted in economic circumstances, but these conditions are reflections of both societal and spiritual conditions that are deeper concerns for Luke and his audience.'[69]

Mary and Elizabeth are given prominent and important roles in 1.39-56. Both are given direct speech and this is the largest section allocated to female-only speech in the New Testament. Their words confirm their status as faithful believers. Both are inspired to be able to interpret God's actions in their lives and they point ahead to significant themes of the Lukan Gospel in salvation, blessedness of believers in God's word and the raising of the lowly. The reader is privy to their conversation and recognizes that Mary and Elizabeth are prophets and models of faith. Within the narrative world, however, no one else (apart from the women themselves) is able to reach the same conclusion as the reader about the women's status. While they hear each other, no other character hears or responds to the inspired content of the women's words. As yet, no woman in the narrative has spoken in a more public setting.

4. *Elizabeth Names Her Son*

With Mary returning to her house after her time spent with Elizabeth (1.56), the stories of the two women once again move in different directions. The women neither meet nor communicate with each other again in the narrative. Elizabeth gives birth to a son (1.57) and goes against public expectation when she announces that her child will be called 'John.' Against her neighbors and relatives who were calling (ἐκάλουν) the child after his father, Elizabeth declares: 'No; he is to be called John' (1.60). The emphatic nature of her negation is communicated by the use of Οὐχί, ἀλλά.[70] While Elizabeth is named in 1.57, this is the last time she is named in the Lukan Gospel. When she names her child she is identified as 'his mother' (1.60) and after this she is not referred to again in the narrative.

While the reader is aware that Elizabeth is faithful and able to discern God's action in her life (1.6, 25), and that filled with the Holy Spirit she has spoken prophetically (1.41-45), the neighbors and relatives who now

---

68. York, *Last Shall Be First*, 54.
69. York, *Last Shall Be First*, 106.
70. Οὐχί, ἀλλά is a strong form of negation. See BAGD, 598; and Marshall, *Luke*, 88.

gather with Elizabeth do not have the same awareness. They have not heard her inspired words. The woman who spoke authoritatively to Mary does not now have the authority to name her child according to those gathered with her.[71] Rather than accept Elizabeth's words, they turn to Zechariah for confirmation of the name. Zechariah confirms in writing that the child's name is John and immediately regains his power of speech and begins to praise God (1.64). Filled with the Holy Spirit, Zechariah prophesies, as Elizabeth had done earlier in 1.42-45, proclaiming a canticle (1.67-79). Unlike Elizabeth, though, Zechariah is explicitly described as prophesying by the use of προφητεύω.

Coleridge describes Elizabeth's announcement in 1.60 as a 'brusque rejoinder to the crowd' and he suggests that it is the task of Zechariah rather than Elizabeth to name the child, as indicated by Gabriel in 1.13.[72] Since Elizabeth's words contain a future passive (κληθήσεται), Coleridge declares that Elizabeth's 'statement is not itself proclamation ... but looks ahead to Zechariah's proclamation,'[73] thus reinforcing Gabriel's prophecy of 1.13. Such an interpretation would appear to marginalize Elizabeth's status. Her 'brusque rejoinder' is actually a pronouncement of God's intended name and her use of κληθήσεται counters the practice of those gathered who were calling (ἐκάλουν) the child Zechariah. If the narrator intends that Gabriel's words in 1.13 determine that Zechariah must name the child, then why is it necessary to have Elizabeth say anything about the name at all? If she merely predicts that Gabriel's prophecy would be fulfilled, as Coleridge suggests, then her speech is superfluous to the narrative. The reader already knows that Gabriel's prophecy is trustworthy (cf. 1.35-36) and that Elizabeth speaks prophetically (cf. 1.42-45). The understanding that Elizabeth is the one who names her son would appear to follow the narrative logic more coherently.[74]

The narrative does not explain how Elizabeth comes to know God's intended name for her child. Marshall considers that Zechariah has communicated the information to her,[75] while Brown concludes that 'the reader is probably meant to think that Elizabeth's decision was a spontaneous and marvellous confirmation of God's plan.'[76] As Reid correctly observes, however, Elizabeth's faithfulness to God has been

71. As Laurentin points out, however, in the Hebrew Scriptures a child is often named by the mother (e.g. Gen. 4.25; 16.11; 19.37; 29.32-35; 38.3-5; Judg. 13.24; 1 Sam. 1.20; 1 Chron. 4.9; 7.16). See Laurentin, *Truth of Christmas*, 472. I was first alerted to this reference from Green, *Gospel of Luke*, 109.

72. Coleridge, *Birth of the Lukan Narrative*, 106–7.

73. Coleridge, *Birth of the Lukan Narrative*, 107.

74. For the understanding that Elizabeth names her son, see Reid, *Choosing the Better Part?*, 78; Tetlow, *Women and Ministry*, 102; and Troost, 'Elizabeth and Mary,' 170.

75. Marshall, *Luke*, 88.

76. Brown, *Birth of the Messiah*, 369.

highlighted (1.6), and it is therefore not unexpected that she announces the intended name.[77] Elizabeth's ability to discern correctly God's action in her life (1.25) and her prophecy inspired by the Holy Spirit (1.42-45) support Reid's comments. The reader is aware that Elizabeth voices God's will regardless of how she has become aware of the name.

The narrative and rhetorical effect of the crowd's response to Elizabeth's words requires further exploration. When Zechariah confirms the name, those gathered are amazed (1.63). While the name does not meet their expectation, however, they do not challenge his written words, in contrast with their response to Elizabeth's declaration of the same name (1.61-62). They recognize the authority of Zechariah's words but not the authority of Elizabeth's words. Coleridge describes his understanding of the crowd's expectation: 'Clearly the crowd expects the dumbstruck patriarch to defend convention and reject the mysterious caprice of his wife.'[78] Such an interpretation reinforces the impression that women's speech is capricious (cf. the women's 'idle tale' in 24.11).[79] In contrast, Zechariah's words are not considered (by either the crowd in the narrative or by interpreters) to be capricious. His written words have the effect of freeing his tongue. Zechariah who was silenced for his disbelief (1.20) is now inspired to praise God and prophesy, proclaiming a canticle interpreting God's actions (1.67-79). What Zechariah lost earlier, therefore, is returned to him with interest.

Elizabeth, in contrast, does not speak again in the narrative once her words are challenged. The rhetorical effect of the crowd's response to Elizabeth's and Zechariah's words has particular significance since Elizabeth's words in naming her son are the first words in the Lukan Gospel spoken by a woman outside the private sphere of women. The prophetic woman who earlier proclaimed to another woman is heard but not listened to in a more public setting.[80] In the group of males and females gathered to circumcise and name her child, Elizabeth's voice has no authority and is eventually rendered silent. As Zechariah is released from his silence, Elizabeth takes over the silent role. Despite Elizabeth's words being vindicated, she is granted no further voice in the Lukan Gospel. Elizabeth is characterized in Luke 1 as faithful to God's purposes but, by the end of the chapter, she loses her potential to proclaim God's word and to be heard. Metaphorically, she 'loses her pound' when she takes the initiative to speak in the presence of men.

Thus, the rhetoric of the opening chapter of the infancy narrative

---

77. Reid, *Choosing the Better Part?*, 79.

78. Coleridge, *Birth of the Lukan Narrative*, 108.

79. The trivialization of women's speech is discussed in the introductory chapter.

80. The term 'public' in relation to women's speech is used to refer to situations where women speak in the presence of men.

reinforces the impression that Elizabeth is an inspired prophet but that her speech is only appropriately expressed in seclusion (1.25) or in the presence of women only (1.42-45). In the wider circle, her voice has no authority and she is effectively silenced. Kahl notes the impact of speech and silence on the Lukan characterizations: '[S]peaking and silence as categories of agency have great significance for the interpretation of Lk. 1. The fact that the messianic time which begins with John is launched by a long speech of the father – and not, for example, by a joint speech by Elizabeth and Zechariah – raises suspicion.'[81]

Though Elizabeth gives the child the name declared by Gabriel and confirmed by Zechariah, no explicit acknowledgment is given in the text that Elizabeth's words were indeed faithful to God's will. Nor is any reproach made on those who did not accept her words. The critique must be supplied instead by the reader who is given sufficient information to make that critique. The reader knows that Elizabeth is correct and that it is those disbelieving her words who are in error.

Zechariah's proclamation of the canticle (1.67-79) and a summary statement (1.80) concerning the child, John, conclude the opening chapter of the Gospel. Despite the women being in the spotlight in this chapter, a patriarchal perspective encompasses the narrative.[82] While Elizabeth disappears from the narrative after the first chapter, Mary's role continues and will now be explored.

5. *Mary Gives Birth*

In Lk. 2.4-5 we are told that Joseph goes to Bethlehem to be registered because he is of the house of David (cf. 1.27), and that he goes with Mary, to whom he is betrothed and who is pregnant. Thus, Joseph's action and lineage are described (2.4) before we learn that Mary travels with him to Bethlehem (2.5). While Joseph is introduced first here, he is not described as acting independently again in the narrative. Several times he acts in conjunction with Mary but never individually. Neither does he speak in the narrative. Thus, Joseph is predominantly a background figure.[83]

81. Kahl, 'Reading Luke Against Luke,' 83. Kahl (pp. 83–84) questions whether this is indicative of a return to the patriarchal household and observes that the patriarchal orientation seems to be evident in Luke 2.

82. See Kozar, 'Reading the Opening Chapter,' 67–68. In contrast, Dornisch, *A Woman Reads*, 27, claims that Luke 1 gives a 'character of dominance' to Elizabeth and Mary.

83. That Joseph is silent in the narrative while Mary sings a song of praise (1.46-55), and that Zechariah is silenced for a time (1.20-22) while Elizabeth cries out a blessing (1.42-44), leads Troost to claim that in these cases the 'traditional attribution of speech-acts is broken.' Troost observes, however, that other parts of the Lukan narrative confirm the traditional attribution, leading to the conclusion that the Lukan treatment is ambiguous. Troost,

In contrast, Mary is the subject of several verbs and acts independently of Joseph. She bears her son, swathes him and lays him in a manger (2.7). These verbs draw attention to the activity of Mary and form the essence of the sign which will later be given to the shepherds by the angel (2.12).[84] When the shepherds find Mary, Joseph and the child and relate what the angel had told them, we learn that all are amazed (2.18).[85] We are also given insight into Mary's individual interior response: 'But Mary treasured all these words [πάντα συνετήρει τὰ ῥήματα ταῦτα] and pondered them in her heart' (2.19). She is portrayed as keeping (συντηρέω) the entire narrative event including all these words: 'While ῥῆμα translates not simply as word, deed or thing, but as all of these and implies in effect an intersection between word, deed and thing, πάντα τὰ ῥήματα ταῦτα encompasses in the narrative context, not only the ῥῆμα passed on by the shepherds but the entire narrative event, namely the beginning or birth of a gospel, in which she has acted.'[86] Mary's 'keeping' activity is similarly pictured in 2.51, making the activity of keeping an integral part of Mary's characterization. This portrayal also has links with the beatitude which Jesus later speaks to a woman in the crowd (11.28).

Mary is portrayed as faithful to the word, just as she was in Luke 1, and she has a more important role in the narrative than Joseph, being highlighted while Joseph remains in the background. This cuts across patriarchal tendencies. Given Mary's portrayal in Luke 1, however, a surprising feature of the birth story is that Mary does not speak. In Luke 1, she speaks to both the angel (1.34, 38) and Elizabeth (1.46-55), yet here she is silent. As we have seen, she is active and takes the initiative with her actions, but she does not speak.

Unlike the naming of John, the naming of Jesus is recorded without detail. While Gabriel announces that Mary will name her son Jesus (1.31), the use of the passive ἐκλήθη in 2.21 means that no one is specified as having this honor. Coleridge explains this as follows: 'In contrast to 1.57-80, we are not told who names the child. What matters for the narrator is not who does the naming, but that the child be named in accordance with

---

'Elizabeth and Mary,' 170–71. Troost does not distinguish, though, between public and private speech. I will argue for consistency in Luke 1–2 with the rest of the Gospel in regard to the treatment of women's private and public speech.

84.   Elvey, 'Birth of the Mother,' 8–9; and Marshall, *Luke*, 106. Johnson, *Luke*, 53, compares the actions of Mary here with the wrapping of Jesus' body and laying in the tomb in 23.53.

85.   The mention of 'all who heard' would suggest a wider audience, yet there is nothing in the narrative to indicate that others have joined the scene. Coleridge sees the reference to 'all who heard' as indicating the public character of the announcement. Coleridge, *Birth of the Lukan Narrative*, 149; also Johnson, *Luke*, 51. For Marshall, *Luke*, 113, the shepherds may have gone and told others.

86.   Elvey, 'Birth of the Mother,' 12.

the divine will communicated by Gabriel.'[87] Yet, earlier in his monograph, Coleridge has argued that Elizabeth does not do the naming (despite declaring that the child is to be called John) because 'the task of implementing the divine choice belongs to Zechariah, as Gabriel has indicated in v. 13.'[88] Hence, in the case of the naming of John, it would seem that Coleridge is concerned with who does the naming, but in the case of the naming of Jesus, the same concern is not displayed. The narrative effect of omitting the details of the naming of Jesus is that Mary's voice is not heard in the naming of her child.

6. *Anna in the Temple*

In fulfilling their religious obligations, Jesus' parents bring him to the temple (2.22-24).[89] This has the dual function of showing that Jesus' parents are faithful to the Torah and of shifting the narrative scene to the temple where two prophets, Simeon and Anna, will be introduced to the stage. Inspired by the Spirit, Simeon praises God proclaiming a canticle (2.29-32), which draws a reaction of amazement from the parents (2.33; cf. 1.63; 2.18). He also blesses Jesus' parents and prophesies to Mary about the destiny of her child (2.34-35). Again, the reader's attention is here drawn to Mary rather than Joseph. Simeon's words are presented so that the reader can savor their significance and nuances. Indeed, interpreters often delve into the importance of his words in great depth.[90] Brown goes so far as to say that the *Nunc Dimittis* 'has struck many as the loveliest of the Lucan canticles.'[91]

Anna is introduced first as a προφῆτις and then as the daughter of Phanuel of the tribe of Asher.[92] The name in Greek is Ἅννα, thus linking Hannah of 1 Samuel with another of the women of the Lukan infancy narrative. We read also of her advanced age and marital history and her present status as a widow (χήρα) who does not leave the temple and worships 'with fasting and prayer night and day' (2.36-37). Her age of eighty-four is of interest since eighty-four is the product of twelve and seven, twelve being a number with Jewish significance and seven being the

87. Coleridge, *Birth of the Lukan Narrative*, 154.

88. Coleridge, *Birth of the Lukan Narrative*, 107.

89. While the law requires the mother to be purified after giving birth, there is no purification requirement made of the father (Lev. 12.2-8). This creates an awkwardness in interpreting 'their purification' (2.22).

90. See, for instance, Brown, *Birth of the Messiah*, 454–66; Coleridge, *Birth of the Lukan Narrative*, 166–78; and Green, *Gospel of Luke*, 146–50.

91. Brown, *Birth of the Messiah*, 456.

92. For the significance of being of the tribe of Asher, see Bauckham, *Gospel Women*, 77–107.

number of completeness.[93] Perhaps her age defines her as the perfect Jewish believer.[94] Being named as a προφῆτις links Anna with Miriam, Deborah and Huldah who are similarly described in the LXX (Exod. 15.20; Judg. 4.4; 2 Kgs 22.14; 2 Chron. 34.22),[95] and Philip's four daughters who have 'the gift of prophecy' (Acts 21.9). A parallel can also be drawn between Anna and Judith, another widow who fasted (Jdt. 8.4-6).[96]

Anna is the first of several widows to feature in the Lukan Gospel (cf. 4.25-26; 7.11-17; 18.1-8; and 21.1-4). The description of Anna corresponds to a number of the features in the description of Christian widows given in 1 Tim. 5.3-16.[97] In particular, her prayer night and day models the description of the real widow in 1 Tim. 5.5. In the LXX, χήρα translates the Hebrew אלמנה which is based on the root אלם carrying the meaning 'silent' or 'unable to speak.'[98] Therefore, the widow can be described as one 'not spoken for,'[99] or one 'without voice in society.'[100] As we will see, though, Anna is here accredited with public speech.

The prophet and widow, Anna, praises (ἀνθωμολογεῖτο) God and speaks about him (ἐλάλει περὶ αὐτοῦ) 'to all who were looking for the redemption of Jerusalem' (2.38).[101] The use of the imperfect suggests an ongoing activity. Though it is generally assumed that Anna speaks here about the child, the Greek is unclear and grammatically could equally be understood as speaking about God. While the context of following Simeon's oracle on the destiny of the child suggests that Jesus is the one being spoken about, the ambiguity diminishes the impact of Anna's prophetic activity on the reader.

---

93. See K. H. Rengstorf, 'δώδεκα,' *TDNT* 2.321-22; and K. H. Rengstorf, 'ἑπτά,' *TDNT* 2.628.

94. Varela sees the number eighty-four as symbolic of Anna's perfect life as a widow. Alfredo T. Varela, 'Luke 2.36-37: Is Anna's Age What is Really in Focus?,' *BT* 27 (1976): 446. Several scholars argue that the phrase – ἕως ἐτῶν ὀγδοήκοντα τεσσάρων (2.37) – should be interpreted as Anna living as a widow for eighty-four years rather than living until she was eighty-four. See, for example, J. K. Elliott, 'Anna's Age (Luke 2:36-37),' *NovT* 30 (1988): 100; and Price, *Widow Traditions*, 48–49.

95. Huldah's name is Ολδαν in the LXX. Also in Isa. 8.3, a προφῆτις bears a son to Isaiah.

96. For more on this comparison, see Reid, *Choosing the Better Part?*, 92.

97. See Brown, *Birth of the Messiah*, 467; Goulder, *Luke*, 1.260; and Seim, *Double Message*, 246–47. Thurston, *Widows*, 23, describes Anna as a 'picture of the prototypical pre-Christian widow.'

98. See BDB, 47–48.

99. Reid, *Choosing the Better Part?*, 93.

100. Seim, *Double Message*, 232.

101. Nolland claims that 'Anna speaks only to a select public ... of those who expectantly wait for God's messianic intervention' Nolland, *Luke*, 1.123. Yet the use of πᾶς suggests a broad announcement. There is no justification for limiting her role here.

Anna and Simeon are often listed as one of the gender pairs of the Lukan narrative. Both are portrayed as faithful and inspired. While Simeon is described as inspired by the Holy Spirit and as prophesying (2.25-27), Anna is named as a prophet (2.36). Both are enabled to interpret the significance of God's actions and to proclaim prophetically (2.28-35; 38). Both display a 'knowledge of salvation' (cf. 1.77).[102] Anna's words are a public proclamation whereas Simeon's prophecy is primarily addressed to the child's parents.[103] While Simeon's direct speech is given in the narrative, however, Anna's prophetic words are not recorded. The reader knows that Anna stands in the tradition of women prophets and a respected widow from the LXX but the reader does not hear this prophet's voice.[104]

In his discussion of Anna's function in the narrative, Coleridge observes that neither the text of Anna's speech nor a report of any reaction to Anna's words is given.[105] He does not consider, however, the impact of these on Anna's portrayal as prophet. Kopas has tried to argue that Anna's testimony is valued no less than Simeon's.[106] One just needs to note the difference in space devoted by commentators to discussing Simeon's and Anna's prophecies, though, to realize that Anna's speech evokes a mere fraction of the response evoked by Simeon's words. Knowing the theme of Anna's prophecy does not have the same impact as knowing the content, and the ambiguity of the subject of her speech further reduces the impact.

An example of a reader's neglect of Anna is found in the words of Darr who, in discussing Lukan characters, observes: 'The ideal character observes the divine, fully recognizes it, comprehends its significance, embraces it immediately and without reservation, and testifies about it to others. The prophet Simeon embodies these ideals early in the story (Luke 2.25-35).'[107] Anna, too, embodies these ideals but this is not acknowledged by Darr. Though Anna testifies to others, her words are not recorded and consequently her action has not made sufficient impact on Darr to be recognized by him.

Accounting for the omission of Anna's words, Robert M. Price argues that a source from the communities of consecrated Christian widows in

---

102. See Byrne, *Hospitality of God*, 34.

103. Seim, *Double Message*, 131.

104. Price, *Widow Traditions*, 47, goes so far as to use the description 'Anna's Silent Song.'

105. Coleridge, *Birth of the Lukan Narrative*, 179–80.

106. Kopas, 'Jesus and Women,' 194–95. Kopas does not clarify here who it is that values Anna's testimony equally. Since she notes that Anna is described as a prophetess (p. 195), it is perhaps the narrator to whom she refers. If so, Kopas fails to recognize how the narrator's choices affect Anna's impact on the reader.

107. Darr, *On Character Building*, 57.

which a canticle was attributed to Anna has been redacted in the Lukan narrative. As a result, the canticle sung by Anna in this source is transferred to Zechariah in the Lukan Gospel.[108] Price claims that this explains why the Lukan narrative prepares the reader for Anna's words but omits them.[109] Using the story of Hannah and Eli in 1 Sam. 1.11-15 as a point of comparison, Price makes a critical judgment of the Lukan author: 'The New Testament Anna speaks without words because Luke no more than Eli trusts the utterances of women which he fears will be as drunken gibberish.'[110] Since the narrative presents Mary's words in proclaiming the *Magnificat* (1.46-55), it is difficult to agree with Price that the Lukan author does not trust the utterances of women. Rather it would seem that the Lukan narrative reinforces the notion that women's speech may be inspired, but that such speech is not suitable for the public arena.

We hear the voice of the narrator rather than the voice of the woman prophet, Anna, while the male prophet, Simeon, speaks for himself. Despite her prophetic status, Anna's role is undermined in the narrative. We do not hear her voice or learn of the response to her words. While this אלמנה is not 'unable to speak,' the reader nevertheless does not hear her words. Anna 'loses her pound,' in that her potential to make an impact on the reader is compromised.

7. *Mary Speaks in the Temple*

The final scene of the Lukan infancy narrative portrays Mary and Joseph searching for the twelve-year-old Jesus and finding him in the temple (2.41-52). Neither Mary nor Joseph is named in this pericope. Instead, they are referred to as his parents (2.41, 43) or as his mother and father (2.48, 51). Thus they are identified in terms of their relationship to Jesus rather than in their own right.[111] They act jointly in all parts of the narrative up to finding Jesus in the temple and being astonished (2.41-48a). Mary then speaks for both of them when she questions Jesus about his actions and reveals their anxiety (2.48b): 'Child, why have you treated us like this? Look, your father and I have been searching for you in great

---

108. Price, *Widow Traditions*, 54–61. Here Price adapts an earlier theory that the *Benedictus* was transferred from Anna to Zechariah. This theory is outlined in A. R. C. Leaney, *A Commentary on the Gospel According to St. Luke*, 2nd edn (London: Adam & Charles Black, 1966), 24–25.

109. Price, *Widow Traditions*, 54.

110. Price, *Widow Traditions*, 61.

111. The last time that Mary is named in the Lukan Gospel is at 2.34 where the reference is to 'his mother, Mary.' After this, she is only referred to as his 'mother' (2.48, 51; 8.19-21), although in Acts 1.14 she is named again. Similarly, the last reference to Elizabeth is as 'his mother' (1.60) before she disappears from the narrative. In both cases the woman's role as mother is the primary focus.

anxiety.' Here Mary is once again brought to the foreground in the narrative and Joseph to the background. Joseph remains silent, as he has done throughout the infancy narrative.

Just as Mary speaks for both parents, Jesus' reply is addressed to both as the use of the second person plural (ἐζητεῖτε and ᾔδειτε) indicates: 'Why were you searching for me? Did you not know that I must be in my Father's house?' (2.49).[112] The play on words here regarding the use of 'father' indicates the different focus of Jesus and his parents. Jesus' priority is faithfulness to God. His response to Mary's words is in the form of a rebuke. The main function of the rebuke is to show the disparate understandings of Jesus and his parents and it is addressed to both of them. The rebuke, however, responds to the words of Mary since she alone speaks. These are the first words spoken by Mary outside a private setting and her words are met with a reproach from Jesus. Hence to this point of the Lukan narrative, no woman's direct speech in a public setting has been affirmed. Mary does not speak again in the Lukan narrative. Though she is the only named woman to appear in both the Gospel and Acts, she is not given voice after her words in the temple. As we shall see, Jesus' rebuke in response to Mary's words is typical of the Lukan Jesus' response to the direct words of Lukan women characters.

While they are portrayed as not understanding Jesus' words (2.50), once again Mary (and not Joseph) is described as keeping 'all these things in her heart' (2.51; cf. 2.19). Thus the portrayal of Mary's 'keeping' activity continues to develop. Joseph remains a silent background figure. The narration that Jesus went to Nazareth with his parents 'and was obedient to them' (2.51) is more in keeping with the expected behavior of a child within the patriarchal family.[113]

8. *Other References to Mary*

While Elizabeth and Anna do not appear in the Lukan Gospel outside of the infancy narrative, there are two further references or allusions to Mary in the Lukan Gospel, though she is named in neither of them. In 8.19, Jesus' mother and family come to him, but fail to reach him due to the presence of a crowd. When informed of their presence outside, Jesus defines his mother and ἀδελφοί as 'those who hear the word of God and do it' (8.21). Thus Jesus defines a new kinship group on the grounds of hearing and doing the word of God. Jesus' words here do not preclude his biological family from membership in this new kinship group, in contrast

---

112. The Greek here is ambiguous and may be translated as 'in my father's house' or 'about my father's affairs.'

113. Balch, 'Luke,' 1110, notes here the expected obedience of children outlined in the later household codes (Eph. 6.1; Col. 3.20; 1 Tim. 3.4).

to the Markan account in which Jesus' biological family remain outsiders (Mk 3.31-35).[114]

Mary, the mother of Jesus, has already been characterized in the infancy narratives as hearing and doing the word of God. The word of God is conveyed to her by the angel Gabriel and she responds with a resounding acceptance (1.26-38). Trusting the word that has been given her, she sets out to visit Elizabeth whom she now knows is pregnant and Elizabeth proclaims a blessing on her for believing the word of God (1.39-45). Thus Mary fulfils the criteria of hearing and doing the word of God, giving her membership in the new kinship group established by Jesus. As such, Mary is portrayed as a model disciple.

Mary is also referred to metonymically in 11.27 when an unnamed woman in the crowd declares: 'Blessed is the womb that bore you and the breasts that nursed you!' (cf. Elizabeth's words of blessing in 1.42). Jesus responds to her: 'Blessed rather are those who hear the word of God and obey [keep] it!' (11.28). Links can be seen here between 11.27-28 and 8.19-21. Once again, Jesus emphasizes characteristics of discipleship rather than biological connections as being worthy of praise. There is an intertwining of hearing and doing the word in 8.21 and hearing and keeping the word of God in 11.28. The implication of 11.28 is that Mary is blessed because she is a hearer and keeper of the word rather than because she is the biological mother of Jesus.[115] As previously noted, Mary's 'keeping' activity is a feature of the infancy narrative (cf. 2.19, 51).

9. Conclusion

The rhetorical effect of the characterization of women in the Lukan infancy narrative is multifaceted. Elizabeth, Mary and Anna are characterized as playing significant roles in the drama. In contrast to Joseph who is a silent character throughout and Zechariah who is silenced for a time (1.8-20), each of these women is portrayed as recognizing God's actions in her life and in the world and as prophetically proclaiming her insight (1.42-45, 46-55; 2.36-38). They have a 'knowledge of salvation' and share that with others. The words of Mary's *Magnificat* are particularly powerful, and give the reader insight into the entire Gospel (1.46-55). That the women act independently and speak out while some of the men are silent cuts across the patriarchal context of the narrative. The additional references to Mary outside the infancy narrative (8.19-21; 11.27-28) confirm her as blessed and as a member of the new kinship group established by Jesus since she is a hearer, keeper and doer of the word.

114. See Lawson, 'Gender and Genre,' 148; Seim, *Double Message*, 66–67; and Reid, *Choosing the Better Part?*, 89.
115. This pericope (11.27-28) will be further explored in Chapter 5.

Hence, there are ways in which the women of the Lukan infancy narrative 'gain' through their characterization.[116]

Another dimension of the text, however, needs to be acknowledged and critiqued. When the women characters speak in the presence of an angel, in strictly female company or in solitude, there is no disparagement of their speech. Their words are shown to be perceptive and inspired. But when the audience moves away from being strictly female there is some marginalization of the women's speech on every such occurrence in the Lukan infancy narrative. Elizabeth's naming of her child is not taken seriously by her neighbors and relatives, while her husband's authority is sought and accepted. Anna's words and the reaction they produce are elided from the narrative while Simeon's words are included. Mary's words to Jesus in the temple receive a rebuke from him. Zechariah who was temporarily silenced is reinstated, regaining his voice and prophesying. The marginalization of each of the women's voices, however, is not explicitly redressed in the narrative, though the reader is able to critique this marginalization. None of the infancy narrative women speaks again in the Lukan Gospel.

Each of these faithful, inspired women 'loses her pound' to varying degrees when she speaks in the presence of men. For these women, the 'pound' they lose is their agency, their power to be heard in the 'male world,' their prophetic speech. When they take the initiative to speak in the 'male world' and challenge an ideal of public female silence, they suffer the consequences. It is only when they speak in private or to other women characters that their words are recorded and not disparaged. The group of neighbors and relatives who do not accept Elizabeth's naming of her son would likely comprise both men and women. Thus women can contribute to the silencing of other women in the presence of men, powerfully reinforcing this oppressive practice. In a similar way, the first two slaves in the Parable of the Pounds reinforce the oppressive practice of their master rather than challenge it. It is the slave who challenges who 'loses his pound.' The following chapter will explore the characterization of women in the remainder of the Lukan Gospel to discover whether the same tension around women's public speech is present throughout the narrative.

---

116. While the usual meaning of 'gain' implies acquiring something they did not have, in this instance it refers to the characteristics which are accredited to the women through their portrayal.

Chapter 5

THE CHARACTERIZATION OF WOMEN IN THE NARRATIVE OF
LUKE 3–24

As we have seen, the women of the Lukan infancy narrative are characterized as prophetic. They show initiative and are affirmed when they speak in a private setting, but in more public settings affirmation of their speech is absent and they can be described metaphorically as 'losing their pound.' Does this pattern continue in the rest of the Gospel of Luke? This chapter presents a reading of the characterizations of women in the narrative context of Luke 3–24,[1] which includes the period of Jesus' ministry. Both actions and speech of the women are important aspects of their characterizations. Also significant is the response by Jesus and/or others to the initiative of women expressed in action or words. As already indicated, this investigation is preliminary to a thematic reading of the women's characterizations through the lens of the Parable of the Pounds which will be undertaken in Chapter 6.

1. Simon's Mother-in-law

The first woman to encounter Jesus in the course of his ministry is Simon's mother-in-law. After Jesus proclaims release (ἄφεσις) for captives and the oppressed at the beginning of his Galilean ministry (4.18-19), a series of exorcisms and healings in Capernaum is narrated which demonstrates this release proclaimed by Jesus. The verb ἐπιτιμάω (to rebuke) links these stories. Jesus rebukes an unclean spirit from a man in a synagogue (4.31-37), rebukes a fever of Simon's mother-in-law (4.38-39) and rebukes the demons of many who come to him (4.40-41).

As in the Markan version of the healing of Simon's mother-in-law (Mk 1.29-31), the woman in the Lukan story is not named and is identified only in terms of her relationship with Simon (4.38). She has no voice in the pericope. Whereas Jesus takes the woman by the hand and lifts her up in

---

1. Other references to Mary, the mother of Jesus, in Luke 3–24 have already been addressed in the previous chapter. Although Herodias is mentioned by the narrator (3.19), she is not a character in the narrative and so will not be included in this study.

Mk 1.31, in the Lukan story Jesus does not touch the woman. Instead he stands over her, rebukes the fever and it releases her (ἀφῆκεν, 4.39). The authority of Jesus' word is highlighted. The use of ἐπιτιμάω suggests that this action of Jesus is an exorcism, whereas that indication is not given in the other Synoptic stories.[2] The association of the woman with demon possession is an addition by the Lukan narrator. That the woman experiences ἄφεσις links the action of Jesus with his proclamation in 4.18.[3]

The woman's response is emphasized by the Lukan addition of παραχρῆμα (4.39). Her immediate response to Jesus' action is to get up and serve/minister to (διηκόνει) them.[4] She is not lifted up by Jesus but gets up on her own in response to Jesus releasing her from the fever. The imperfect form of διηκόνει indicates an ongoing action on her part. The same verb is used in the Markan version (Mk 1.31) aligning the action of Simon's mother-in-law with the actions of the angels who minister to Jesus in the desert (Mk 1.13). In the Lukan text, however, the angels are not present with Jesus in the corresponding desert scene (4.1-13) so that this is the first use of διακονέω in this Gospel.

The nature of the woman's serving/ministering has evoked different explanations. Some argue that the woman's serving should be equated with waiting on tables, implying duties of hospitality.[5] A further suggestion is that there may also be overtones of a diaconal role for the woman within the context of a Christian meal, given the function of deacons by the time of the Lukan author.[6] These nuances in the meaning of διακονέω will be further explored later in this chapter. As we will see, noting common elements between the characterization of Simon's mother-in-law and that of other women of the Lukan Gospel may open up added dimensions of the woman's response. The overtones of exorcism in 4.39 particularly align the actions of Simon's mother-in-law with the women of 8.2-3 who are with Jesus and the twelve and who have been cured of evil spirits and infirmities. These women, too, serve/minister to (διηκόνουν) them.

In both 4.38-39 and 8.2-3 the association of the women with evil spirits or demon possession is unique to the Lukan narrative. Malevolent spirits

---

2. For the linking of exorcism and healing, see Johnson, *Luke*, 85; Evans, *Saint Luke*, 282; and John J. Pilch, 'Sickness and Healing in Luke-Acts,' in *The Social World of Luke-Acts: Models for Interpretation*, (ed.) Jerome H. Neyrey (Peabody, MA: Hendrickson, 1991), 196–97.

3. Elaine Wainwright, 'The Lucan Demon Possessed Women – Were They Healers?,' (paper presented at the Catholic Biblical Association of America's Annual Meeting, Cleveland, OH, 2002), 5.

4. The identity of 'them' is not specified, being the same group who earlier ask Jesus about the woman. (cf. Mt. 8.15 where the woman serves 'him,' Jesus, rather than 'them').

5. See, for instance, Corley, *Private Women*, 120–21; and Seim, *Double Message*, 60–61.

6. Via, 'Women,' 42. Melzer-Keller, *Jesus und die Frauen*, 193, also describes the translation of table-service as too limiting and claims a greater significance in the use here.

feature prominently in descriptions of the ailments afflicting women in the Lukan Gospel.[7] Although she does respond to Jesus' healing with ongoing action, the unnamed woman of 4.38-39 does not take the initiative in seeking a cure for herself and remains silent.

2. *The Widow at Nain*

After healing the slave of a centurion in Capernaum (7.1-10), Jesus raises to life a dead man, the only (μονογενής) son of a widow, at Nain (7.11-17).[8] The story is unique to the Lukan Gospel. Unlike the previous healing, there is no request made to Jesus in this case (cf. 7.3, 6-7). It is Jesus' compassion for the woman when he sees her rather than any initiative on her part that elicits Jesus' action (7.12-13).[9] Furthermore, faith is not portrayed as a requirement for healing (cf. 8.48; 18.42). The woman is unnamed and is identified as the mother of the dead man and as a widow. Thus, she is identified by her relationships to men. She is not given voice. Neither is any direct action accredited to her, though Jesus' words suggest that she is weeping (7.13).

Jesus is the protagonist in the pericope, with the core of the story formed around his actions. Jesus sees the woman and speaks to her (7.13); he approaches, touches the bier and instructs the dead man to rise (7.14). Again the power of Jesus' word is made manifest,[10] as the man sits up and speaks, though we are not informed of his words, and Jesus gives him to his mother (7.15, cf. 1 Kgs 17.23). The woman's individual reaction is not given. Instead we are given a general response, being informed that they are all fearful and that they glorify God, recognizing Jesus as a great prophet (7.16). Their further words – ἐπεσκέψατο ὁ θεὸς τὸν λαὸν αὐτοῦ (7.16) – continue the theme of divine visitation to describe God's action and presence in Jesus (cf. 1.68, 78). Thus, while Jesus is identified as a prophet, he is portrayed as more than that since he is also recognized by 'all of them' as the agent of the divine visitation. Whether the 'all' and 'they' include both the crowd which is with the woman (7.12) and the crowd and disciples accompanying Jesus (7.11) is not clear.

The raising of her son alleviates the widow's vulnerable position.[11] In

7.   See Pilch, 'Sickness and Healing,' 196–97. The woman in 13.10-17 has a spirit of infirmity and she is described as being bound by Satan (13.16). This story is unique to the Lukan Gospel.

8.   The passage is reminiscent of Elijah raising the son of a widow in 1 Kgs 17.17-24. For discussion of the comparison, see Reid, *Choosing the Better Part?*, 104–5; and Fitzmyer, *Luke*, 1.656-59. μονογενής is also used in 8.42 and 9.38.

9.   The first occurrence of the narrator referring to Jesus as κύριος is given in 7.13.

10.   Fitzmyer, *Luke*, 1.656.

11.   For a discussion on the status and situation of Jewish widows in Greco-Roman Palestine, see Tal Ilan, *Jewish Women in Greco-Roman Palestine: An Inquiry into Image and*

effect, Jesus' action responds to *her* need as well as the son's. In his response to the widow, Jesus enacts the bringing of good news to the poor (cf. 4.18; 7.22). He liberates her from the effects of death. Jesus' words to her suggest that she is weeping when he sees her (7.13) though this is not narrated. As the agent of the divine visitation, Jesus is thus portrayed as hearing the cry of the poor (cf. Exod. 3.7; Neh. 9.9; Pss. 106.44; 145.19). Apart from her weeping, however, the woman does not speak or act. She remains a passive recipient throughout the pericope. She does not request help and her response to Jesus is not narrated. Reid considers that the woman 'prompts Jesus to take up the cause of one who is voiceless. It is her very silence that brings Jesus to compassion.'[12] Yet it would appear that Jesus' action is prompted by *seeing* the woman (7.13). Regardless of what triggers Jesus' action, it does not result in the woman finding voice to speak. The narrator chooses to envelop the woman's response with that of the wider group.

The widow at Nain is not the only beneficiary of Jesus' miracles in the Lukan Gospel who is portrayed as silent and passive throughout, making no request or response to the miracle. The man with a withered hand and the man with dropsy are similarly portrayed (6.6-11; 14.1-6). In both of these cases no request or response, either verbal or symbolic, on the part of the men is narrated.[13] In the miracle stories of a male being healed in the Lukan Gospel, however, it is far more common for Jesus not to initiate the interaction. The leper, the ten lepers and the blind beggar make the request of Jesus themselves (5.12-16; 17.11-19; 18.35-43) while a centurion and a father request Jesus' help for a male slave and son (7.1-10; 9.38-42). Men carry the paralytic to Jesus (5.17-26) and the man with an unclean spirit and the Gerasene demoniac call out to Jesus (4.31-37; 8.26-39). Thus, it is usual for men to initiate the interaction with Jesus in these healing stories.[14]

As in the case of the raising of the widow's son, we will see below that Jesus takes the initiative to heal the crippled woman (13.10-17). Jairus begs Jesus to come to his daughter (8.40-42) and an unspecified 'they' ask Jesus about Simon's mother-in-law (4.38-39). The woman with a hemorrhage takes the initiative in coming to Jesus, though she comes from behind not wanting to be noticed (8.43-48). While it is common for male characters in these miracle stories to come to Jesus to elicit his help,

---

Status (Tübingen: J. C. B. Mohr, 1995), 147–51. Johnson states that a consequence of the widow losing her only son is that she would have no economic support. See Johnson, *Luke*, 118; and Price, *Widow Traditions*, 91.

12. Reid, *Choosing the Better Part?*, 106.

13. In summary statements of Jesus' healings (e.g. 4.40-41; 6.17-19) individual requests and responses are not recorded.

14. In the case of the healing of the mute demoniac (11.14) it is not narrated whether a request for healing was made or whether the healing was the result of Jesus' initiative.

the same cannot be said for the women characters in these stories. Women receive help through the initiative of Jesus and from the intercession of others (presumed male in 4.38) on their behalf but they never openly make a request of Jesus in the miracle stories.[15] In Chapter 6 of this study, the widow of Nain will be grouped with several other Lukan women characters who are given neither direct nor narrated speech.

3. *The Woman who Anoints Jesus' Feet*

The healing of a centurion's slave and the raising of the widow's son (7.1-17) leads into the summary statement of Jesus' ministry which he makes to the messengers of John the Baptist, outlining the benefits the poor are experiencing from the divine visitation (7.22). A further description in 7.34 informs us that Jesus is considered 'a friend of tax collectors and sinners,' demonstrating inclusion in the community of God, an aspect of salvation in the Gospel of Luke. The following story (7.36-50) expands the theme of knowledge of salvation experienced by those considered sinners.

The scene takes place within the context of a meal in the house of a Pharisee, later identified as Simon. Since Jesus teaches within this formal meal context, a symposium setting is suggested.[16] After the scene is set a woman takes center stage, the first Lukan woman during Jesus' ministry to take the initiative to approach him. The woman is unnamed while the male characters, Simon and Jesus, are named. She is identified by the description 'a woman in the city, who was a sinner' (7.37). Corley argues that the combination of being labeled a sinner and being known in the city 'makes it more than likely that Luke intends for his readers to identify her as a prostitute.'[17] The label of sinner, however, may reflect other circumstances, such as the woman's contact with Gentiles,[18] so it should

15. Dewey, 'Seen but not Heard?,' 54–57, demonstrates that women in the healing narratives of the Gospel of Luke are presented with less mimetic emphasis than those in the healing narratives of the other Synoptic Gospels.

16. See Dennis E. Smith, 'Table Fellowship as a Literary Motif in the Gospel of Luke,' *JBL* 106 (1987): 614; also Darr, *On Character Building*, 23, 32–35.

17. Corley, *Private Women*, 124. Others who understand the woman to be a prostitute include Schottroff, *Let the Oppressed*, 150–51; Judith K. Applegate, ' "And She Wet His Feet With Her Tears": A Feminist Interpretation of Luke 7.36–50,' in *Escaping Eden: New Feminist Perspectives on the Bible*, (eds.) Harold C. Washington, Susan Lochrie Graham, and Pamela Thimmes (Sheffield: Sheffield Academic Press, 1998), 78; Ben Witherington, *Women in the Ministry of Jesus: A Study of Jesus' Attitudes to Women and their Roles as Reflected in His Earthly Life* (Cambridge: Cambridge University Press, 1984), 54; and Schüssler Fiorenza, *In Memory of Her*, 129.

18. See the argument in Reid, *Choosing the Better Part?*, 116. From a survey of the use of ἁμαρτωλός in the ancient world, Teresa Hornsby explains that the term has two primary connotations – one of social deviance and one of imperfection. The latter requires an ideal standard against which everything is measured. In Aristotle's concept of the ideal as male,

not be assumed that the woman is a prostitute. Furthermore, the woman does not undertake the typical actions of a courtesan.[19] The woman's actions are highlighted: she learns of Jesus' whereabouts, brings an alabaster jar of ointment, places herself at Jesus' feet, weeps, bathes his feet with her tears, dries them with her hair, continues to kiss his feet and anoints them with ointment (7.37-38).

Each of the Gospels has a story of a woman anointing Jesus. In Mk 14.3-9, Mt. 26.6-13 and Jn 12.1-8, the meal takes place in Bethany and leads into Jesus' passion. Only in the Lukan narrative is the scene placed at an earlier stage in Jesus' ministry. In the Gospels of Matthew and Mark the woman anoints Jesus' head whereas in the Gospels of Luke and John she anoints his feet and wipes them with her hair. The anointing of the head is reminiscent of the prophet anointing the head of the king in 1 Sam. 10.1 and 2 Kgs 9.3. In this sense the woman in the Markan narrative may be said to have a prophetic role anointing Jesus before his burial, proclaiming him as Messiah, the anointed one. Offering a different reading, Wainwright has identified the language of the Markan pericope as evoking a context of healing and argues convincingly that the Markan woman is portrayed as a healer for Jesus who is facing impending death.[20] Within the Lukan pericope, though, a number of features – the different context for the story, the lack of Jesus' words to connect her action to preparation for burial, the anointing of the feet rather than the head – weaken the characterization of the woman as healer. Nevertheless, as we shall see, the actions of the woman have significance.

In the Lukan pericope Jesus is portrayed as a prophet (7.39-47),[21] though as the agent of the divine visitation he is also much more than that. The woman's response to Jesus signifies her understanding of God's action in her life. She is one of a number of characters in the Gospel who find themselves at Jesus' feet or knees (7.38, cf. 5.8; 8.35, 41, 47; 10.39, 17.16). Like the Gerasene demoniac who is 'in his right mind' when at the feet of Jesus (8.35), those at Jesus' feet demonstrate insight and faith. The

---

"sinner" 'may be seen as being gendered female.' Teresa J. Hornsby, 'The Woman is a Sinner/The Sinner is a Woman,' in *A Feminist Companion to Luke*, (eds.) Amy-Jill Levine and Marianne Blickenstaff (London: Sheffield Academic Press, 2002), 125–26.

19. Reid, *Choosing the Better Part?*, 116–17; and Teresa J. Hornsby, 'Why is She Crying? A Feminist Interpretation of Luke 7.36–50,' in *Escaping Eden: New Perspectives on the Bible*, (eds.) Harold C. Washington, Susan Lochrie Graham, and Pamela Thimmes (Sheffield: Sheffield Academic Press, 1998), 95.

20. Elaine Wainwright, 'The Pouring Out of Healing Ointment: Rereading Mark 14:3-9,' in *Toward a New Heaven and a New Earth: Essays in Honor of Elisabeth Schüssler Fiorenza,* (ed.) Fernando F. Segovia (Maryknoll, NY: Orbis Books, 2003), 163–69.

21. See Talbert, *Reading Luke*, 86; and Luise Schottroff, 'Through German and Feminist Eyes: A Liberationist Reading of Luke 7.36–50,' in *A Feminist Companion to the Hebrew Bible in the New Testament*, (ed.) Athalya Brenner (Sheffield: Sheffield Academic Press, 1996), 335.

woman takes over the role of host, displaying hospitality to the one who embodies the hospitality of God. Since hospitality is an important motif in the Lukan Gospel, the woman's display of hospitality to Jesus underlines that her actions are a faithful response to him. Jesus contrasts the hospitality of Simon the Pharisee with that shown by the woman. Three times Jesus pronounces a lack in Simon's response and uses the words αὕτη δέ to introduce the woman's extravagant response in comparison (7.44-46).

The interpretation of 7.47 is debated. At issue is whether the woman's sins are forgiven because she has shown great love or whether her great love is a consequence of having been forgiven. The conjunction ὅτι can carry the sense of either understanding. The perfect tense of ἀφέωνται, however, is significant in interpreting the verse. The perfect should be understood as an ongoing effect of a past action. Further, the passive form suggests the theological passive – that it is God who has acted. This leads to the interpretation that God has forgiven the woman *before* she anoints Jesus.[22] Jesus' words to her, 'Your sins are forgiven' (7.48), are an assurance of her forgiveness by God, deepening the knowledge of her salvation. His final words to the woman, 'Your faith has saved you; go in peace' (7.50, cf. 8.48) further this knowledge. While God has forgiven the woman, her loving actions to Jesus and the question of those at table (7.49) indicate that Jesus is integral to bringing the woman to a knowledge of her salvation.[23] More particularly, Jesus' announcement of her forgiveness means that the wider community learns of her status, enabling her to be restored to the community.[24]

The woman has experienced the expansive hospitality of God, the welcome of sinners into the presence of God embodied by the actions of Jesus. She responds with an extravagant demonstration of her love. In terms of her response to Jesus and her awareness of God's action in her life, the woman is characterized more positively than Simon. In a sense, she has acted prophetically by drawing attention to the agent of the divine visitation in their midst. The woman takes the initiative in her encounter with Jesus. He affirms the woman's actions and faith and restores her status within the community.

At the same time, there are aspects of the text which marginalize the significance of the woman. She is first marginalized by the physical setting of the scene, 'with the two men reclining toward one another and the

22. See Evelyn R. Thibeaux, ' "Known to be a Sinner": The Narrative Rhetoric of Luke 7:36-50,' *BTB* 23 (1993): 152. In contrast, Applegate contrasts the woman's tears with those who refuse to weep in the previous pericope (7.32). She claims then that the woman's tears indicate repentance rather than gratitude. See Applegate, 'She Wet His Feet,' 76.
23. See John J. Kilgallen, 'A Proposal for Interpreting Luke 7, 36-50,' *Bib* 72 (1991): 328.
24. Thibeaux, 'Known to be a Sinner,' 156.

woman standing behind Jesus.'[25] Furthermore, as Evelyn Thibeaux observes, after the description of her actions in 7.38, the woman is portrayed more as object than subject. She is the object of the men's gaze (7.44) and the object of their conversation (7.44-47), but she is not involved in the conversation until Jesus addresses her (7.48).[26] Jesus and Simon both speak and have their words recorded as do the others at table, but the woman does not speak at any stage of the pericope. The narrator gives no indication of the woman's response to Jesus' words to her. While it is the woman's actions which set the scene in motion, the narrator ensures that the woman does not take the initiative with her words.

According to Bauckham, 'her action is more eloquent than words ... We do not need to be told her feelings.'[27] Yet the different views of scholars on whether the woman's tears reflect gratitude or repentance, suggest that the woman's feelings are not as transparent as Bauckham suggests. He further claims that while the story abides by 'androcentric social conventions,' it 'brilliantly foregrounds the woman.'[28] The brilliant foregrounding, however, does not include a response by the woman to Jesus' words to her and the conventions which marginalize women's speech are not challenged.

The interaction between the woman who was a sinner and Jesus can be contrasted with the interaction between Jesus and Peter who declares himself a sinner (5.1-11). Peter is granted direct speech on two occasions in this pericope (5.5, 8) and follows Jesus (5.11), becoming an apostle (6.13-14) and an important character in the narrative of Luke-Acts. The woman, on the other hand, has no speech (neither direct nor implied) in the story and plays no further part in the narrative after being told by Jesus to 'go in peace.'[29]

4. *Women With Jesus*

Immediately following the pericope of the woman anointing Jesus' feet, the twelve and a group of women are identified as being with Jesus as he travels through cities and villages, continuing to proclaim and bring the good news of the βασιλεία of God (8.1-3). Despite Witherington describing women traveling with Jesus as 'unheard of and considered scandalous in Jewish circles,'[30] it can be argued cogently that women

---

25. Thibeaux, 'Known to be a Sinner,' 155.
26. Thibeaux, 'Known to be a Sinner,' 158.
27. Bauckham, *Gospel Women*, 201.
28. Bauckham, *Gospel Women*, 201.
29. Applegate, 'She Wet His Feet,' 89.
30. Witherington, *Genesis of Christianity*, 110. See, too, Tannehill, *Narrative Unity*, 138; and Talbert, *Reading Luke*, 93.

joining the Jesus movement was 'not altogether unique or alien to the Jewish background from which it sprang.'[31]

In the Gospel of Mark, a list of women followers (including Mary Magdalene) is not given until after the crucifixion (Mk 15.40). The Lukan list of women followers therefore occurs far earlier in the Gospel narrative. Tannehill claims that the women's earlier mention indicates their importance to the Lukan narrator,[32] which suggests that the move raises the profile of the women. A list of women to parallel a list of twelve male followers (6.12-16), however, makes women visible but also serves to distinguish them from the male group.[33]

Mary Magdalene is the only named woman from the Markan list who also appears in the Lukan list. The other named women in the Lukan list are Joanna, the wife of Chuza, a steward of Herod, and Susanna (8.2-3). Mary Magdalene is identified in terms of a place and Joanna is described in terms of her relationship to a man.[34] Susanna, however, is identified in relationship to neither a geographic location nor a man. As well as these three named women there are many unnamed women who are also with Jesus.

These Lukan women followers are introduced as having been cured of evil spirits and infirmities. Mary Magdalene is described as one 'from whom seven demons had gone out' (8.2). In Semitic interpretation, the number seven is linked with the character of totality so that, regarding the description of Mary Magdalene, 'the number seven points to the fact that there could be no worse state of corruption.'[35] It should be noted that if the number seven indicates the extent of her possession, it also indicates the extent of her cure. Mary Magdalene is characterized as 'someone who

---

31.   Tal Ilan, 'In the Footsteps of Jesus: Jewish Women in a Jewish Movement,' in *Transformative Encounters: Jesus and Women Re-viewed*, (ed.) Ingrid Rosa Kitzberger (Leiden: Brill, 2000), 117. Ilan argues that Jewish women were able to join religious sects at the time of Jesus (pp. 115–28). Moreover, Corley, *Women and the Historical Jesus*, 144, suggests that 'given the predominance of a number of women in social, religious and philosophical contexts across the Mediterranean world, ... it would be surprising if Jesus' company had not included at least a few women.'

32.   Tannehill, *Narrative Unity*, 138.

33.   Seim, *Double Message*, 19. See, also, Fitzmyer, *Luke*, 1.696; and Ben Witherington, 'On the Road with Mary Magdalene, Joanna, Susanna, and Other Disciples – Luke 8.1-3,' *ZNW* 70 (1979): 245.

34.   According to Carolyn Osiek, Joanna may have some status on 'the Herodian ladder.' See Carolyn Osiek, 'The Women at the Tomb: What are They Doing There?,' *Ex Auditu* 9 (1993): 99; also Bauckham, *Gospel Women*, 135–45. Marianne Sawicki argues that Joanna is 'the link between the Herodians and the Jesus movement' and may have protected Jesus from Herod. Marianne Sawicki, 'Magdalenes and Tiberiennes: City Women in the Entourage of Jesus,' in *Transformative Encounters: Jesus and Women Re-viewed*, (ed.) Ingrid Rosa Kitzberger (Leiden: Brill, 2000), 190–91.

35.   Rengstorf, 'ἑπτά,' *TDNT* 2.628–31.

has experienced the unlimited (seven) liberating power of the *basileia* in her own life.'[36] The women followers are portrayed as having experienced the good news of the βασιλεία themselves, being released from their burdens and responding by serving/ministering to (διηκόνουν) Jesus and the twelve from their own means (ἐκ τῶν ὑπαρχόντων αὐταῖς).[37] The twelve, on the other hand, are not portrayed as having been healed of illness or possession before following Jesus, though Simon describes himself as a sinner before following Jesus (5.8-11).

Malina and Neyrey argue that, in the first-century Mediterranean world, being described as possessed by a demon was a label of deviance, and that physical mobility would be sufficient cause for such a label.[38] This reasoning gives an explanation for the women accompanying Jesus being labeled as demon-possessed (8.1-3) but it does not account for the fact that the twelve who also travel with Jesus are not so labeled.

As in Lk. 4.39, the nature of the women's service evokes a range of views. Some interpret the women's service as financial support, under-standing the women as benefactors.[39] Such an interpretation brings the women's actions in line with the ideal description in Acts 2.44-45 and 4.32 of believers sharing their possessions. While the roles of these Lukan women, including their provision from their own means, has been described as 'surprising for their day,'[40] inscriptional evidence indicates

36. Schüssler Fiorenza, *In Memory of Her*, 124.

37. Some texts, including ℵ, A and L, have διηκόνουν αὐτῷ, rather than διηκόνουν αὐτοῖς, (B D W and others). The former is likely to be a change intended to draw the focus onto Jesus, or harmonize with Mk 15.41 and Mt. 27.55. See Metzger, *Textual Commentary*, 120–21; and Fitzmyer, *Luke*, 1.698. For an argument for διηκόνουν αὐτῷ, see C. Ricci, *Mary Magdalene and Many Others: Women Who Followed Jesus*, trans. Paul Burns (Minneapolis, MN: Fortress, 1994), 156–58. In a different interpretation, Maria-Luisa Rigato contends that the women, including Mary Magdalene, referred to in 8.2 are not included among those women who provide for them (8.3). See Maria-Luisa Rigato, ' "Remember" … Then They Remembered: Luke 24:6-8,' in *Luke and Acts*, (eds.) Gerald O'Collins and Gilberto Marconi (Mahwah, NJ: Paulist Press, 1991), 234. Esther De Boer argues that the appropriate interpretation is that the unnamed women of 8.3 provide for Jesus, the twelve and the named women. Further, she suggests that it is only the named women who are healed. Esther A. de Boer, 'The Lukan Mary Magdalene and the Other Women Following Jesus,' in *A Feminist Companion to Luke*, (eds.) Amy-Jill Levine and Marianne Blickenstaff (London: Sheffield Academic Press, 2002), 144–46. In 24.10, however, the named group of women and the other women with them are clearly involved in the same activity. The only distinguishing feature is that some are named and some are not. This suggests that 8.2-3 be interpreted in the same way – that all the women are healed and that all the women minister to Jesus and the twelve.

38. Bruce J. Malina and Jerome H. Neyrey, *Calling Jesus Names: The Social Value of Names in Matthew* (Sonoma, CA: Polebridge, 1988), 21–23; also Wainwright, 'Demon Possessed Women,' 1–2.

39. See, for example, Corley, *Private Women*, 111; Johnson, *Luke*, 131; and Bauckham, *Gospel Women*, 113–14.

40. Fitzmyer, *Luke*, 1.696.

that women could own property independently and that some did act as benefactors.[41]

The nature of the women's ministering needs further consideration, however. In his monograph, John N. Collins presents a detailed study of διακονία and its cognates in both non-Christian and Christian literature. He finds that the words occur in three kinds of contexts: message; agency; and attendance upon a person or within a household.[42] In each context the sense is of 'activity of an in-between kind.' Thus, for the verb form, the respective contexts carry the sense of: acting as a go-between, performing an errand; effecting, officiating or mediating; and attending or fetching.[43]

The verb διακονέω invokes a range of meaning. Collins claims that the meaning 'to wait at table' is not basic to the interpretation but is only one expression of the idea of 'go-between.'[44] Further, he notes that the words were not part of everyday language and occurred in passages of a 'profoundly religious nature.' Within Christian literature, Collins finds the words refer mainly to messages from heaven or between churches, and commissions within a church: 'Whether the words apply to message or to another type of commission, they necessarily convey the idea of mandated authority from God, apostle, or church.'[45] The only distinguishable difference that he notes between Christian and non-Christian usage of the words lies in the Christian designation of 'deacon': 'The word was chosen as a title of this Christian officer because the word had currency in religious language.'[46]

For διακονία and its cognates, the context in which a word appears is significant for understanding its use.[47] Within the Lukan Gospel, the verb διακονέω is used in regard to women's activity on three occasions (4.39; 8.3; 10.40). Collins concludes that, in these instances, the verb refers to table attendance. When the verb or its cognates are used of the male leaders in Acts, however, he argues for a different meaning (cf. Acts 1.17, 25; 11.29; 12.25; 19.22; 20.24; 21.19):

> The reason the words apply to women in three instances in the Gospel is simply that the narrative requires appropriate words for attendance

41. See Ilan, *Jewish Women*, 170–72; also Brooten, *Women Leaders*, 141–44, 157–65. For sources of independent property for Jewish women, see Bauckham, *Gospel Women*, 121–35. For a discussion of the circumstances under which women may sell or give away their inherited means, see Wegner, *Chattel or Person?*, 88–90.
42. John N. Collins, *Diakonia: Re-interpreting the Ancient Sources* (New York, NY: Oxford University Press, 1990), 335.
43. Collins, *Diakonia*, 335.
44. Collins, *Diakonia*, 335.
45. Collins, *Diakonia*, 336.
46. Collins, *Diakonia*, 337.
47. Collins, *Diakonia*, 336; also John N. Collins, 'Did Luke Intend a Disservice to Women in the Martha and Mary Story?,' *BTB* 28 (1998): 110.

upon guests or master; on the other hand, they apply to men in the public roles of mission and proclamation in Acts ... because the words properly designate such activities, especially as these are of a religious character.[48]

Hence, Collins assumes that, when the words are predicated of women in the Gospel of Luke, they do not refer to mission or proclamation. These activities are the domain of men.[49] He asserts, however, that this does not reflect a Lukan bias against women but rather reflects the sociological conditions of the time: 'The simple fact is that mission and proclamation were activities carried out basically by men.'[50]

Having decided that women did not engage in mission and proclamation, Collins can only interpret the Lukan women's διακονία in terms of table-attendance. Despite acknowledging one instance when διακονία and its cognates in relation to women reflect the usage of mission and proclamation (Phoebe in Rom. 16.1),[51] Collins is not prepared to grant any other instance from the Lukan narrative. His research on the use of the words, however, would suggest that it is possible to interpret the women's activities in the Gospel of Luke in this broadened sense.

We have seen that διακονέω and its cognates hold significance in the Greek literature. They suggest a religious context and commission. Considering the women of 8.2-3, it can be argued that Collins' research 'offers an alternative to the dominant interpretation of the nature of the women's ministry: the women are sent out on a prophetic mission in God's name.'[52] At the same time, this element of mission is not developed in the Lukan narrative: 'it would seem that in the Lukan narrative the prophetic-missionary dimension of the women's serving is subordinated to the practical domestic dimensions of their ministry.'[53] The imperfect tense of διηκόνουν indicates that the ministering of the women is ongoing.

The terms διακονία and διακονεῖν have been described as 'technical terms for ecclesial leadership' in the early church, with διακονία in the early Christian usage referring to 'eucharistic table service' and

---

48. Collins, 'Disservice to Women?,' 109–10.

49. For a critique of interpretation that distinguishes between the διακονία of women and men though the same language is used, see Schottroff, *Lydia's Impatient Sisters*, 218–20.

50. Collins, 'Disservice to Women?,' 110.

51. Collins, 'Disservice to Women?,' 110.

52. Lawson, 'Gender and Genre,' 159. See also Karris, 'Women and Discipleship,' 9.

53. Lawson, 'Gender and Genre,' 160. The 'practical domestic dimensions' are emphasized by Evans who claims that 8.3 'establishes the function of women disciples as material care and not preaching and healing.' See Evans, *Saint Luke*, 366–37. Witherington, 'On the Road,' 247, also argues that the women of 8.2-3, though they are disciples, do not abandon their 'traditional roles in regard to preparing food, serving, etc.'

'proclamation of the word' (Acts 6–8).[54] Furthermore, leadership and the verb διακονεῖν are particularly linked in the Gospel of Luke in 22.26. Thus, the women model appropriate characteristics of leadership. While the women in 8.3 are portrayed as ministering (διηκόνουν), however, the additional phrase ἐκ τῶν ὑπαρχόντων αὐταῖς gives the impression of 'a more general sense of support and provision.'[55] Other uses of ὑπάρχοντα in the Gospel of Luke suggest the term refers to possessions or property (11.21; 12.15, 33, 44; 14.33; 16.1; 19.8).[56] The added phrase, therefore, lessens the likelihood of a diaconal context within Christian ministry being evoked in this use of διακονέω. While the verb has multiple dimensions, the effect of the addition is to move the focus away from leadership activity and onto practical provision. Esther De Boer argues that within the Lukan Gospel the verb διακονέω refers to preparing food and waiting at table, but that this is a discipleship role for both men and women (cf. 9.14-16; 22.7-13):[57] '[W]hen one reads Lk. 8.1-3 within the context of the gospel as a whole, it becomes apparent that Luke is portraying the serving women in a leadership role. They are practicing an important Christian ideal, not one restricted to women, but one meant for all believers.'[58] The women's leadership role, though, never takes the form of preaching.[59] Proclamation is portrayed as a role for male disciples.

The response of the women followers to Jesus can be interpreted as an act of gratitude for being healed.[60] The implication that they are with Jesus out of gratitude undermines the significance of the women's discipleship as presented in the Markan Gospel. Further, since the women serve *them* (Jesus and the twelve), the importance of the twelve is highlighted. The twelve are given a superior status to the women.[61] Hence, it would seem that the narrator's changes function in some ways to reduce the significance of the women's roles. This can be seen further in a

54. Schüssler Fiorenza, *But She Said*, 64. For a critique of Schüssler Fiorenza's claims here, see Collins, 'Disservice to Women?,' 104–11.
55. Seim, *Double Message*, 62.
56. David C. Sim, 'The Women Followers of Jesus: The Implications of Luke 8:1-3,' *HeyJ* 30 (1989): 57, therefore argues that the women's provision is only in an economic sense.
57. de Boer, 'Lukan Mary Magdalene,' 143. It should be noted, though, that the verb διακονέω is not used to refer to the actions of the disciples in either 9.14-16 or 22.7-13.
58. de Boer, 'Lukan Mary Magdalene,' 144.
59. de Boer, 'Lukan Mary Magdalene,' 158–60.
60. See Melzer-Keller, *Jesus und die Frauen*, 198; and Schüssler Fiorenza, *But She Said*, 64. For a contrary view, see Bauckham, *Gospel Women*, 165.
61. Lawson states that the women's subordination to the men is highlighted here. Lawson, 'Gender and Genre,' 157. For a contrary opinion, see Karris, 'Women and Discipleship,' 9.

comparison of the observers to the crucifixion in the Markan and Lukan narratives, as we will see later in this chapter.[62]

As in the case of Simon's mother-in-law who also ministers to Jesus and others (4.38-39), the connection of evil spirits with the women is unique to the Lukan Gospel. The combination of evil spirits and διακονέω in both these pericopes needs further investigation. Exploration of the ancient Greco-Roman world enables some links between healing powers and labels of demon possession to be made. Discussing attitudes to the art of healing, Tal Ilan claims that 'Jews, like their neighbours, viewed with suspicion the healing powers of certain individuals, and often identified them as originating in the domain of evil.'[63] This may explain why, in the Lukan Gospel, Jesus' healing of a mute man causes some to consider him as using demonic power (11.14-15). From investigating Greco-Roman Palestinian Judaism, Ilan also comments on the large number of women who operated as healers.[64] Moreover, she notes examples in the New Testament where a possessed individual displays prophetic insight (Mk 5.7/pars.; Acts 16.16-17) and that Jesus himself is accused of being out of his mind (Mk 3.21). She insightfully concludes that exorcism, possession and prophecy are 'truly confused in the New Testament.'[65]

The links between demonic possession, healing and prophecy in the Gospel of Luke are developed further by Wainwright. Drawing intertextually on the portrayal of Circe in the works of Homer and Pliny, she questions whether the women are labeled as demon-possessed because they are female healers who work with drugs or herbs, like Circe whose power is portrayed as evil.[66] Such a question raises significant issues:

> [T]he emerging Christian movement may have been labelled and demonised because of its association with women's healing power. Or did the Lucan community seek to demonise women's healing powers over against those of Jesus and the Twelve who are commissioned to heal in 9.1 just as the healing power of Odysseus was pitted against the supposedly harmful power of Circe. In these questions, text and context permeate one another.[67]

---

62. For a discussion on the devaluing of the roles of the women disciples, see Lawson, 'Gender and Genre,' 156–61.

63. Ilan, 'Footsteps of Jesus,' 128–29.

64. Ilan, 'Footsteps of Jesus,' 129. For women as healers in the Greco-Roman period, see Elaine M. Wainwright, '"Your Faith Has Made You Well." Jesus, Women and Healing in the Gospel of Matthew,' in *Transformative Encounters: Jesus and Women Re-viewed*, (ed.) Ingrid Rosa Kitzberger (Leiden: Brill, 2000), 228–37.

65. Ilan, 'Footsteps of Jesus,' 134–35.

66. Wainwright, 'Demon Possessed Women,' 3–4.

67. Wainwright, 'Demon Possessed Women,' 4. A similar dynamic is described by Gloria Kehilwe Plaatjie in relation to modern-day Sotho-Tswana communities. The accusation of

If the Lukan Gospel women who are portrayed as possessing evil spirits or demons are stereotyped, just as women in classical literature who have healing power are stereotyped, then the διακονία which these women perform becomes caricatured.

On two occasions the women depicted as evil spirit- or demon-possessed are said to minister (διακονέω) to Jesus and others (4.39; 8.3) and the use of the imperfect tense on both occasions indicates that their ministry is an ongoing activity. If this ministry becomes caricatured, however, then the significance of the ministry is marginalized. This marginalization has often been articulated. As Ross S. Kraemer recognizes, '[t]he author of Luke-Acts … may prefer to represent women around Jesus as marginalized women to minimize women's stature within early Christian churches.'[68] Joanna Dewey also interprets the attribution of demonic possession to women as continuing the Lukan pattern of restricting women to subordinate roles.[69]

When Jesus commissions the twelve (9.1-2) and the seventy (10.1-12), his commission to heal is linked with his commission to proclaim the βασιλεία of God (9.2; 10.9). The twelve and the wider group of disciples are sent to do both activities. Hence, any marginalization of women's healing ministry also has consequences for women's proclamation of the βασιλεία and vice versa. While the demonization of the women characters may marginalize women's διακονία, it may also compromise their public voice. In both these ways, the women can be described metaphorically as 'losing their pound.'

5. *Jairus' Daughter and a Woman With a Hemorrhage*

Following the Markan order, the Lukan narrative follows the story of the healing of the Gerasene demoniac (8.26-39) with the entwined stories of two females, neither of whom is named (8.40-56). The first is identified as the only daughter (θυγάτηρ μονογενής, 8.42; cf. 7.12; 9.38) of Jairus, a leader of the synagogue. Thus she is identified in terms of her relationship to a man. We also learn that she is about twelve years old and is dying (8.42). The girl does not appear as a character until later in the narrative.

---

witchcraft is used to 'distance and discourage women' from some public positions. 'Women tend to be labeled witches, thereby preserving the public profession of healing, public leadership, and property ownership for men.' Gloria Kehilwe Plaatjie, 'Toward a Post-apartheid Black Feminist Reading of the Bible: A Case of Luke 2:36-38,' in *Other Ways of Reading: African Women and the Bible*, (ed.) Musa W. Dube (Atlanta, GA: SBL, 2001), 132.

68.   Kraemer, 'Some Caveats,' 46.

69.   Joanna Dewey, 'Jesus' Healings of Women: Conformity and Non-Conformity to Dominant Cultural Values as Clues for Historical Re-construction,' *BTB* 24 (1994): 124. See also Tetlow, *Women and Ministry*, 103.

We know of her initially only through the narrator's description of her father's actions. It is Jairus who takes the initiative, falls at Jesus' feet and makes the request for healing of his daughter (8.41-42).[70]

As in the Markan narrative, the story of another woman intrudes into the journey of Jesus to the house of Jairus and the combination of stories is presented in such a way that one story informs the other. The second woman is identified in terms of her illness. She has been hemorrhaging for twelve years and has been unable to find a cure (8.43).[71] The woman takes the initiative to approach Jesus, coming from behind amidst the crowd to touch the hem of his garment, and is immediately cured (8.44).[72] The Markan version informs us that the woman had heard about Jesus and includes the words which she speaks: 'If I but touch his clothes, I will be made well [saved]' (Mk 5.28). Almost identical words are spoken by the woman in the Matthean version (Mt. 9.21). These features are lacking, however, in the Lukan story. Hence the women's motivation to touch Jesus' garment is not given at this point and we do not hear her words.[73]

A further difference from the Markan story can be seen in the response to Jesus' question to identify who had touched him. Only in the Lukan version does everyone deny it (8.45). Peter's dismissal of the question causes Jesus to insist that someone had touched him because he is aware of the flow of power from him (8.45-46). This insistence is made via the direct speech of Jesus whereas it is a narrated comment in the Markan version (Mk 5.30). It is only when the woman sees she cannot remain hidden that she falls down before him (8.47). The woman who initially comes from behind is now before Jesus. In the Markan story, when Jesus asks the question the woman comes forward because she knows what has happened to her (Mk 5.33). In the Lukan version, however, the woman's reasoning is only 'obliquely' reported (8.47).[74] The rhetorical function of the Lukan redaction is to highlight Jesus and detract attention from the woman since it is Jesus' understanding rather than the understanding of the woman which is recorded.[75]

Within the Lukan version, the woman declares in the presence of all the

70. By falling at Jesus' feet, Jairus does not act to maintain his public honor. See Dewey, 'Jesus' Healings,' 126.

71. Some texts include ἰατροῖς προσαναλώσασα ὅλον τὸν βίον but P[75] and B, among others, omit the phrase. The inclusion of the phrase is uncertain.

72. While some texts lack ὄπισθεν an overwhelming majority of witnesses, including P[75] א A B, attest to its inclusion.

73. Evans, *Saint Luke*, 390.

74. Vernon K. Robbins, 'The Woman Who Touched Jesus' Garment: Socio-Rhetorical Analysis of the Synoptic Accounts,' *NTS* 33 (1987): 512.

75. Robbins, 'Woman Who Touched,' 512. Reid, *Choosing the Better Part?*, 142, also notes three links between the woman and Jesus which are present in the Markan narrative but not the Lukan version.

people her motivation for touching Jesus and her healing (8.47). Thus, the narrator emphasizes the public nature of her declaration. As in the Markan version, however, the woman's words of declaration are not provided so the woman's motivation is not made explicit to the reader. Neither is the woman's voice heard by the reader. Jesus affirms her with the words: 'Daughter, your faith has made you well [saved you, σέσωκέν σε]; go in peace.' (8.48, cf. Mk 5.34). Apart from the designation of daughter, identical words are spoken to the woman who anoints Jesus (7.50). The term 'daughter' indicates that she is included in the community (cf. 13.16).[76]

Though she tries to remain hidden, the result is that the woman speaks in a public situation and is affirmed by Jesus (8.47-48). She is the first woman in the Gospel to speak since the beginning of Jesus' ministry and it is the Lukan Jesus who draws her out of the crowd to speak publicly (8.45-46). This focused attention from Jesus counters Peter's efforts to direct Jesus' attention elsewhere (8.45). The Lukan narrator (consistent with the Markan narrative) does not include the woman's words after her healing (8.47), so that it is the narrator's description of her words rather than her voice that we hear. Further, the Lukan narrator (unlike the Markan narrative) emphasizes that the woman does not come forward and speak out of her own initiative but only speaks when she can no longer remain hidden.

The inconsistency of the Lukan narrator is evident here. While the narrator portrays Jesus as drawing the woman out of the crowd and eliciting her voice, the narrator ensures that the woman's initiative is cast into the background. She takes the initiative with her initial action (though she does not want her action to be known) but not with her words, and we do not hear her own words. Furthermore, the narrator emphasizes that she only speaks when it is no longer possible to be silent. Jesus' actions, on the other hand, lead the woman to proclaim publicly and he then affirms her words (8.48). Hence, on this occasion Jesus affirms the woman's speech. Jesus and the narrator therefore operate to different effect in this pericope. Jesus responds to the woman's speech with affirmation but the narrator, while noting the public nature of the woman's speech, ensures that the influence of the woman's words on the reader is significantly diminished. Marie-Eloise Rosenblatt writes: 'When the haemorrhaging woman achieves her healing, she experiences a

76. Annette Weissenrieder, 'The Plague of Uncleanness? The Ancient Illness Construct "Issue of Blood" in Luke 8:43-48,' in *The Social Setting of Jesus and the Gospels*, (eds.) Wolfgang Stegemann, Bruce J. Malina, and Gerd Theissen (Minneapolis, MN: Fortress Press, 2002), 218.

transformation which is more than physical: she acquires a public voice.'[77] Her public voice, however, is not heard by the reader.

While the woman described as 'daughter' demonstrates her faith, word comes that the other daughter, that of Jairus, has died. Jesus enjoins Jairus to have faith and his daughter will be saved (σωθήσεται), recalling that the other woman's faith has saved (σέσωκέν) her (8.48, 50). Following the Markan story, Jesus takes her hand and tells her to get up. She responds at once (8.54-55). The power of Jesus which earlier healed the woman is evident once again.[78] The girl remains silent. We are not given any verbal response from her. Rather we are informed of the astounded reaction of the parents. While the woman tells her story openly (8.47), the parents are told not to tell anyone what has happened to their daughter (8.56).

The weaving of the two stories allows us to see parallels between the two female characters who are saved/healed. They are linked by the time frame of twelve years and by the designation of daughter. They are also linked by their situation (or possible situation) of ritual uncleanness and by being 'restored to life' by Jesus.[79] The woman and Jairus are linked by their need and their faith and the initiative they take in coming to Jesus. A contrast, however, can also be drawn between the two. He is named, but she is not. He has status, but she does not. He comes to Jesus

---

77. Marie-Eloise Rosenblatt, 'Gender, Ethnicity, and Legal Considerations in the Haemorrhaging Woman's Story Mark 5:25-34,' in *Transformative Encounters: Jesus and Women Re-viewed*, (ed.) Ingrid Rosa Kitzberger (Leiden: Brill, 2000), 145. While Rosenblatt is discussing the Markan version here, the situation is similar in the Lukan version.

78. Fitzmyer, *Luke*, 1.744.

79. Amy-Jill Levine puts the effects of ritual 'uncleanness' into context, explaining that one should read the 'purity legislation as a social system concerned, in Jesus' time, primarily with participation in Temple sacrifice.' Amy-Jill Levine, 'Lilies of the Field and Wandering Jews: Biblical Scholarship, Women's Roles, and Social Location,' in *Transformative Encounters: Jesus and Women Re-viewed*, (ed.) Ingrid Rosa Kitzberger (Leiden: Brill, 2000), 337. Further, it is not definite that the hemorrhage is menstrual. Thus, it is possible that the hemorrhage may not render the woman ritually unclean. See also Amy-Jill Levine, 'Discharging Responsibility: Matthean Jesus, Biblical Law, and Hemorrhaging Woman,' in *Treasures New and Old: Recent Contributions to Matthean Studies*, (eds.) David R. Bauer and Mark Allen Powell (Atlanta, GA: Scholars Press, 1996), 379–97; Amy-Jill Levine, 'Second Temple Judaism, Jesus and Women: *Yeast of Eden*,' in *A Feminist Companion to the Hebrew Bible in the New Testament*, (ed.) Athalya Brenner (Sheffield: Sheffield Academic Press, 1996), 311–13; and Rosenblatt, 'Gender, Ethnicity, and Legal Considerations,' 151. Moreover, Annette Weissenrieder points out that, since Lev. 15.25-30 does not specify that anyone touching an irregularly bleeding woman shall be unclean (in contrast to Lev. 15.19), Jesus is not contaminated by the woman's touch. She argues that the purity code is not the focus of any of the characters in the pericope. Rather the pericope shows the extent of the woman's illness and the effect of Jesus' healing in restoring her physically and socially. See Weissenrieder, 'Plague of Uncleanness?,' 207–22. For a different view, see Dewey, 'Jesus' Healings,' 126–27.

directly to appeal for help. She comes from behind without any direct appeal. He speaks publicly. She keeps hidden and only speaks publicly when she knows that she cannot remain hidden. The speech of neither character is reported directly. Jairus' words of request and the woman's words expressing her motivation are given in the Gospel of Mark but are not given by the Lukan narrator. Hence the significance of the words of both Jairus and the woman here are lessened in the Lukan version.[80] In a sense, then, both have their 'pound' compromised. The women's words of declaration are in neither the Markan nor Lukan accounts. Thus, while the woman cured of the hemorrhage is the first woman in the Lukan Gospel to speak in the course of Jesus' ministry, we do not hear her voice.

The restoration to life of Jairus' only daughter links with the raising by Jesus of another only child, the son of the widow from Nain (7.11-17). The main contrast in these two stories, however, is between the widow and Jairus. While Jairus takes the initiative to beg for help, the widow makes no such request and remains a passive recipient throughout.

6. *Martha and Mary*

The story of Martha and Mary (10.38-42) is unique to the Lukan Gospel. It follows on from the Parable of the Good Samaritan (10.25-37), leading some to claim that the parable elucidates love of neighbor while the story of Martha and Mary elucidates love of God.[81] Martha is introduced as welcoming (ὑπεδέξατο) Jesus when he enters a certain village (10.38; cf. 19.6). Some texts, such as A, D and W, include a reference to her welcoming him 'into her house' (εἰς τὸν οἶκον αὐτῆς) and others, such as P³ and ℵ*, include 'into the house' (εἰς τὴν οἰκίαν) but some strong witnesses (P⁴⁵, ⁷⁵ B) have no mention of the house, so that the inclusion has doubtful status. Not only is Martha named, she is not linked in relationship to any man. She is given an independent status. The included reference to Martha welcoming Jesus into her house also reflects the understanding that she is a woman of independent means.[82] The context of Jesus journeying and Martha welcoming him presents hospitality as central to the pericope (cf. 19.6). Seim comments that Martha performs the practical tasks of hospitality herself and that she is portrayed as a

80. Melzer-Keller argues that the Lukan interest in this pericope is exclusively Christological and that this influences the changes made to the Markan narrative. See Melzer-Keller, *Jesus und die Frauen*, 284.

81. See, for example, Marshall, *Luke*, 450; and Talbert, *Reading Luke*, 120.

82. For a discussion outlining the possibility of Jewish women having their own property, see Ilan, *Jewish Women*, 167–72. The situation in Roman law is outlined in Gardner, *Women*, 163–203.

'patroness in comfortable circumstances.'[83] While she is portrayed as independent, however, it is difficult to argue from the text that she has comfortable circumstances. Seim assumes the service refers to domestic service, but it is likely that someone of comfortable means would have a slave perform the practical tasks.[84]

By considering the various uses of the verb δέχομαι and its compound ὑποδέχομαι in Luke-Acts, Reid notes that they are used in reference to welcoming a person (e.g. 9.5, 48, 53; 10.8, 10; 19.6; Acts 17.7) and also to hearing the word (e.g. 8.13; 18.17; Acts 8.14; 11.1; 17.11).[85] She concludes that Martha welcoming (ὑπεδέξατο) Jesus can, therefore, be understood as a faithful response corresponding to Mary hearing Jesus' word.[86] By welcoming Jesus, Martha demonstrates the appropriate response to the agent of the divine visitation. The one who welcomes Jesus welcomes the one who sent him (9.48).

Mary is introduced as Martha's sister and is described as sitting at the feet of the κύριος (cf. 8.35) and listening to his word (10.39). The narrator here again uses the title κύριος to refer to Jesus. Mary is one of several Lukan characters who find themselves at Jesus' feet or knees (10.39, cf. 5.8; 7.38; 8.35, 41, 47; 17.16), demonstrating insight and faith. Identifying Mary as sitting in the position of a student (cf. Acts 22.3), Seim describes this as noteworthy since '[w]ithin Judaism, the study of the Law was, as far as we know, at that period restricted to men. Women had neither the right nor the obligation to be taught.' She draws on a rabbinic saying (*b. Kid.* 29b), which prohibits the teaching of women, to support her view.[87] It is, however, somewhat anachronistic to use the rabbinic documents,

---

83. Seim, *Double Message*, 98–99.

84. In Acts 12.13 Rhoda, a female slave (παιδίσκη), answers the door to Peter in the house of Mary. It is not clear from the text, however, whether Rhoda is the slave of Mary. Ivoni Richter Reimer writes that, if Rhoda is Mary's slave, opening the door may be one of her duties, though not necessarily her only task. See Ivoni Richter Reimer, *Women in the Acts of the Apostles: A Feminist Liberation Perspective*, trans. Linda M. Maloney (Minneapolis, MN: Fortress Press, 1995), 241–42.

85. Reid, *Choosing the Better Part?*, 156–57.

86. Reid, *Choosing the Better Part?*, 157. See also Warren Carter, 'Getting Martha Out of the Kitchen: Luke 10:38-42 Again,' in *A Feminist Companion to Luke,* (eds.) Amy-Jill Levine and Marianne Blickenstaff (London: Sheffield Academic Press, 2002), 218.

87. See Seim, *Double Message*, 102–3. Seim does, however, note an exception to the rule and also suggests that further investigation from a feminist perspective may nuance the picture presented (n. 15). Witherington claims that while women could learn, 'for a rabbi to come into a woman's house and teach her specifically is unheard of.' Witherington claims further that the roles which Mary and Jesus assume in this pericope contrast with the expected roles for Jewish men and women. Witherington, *Women in the Ministry of Jesus*, 101. Critiquing Christian interpretation, Reinhartz notes that often studies on New Testament passages, including the Martha and Mary story, have fostered anti-Judaism sentiments. In particular, the roles accorded women in Judaism are contrasted negatively

which were edited at a much later stage than either the life of Jesus or the period of Lukan writing, to argue against women studying the Law in the first century. Furthermore, since rabbinic literature presents a range of opinions, it cannot be assumed that a particular rabbinic saying describes typical views.[88] Rather, other evidence suggests that some women were educated in the Law.[89] Thus, assertions about the exclusion of Jewish women from studying cannot be justified.

While Mary is portrayed as listening to Jesus, she is not granted any speech.[90] The use of the particle δέ casts Martha's activity into contrast with Mary's position: ἡ δὲ Μάρθα περιεσπᾶτο περὶ πολλὴν διακονίαν (10.40) and her request to Jesus seeks to elicit Mary's help with the διακονία. Martha is the first woman to have her words recorded in the Lukan narrative since the start of Jesus' ministry. Martha's διακονία connects her with other Lukan women who serve/minister (διακονέω),[91] Simon's mother-in-law (4.39) and the women who follow Jesus (8.2-3). Her διακονία links her both with Jesus who describes himself as ὁ διακονῶν and with the appropriate actions for leadership among the disciples (22.26-27).

Most interpret the διακονία of Martha as serving at table, providing a meal for Jesus.[92] The text, however, does not specifically refer to a meal.[93] As noted earlier, the term διακονία has far-reaching significance. Its use in the contexts of commission and religious ritual, as well as its early Christian usage, suggest that Martha's διακονία may be understood as embracing more than meal provision. It is possible to argue that her διακονία incorporates aspects of ecclesial leadership.[94] The use of the title κύριε in the narrative suggests a post-resurrection context for the story.[95]

---

with those of women in Christianity. See Adele Reinhartz, 'From Narrative to History: The Resurrection of Mary and Martha,' in *A Feminist Companion to the Hebrew Bible in the New Testament*, (ed.) Athalya Brenner (London: Sheffield Academic Press, 1996), 200–3, 223.

88.   Kraemer, 'Some Caveats,' 37.

89.   Reid, *Choosing the Better Part?*, 153, presents a range of evidence to support this statement.

90.   From an Asian woman's perspective, Ranjini Rebera interprets Mary's position at the feet of Jesus as being in a training process that will lead into her role as teacher. 'When viewed from this standpoint, Mary ceases to be a silent receiver. She becomes an active participant.' Ranjini Rebera, 'Polarity or Partnership? Retelling the Story of Martha and Mary from Asian Women's Perspective,' *Semeia* 78 (1997): 101.

91.   In both these instances, though, the women serve 'them' and not Jesus alone.

92.   See, for example, Fitzmyer, *Luke*, 2.892; and Marshall, *Luke*, 452.

93.   See Schüssler Fiorenza, *But She Said*, 64; Schüssler Fiorenza, 'Martha and Mary,' 30; Reid, *Choosing the Better Part?*, 147; and Thurston, *Women in the New Testament*, 110.

94.   See Schüssler Fiorenza, *But She Said*, 64; Price, *Widow Traditions*, 184; Carter, 'Martha,' 222; and D'Angelo, 'Women in Luke-Acts,' 454.

95.   Schüssler Fiorenza, *But She Said*, 62. For a critique of Schüssler Fiorenza's context for the story, see Seim, *Double Message*, 99–100.

The phrase περιεσπᾶτο περὶ πολλὴν διακονίαν (10.40) is usually interpreted as Martha being burdened, however διακονία is understood. Yet the verb περισπάω also carries the meaning 'be pulled or dragged away,'[96] opening up the possibility that Martha is 'being pulled away from her diaconal ministry by those who disapprove' of women's involvement in such ministry.[97] In this interpretation, the pericope is concerned with the appropriate roles for women rather than appropriate meal provision.

In 12.13 a man makes a request concerning his brother to Jesus. This request can be compared with that of Martha. Both ask Jesus to tell a sibling to do something. In the case of the man and his brother, however. Jesus refuses to act as judge over them (12.14). In contrast, Jesus' response to Martha does judge between the two sisters.[98] Mary is said by Jesus to have 'chosen the better part' while Martha is described as worried and distracted περὶ πολλὴν διακονίαν (10.41-42). The uncertainty of the text of 10.41-42, indicated by the variations attested, makes it difficult to be specific about the context for ἑνὸς δέ ἐστιν χρεία.[99]

Jesus' rebuke of Martha creates a narrative tension if it is interpreted as a belittling of Martha's διακονία. 'Against the background of the positive portrayal of the διακονία role elsewhere in the gospel, … it is difficult to accept that it should suddenly come here to represent the mistaken choice.'[100] One way that this narrative tension has been explained is to argue that Jesus' objection is not in regard to Martha's serving but in the way she goes about it, displaying fuss and agitation.[101] Such an explanation interprets περισπάω as being 'overburdened' rather than 'being pulled away.' That being anxious is not desirable behavior for disciples is indicated by Jesus elsewhere in the Gospel (cf. 8.14; 12.25-26).

Some interpret the pericope as liberating for women. Witherington, for instance, insists that Jesus is here defending the right of women to be disciples. He argues that Jesus' words neither 'devalue Martha's efforts at hospitality' nor 'attack women's traditional role.' Rather they are said to underscore the notion that women, too, are able to sit as disciples at the feet of the teacher.[102] Other elements of the text, however, make it difficult to perceive the text in a liberating light. Mary, who is affirmed by Jesus, is

---

96. BAGD, 650.

97. Reid, *Choosing the Better Part?*, 157.

98. Goulder notes the similarities between 10.38-42 and 12.13 but does not appear to notice that only in the Martha and Mary story does Jesus judge between the two. Goulder, *Luke*, 2.494. Gooding, *According to Luke*, 209, also links the two stories.

99. For a discussion of the various textual variants, see Marshall, *Luke*, 452–53; and Fitzmyer, *Luke*, 2.894.

100. Seim, *Double Message*, 106.

101. See Seim, *Double Message*, 104–5; and Carter, 'Martha,' 227–28.

102. Witherington, *Women in the Ministry of Jesus*, 101. See also Danker, *New Age*, 224–25.

silent throughout and her listening does not lead to any further action. Thus, while she sits in the position of a disciple, Mary's discipleship role is not portrayed as progressing beyond this. We have previously been told that those who hear the word and do it are members of Jesus' family (8.21). Mary hears the word but is not portrayed as doing it. The active διακονία is associated with Martha. Martha is also the one who takes the initiative, first by welcoming Jesus and then with her words of request. The one who takes the initiative with her words is the one who is reprimanded by Jesus. Hence, the first words of a woman to be recorded in the ministry of Jesus are corrected by him: 'Mary, who receives positive approval, is the *silent* woman, whereas Martha, who argues in her own interest, is *silenced*.'[103] While Martha has the first word in the pericope, it is Jesus who has the last and authoritative word.[104]

A further attempt at reading the pericope in an affirming light presumes an implicit call of Mary to action. Carter assumes that Jesus' commendation of Mary incorporates the requirement that she not just listen to the word but also do it (cf. 8.14; 11.28). For Carter, then, the pericope warns against being distracted from the source of one's ministry and also warns about being absorbed with listening to the teaching without passing it on. Both actions threaten partnership in leadership. As such, he sees the pericope as affirming the ministry and leadership of Martha and Mary rather than rendering them silent.[105] That no reference to Mary's 'doing' of the word is provided in the pericope would seem to challenge Carter's views, however.

Martha is often perceived in a poor light.[106] The narrative portrays Mary's response to Jesus as superior to that of Martha. The words of Jesus make this abundantly clear. The narrative reinforces the impression that the woman who took the initiative in her words and actions should follow the example of the one who listens attentively to Jesus but does not otherwise act or speak. Thus the two Lukan women are set against each other.[107] The story develops in such a way that one woman will be affirmed and one will be reproved.[108] Nonetheless,

---

103.   Schüssler Fiorenza, *But She Said*, 62.

104.   Pamela Thimmes, 'The Language of Community: A Cautionary Tale (Luke 10.38–42),' in *A Feminist Companion to Luke*, (eds.) Amy-Jill Levine and Marianne Blickenstaff (London: Sheffield Academic Press, 2002), 238.

105.   Carter, 'Martha,' 229–31.

106.   While Johnson, for example, describes the two sisters as showing hospitality to Jesus and together representing the proper response to the prophet, he adds that Martha's 'self-preoccupation and resentment led her to break the rules of hospitality.' Johnson, *Luke*, 175.

107.   Against this view, see Rebera, 'Polarity or Partnership?,' 102–3.

108.   While Martha and Mary are set against each other in the Lukan Gospel, their characterization in the Johannine Gospel is very different. Satoko Yamaguchi describes the characters of Martha and Mary in the Johannine Gospel as engaging in collaborative co-ministries, not pitted against each other. See Yamaguchi, *Mary and Martha*, 140.

Mary, the one affirmed, does not hear the word and do it (cf. 8.21), she only hears it.

The recognition that Mary's listening does not lead to further action illuminates rhetorical strategies. As Schüssler Fiorenza argues, the pericope diminishes the leadership role of women, encouraging women to listen but not preach. While Mary is portrayed as a disciple of Jesus, she is not a minister of the word. This supports the Lukan rhetorical strategy of including women as members of the Christian communities but curtailing their apostolic leadership and silencing women leaders.[109] For Schüssler Fiorenza, 'it is not the *Kyrios* but the writer of Luke 10.38–40 who promotes such patriarchal restrictions.'[110] Yet the κύριος is the character with the authority in this Lukan pericope,[111] and it is the words of the κύριος which determine how the sisters' responses are evaluated. Hence, the restrictions are promoted by the κύριος as characterized in the Lukan narrative.

Critiquing Schüssler Fiorenza's views, Karris claims that the Martha and Mary story should be placed within the context of the Lukan theme of meals. He notes that many of Jesus' table partners – men, women, disciples and Pharisees – are criticized by Jesus: 'Martha takes her place in the same line as others in Luke's gospel who might complain that they have gotten a "raw deal" from Jesus.'[112] Karris, however, fails to place the story also within the context of Lukan characterization of women's speech. As we will see, rebuke of women's direct speech occurs in several places within the Lukan Gospel. The affirmation of the silent woman and the correction of the woman who speaks in this pericope continues this rhetoric regarding women's speech.

7. *A Woman in the Crowd*

As discussed in the previous chapter, Mary the mother of Jesus is metonymically referred to by an unnamed woman in the crowd: 'Blessed is the womb that bore you and the breasts that nursed you!' (11.27). Jesus' response to the woman highlights Mary's blessedness because she hears and keeps the word of God (11.28). This interaction follows Jesus' exorcism of a demon from a mute man, enabling the man to speak (11.14), and a discourse by Jesus on the demonic (11.17-26). The beginning of 11.27 intimates that the words of the woman form an interruption to those

109. Schüssler Fiorenza, *But She Said*, 65–68; and Schüssler Fiorenza, 'Martha and Mary,' 30–31.

110. Schüssler Fiorenza, *But She Said*, 68.

111. This is demonstrated by the way Martha asks Jesus to speak to Mary rather than speaking to Mary herself (10.40).

112. Karris, 'Women and Discipleship,' 4.

of Jesus, but the woman's speech is also a response to the healing power of Jesus.[113] Though the woman's words have been described as a blessing of Jesus rather than of Mary since it is the son who makes the mother honorable,[114] the woman's blessing does also flow on to the mother.

Scholars provide varying understandings of the nature of Jesus' response to the woman. Fitzmyer explains that the Greek particle μενοῦν can have three senses – adversative ('on the contrary'), affirmative ('indeed') and corrective ('yes, but rather') and he argues that Lukan stylistic tendencies make the corrective sense the preferred sense in 11.28.[115] This sense of μενοῦν suggests that Jesus' words do not deny the blessedness of his mother, but they add further qualification to the category of blessedness. For Marshall, however, μενοῦν indicates that Jesus emphatically corrects the woman ('nay, rather'),[116] while Arlandson states that Jesus contradicts the woman and describes Jesus' words to her as a rebuke.[117] Certainly, Jesus' words cannot be read here as affirmation of the woman's words. Moreover, it is difficult to read Jesus' words without recognizing an element of censure. In contrast, when a man speaks a beatitude to Jesus, his words are not corrected (14.15-24).[118]

Considering the implications of the woman's words triggers further insight into the dynamics of the pericope. Craig and Kristjansson helpfully explore the approaches of the woman and Jesus. They argue that '[t]he woman and the elements of her speech are in opposition to Jesus and the elements of his speech.'[119] For Jesus, blessing comes from hearing and keeping the word of God, whereas for the woman, blessing comes from the 'bodily realities of life.'[120] In the Gospel of Luke, Jesus is identified as the agent of the divine visitation. As such, Jesus is portrayed as the one with authority and his words and actions influence how the reader perceives the words and actions of others.

The rhetoric of the narrative at this point needs closer investigation. Craig and Kristjansson believe the puzzle of Jesus' apparent negative response to the woman's comment is understandable in terms of the patriarchal ideology which the text exhibits: 'The woman speaks a truth about the importance of the body (incarnation) and the female which patriarchy cannot admit as truth. Thus her speech is presented as both irrelevant and wrong.'[121] Metaphorically, she has her 'pound' taken away.

113. Craig and Kristjansson, 'Women Reading as Men,' 124.
114. Seim, *Double Message*, 114.
115. Fitzmyer, *Luke*, 2.928–29.
116. Marshall, *Luke*, 482.
117. Arlandson, *Women, Class, and Society*, 123.
118. D'Angelo, '(Re)Presentations of Women,' 187.
119. Craig and Kristjansson, 'Women Reading as Men,' 125.
120. Craig and Kristjansson, 'Women Reading as Men,' 126.
121. Craig and Kristjansson, 'Women Reading as Men,' 126.

Because of her 'distinctly female speech,' the woman dooms herself to 'silence and invisibility within that universe.'[122] Ironically in Luke 11, after Jesus heals a mute man so that he is enabled to speak, a woman who takes the initiative to speak (and perhaps even interrupt) is effectively silenced by the Lukan Jesus in a pericope which is unique to the Lukan Gospel.

8. The Woman With a Spirit of Infirmity

The healing of a woman who is bent over (13.10-17) and the healing of a man with dropsy (14.1-6) are often described as another example of a Lukan male–female pair, with the story of a woman paralleled with the story of a man.[123] Both healings take place on a Sabbath (13.10; 14.1) and in both Jesus takes the initiative to heal (13.12; 14.4). Further, both include a reference to the treatment of an ox on the Sabbath (13.15; 14.5). The healed woman has a more significant role, however, than the healed man. The healing of the woman is the longer pericope and more detail is given in the characterization of the woman, her healing by Jesus, her response and the opposition to Jesus' action. The story is unique to the Lukan Gospel.

The setting for the story is a synagogue on a Sabbath day (13.10). The woman is unnamed and is presented as having had a spirit of infirmity (πνεῦμα ἔχουσα ἀσθενείας) for eighteen years. As a result, the woman is bent over and unable to stand erect (13.11). Since Jesus describes the woman's situation as being bound by Satan (13.16), the infirmity is portrayed as being caused by demonic possession.[124] This characterization continues the Lukan tendency to associate women with evil spirits (cf. 4.38-39; 8.2-3). Unlike the woman, the man with dropsy (14.1-6) is not characterized as possessing a malevolent spirit or demon. Thus the parallel between the characters does not extend to demonic possession.

Like the man with dropsy (14.1-6), the woman makes no request and takes no initiative in the healing. It is Jesus' actions and initiative which are highlighted. He sees her, calls out to her, tells her that she is set free from her infirmity and lays his hands on her (13.12-13). Immediately the woman is restored and she glorifies God. The passive form of ἀνωρθώθη has the sense of a theological passive, indicating that God has acted.[125] This explains the woman's response, and the imperfect tense of ἐδόξαζεν

---

122. Craig and Kristjansson, 'Women Reading as Men,' 133.

123. See, for example, Seim, *Double Message*, 16–17; and Tannehill, *Narrative Unity*, 135.

124. Johnson, *Luke*, 212; also Marshall, *Luke*, 557.

125. See Fitzmyer, *Luke*, 2.1013; also Schüssler Fiorenza, *But She Said*, 199.

indicates the ongoing nature of her action (13.14). Her action and words are in response to the initiative of Jesus.

In two other Lukan healings on a Sabbath, the men healed remain silent and make no response to Jesus' action (6.6-11; 14.1-6). That the woman glorifies God, therefore, gives her a response which is not accredited to these two men.[126] Schüssler Fiorenza describes the woman in the healing as moving 'from margin to center, from invisibility to presence, from silence to the praise of G-d.'[127] At the same time, however, that she is not accorded direct speech reduces the impact of her response on the reader.

The verb δοξάζω is used nine times in the Lukan Gospel and in eight of these it is associated with θεός, so that the action is a glorifying of God.[128] As Doble points out, the verb in relation to God is used to describe the response of those who have recognized God's action in the activity of Jesus.[129] On three of these occasions, the direct speech of those glorifying God is recorded by the narrator (5.26; 7.16; 23.47). On three more of these occasions, the direct words of glorification are not given but those who glorify God are given direct speech elsewhere in the pericope (2.20; 17.15; 18.43). Along with the paralytic (5.25), the woman healed of a spirit of infirmity glorifies God (13.13) but the narrator does not present any words of glorification, nor does she speak elsewhere in the pericope.

Thus, on six out of seven other occasions those who are portrayed as glorifying God are given direct speech at some point in the narrative. One might expect then that the healed woman would have been given direct speech but the narrator does not meet these expectations. Regarding the response of the centurion witnessing Jesus' death (23.47), Doble comments: 'Luke's use of ἐδόξαζεν τὸν θεόν at this point strongly suggests that his readers should, consequently, take seriously what his centurion said.'[130] Despite the same phrase being used to describe the healed woman's response in 13.13, however, the reader cannot focus on her words because they are not provided. Her influence, her 'pound,' is compromised.

After the healing, the focus of the narrative moves to the conflict caused by Jesus healing on the Sabbath. The direct speech of the leader of the synagogue and Jesus are recorded, with Jesus again being given the title

126. See Dewey, 'Jesus' Healings,' 124–25.
127. Schüssler Fiorenza, *But She Said*, 199. Schüssler Fiorenza notes, however, that in the ensuing controversy the woman does not have a subject-position in the text. By combining the Sabbath controversy with the healing story, the text moves from 'a woman-focused to a male-centered sacred text' (p. 208). The term 'G-d' is used by Schüssler Fiorenza to indicate that God is ineffable (p. 220, n. 10).
128. These eight occurrences are in 2.20; 5.25, 26; 7.16; 13.13; 17.15; 18.43; 23.47. The other occurrence of δοξάζω is in 4.15 when it is Jesus who is praised.
129. Doble, *Paradox of Salvation*, 46.
130. Doble, *Paradox of Salvation*, 68.

κύριος by the narrator (13.14-16).[131] The woman is not spoken to again by Jesus but she is the subject of his speech. Jesus describes her as one who had been bound by Satan for eighteen years and names her a daughter of Abraham, affirming her place in the faith community (cf. 8.48; 19.9). Jesus' question (13.16) identifies the healing as a setting free from bondage, in line with Jesus' pronouncement in 4.18-19.[132]

The portrayal of the woman in this story has similar elements to the portrayal of some of the other Lukan women whom we have already met in Jesus' ministry. She is associated with a malevolent spirit (cf. 4.39; 8.2-3). She does not request healing nor take any initiative which leads to the healing (cf. 4.38; 7.12-14). She immediately responds in deed or word to the action of Jesus (cf. 4.39; 8.55) but her words are not recorded by the narrator (cf. 8.47). She is the object of men's conversation but she does not contribute to that conversation (cf. 7.44-47). Jesus names her a daughter of Abraham, just as he gives the woman healed from a hemorrhage the title of 'daughter' (cf. 8.48). Since it is implied that the woman speaks but her voice is not heard by the reader, the narrative effect is that the woman is rendered 'visible in the narrative, but in a suitably restricted role.'[133]

9. *The Widow With Two Coins*

Following the Gospel of Mark, the Lukan narrative includes a story of a woman contributing to the treasury (21.1-4; cf. Mk 12.41-44). The woman is unnamed and is introduced as a poor widow. Thus, she is identified in terms of her marital and economic status. She does not speak in the pericope but she does act to throw her two coins into the treasury coffers (21.2). The widow does not draw attention to herself, but Jesus draws the attention to her by stating that she has given more than the rich people because she has put in πάντα τὸν βίον ὅν εἶχεν (21.3-4).

While some suggest that Jesus highlights the woman's action to exemplify the righteous poor,[134] the context can also suggest another dimension. The story follows on from Jesus' denouncement of the scribes (20.45-47). One of Jesus' criticisms is that the scribes devour widows' houses (20.47). Encouraging the widow to donate her all can be seen as a way in which the scribes devour her house or livelihood: 'Jesus' comment

---

131. Schüssler Fiorenza argues that the conflict between the synagogue leader and Jesus encourages an anti-Jewish sentiment. See Schüssler Fiorenza, *But She Said*, 207–10.

132. See Seim, *Double Message*, 42.

133. Dewey, 'Jesus' Healings,' 125.

134. See Johnson, *Luke*, 316. Seim, too, writes of the exemplary actions of the widow. Seim, *Double Message*, 245–46.

contains words of lament, not of praise.'[135] Given that the passion narrative begins in the following chapter, Reid claims that the context encourages a reading in which the widow contributes her whole life, as will Jesus in that passion narrative.[136] It would seem, then, that the text can support a range of interpretations.

While the Lukan characterization of the widow is based on the corresponding Markan characterization, it also parallels the depiction of two women unique to the Lukan Gospel. Like the nameless woman who anoints Jesus and the nameless woman who is bent over, the nameless widow is the subject of Jesus' conversation but her voice is not part of that conversation (cf. 7.44-47; 13.15-16).

10. *A Slave-Woman*

After the arrest of Jesus, an unnamed slave-woman (παιδίσκη) is involved in the scene of Peter's denial of Jesus (22.54-62). As in the parallel Markan version, the woman sees Peter and stares at him before speaking (22.56; cf. Mk 14.66-69),[137] but the woman's narrative role is more limited in the Lukan version. She is given direct speech in 22.56 – 'This man [οὗτος] also was with him' – identifying Peter as a follower of Jesus, but she is met with a denial by Peter – 'Woman [γύναι], I do not know him' (22.57). This slave-woman is one of three people who individually identify Peter as a follower of Jesus, only to have him deny it (22.54-60). The use of the vocative in the words to the woman is significant: 'Peter addresses the woman as γύναι, an unusual form of address for a slave, but probably her slave status is not at issue here.'[138] Rather, the use of γύναι draws the focus onto gender.[139] Despite Peter's denials, it is clear from the narrative that the slave-woman's words (and the words of the other two who identify Peter) are correct, and that it is Peter who is lying (22.61-62). Peter has an important and ongoing speaking role in Luke-Acts, however, while none of Peter's three challengers speaks again after the denials.

The preceding narrative enables the slave-woman to be linked with Satan's designs. In 22.1-6, '*Satan*-inspired Judas Iscariot' plots with religious leaders to destroy Jesus. Further, prior to his arrest, Jesus

---

135. Fitzmyer, *Luke*, 2.1321. Instead, Reid argues that it is not clear from the text as to whether Jesus' words reflect praise or lament and ultimately sees it as open-ended. See Reid, *Choosing the Better Part?*, 196–97.

136. Reid, *Choosing the Better Part?*, 195–96.

137. Different verbs (ἐμβλέπω and ἀτενίζω) are used in the two versions to indicate staring.

138. Osiek, 'Female Slaves,' 267.

139. Only in the Lukan account does Peter use the term γύναι to address the slave-woman here.

predicts that Satan will test Peter (and the other apostles) and that Peter will deny Jesus three times (22.31-34):[140] 'Against this backdrop, the slave-girl emerges as the *agent of Satan* intent on undermining Peter's faith and discipleship.'[141] Such an insight continues the portrayal of Lukan women as linked to demonic forces. Moreover, this link between the woman and Satan is not made in the other Synoptic narratives. The rhetoric regarding women's speech continues in this pericope. The slave-woman speaks in a public setting but her voice is not affirmed.[142] Rather, the woman who correctly identifies a disciple of Jesus is aligned with Satan, and thus vilified, 'losing her pound.'

11. *The Daughters of Jerusalem*

Like the woman with a hemorrhage (8.48) and the woman who is bent over (13.16), the women who lament for Jesus as he is led away to his crucifixion are identified by Jesus as 'daughters' – in this case, 'daughters of Jerusalem' (23.28).[143] The women are included among the great number of people who follow Jesus to his crucifixion and are presented as 'beating their breasts and wailing for him' (23.27). The particle δέ in 23.28 contrasts Jesus' words with the women's actions. He tells them not to weep for him, but for themselves and for their children. His further words to the women speak of the days to come when the barren will be declared blessed (23.29). While barrenness normally brought disgrace (cf. Elizabeth in 1.25) Jesus warns that in the days ahead to be childless will be considered a blessing (cf. 21.23). While the women lament for Jesus, he laments for Jerusalem (cf. 13.34; 19.41-44). Jesus thus draws attention to the suffering which the women and their children will experience.

The title 'daughters of Jerusalem' distinguishes these women from the women from Galilee who have been introduced in 8.2-3 and will feature in the narrative of the death, burial and resurrection of Jesus. The distinction causes some to interpret the women of Jerusalem as professional mourners rather than disciples.[144] Yet the women as part

140. F. Scott Spencer, 'Out of Mind, Out of Voice: Slave-girls and Prophetic Daughters in Luke-Acts,' *BibInt* 7 (1999): 141.

141. Spencer, 'Out of Mind,' 141.

142. For a discussion of the private or public nature of the scene, see Spencer, 'Out of Mind,' 140.

143. For a discussion of women's role in lamentation and mourning, see Corley, *Women and the Historical Jesus*, 108–18. See also Osiek, 'Women at the Tomb,' 103; and Ilan, *Jewish Women*, 189–90.

144. Marshall describes them as local women who turn out to witness executions. See Marshall, *Luke*, 864. Fitzmyer understands them as in the character of professional mourners and not necessarily disciples. See Fitzmyer, *Luke*, 2.1495-97.

of the crowd have followed Jesus and the verb ἀκολουθέω has
connotations of discipleship (23.27; cf. 5.11, 27, 28; 9.23, 57, 59, 61;
18.22, 28, 43).[145] Seim observes that the third person plural rather than
second person gives a more general scope to Jesus' words to the women in
23.31. She rightly argues that the 'women are to be understood as *victims*
of the catastrophe and not its cause, either concretely or symbolically.'[146]
There is no reason to view this characterization of the daughters of
Jerusalem negatively.

Jesus' words to the women (23.29) are a negative version of the words
of the woman in the crowd (11.27). As in that case, Jesus here corrects the
women. Whereas the woman in the crowd is silenced by Jesus' words to
her, however, these women are not told to stop their weeping. Rather,
Jesus' words to them suggest they should continue their weeping, but not
on his account. The correction therefore shifts the focus of their tears but
does not serve to silence the women. Thus, Jesus' words to the women
here have a different effect on the women's voices from his words to the
woman in 11.28 and another mourning woman, the widow of Nain, who
is told not to weep (7.13). In 23.28-31, Jesus first draws attention to the
women's tears then directs the 'daughters of Jerusalem' to continue their
mourning but to lament for themselves not for him. Jesus encourages
them to continue in a role of mourning, traditionally associated with
women. Their role is not challenged, just the focus of their tears. While
Jesus shows compassion to the women here, the pattern of Jesus
correcting women's voices nonetheless continues.

12. *The Women from Galilee*

The women introduced in 8.2-3 as traveling with Jesus are featured again
in 23.49 at the death of Jesus and become central characters in the ensuing
narrative. In the Markan Gospel, the women watch the crucifixion from a
distance, the male disciples having earlier betrayed, denied and aban-
doned Jesus (Mk 15.40-41). In the Lukan version, *all* Jesus' acquaint-
ances, 'including the women who had followed him from Galilee,' watch
the crucifixion (23.49). Hence, the male disciples in the Lukan narrative
are presented more sympathetically than in the Markan version and the
Lukan women are no longer the unique witnesses among the disciples,
decreasing their profile at this critical stage.[147] The Lukan narrator

---

145. Johnson, *Luke*, 374.
146. Seim, *Double Message*, 207. See also Johnson, *Luke*, 374.
147. See, for instance, Brock, *Mary Magdalene*, 33; and Lawson, 'Gender and Genre,'
156–57.

downplays the failure of the male disciples and raises their status to the detriment of the status of the women witnesses.[148]

While the women *and* men disciples are portrayed as watching on, the use of the feminine plural participle ὁρῶσαι (23.49) suggests that the male witnesses are a Lukan insertion.[149] These same women, specifically the women who had come with him from Galilee, witness Jesus' body being laid in the tomb and prepare spices and ointments for the body. The preparations for anointing the body give the women a more active role than at the corresponding point in the Markan narrative.[150] We are also told they uphold the Sabbath rest (23.55-56), in accord with the Torah.

When the same women return to the tomb on the first day of the week to anoint the body they become the first witnesses to the empty tomb (24.1-2). They are informed by two men in dazzling clothes that Jesus is not there but has been raised (ἠγέρθη, 24.4-5).[151] The passive form of the verb suggests the divine passive, that it is God who has raised Jesus.[152] The repeated description that the women have followed from Galilee (23.49, 55) gives the background for the next words spoken to the women. They are told to remember what Jesus had said to them in Galilee about his death and resurrection (24.6-7).

The instruction to the women to remember raises the question of when Jesus said these words. Maria-Luisa Rigato observes that the wording of the two men at the tomb corresponds most closely with the wording of the passion predictions which Jesus makes to the twelve in 18.31-34 and to the disciples in 9.22. She claims further that the women belong to the groups which heard both of these predictions, despite not being described as present for the prediction of 18.31-34.[153] Rigato accounts for their lack of mention here by referring to the social situation of the first century, but asserts that after the resurrection a different picture is presented in the Lukan Gospel: '*Before* the resurrection, the women did not count; this was due to the mindset of the time … *After* the resurrection, the women belong with those who count, namely, the men, and form but a single group with them.'[154] Despite Rigato's statement that the women are included in 'those who count,' we will see below that their words are not

---

148. Seim, *Double Message*, 20, claims that the addition of other witnesses does not diminish the women's role but rather expresses gender complementarity. This argument does not adequately address, however, the reduction of the women's role which results in their not being the unique witnesses.

149. Schaberg, 'Luke,' 378.

150. Seim, *Double Message*, 149.

151. 'He is not here but has been raised' is not in some manuscripts (including D) but is strongly attested, being included in P[75] ℵ A B among others.

152. Fitzmyer, *Luke*, 2.1545.

153. Rigato, 'Remember,' 99–101.

154. Rigato, 'Remember,' 102.

believed nor do they explicitly bear witness in Acts. This suggests that distinctions are made within the 'single group.' Nevertheless, the instruction to remember does indicate the inclusion of the women in Jesus' ministry.

The women remember as instructed and tell the news 'to the eleven and to all the rest' (24.8-9). That the women remember suggests that the women have come to understanding and faith in the resurrection event.[155] Both 'their discipleship and the instruction they have received as disciples' are confirmed.[156] They have heard the word and kept it (cf. 8.15; 11.28). Each of the other canonical Gospel narratives includes a commission to the women to tell the disciples that Jesus is risen (cf. Mk 16.7; Mt. 28.7; Jn 20.17-18). Only in the Lukan version are the women given no such commission. They are told to remember but they are not told to do anything with their remembrance. Thus, the women's pronouncements 'to the eleven and to all the rest' (24.9) result from their own initiative. The narrator does not give us the direct speech of the women. We know only that the women proclaimed all these things.[157]

In Luke 24, the women are clearly portrayed as included among the disciples, a group wider than the twelve, or eleven at this stage (see 24.9, 13, 22), suggesting that the women are also included in the group of disciples who receive a resurrection appearance and are commissioned (24.36-49).[158] Bauckham dismisses the effect of the lack of a resurrection appearance to the women who go to the tomb and lack of a commission to the women, claiming that the women are included in the wider group 'without having to single them out for special attention.'[159] Thus, he disregards the significance which accrues to the women characters by being singled out for particular focus (cf. Mt. 28.1-10; Mk 16.6-7; Jn 20.11-18).

Also arguing that women as well as men received Jesus' commission as witnesses (24.48), Karris queries whether Jewish women could testify in

155. Johnson, *Luke*, 391; and Karris, 'Women and Discipleship,' 14–15. Both Tannehill and Evans, though, claim that it is not clear whether the women have immediately come to faith at this point. See Tannehill, *Narrative Unity*, 139; and Evans, *Saint Luke*, 898.

156. Seim, *Double Message*, 151.

157. Seim argues that telling all emphasizes the integrity of the women's testimony which is also later demonstrated to be reliable in the Emmaus story (24.22-24). See Seim, 'The Gospel of Luke,' 750.

158. For detailed discussion, see Bauckham, *Gospel Women*, 281–83; and Lawson, 'Gender and Genre,' 139–40. Quentin Quesnell, 'The Women at Luke's Supper,' in *Political Issues in Luke-Acts*, (eds.) Richard J. Cassidy and Philip J. Scharper (Maryknoll, NY: Orbis, 1983), 59–79, extends the inclusion of women among the disciples by arguing that women are present at the last supper in the Gospel of Luke. For a counter-argument to Quesnell's views, see Corley, *Private Women*, 115.

159. Bauckham, *Gospel Women*, 281.

the public sphere.[160] He concludes, 'whereas the women of Lk. 24 might not be able to testify in the public forum as Luke depicts Peter doing in Acts 2, they surely could do so in other non-public, extradomestic contexts.'[161] Hence, Karris is aware of the different portrayals of public speech of men and women in Luke-Acts, but reinscribes the proscription of women speaking in the public sphere.

The names of three of the women are given at this stage of the narration. We learn that 'Mary Magdalene, Joanna, Mary the mother of James, and the other women with them' announce this to the apostles (24.10). Mary Magdalene and Joanna were named in 8.2-3 while Mary the mother of James is named at this point for the first time in the Lukan narrative. Her name is given as well as her relationship to a male figure. She is one of the women who have followed Jesus from Galilee (23.49, 55) but has not been identified previously. The naming of Mary Magdalene and Joanna ensures the continuity between the group of women followers introduced in 8.2-3 and the women who come to the tomb and proclaim the news to the apostles.

In 24.9 the audience to the women's pronouncement is identified as the eleven and all the rest, but in 24.10 we are told that the women said these things to the apostles. The imperfect form of ἔλεγον suggests that the women repeatedly related these things.[162] The term 'apostles' refers to the twelve (6.13), now eleven without Judas. Thus the focus is drawn away from the rest and on to the eleven male disciples by the use of this term and the plural pronoun αὐτῶν in 24.11 refers to the eleven. As Lawson identifies, the focus on the eleven here points to the importance which the eleven/twelve will have in Acts:

> In this perspective, the shift of narratorial focus in Lk 24:9 from the broader group of disciples to the male leaders in Lk 24:10 is paradigmatic of the more decisive focal shift that takes place between the end of the Gospel, where others are more explicitly linked with the eleven, and the beginning of Acts, where others are defocussed in order to highlight the decisive role of the twelve in the creation of the new Israel.[163]

The eleven consider the women's words idle talk, nonsense (λῆρος) and they do not believe them. This is the only use of λῆρος in the New Testament.[164] 'The term *lēros* ('nonsense') could scarcely be more condescending. It forms the basis for the English word "delirious."

160. Karris, 'Women and Discipleship,' 17–19.
161. Karris, 'Women and Discipleship,' 19. See also Bauckham, *Gospel Women*, 303.
162. See Marshall, *Luke*, 888.
163. Lawson, 'Gender and Genre,' 139.
164. Brock, *Mary Magdalene*, 35.

There is a definite air of male superiority in this response.'[165] Moreover, that others see the empty tomb (24.12, 24) suggests that the women do not need to be believed 'since what they have to relate is not unique.'[166]

D'Angelo writes that the disbelief of the women's words by the disciples in 24.11 does not seek to disparage the women since the reader knows the women are right, 'but rather defends the community from the charge of easy credulity' or answers the charge 'that Christians believed the resurrection on the word of a few hysterical women.'[167] Even if this is the case, however, it does not explain why the women's ongoing characterizations should be affected. The women who are disbelieved do not witness to the resurrection in the story of the early Church, despite being the first to hear and proclaim the good news.

For Goulder, 'Luke comes from a world of male chauvinists.'[168] This does not adequately account, though, for Goulder's interpretation of this pericope which reinforces a caricature of the women: 'Being women, the receivers of this message do not presume to rise to faith before the apostles, but limit themselves to remembering his "sayings" (a Lucanism), and scuttling off to the Eleven.'[169] Moreover, in describing the reaction of the eleven to the women's words (20.11), Goulder writes: 'Such is to be the pattern throughout the Resurrection story, disbelief turning reluctantly to conviction; for only so can the hearer be reassured that his vital witnesses are hard-headed and trustworthy men, and not credulous simpletons.'[170] Such interpretations or charges reinforce the rhetoric that a woman's witness is unreliable, resulting from hysteria, and that trustworthy men do not believe women's words. Furthermore, the connotation that 'vital witnesses' are men overlooks the women's witness. Thus interpreters can contribute to the marginalization of the women's witness.

Peter is described as running to the tomb, seeing the linen cloths and being amazed, though it is not clear what he understands at this point (24.12, cf. Jn 20.3-10).[171] The narrative of the appearance of Jesus to two disciples on the road to Emmaus relates that some went to the tomb and confirmed what the women had said about it (24.24).[172] Jesus describes

165.   Johnson, *Luke*, 388.

166.   de Boer, 'Lukan Mary Magdalene,' 155.

167.   D'Angelo, 'ANHP Question,' 51–52.

168.   Goulder, *Luke*, 2.775.

169.   Goulder, *Luke*, 2.775.

170.   Goulder, *Luke*, 2.776.

171.   Fitzmyer claims that Peter is not yet believing at this point. Fitzmyer, *Luke*, 2.1543; also Johnson, *Luke*, 391. While 24.12 is strongly attested (P^{75} ℵ A B W), it is omitted in some texts, including D.

172.   The second disciple is unnamed and does not act individually. While it is possible that the other disciple with Cleopas on the way to Emmaus is female, the text does not allow for identification. A Mary is linked with Clopas, however, in the Johannine Gospel – Μαρία

the two disciples as 'foolish' and 'slow of heart to believe all that the prophets have declared' (24.25), but does not explicitly comment on their foolishness and slowness of heart for disbelieving the women. When they return to Jerusalem, they find the eleven and those with them saying: 'The Lord has risen indeed, and he has appeared to Simon!' (24.34). Thus, Simon Peter is described as the first to receive a resurrection appearance.[173] Male witness, rather than the words of the women, confirms the resurrection. Fitzmyer states that the women's testimony 'does not engender faith; it does not give "assurance." '[174] Such an interpretation suggests that there is something lacking in the women's testimony although this is not warranted by the text.

The women are faithful witnesses and the reader knows that their words are true. By implication, it is the eleven and not the women who are in error. This leads some to detect irony in the pericope since the women are perceived as faithful while the apostles are ignorant.[175] The reader has the information to critique the response of the eleven despite the narrator not providing an explicit critique. In the added verses to the Markan Gospel, Jesus upbraids the eleven for not believing the witness of Mary Magdalene and others (Mk 16.9-14) but no such explicit critique is provided in the Lukan account. Elsewhere in the Lukan Gospel, Zechariah disbelieves the angel but he is subsequently silenced by the angel and comes to recognize his lack of faith (1.8-23, 59-79); Peter is skeptical of Jesus' instruction to make a catch but later acknowledges his inadequacy (5.4-9). In the case of the women witnesses, however, the eleven make no such acknowledgment of inadequacy.

Within the Lukan resurrection narrative, women do not receive the first resurrection appearance. Neither are they commissioned to act as witnesses to the resurrection. When they use their own initiative to proclaim the resurrection, they are disbelieved and their words are dismissed as idle talk by the eleven. When they take the initiative to speak to the male apostles, they are effectively silenced.

Despite the later implicit vindication of the women's words, these women do not speak again in the Gospel, except perhaps as part of a group that includes men (24.33-34). The distinct women's voice is lost. While women are included in the upper room with the eleven in Acts 1.14, the only named woman is Mary, the mother of Jesus. None of the women

---

ἡ τοῦ Κλωπᾶ (Jn 19.25) – suggesting the possibility that the pair are known in a common tradition. (Quesnell, 'Women at Luke's Supper,' 68, wonders whether the two disciples on the way to Emmaus are Cleopas and his wife.)

173. In contrast, Mary Magdalene is among those who are the first to see the risen Jesus in Mt. 28.9-10 and Jn 20.11-18, as well as the addition to the Markan Gospel, Mk 16.9-11.

174. Fitzmyer, *Luke*, 2.1543.

175. See, for instance, Arlandson, *Women, Class, and Society*, 166–67; and Dornisch, *A Woman Reads*, 224.

from Galilee who have been identified in the Lukan Gospel as following Jesus is named in Acts and none of them is accorded direct speech. Thus, the disregard of the women's resurrection words by the apostles effectively silences their voices in the ongoing story of the early Church.[176] It is the witness of Simon Peter that confirms the resurrection and his witness is not doubted (24.34). As in the case of the naming of John the Baptist (1.59-66), it is the male voice that has authority. Peter becomes the major character in Acts 1–12. Since the women have followed Jesus from Galilee they are included among his witnesses to the people, according to Acts 13.31.[177] Yet no woman is explicitly portrayed as witnessing (μαρτυρέω) in Acts.[178]

While Bauckham acknowledges that there is a change of focus between the end of the Lukan Gospel and the beginning of Acts,[179] he does not analyze its effect. In Luke 24.48, it is likely that women are included in the group which the risen Jesus addresses with the words: 'You are witnesses of these things.' In Acts 1.2-3, however, it is the apostles who are highlighted. That the words of the risen Jesus – 'you will be my witnesses in Jerusalem, in all Judea and Samaria, and to the ends of the earth' (Acts 1.8) – are addressed to men is indicated by the title given to them in Acts 1.11 –῎Ανδρες Γαλιλαῖοι. The women of Luke 24 are explicitly excluded from this commission.[180] That the Lukan narrative includes women as disciples but does not portray them as witnessing to the resurrection may be considered an example of the sophisticated strategies for silencing described in the opening chapter, which 'assign women to silence while simultaneously placing them at the very heart of [the] domain.'[181] The inclusion of women as disciples does not necessarily grant them agency and subjectivity. The women's witness is marginalized and, using the categories of Iris Marion Young outlined in the introductory chapter, it can be said that the women are subjected to a form of oppression. They 'lose their pound.'

13. *Women in Parables*

Thus far, we have been exploring the portrayals of women characters within the Lukan Gospel narrative. The women who appear in Jesus'

176. Bauckham, *Gospel Women*, 190, states that 'women are prominent in Acts, though to a lesser extent' than in the Lukan Gospel. Given that only three women are accorded direct speech in the entire narrative of Acts, this claim is difficult to justify.
177. Osiek, 'Women at the Tomb,' 100; and Rigato, 'Remember,' 102.
178. See the discussion in Reid, *Choosing the Better Part?*, 34–35.
179. Bauckham, *Gospel Women*, 283.
180. Lawson, 'Gender and Genre,' 141.
181. Walker, *Reading Silence*, 2.

parables and teachings, however, are yet to be considered. These women can be considered characters in a story within a story since they are not Gospel characters in their own right but appear only in the words of Jesus. Are the portrayals of these women similar to those of the women characters in the Lukan Gospel? There are several references to women in Jesus' parables and teachings where the woman is not a Gospel character in her own right: the widow at Zarephath (4.26); the queen of the south (11.31); female slaves (12.45); mother, daughter, mother-in-law and daughter-in-law (12.53); the woman working with yeast (13.21); the wife of an invited dinner guest (a woman in a story within a story within a story – 14.20); mother, wife and sisters (14.26); the woman with ten coins. her female friends and neighbors (15.8-10); prostitutes (again, women in a story within a story within a story – 15.30); a wife and divorced woman (16.18); two women grinding together (17.35); a widow seeking justice (18.3-5); a mother (18.20); a wife (18.29); widows (20.47); and those pregnant and nursing infants (21.23).

Many of these references to women are merely passing allusions. Few are accorded action or speech by the words of Jesus. Nevertheless, there are some exceptions to this general rule. The queen of the south (11.31), the woman working with yeast (13.21), the woman with ten coins (15.8-10), the two women grinding (17.35) and the widow who seeks justice (18.3-5) are all the subjects of actions. Further, it is implied that the queen of the south speaks though her words are not recorded (11.31), and both the woman with ten coins and the widow seeking justice are accorded direct speech (15.9; 18.3). Of the women that come to life in Jesus' words. these latter two women will be addressed in more detail. Both are characters in parables of Jesus. Both are the subject of several actions and both have their voice heard in Jesus' words.

a. *The Woman With Ten Coins*

The Parable of the Woman with Ten Coins is one of three parables in Luke 15 told in response to the grumbling of the Pharisees concerning Jesus' inclusive table-fellowship (15.1-2). By eating with sinners, Jesus embodies God's welcome to all who are 'lost' according to the law. The three parables continue this theme. Each is concerned with the condition of being lost and describes the seeking out of the lost and the joy when that which is lost is found. The first parable concerns a shepherd and a lost sheep (15.3-7); the second, a woman and a lost coin (15.8-10); and the third, a father and two lost sons (15.11-32).[182] The Parable of the Woman with Ten Coins is the shortest of the three and is framed by the other two

---

182. A version of the parable of the lost sheep is also found in Mt. 18.12-14. The other two parables are unique to the Lukan Gospel.

which have male protagonists. In particular, the parable describing the
woman and her coins can be linked with that of the man and his sheep as
male and female examples of a similar storyline.

The woman is described as having ten coins (δραχμάς) and losing one
of them (15.8).[183] The woman's response to one being lost is highlighted
by the number of actions which are predicated to her. She lights a lamp,
sweeps the house, searches and finds it. She then calls together her female
friends and neighbors (τὰς φίλας καὶ γείτονας) and tells them to rejoice
with her (15.8-9). Further her direct speech is recorded by the narrator:
'Rejoice with me, for I have found the coin that I had lost' (15.9). Hence
the woman is characterized in the parable as a woman of actions and
words. Her response is likened to the joy among God's angels because of
one sinner's repentance (15.10), thus affirming her actions and words. The
woman images God's welcome of the lost. There are clear parallels
between this parable and the preceding parable of a man finding a lost
sheep. After searching and finding, he too calls together his friends and
neighbors (τοὺς φίλους καὶ τοὺς γείτονας) and his direct speech is given:
'Rejoice with me, for I have found my sheep that was lost' (15.6). His
response is likened to the joy in heaven because of one sinner's repentance
(15.7).

Attention has been paid to the woman searching and finding the lost
coin as an image of God seeking out the lost. The woman who searches
for her lost coin is an image of God just as the shepherd who searches for
his lost sheep.[184] Susan Durber argues, however, that there is a subtle
difference between the comparison of the shepherd's joy with the joy in
heaven and the comparison of the women's joy with the joy among the
angels of God. She claims that the difference suggests that the woman can
less easily be compared with God and she notes that the shepherd and
father images of Luke 15 have readily been taken to be images of God but
not the image of housewife.[185] Marshall's interpretation reinforces these
comments since he describes the reference to the angels as 'hardly a
periphrasis for the name of God.'[186] He further distinguishes between the
rejoicing of the two parables, claiming that the man calls his friends and
neighbors 'to share in his rejoicing, no doubt at a feast,' whereas the

183.   The drachma was a Greek silver coin similar in value to the Roman denarius. It was
roughly equivalent to the value of a sheep around 300 BCE but was devalued by the first
century CE. See Marshall, *Luke*, 603; and Linda Maloney, ' "Swept Under The Rug":
Feminist Homiletical Reflections on the Parable of the Lost Coin (Lk. 15.8-9),' in *The Lost
Coin: Parables of Women, Work and Wisdom*, (ed.) Mary Ann Beavis (London: Sheffield
Academic Press, 2002), 36.

184.   See Via, 'Women,' 48; Kopas, 'Jesus and Women,' 199; Maloney, 'Swept Under The
Rug,' 37.

185.   Susan Durber, 'The Female Reader of the Parables of the Lost,' *JSNT* 45 (1992): 70.

186.   Marshall, *Luke*, 604.

rejoicing which the woman's neighbors (ignoring her friends) are invited to share is 'no doubt on a modest scale.'[187] Such a distinction cannot be justified by the text. While Fitzmyer asserts that the woman 'serves to portray divine initiative in seeking out what was lost,' he also claims that 'Luke may intend to depict her as miserly.'[188] Again this cannot be justified by the text, and such an interpretation undermines the woman's ability to image God.

Rather than presenting a miserly picture, the parable may highlight the woman's need. Luise Schottroff interprets the parable as indicating that the drachma is indispensable to the woman. Arguing that wages for women's paid work were roughly half of that paid to male workers, she contends that it is a struggle for the woman to survive.[189] In this sense, the women's struggle can be interpreted theologically: 'The very struggle for survival of women, who have to work twice as long as men to earn one drachma, is a parable for the struggle of God, the One searching for lost human beings who repent.'[190]

The parables of Luke 15 reflect an androcentric portrayal of the audience. This can be discerned from Jesus' opening words in the first two parables: 'Which one of you, having a hundred sheep ...' (15.4) followed by the use of male participles and pronouns, compared with 'Or what woman having ten silver coins ...' (15.8). Unlike the shepherd, the woman is not compared with the audience. The audience or reader is therefore constructed as male.[191] Durber agues that a female reader of these parables cannot make sense of the text unless she allows herself to be constructed as male.[192] Alternatively, the female reader can critique the androcentrism of the text but still embrace the liberative aspects of the text.[193] The woman images God and the parables describe the power of the woman, as well as the shepherd and father, to search for the lost: '[T]his woman has the power to restore wholeness and order and to celebrate that restoration.'[194]

The woman is portrayed in a domestic situation, celebrating with

187. Marshall, *Luke*, 602–3.
188. Fitzmyer, *Luke*, 2.1080.
189. Schottroff, *Lydia's Impatient Sisters*, 94–96.
190. Schottroff, *Lydia's Impatient Sisters*, 100.
191. Durber, 'Female Reader,' 70–71. Schottroff assumes that women are part of the crowd but are not addressed. See Schottroff, *Lydia's Impatient Sisters*, 92.
192. Durber, 'Female Reader,' 77. In response to Durber, Carol Schersten La Hurd argues that Eastern women may respond differently from Western women to the text and that Eastern women may see 'themselves and their realities positively portrayed' in the Parable of the Lost Coin. Carol Schersten La Hurd, 'Rediscovering the Lost Women in Luke 15,' *BTB* 24 (1994): 74.
193. Reid, *Choosing the Better Part?*, 184.
194. La Hurd, 'Lost Women,' 72.

female friends and neighbors. She is accorded direct speech and her words are affirmed since they are likened to the rejoicing of the angels (15.10). No male character within the world of the parable hears her voice. The only other women mentioned in Luke 15 are prostitutes in the Parable of the Two Sons (15.30). The mother and sisters are not included in this parable (15.11-32). According to Durber, '[t]hey are unimportant for the text because the story is structured around a patriarchal legal and inheritance system.'[195] Arab Christian women interviewed by Carol Schersten La Hurd, however, present a different view. They interpret the absence of the mother from the story as resulting from women of the first century having 'no public voice': 'The mother's realm was inside the home; so it is not surprising that it was the father who was "outside" to welcome the son and instruct the servants.'[196] The concept of public voice, therefore, may shape the telling and interpretation of these parables. The woman with the coins is portrayed as speaking to other women only. In a more public setting in which males are present, no woman is given voice in the parables of Luke 15.

b. *The Widow Seeking Justice*

The Parable of a Widow Seeking Justice (18.2-5) is introduced by a comment from the Lukan narrator (18.1; cf. 19.11) that attributes the reason for Jesus telling the parable to exhorting the disciples to persist in prayer.[197] Two characters – a judge and a widow – are featured in the parable which is set in a city. Neither of the characters is named. The judge is introduced by his characteristics. He neither fears God nor respects people (18.2).[198] The widow initiates the action in the parable by continuing to come to the judge to seek justice. The imperfect form of ἤρχετο indicates the ongoing nature of her requests. Her direct words of request are given: 'Grant me justice against my opponent' (18.3). The judge is portrayed as granting her request, though not because he wants justice to prevail. Rather he fears the consequences of the woman's actions (18.5). The word ὑπωπιάζω literally means 'strike under the eye' and its use in 18.5 has been described as the actions of 'a woman driven to

---

195. Durber, 'Female Reader,' 70.

196. La Hurd, 'Lost Women,' 68.

197. The relationship between the parable and its frame has attracted considerable scholarly attention. For a list of different views, see Stephen Curkpatrick, 'A Parable Frame-Up and Its Audacious Reframing,' *NTS* 49 (2003): 22. For a more detailed discussion on the issue, see Stephen Curkpatrick, 'Dissonance in Luke 18:1-8,' *JBL* 121 (2002): 107–21.

198. J. D. M. Derrett, 'Law in the New Testament: The Parable of the Unjust Judge,' *NTS* 18 (1971–72): 191, claims that the judge showing no respect for people indicates that the judge is impartial. The label of the judge as ἀδικίας (18.6) would suggest otherwise, however.

desperation.'[199] In a weakened sense the verb could be interpreted as 'annoy greatly.'[200]

The usual interpretation of the judge's words accepts this weakened sense of the verb. Some describe the woman as 'nagging' the judge.[201] Such a description, using the pejorative term 'nagging,' undermines the woman's actions.[202] She seeks justice, her rights. In the Hebrew Scriptures we read 'Justice, and only justice, you shall pursue' (Deut. 16.20). In seeking justice, the widow's actions are thus not only acceptable but to be modeled. Persistence in seeking justice is surely different from 'nagging.' According to Price, 'the original point of the story of the persistent widow was to inculcate the doggedness (bitchiness?) she showed.'[203] Associating the woman's actions with bitchiness, however, also serves to undermine her actions.

The words of the κύριος, coming after the parable, label the judge as unjust and encourage the understanding that if an unjust judge will grant justice, how much more can we be sure that God will grant justice to those who cry for help (18.6-8). The term κύριος refers here to Jesus so that the words are given authority. It has been suggested that the objective of the parable is to contrast the judge with God.[204] The description of God as judge in Sir. 35.14-22, executing justice and not ignoring the widow, certainly contrasts with the presentation of the judge in the parable.[205] To focus on this contrast, however, overlooks the role of the widow in the parable. Some understand the judge as an image of God,[206] but the injustice of the judge makes this questionable. It is the widow and not the judge who pursues justice, and thus more closely models God's action.

Some focus on the perceived helplessness of the widow based on the image in the Hebrew Scriptures of widows being among the most vulnerable (Exod. 22.22-24; Deut. 10.18; 24.17; Ps. 68.5).[207] Yet the widow in this parable proves not to be helpless.[208] She takes the initiative and cries out for justice until she achieves it. She acts on her own behalf, asserting herself, and her words eventually prevail. The widow uses what

199. BAGD, 848.

200. BAGD, 848.

201. See Marshall, *Luke*, 673; Fitzmyer, *Luke*, 2.1179; and Jeremias, *Parables of Jesus*, 154.

202. The term 'nagging' evokes the stereotype of a nagging woman who henpecks a man. See Carter Shelley, 'A Widow Without Wiles,' in *The Lost Coin: Parables of Women, Work and Wisdom*, (ed.) Mary Ann Beavis (London: Sheffield Academic Press, 2002), 56.

203. Price, *Widow Traditions*, 198.

204. Marshall, *Luke*, 670.

205. The comparison with Sirach 35 is noted, for example, in Reid, *Choosing the Better Part?*, 192; Schottroff, *Lydia's Impatient Sisters*, 102; and Johnson, *Luke*, 269.

206. See Fitzmyer, *Luke*, 2.1177; and Derrett, 'Law,' 179, 187.

207. See Johnson, *Luke*, 269; Fitzmyer, *Luke*, 2.1178; and Marshall, *Luke*, 672.

208. Curkpatrick, 'Parable Frame-Up,' 31; and Reid, *Choosing the Better Part?*, 190–91.

she has, her voice and her time, to challenge the injustice.[209] Her vulnerable situation is therefore integrated with an image of her efficacy.

The introduction to the parable (18.1) focuses on persistence in prayer. This brings the parable in line with the theme of the Parable of the Friend at Midnight (11.5-8). In this understanding, the widow models persistent prayer more than pursuing justice. According to Reid, the Lukan introduction 'sidetracks the reader' from the message of relentlessly seeking justice which is the concern of the parable. 'Since this kind of role is not what he would encourage for women, he softens the parable's impact by posing the widow as an example of persistent prayer, a docile and acceptable role.'[210] An exploration of Luke-Acts shows that Jesus and the early Christians are often portrayed as praying (Lk. 3.21; 5.16; 6.12, 28; 9.18, 28-29; 10.21-22; 11.1-4; 22.40-46; 23.46; Acts 1.14, 24; 2.42; 4.31; 6.4, 6; 7.59; 8.15; 9.40; 11.5; 12.5, 12; 13.3; 14.23; 16.25; 20.36; 21.5; 22.17; 26.29; 28.8) and that prayer is the source of dynamic activity. In the Lukan narrative, therefore, the fullest picture of the widow can perhaps be obtained by linking prayer with the pursuit of justice so that both are highlighted.

Like Reid, Stephen Curkpatrick also argues that the parable's frame eclipses the widow's prophetic voice for justice: 'The parable depicts and therefore says more than its immediate frame (vv. 1, 6-8) allows.'[211] He argues that the parable strikingly depicts the vision of justice for the oppressed as expressed in the *Magnificat* but that this correspondence is mitigated by the frame.[212] Curkpatrick is critical of the effect of the Lukan framing:

> He has effectively achieved in the frame what the judge could not achieve in the parable, inadvertently and effectively silencing the widow's voice, and thereby silencing a demonstrative expression of the vision of the Magnificat. Perhaps, then, it could be argued that Luke's framing, and not the judge, is the widow's greatest adversity.[213]

Actually, the widow's voice is not silenced. Not only does she continually cry out but also her words are recorded. The widow achieves her aim of attaining justice. The frame does not function to silence the widow but it does affect the reader's understanding of the widow's actions. Therefore, it is the reader's interpretation and not the actions of the widow that is influenced by the framing of the Lukan narrator here.

The reader of the parable is invited to model the widow's actions. She images God who continuously seeks justice. The two themes of justice and

---

209. Shelley, 'Widow Without Wiles,' 58.
210. Reid, *Choosing the Better Part?*, 194.
211. Curkpatrick, 'Parable Frame-Up,' 29.
212. Curkpatrick, 'Parable Frame-Up,' 27.
213. Curkpatrick, 'Parable Frame-Up,' 33.

prayer can be combined so that relentlessly pursuing justice and resisting injustice should model the reader's behavior in the community. At the same time, the reader is encouraged to cry out to God for justice, knowing that God responds differently from the unjust judge.[214] It is the widow rather than the judge who images God. That the woman is accorded direct speech in a public setting and achieves the outcome which she seeks cuts across the general portrayal of women's speech in the ministry of the Lukan Jesus. This women's words are efficacious rather than silenced. She 'gains' rather than 'loses.'

14. *Conclusion*

Within the Gospel of Luke, women's speech is not as prominent in the ministry of Jesus as it is in the infancy narrative. While women are depicted as benefiting physically, economically and socially from Jesus' proclamation of the βασιλεία, direct speech is accorded to women characters on only a few occasions during Jesus' ministry and on none of these occasions is the woman affirmed for her speech. Rather, there is a sense in which each woman granted direct speech can be said to have 'lost her pound.' On the other hand, there are examples of women's actions being affirmed by Jesus and some of the women are portrayed as models of faith. Hence, the Lukan Jesus is portrayed as responding differently to women's initiative in regard to action and speech. The situation of women's speech changes, however, for the women in parables. Here, in stories within a story, women are portrayed as initiating speech and they have their words recorded without being corrected, without 'losing out.' The association of women with demon-possession is another prominent feature of Lukan women's characterizations in the ministry of Jesus and is another way in which the women's 'pound' may be compromised. In the following chapter, a thematic approach to the women's characterizations will be presented. The lens of the Parable of the Pounds will be used to focus and analyze the women's characterizations in order to manifest the rhetoric of the Lukan text.

---

214. See Schottroff, *Lydia's Impatient Sisters*, 102.

Chapter 6

WOMEN, THE PARABLE OF THE POUNDS AND LUKAN THEOLOGY

In Chapters 4 and 5, the Lukan women's characterizations have been analyzed within their narrative Gospel context. The findings emerging from the study to this point provide some indications that the Parable of the Pounds (19.11-28) can be interpreted metaphorically to elucidate the nature of these characterizations. Drawing together the insights of the previous two chapters, this chapter will employ a thematic reading in order to focus more explicitly the women's characterizations through the lens of the parable.

Following the reading presented in Chapter 2, the Parable of the Pounds depicts an oppressive nobleman who gives his slaves a pound each. Those who continue the oppressive practices of their master are rewarded generously but the slave who refuses to continue the oppression has his pound taken away from him. That slave knows that his action is likely to have repercussions, but he is resolved not to participate in the oppression. Furthermore, the citizens who oppose the oppressive rule of the nobleman are slaughtered. Therefore, those who take a stand against the oppressive practices suffer the consequences of their actions. One with power over them rules that they should 'lose their pounds,' their status, the possibility of future manumission, or the chance to influence their future. Some climactically lose their lives. At the same time, those who do not challenge the system can benefit from it. The same oppressive system promotes different responses and different outcomes.

As we have seen, the 'pound' can be used as a metaphor for what one has that can potentially be taken away by an oppressive other, not only in the context of this parable, but within a wider context in the Lukan narrative. Thus the parable can be read metaphorically to describe a dynamic operating in the Lukan Gospel narrative. That the parable describes different responses to an oppressive system and portrays different outcomes for the slaves makes the Parable of the Pounds particularly pertinent to the Lukan women's characterizations. The parable helps to interpret the different outcomes for the various women characters. Using this parable as a lens through which to view the characterization of the Lukan women also draws some significant questions into focus:

- What do the women characters of the Gospel of Luke 'gain' by their characterization?[1]
- Does any woman have her 'pound' taken away by her characterization?
- If so, what is taken away and who is it that takes away the woman's 'pound'?
- What action by the woman triggers the taking away of her 'pound'?
- Who does not 'lose her pound'?

Since some women both 'gain' and 'lose' by their characterization, their situations are more ambiguous than the situation of the third slave in the Parable of the Pounds. There is a sense, then, in which the women 'losing their pound' both 'is' and 'is not' like the third slave 'losing his pound.'[2] When they 'gain,' the women can be compared instead with the first two slaves who benefit greatly from their master's decisions. Of importance is to consider what determines whether women 'gain' or 'lose.'

1. *What is 'Gained'?*

As we have seen, much is 'gained' by the women of the Lukan infancy narrative (Lk. 1–2). Women have central roles within this infancy narrative. Elizabeth, Mary and Anna are portrayed as faithful and prophetic, and as taking initiative. Each proclaims her 'knowledge of salvation' to others. In the case of Elizabeth and Mary, the reader learns from the mouths of these women themselves of the insight with which they have been gifted by the Spirit. Mary is portrayed as a hearer, keeper and doer of the word (cf. 8.19-21; 11.27-28).

There is a sense in which women in the ministry of Jesus also 'gain' much by their characterization. Women model the appropriate actions for leadership among the disciples (22.26) and are portrayed as following him from Galilee (23.49). Hence the portrayal of women as disciples is reinforced. Some women initiate their interaction with Jesus (7.37-38; 8.43-44; 10.38-40; 11.27). Two of these – the woman who anoints Jesus' feet (7.37-38) and Martha (10.38-40) – are depicted as welcoming Jesus or offering him hospitality. Women are thus portrayed as initiating the appropriate response to the divine visitation.

Martha's sister, Mary, is affirmed by Jesus for sitting at his feet and listening to his word (10.39-42). Two other women are also affirmed by Jesus for their faith. The woman who anoints Jesus and the woman cured of a hemorrhage are both explicitly referred to by Jesus as demonstrating

---

1. The terms 'gain,' 'take away' and 'lose' are used here in a metaphorical sense, extending the metaphor of the parable.

2. For some discussion on the 'is' and 'is not' nature of metaphor, see Schneiders, *Revelatory Text*, 29–32.

faith (7.50; 8.48). Similar affirmations are addressed to the leper and the blind man (17.19; 18.42), and the centurion and the men carrying the paralytic are also portrayed as having faith (5.20; 7.9). Women as well as men are models of faith in the Lukan Gospel. Moreover, the widow who gives all that she has (21.3-4) can be aligned with Jesus who gives his life.

As in the other three canonical Gospels, in the Gospel of Luke women are the first to receive the good news of the resurrection (24.5-6; cf. Mt. 28.1-10; Mk 16.5-7; Jn 20.11-18). Further, unlike the reaction of the women in Mk 16.8, the Lukan women tell the good news to the eleven and all the rest (24.9-10). The women are portrayed as faithful witnesses and they are the first to tell the good news to the other disciples.

Along with many men, several women in the Lukan narrative benefit from Jesus' healing ministry.[3] Simon's mother-in-law (4.38-39), the woman with a hemorrhage (8.43-48), the women healed of evil spirits (8.1-3), Jairus' daughter (8.40-42, 49-56) and the woman with a spirit of infirmity (13.10-13) are all healed by Jesus. While it is the widow of Nain's son who is restored to life by Jesus, it is compassion for the widow that initiates Jesus' action. She is liberated from the effects of her son's death, so she also benefits from Jesus' healing (7.11-17). The woman who anoints Jesus is not in need of physical healing, yet she is in need nevertheless (7.36-50). Jesus' announcement of her forgiveness (by God) to the wider community assures her knowledge of salvation and restores her status within the community. Thus, she is socially healed in her community. The two women called 'daughter' by Jesus (8.48; 13.16) are similarly confirmed within the community.

Women can be seen to 'gain' much, therefore, by their characterization in the Lukan Gospel. Some women are portrayed as exercising agency and power. Some are prophetic, able to identify God's actions in their life and to proclaim this. Some are women of faith who minister and model leadership qualities among the disciples. Some show hospitality to the agent of the divine visitation and are thereby drawn into the wider hospitality of God. Some receive the benefit of Jesus' ministry, being healed physically and/or socially. Some follow Jesus, witness his death and burial, and receive the good news of the resurrection that they share with others. Some women are affirmed as listeners to the word of Jesus. In particular, Mary the mother of Jesus is portrayed as one who hears the word of God and keeps it and she is included in the new kinship group established by Jesus. Women, along with men, are disciples of Jesus.

---

3. Males are healed by Jesus in the following pericopes: 4.31-37; 5.12-16, 17-26; 6.6-11; 7.1-10, 11-17; 8.26-39; 9.37-43; 11.14; 14.1-6; 17.11-19; 18.35-43.

2. *The Pound Taken Away*

While women 'gain' much through the Lukan Gospel, that is not the only side of the story. The exploration in previous chapters of the women's characterizations reveals that at times women also 'lose' what they have 'gained.' Sometimes this results from the actions of other characters within the Gospel. Sometimes it is the strategies of the Lukan narrator which take away from the women's characterizations. While the characters and narrator are ultimately shaped by the Lukan author, it is helpful to distinguish them in order to explore the range of ways in which women may be seen to 'lose their pound' within this Gospel. The following categories will be examined in this exploration:

- Women disbelieved by other characters
- Women corrected
- Women's words not recorded
- Women as demon-possessed
- Women who do not speak

a. *Women Disbelieved By Other Characters*

Some Lukan women speak out but are not believed by other characters within the Gospel. Elizabeth is portrayed as spirit-filled and proclaiming prophetically to Mary (1.41-45) but her authoritative words are not recognized when she names her son in a more public context (1.60). While Elizabeth's portrayal in Luke 1 offers much, by the end of the chapter she 'loses her pound.' For Elizabeth, the 'pound' metaphorically refers to her potential to proclaim publicly and be heard. In this case those who 'take the pound away' are the neighbors and relatives gathered at the circumcision who do not accept Elizabeth's words. The effect, however, is compounded by interpretations that reinforce the impression that women's words are capricious rather than authoritative and that thus marginalize Elizabeth's status.

Other Lukan women who are not believed when they speak the truth are the women who announce the good news of the resurrection (24.1-12). Despite their portrayal as faithful disciples (23.49–24.12), their words are not accepted by the eleven. Moreover, none of the women is named or given voice in the ongoing story of the Church told in Acts. The eleven's disbelief of the women impacts detrimentally on the women's continued characterizations but not on those of the male apostles.

The eleven effectively take away the women's 'pound' – their efficacy and witness. Their distinction of being the first to proclaim the good news is also compromised. While the eleven are portrayed as taking the women's 'pound' away, some of the strategies of the narrator reinforce this loss. Furthermore, interpretations which suggest that a woman's witness is unreliable can also contribute to this effect. Both text and interpretation can marginalize the women's witness.

b. *Women Corrected*

Only five women characters are accorded direct speech in the Lukan Gospel – Elizabeth, Mary the mother of Jesus, Martha, a woman in the crowd and a slave-woman.[4] Elizabeth speaks to herself (1.25) and proclaims to Mary (1.42-45). In both instances, she is portrayed as recognizing and speaking about God's action in her life. The only other time she speaks is to relatives and neighbors at the naming of her child (1.60). As we have seen, in this instance she is disbelieved.

Mary first speaks to the angel Gabriel (1.34, 38) and her next recorded words are proclaimed in the presence of Elizabeth (1.46-55). The only other time that she is accredited with speech is in the temple (2.48). Here she speaks to Jesus on behalf of Joseph and herself. Jesus' words in response are in the form of a rebuke addressed to both of them.

Martha speaks to Jesus in 10.40. Jesus' response is again in the form of a censure. His words reprimand Martha and affirm her silent sister, Mary. Mary, rather than Martha, is said to have 'chosen the better part' (10.42). A woman in the crowd who raises her voice and speaks to Jesus is met by a correction from Jesus (11.27-28). A slave-woman's words, correctly identifying Peter as being one of those with Jesus, are denied by Peter (22.56-57). No woman in the Lukan Gospel who is corrected or rebuked when she speaks is explicitly given voice at a later stage of the narrative. No other woman character has her words recorded in the Lukan Gospel narrative.

It can be observed then that women's words in the Lukan Gospel are affirmed, or at least not undermined, when they are spoken to an angel or within the presence of a strictly female audience. On each other occasion, however, women's reported words are met with disbelief, rebuke, correction or denial. This includes the three occasions, each unique to the Lukan Gospel, in which women speak to Jesus and have their words recorded (2.48-49; 10.40-42; 11.27-28). On each of these three occasions, the woman initiates the conversation with Jesus.

Women are not the only ones to be censured or corrected for their direct speech to Jesus. Words inspired by unclean spirits or demons are rebuked by Jesus (4.34-35).[5] Scribes, Pharisees, lawyers and religious leaders are often censured or corrected by Jesus (for example, 5.21-24, 30-31, 33-35; 6.2-5; 7.39-47; 11.45-52; 13.14-16; 19.39; 20.1-8, 20-26; 22.66-

---

4. The women in Jesus' teachings and parables are not considered here since they are not characters in their own right.

5. In 8.28-29 the words of the demoniac are implicitly rebuked because Jesus commands the unclean spirit to come out of the man.

70). The same can be said of disciples and followers of Jesus (for example, 8.24-25; 9.12-13; 9.49-50, 54-55, 57-61; 10.17-20; 17.5-6; 22.33-34; 24.17-26). Some other instances of men being censured or corrected by Jesus when they speak are given in 12.13-15; and 18.18-19.[6]

There are also many examples, however, of men speaking directly to Jesus and not being rebuked or corrected by him. Peter speaks to Jesus at the time of his call. He is given a new role by Jesus and follows him (5.4-11). The leper who requests healing from Jesus is healed (5.12-13). The Jewish elders who appeal to Jesus on behalf of the centurion succeed in getting Jesus to go with them (7.3-6). The words of the centurion relayed to Jesus draw praise for his faith from Jesus (7.6-9). The messengers from John the Baptist pass on John's question to Jesus and receive a response (7.20-23). Questions from Peter and a dinner guest result in Jesus teaching (12.41-48; 14.15-24). Ten leprous men call out to Jesus and are healed (17.12-14). Peter's words draw affirmation from Jesus in 18.28-30. The blind man, whom the crowd attempts to silence, requests healing and is both healed and affirmed by Jesus for his faith (18.35-43). Zacchaeus' words lead into Jesus' description of him as a son of Abraham (19.8-10). Peter and John ask a question of Jesus and are given instructions about the preparation for the Passover meal (22.9-12). The apostles converse with Jesus at the last supper (22.35-38). A criminal put to death with Jesus asks Jesus to remember him and his salvation is assured by Jesus (23.42-43).[7]

Not only is it evident from this that men speak and are spoken to by Jesus far more than is the case for women, but also that there are differences in the way Jesus is characterized as responding to the speech. Each woman who speaks to Jesus and has her words recorded is met with censure or correction. Sometimes men are also met with such a response. In particular, Pharisees, scribes and religious leaders are typically censured by Jesus when they speak to him. Since they are stereotypically characterized as opponents of Jesus, this may not be surprising. Disciples, too, are often corrected but this is combined with times when Jesus does not censure them for their words. As well, several times men petition Jesus' help and receive it without their words being undermined.

---

6. In 9.38-41 the direct speech of a father of a possessed child results in a censure by Jesus, though it would appear that this censure is not directly addressed to the father. It may be addressed to the disciples or more generally to the wider audience. See Fitzmyer, *Luke*, 1.809. Also, one of the criminals put to death with Jesus speaks to Jesus and is rebuked by the other criminal (23.39-41).

7. In 10.25-37 the lawyer who asks questions of Jesus to test him is not specifically censured by Jesus but there is an implicit correction in Jesus' use of the parable. Similarly, while there is no explicit correction of the Sadducees and scribes in 20.27-40, it is clear that the words of the scribes confirming Jesus has spoken well are ironic. The attempts to trap Jesus have failed.

The result is that men's words to Jesus in the Lukan Gospel are often affirmed and considered appropriate whereas women's words to Jesus are never given that assurance. Thus, there is inconsistency in the portrayal of men's and women's direct speech. As the agent of the divine visitation, Jesus is portrayed as the one with authority in the Lukan Gospel and his response to other characters influences the reader's reaction to those characters. The narrative technique of giving Jesus the last word in these interactions highlights his response to them. While Jesus affirms women for their faith, the lack of affirmation by Jesus of any woman's direct words in the Lukan Gospel has the rhetorical effect of reinforcing an understanding that women's words are not appropriate in a public situation.

Women characters 'lose their pound,' their ability to speak and be heard in the public arena, and their initiative and agency are compromised. The characterization of Jesus in the Lukan Gospel sometimes contributes to this loss. The issue is not that some women characters in the Gospel are corrected or rebuked by Jesus. (As we have seen, many men receive a similar response from Jesus.) The issue is that *no* woman character's direct words are affirmed by Jesus.[8]

c. *Women's Words Not Recorded*

Some further narrative strategies limit the efficacy of women's speech. In particular, at times the Lukan narrator does not record women's words when they do speak, undermining the effectiveness of their words. 'Luke regularly introduces women whom the reader is to imagine speaking, but who at the same time are silenced since Luke grants them no actual voice.'[9]

While the reader is informed that the prophet, Anna, continually speaks out, we are not informed of her words (2.36-38). As a result, Anna's prophetic activity rarely receives the same attention from the reader as Simeon's activity (2.25-35). Thus, narrative strategies impact on the characterization of the prophet, Anna. All those seeking the redemption of Jerusalem in the narrative benefit from Anna's continual speech (2.38), but the benefit to the reader is limited by the narrator. Similarly, when the woman with a hemorrhage speaks her words are not recorded by the narrator (8.47). While the characters in the story hear her words, the reader does not.

The woman who is healed of a spirit of infirmity is likewise not given direct speech (13.10-17). The impact of her response is diminished by the

---

8. The woman cured of a hemorrhage is described as speaking but her direct words are not given (8.47).

9. de Boer, 'Lukan Mary Magdalene,' 151.

narrative device of informing the reader that the woman glorifies God (13.13) without attributing to her any direct speech. As in the case of Anna and the woman healed of a hemorrhage, other characters in the narrative hear the woman's words but the reader does not benefit from hearing her speech.

Thus the narrator compromises the 'pound' of these three women. Here the 'pound' refers to the women's capacity to have their words impact on the reader.[10] The women's significance is thus marginalized: 'silencing through unreported speech ... means the erasure of their contribution.'[11] Likewise, the words of the women who tell the good news of the resurrection to the eleven are not provided in the narrative (24.10-11). This, along with the reaction by the eleven to the women's words, is a further marginalization of the women's roles.

It is not only women who are accredited with implied speech without having their words recorded. Several times groups (such as crowds, disciples, Pharisees) are described as speaking but we do not hear their direct words. Further, many times a male character's words are not recorded on a particular occasion but they are given direct speech elsewhere in the Lukan Gospel.[12] In the case of the following individual male characters, however – the paralyzed man (5.25); the widow's son (7.15); Jairus (8.41); the former mute man (11.14); Judas (22.4, 6); and Joseph of Arimathea (23.51) – the male character's words are not recorded, neither are they accorded direct speech elsewhere in the Gospel of Luke.

In some of these cases, no words of the individual are recorded in the corresponding version in the Gospel of Mark or Q (11.14; 22.4, 6; 23.51). Moreover, the paralyzed man has implied speech only in the Lukan version (5.25). He has no voice in the Markan version. In these instances, therefore, the Lukan narrator does not lessen the significance of the male character from the other versions (and in one case, increases the significance). In the case of Jairus (8.41), however, the Lukan narrator reduces the impact of this man's words, as well as those of the woman with the hemorrhage, compared with the Markan version. The story of the raising of the widow's son from Nain is unique to the Gospel of Luke.

Given the frequency of male direct speech reported in the Lukan

10.   The significance of direct speech is highlighted by Dewey, 'Seen but not Heard?,' 54-58, who uses direct speech as an indicator of mimetic development of characters in the Synoptic Gospels.

11.   Jane Schaberg, 'Magdalene Christianity,' in *On the Cutting Edge: The Study of Women in Biblical Worlds*, (eds.) Jane Schaberg, Alice Bach, and Esther Fuchs (New York, NY: Continuum, 2003), 198.

12.   I include the Pharisee of 11.37 in this section since the man is unnamed and identified solely as a Pharisee, and groups of Pharisees are accorded direct speech on other occasions (5.21, 30; 6.2; 15.2).

Gospel, it is rare that a male who is given only implied speech is not heard speaking directly at some point in this Gospel. On the other hand, of the eight women characters who are accorded individual speech (direct or implied),[13] three never have their voices heard in the Lukan Gospel. A far greater percentage of women characters are affected in this way by the Lukan narrative strategies. Furthermore, while the reader is likely not to be expecting to hear the voice of a dead man who has been raised, the voice of a prophet presents a different expectation. The non-reporting of Anna's words is surprising since 'a prophetess is someone whose vocation requires speech.'[14] As already noted, one may well expect to hear the words of the bent-over woman who glorifies God. The narrator's choices regarding the speech of women characters, once again, however, fail to meet these expectations.

d. *Women as Demon-Possessed*

As we have seen, healed women are associated with malevolent spirits or demon possession in 4.38-39, 8.2-3 and 13.10-17. Each of these associations is unique to the Lukan Gospel. Jesus heals men associated with malevolent spirits in 4.31-37, 8.26-39, 9.37-43, and 11.14.[15] In the first three of these references, the association with possession is taken over from the Markan version. In the last reference, the association is from Q.[16] Hence, of the male Lukan characters healed by Jesus, none of the depictions of demon possession or association with malevolent spirits is unique to the Lukan Gospel.[17] In contrast, each of the women associated with demon possession in the Gospel of Luke is either not portrayed as such in the other Gospels or is a uniquely Lukan character. Further, as we have seen, the portrayal of the slave-woman in 22.54-57 links the woman with Satan's designs (22.31-34). This specific connection of the woman with Satan is unique to the Lukan Gospel. At the same time, the linking of Peter with Satan in Mk 8.33 and Mt. 16.23 is not included in the Lukan Gospel.[18]

It would seem to be a choice by the Lukan narrator to depict the women in 4.38-39, 8.2-3 and 13.10-17 as possessing evil and unclean spirits or as being demon-possessed. The uniquely Lukan material presents only

---

13. This figure does not include the women in parables.

14. Troost, 'Elizabeth and Mary,' 169.

15. In addition, there are summary statements of Jesus' healing that incorporate Jesus healing those with demons and unclean spirits (see 4.40-41, 6.18, and 7.21). It is also implied that the twelve have authority over demons and that the seventy have cast out demons (9.1-2; 10.17-20). Judas is linked with Satan in 22.3 and the apostles are described as being tested by Satan in 22.31.

16. Fitzmyer, *Luke*, 2.917–18.

17. Dewey, 'Jesus' Healings,' 124.

18. Brock, *Mary Magdalene*, 24.

females in this way. While it is possible that a number of Lukan women are portrayed as possessed so that both women and men are characterized thus in the Lukan Gospel, it is surprising that the man with dropsy (14.1-6) is not similarly portrayed as possessed if gender parallelism in regard to possession of unclean and evil spirits is the motive.

The first-century world associated some illnesses with malevolent spirits and the activity of spirits is featured more prominently in the Lukan Gospel than in any of the other Gospels. Indeed, it has been said that '[t]he malevolent presence of demons and unclean spirits in Luke-Acts is truly considerable.'[19] Even so, it is striking that in most healing stories in the Lukan Gospel those healed are not specifically characterized as possessed. The woman with the hemorrhage and Jairus' daughter, however, are the only females healed by Jesus who are not characterized as possessed (8.40-56). Against this, none of the leper (5.12-13), the paralytic (5.17-26), the man with the withered hand (6.6-11), the centurion's slave (7.1-10), the son of the widow at Nain (7.11-17), the man with dropsy (14.1-6), the ten lepers (17.11-19) nor the blind man (18.35-43) is characterized as demon-possessed and all are healed by Jesus.[20] A far greater percentage of women than men is portrayed in the Lukan Gospel as having been possessed.

The discussion in the previous chapter indicated how women's healing ministry may be caricatured by their depiction as demon-possessed. Furthermore, since healing is linked to proclamation of the βασιλεία of God (9.2; 10.9), the demonization of the women may also compromise the women's public voice. These, then, become other ways in which the Lukan narrator compromises the women's 'pound,' where here the 'pound' refers to the significance of the women's διακονία as well as their ability to proclaim publicly.

Noting that Jesus is himself labeled as possessed by Beelzebul (11.15), and that Jesus describes his ministry in terms of διακονία (22.27), Wainwright questions whether the demon-possessed women are aligned with Jesus as healers or prophetic teachers, and whether they can therefore be considered ultimately acclaimed as Jesus is acclaimed despite his labeling. Or, rather, does the label of demon possession function to marginalize the διακονία of the women? Wainwright argues that an issue of conflict is depicted here.[21]

While the characterization of women as demon-possessed by the Lukan narrator may function to stereotype the women's διακονία, can a counter-

19. Pilch, 'Sickness and Healing,' 202.
20. Those healed of evil spirits who are mentioned in the summary statements of Jesus' healing (4.40-41, 6.18, and 7.21) are not included here because it is not possible to determine whether they are men or women.
21. Wainwright, 'Demon Possessed Women,' 5–6.

narrative be discerned within the text, operating to restore the women's
'pound' which is compromised by the dominant narrative?[22] While the
women's 'pound' may in one sense be compromised by their portrayal as
demon-possessed, it may be restored in another sense. That a counter-
narrative may function to restore the women's 'pound' is considered later
in this chapter.

e. *Women Who Do Not Speak*

Several women characters in the Lukan Gospel are given neither direct
speech nor narrated speech. Simon's mother-in-law (4.38-39), Jairus'
daughter (8.40-42, 49-56) and Mary, the sister of Martha (10.38-42) are
silent throughout their portrayal. The widow at Nain (7.11-17), the
woman who anoints Jesus (7.36-50), and the daughters of Jerusalem
(23.27-31) are depicted as weeping, so they are not necessarily silent, but
none of them speaks. Only a few of the many male characters, including
Joseph (2.1-52), the man with a withered hand (6.6-11) and the man with
dropsy (14.1-6), also remain silent throughout their characterization. Levi,
too, is not described as speaking though perhaps it may be implied given
that he gives a banquet for Jesus (5.27-29). Once again we can see that a
far greater percentage of women than men characters are never portrayed
as speaking in the Lukan Gospel narrative.

Simon's mother-in-law, Jairus' daughter and the widow at Nain all
benefit from Jesus' healing ministry. None of these requests action from
Jesus and none of these responds in word to Jesus' actions. The widow at
Nain remains passive throughout and challenges no oppressive structures.[23] No action is predicated to her. Simon's mother-in-law and Jairus'
daughter each stand up immediately in response to being healed (4.39;
8.55). The only other action by a woman in these healing stories is Simon's
mother-in-law ministering to 'them,' Jesus and unspecified others (4.39).
None of these three women receives a rebuke or correction from another
character in the narrative and none is discredited. No other character
explicitly takes away these women's 'pound,' though, as noted above, the
ministry of Simon's mother-in-law may be caricatured by her depiction as
possessed.

The woman who anoints Jesus is a woman of action (7.36-50). She
initiates her interaction with Jesus and is the subject of much activity
(7.37-38). Jesus is portrayed as affirming her actions at length (7.44-46).
Further, Jesus' words make clear that she is forgiven and that she is a

22. See Wainwright, 'Demon Possessed Women,' 7.
23. Melzer-Keller notes that the solution to the widow's problem remains inside the
traditional patriarchal framework – the widow relies on her son who can give her material
security. See Melzer-Keller, *Jesus und die Frauen*, 291. Dewey describes the story as 'culture-
maintaining.' Dewey, 'Jesus' Healings,' 125.

woman of faith (7.47-50). The woman 'gains' much through her characterization and none of what she 'gains' is explicitly taken away from her. This woman of action is not, however, a woman of words. Martha, on the other hand, is a woman of both action and words (10.38-40). As we have seen, Jesus contrasts Martha unfavorably with her sister, Mary, who remains silent throughout (10.41-42). Like the woman who anoints Jesus, Mary is explicitly affirmed by Jesus. She is said to have 'chosen the better part' and Jesus announces that this 'better part' will not be taken away from her (10.42). No character in the pericope explicitly takes away the 'pound' of the silent Mary.

3. *The Cumulative Narrative Effect*

The above discussion enables the questions asked at the beginning of the chapter to be addressed. As demonstrated above, women at times 'gain' much by their characterization. In various ways, however, women in the Gospel of Luke can also be seen to 'lose their pound,' or at least have it somewhat compromised. The narrator and other characters within the narrative succeed in reducing the efficacy of the women character's speech and their agency, as well as their impact on the reader. Furthermore the women's διακονία may be marginalized. Ultimately it is the Lukan author who shapes the characters and narrative strategies within the Lukan Gospel, so ultimately it is the Lukan author whose rhetorical strategies compromise the 'pound' of the women characters.

It can be seen that it is often women's speech which triggers the actions which take away or compromise the women's 'pound.' The women who speak to an angel or within strictly female company are not compromised. Moreover, most women who remain silent throughout the narrative do not explicitly 'lose their pound.' No silent woman stands corrected or disbelieved by other characters.[24] Rather, two women without speech receive explicit praise from Jesus. Silent women benefit from Jesus' ministry, in the sense of being restored and affirmed, without explicitly 'losing out.' Hence, while those women who take the initiative to speak out in a 'public' situation have their 'pound' taken away, those who do not speak can benefit without explicitly 'losing out.'[25]

As explained in the introductory chapter, marginalization, cultural imperialism and violence are some of the faces of oppression, and silence, vilification and trivialization are particular expressions of these. The trivialization of women's speech and the strategies which lead to the silencing of women's public voice in the Lukan Gospel narrative are thus

---

24. While the synagogue leader criticizes the woman healed of a spirit of infirmity for coming to be healed on the Sabbath (13.14-16), Jesus defends her action.

25. 'Public' here refers to situations where those present are not all female.

oppressive. So, too, are the marginalization and vilification of women by caricaturing them as demon-possessed. Those women characters in the narrative who challenge the oppressive stricture of public silence for women are seen to 'lose their pound.' On the other hand, those who do not challenge this oppressive ideal are able to 'gain.' As in the Parable of the Pounds, those who challenge the oppressive structure suffer the consequences while those who do not challenge it can benefit.

The cumulative rhetorical effect of all these strategies by the Lukan author is to reinforce the patriarchal ideal that women's speech is not authoritative in a public setting and that the appropriate role of women in such a setting is a silent one. As we have seen, some women characters do initiate actions and are affirmed by Jesus (7.36-50; 8.43-48). Hence, a woman initiating action does not trigger the taking away of her 'pound' whereas a woman initiating public speech has her agency compromised. Thus, while both action and speech are important elements of characterization, Lukan narrative strategies operate to different effect regarding women's initiated action and speech. This may suggest that women's public speech is perceived as more of a threat to the patriarchal system than women's silent actions. Since women's speech is sometimes portrayed as correct despite not being believed, it is not the truthfulness or correctness of women's words which is at issue, but rather the appropriateness of women speaking in a public setting.

The overall strategy concerning women's speech and demonization in the Lukan Gospel prepares for women's characterization in Acts, the second book of the Lukan narrative. Having lost the efficacy of their public voice by the end of the Lukan Gospel, the women's voice in the ongoing story of the Church is marginalized. Women's speech is more rare in Acts than in the Lukan Gospel. Direct speech is given to women on only three occasions (Acts 5.8; 16.15, 17), with indirect or implied speech attributed to women in Acts 12.14-15 and 18.26. Sapphira is accorded two words in a public setting (Acts 5.8) and then two verses later we read that she falls down and dies: 'The famous, or rather infamous, first words from a woman in Acts are her last!'[26] Lydia is accorded direct speech in inviting Paul and his companions to her home (Acts 16.15).[27] While a female slave (παιδίσκη) speaks in a public setting in Acts 16.17, her voice is attributed to the pythonic spirit within her.[28] When a παιδίσκη, Rhoda, twice speaks in Acts 12.14-15 the narrator does not record her words whereas those to

26. Spencer, 'Out of Mind,' 136.
27. Thus, Lydia, alone of the women in Acts, is given direct speech without explicitly 'losing out' in some way. While Spencer, 'Out of Mind,' 147, describes Lydia's role as 'passive hearer and helper,' her prevailing upon Paul and his companions suggests more than passivity.
28. Lawson, 'Gender and Genre,' 264.

whom she speaks are twice accorded direct speech in response to her. Moreover, like Elizabeth and the women at the tomb, Rhoda's truthful words are met with disbelief, and she is thought to be out of her mind.[29] Priscilla's words to Apollos are not recorded (Acts 18.26). In contrast, the male leaders in Acts are often accorded direct speech, with several lengthy speeches highlighted.

An important narrative effect of the women 'losing their pound' by the end of the Lukan Gospel, that is, losing the efficacy of their speech, having their agency compromised, is that women do not prophesy, teach or proclaim in Acts. Since the commission to heal is linked with proclamation of the βασιλεία, having lost the efficacy of their public speech, it is also not surprising that no woman is engaged in healing ministry in Acts. While the words of the prophet Joel, that sons and daughters shall prophesy, are spoken by Peter (Acts 2.17), no woman actually prophesies in Acts. Though the four daughters of Philip are described as having the gift of prophecy (Acts 21.9), they are not portrayed as using that gift. Instead, the male prophet, Agabus, prophesies to Paul when he stays in Philip's house (Acts 21.8-11). Lawson observes 'the almost incidental nature of the reference to the prophesying daughters and their subordination to a prophesying male; the naming of the male prophet in contrast with the non-naming of the female prophets.'[30] Agabus is earlier introduced as a prophet in Acts 11.27-28.

Men are often portrayed as teaching (διδάσκω) in Acts,[31] but the only woman portrayed in a teaching role is Priscilla. With her husband, Aquila, she explains the way of God to Apollos (Acts 18.26). The verb διδάσκω is not used in this instance, however. Instead, the verb ἐκτίθημι (to explain) is used.[32] As Reid comments, 'One wonders if this is deliberate, so as to restrict the teaching ministry to male disciples.'[33] Moreover, as we have seen, Priscilla's words of explanation are not recorded. Similarly, in Acts it is only men who proclaim. No female voice is engaged in proclamation.[34] Furthermore, men are often portrayed as healing in Acts,[35] but no woman is so portrayed. While women are included as beneficiaries of these healings, the healing ministry is portrayed as a man's domain.

29. Spencer, 'Out of Mind,' 136–37, highlights that, on three occasions in Luke-Acts (Lk. 22.54-57; Acts 12.13-15; 16.16-18), the word of a παιδίσκη is 'squelched or challenged in some way' and she is stigmatized.

30. Lawson, 'Gender and Genre,' 242.

31. For example, Acts 4.2, 18-20; 5.21, 25, 28, 42; 11.26; 15.35; 18.1, 25; 20.20; 21.21, 28; 28.31.

32. Reid, *Choosing the Better Part?*, 43–44.

33. Reid, *Choosing the Better Part?*, 44.

34. For a thorough investigation of those engaged in proclamation in Luke-Acts, see Reid, *Choosing the Better Part?*, 30–34.

35. See Acts 3.1-10; 5.12-16; 8.6-7; 9.32-35; 14.8-10; 19.11-12; 28.8-9.

Though women follow Jesus from Galilee to Jerusalem (23.49) and witness to his resurrection (24.1-12), thus fulfilling the criteria outlined for the replacement of Judas among the apostles, they are considered ineligible. It is explicitly stated by Peter that one of the *men* (ἄνδρες) who had traveled with Jesus must be chosen to be a witness to the resurrection (Acts 1.21-26).[36] Ultimately, women are not considered eligible for a position of public teaching and proclamation of the βασιλεία of God. Having lost the efficacy of their speech by the end of the Gospel of Luke, the women disciples are not considered suitable for a role incorporating public proclamation within the continuing story of the early Church in Acts. Mark Allan Powell claims that 'Luke's primary concern is to assure the reliability of the witnesses on which his Gospel depends.'[37] The irony is that, though the Lukan Gospel portrays women as reliable and faithful witnesses to the resurrection, women's role as witness does not continue in the ongoing Lukan narrative.

Given this cumulative narrative effect, it is possible to look back over the Lukan Gospel and see a sense in which Mary, the sister of Martha, also 'loses her pound' although it is not made explicit in the text. Mary is portrayed as sitting at the feet of Jesus and listening to his word (10.39). As such, while she is not corrected or disbelieved, there is a sense in which she too 'loses her pound' since she symbolizes the central position of hearing the word (cf. 8.15; 11.28), but does not progress to the stage of proclamation, the 'doing.' For Mary, the sister of Martha, 'losing her pound' means losing the opportunity to publicly proclaim the word.

Similarly, Mary of Nazareth is a hearer and keeper of the word, one of the good soil (8.15). She is also the only named woman among those devoting themselves to prayer (Acts 1.14), as Jesus has taught them (11.1-13; 18.1). Like her namesake, however, Mary of Nazareth does not publicly proclaim. Both these women called Mary are faithful disciples but do not have an apostolic role of proclamation. In Acts 6.2-4, the twelve give priority to ministry of the word over other ministry (διακονία).[38] That the word of God continues to spread (Acts 6.7) indicates that the twelve continue to proclaim the word publicly. The public proclamation involved in the role of the twelve, the apostles (6.13), prohibits women from having an apostolic role in Acts since the Lukan women have effectively 'lost their pound,' their capacity and opportunity to proclaim publicly, by the end of the Lukan Gospel.

36. See Seim, 'The Gospel of Luke,' 748; Lawson, 'Gender and Genre,' 158; and Caroline Vander Stichele, 'Gender and Genre: Acts in/of Interpretation,' in *Contextualizing Acts: Lukan Narrative and Greco-Roman Discourse*, ed. Todd Penner and Caroline Vander Stichele (Atlanta, GA: SBL, 2003), 313.

37. Mark Allan Powell, *What are they Saying About Luke?* (Mahwah, NJ: Paulist Press, 1989), 48.

38. See Schüssler Fiorenza, *But She Said*, 65.

At both the beginning and end of the Lukan Gospel narrative, women display greater faith and insight than men (Luke 1.5-55; 24.1-25). Yet those who are most qualified to proclaim on the basis of their faith are not portrayed in an apostolic role. This is a profound irony of the Lukan narrative. Lukan women can listen to and treasure the word, but they cannot publicly announce the word. Noting that public proclamation is depicted as a male prerogative in Acts, Seim clarifies this dynamic of absence: 'The invisibility of the women does not necessarily reflect the actual reality but is a construction that is ideologically undergirded and maintained.'[39]

4. *Women in Lukan Parables*

The above conclusions are drawn from consideration of the women characters in the Lukan Gospel. It remains to draw the women of the Lukan parables, the characters in a story within a story, into these considerations. The two women who are given direct speech in the parables are the woman with the ten coins (15.8-10) and the widow who seeks justice (18.1-8).

When the woman who finds a lost coin rejoices, a female audience within the parable hears her words. The woman's direct speech is recorded and not marginalized by other characters (15.9). The woman does not 'lose her pound,' rather she images God's seeking out the lost. This characterization does continue the pattern of women's speech outlined above. Like Elizabeth and Mary who speak to each other and are not corrected or discredited (1.39-56), the woman's speech is not critiqued when she speaks in female company. Rather the narrative affirms her speech.

The widow who seeks justice speaks in a public setting. Her words are recorded and she finally succeeds in her task of claiming justice for herself (18.3-5). Rather than 'lose her pound,' the widow gains justice. Hence, within this parable the pattern observed above is broken. This woman asserts herself by initiating public speech and does not 'lose her pound.' The efficacy of her speech produces the desired result. Here then is the only example of women's direct speech in a public setting in the Lukan Gospel that is not discredited in some way.[40]

Perhaps the situation of the woman as a widow may be significant in the response to her speech. While the status of widow potentially makes this woman more vulnerable, it also grants her more independence from

39. Seim, 'The Gospel of Luke,' 752.
40. As we have seen, there is also one example in Acts – Lydia speaks publicly in Acts 16.15 without 'losing her pound.'

patriarchal structures.[41] Since there is no one to speak for her, she is more able to speak for herself in public. There is less likelihood that a male relative is shamed by her public speech. Does the widow's increased independence, therefore, enable her to speak in a public setting and not 'lose her pound'?[42]

For whatever reason, the widow who seeks justice from a judge does not lose the efficacy of her speech. The narrator portrays a persistent woman in the parable. Yet the characterization of women in the rest of the Gospel has them 'losing their pound' when they speak publically. While the widow in the parable can persist in claiming justice and not 'lose out,' the women characters in the Lukan Gospel cannot persist in other ways. The public voice of women is diminished by the end of this Gospel so that women do not persist in public roles of prophesying, teaching, proclaiming or healing in Acts. Thus, there is inconsistency on the part of the Lukan narrator in presenting women's continuing role. What is granted the widow in the parable is not granted the women characters in the rest of the Lukan Gospel.

5. *Women's Resistance*

Where oppressive structures operate, elements of resistance also spring to life. The second-century extracanonical *Acts of Paul and Thecla* is described by Schottroff as 'a significant document of women's resistance in early Christianity' and she considers that there are traditions of women's resistance in the New Testament.[43] She argues that women's resistance results from the rejection of roles forced on them by the patriarchal order: 'It would be inappropriate to interpret this resistance of women as resistance of women against men per se. ... It is rather the resistance of women against the patriarchal system that, through the enforcement of women's roles, plunges them into unfreedom.'[44] Women as well as men can act as agents of the patriarchal order. Schottroff notes,

41. As D'Angelo outlines, '[i]n antiquity, widows with either property or family might well have a relative degree of autonomy.' See D'Angelo, '(Re)Presentations of Women,' 186; also Curkpatrick, 'Parable Frame-Up,' 25.
42. The independence accorded Lydia (Acts 16.13-15, 40) leads some scholars to suggest that she is a widow. See, for example, Lilian Portefaix, *Sisters Rejoice: Paul's Letter to the Philippians and Luke-Acts as Received by First-Century Philippian Women* (Stockholm: Almqvist & Wiksell International, 1988), 159. The text does not specifically identify Lydia as a widow, however.
43. Schottroff, *Lydia's Imapatient Sisters*, 105. Schottroff refers to this writing as *The Acts of Thecla*.
44. Schottroff, *Lydia's Imapatient Sisters*, 109.

for instance, that Thecla's mother was a harsh critic of her daughter's decision not to marry.[45]

We have seen in the introductory chapter that different voices from different social locations can be recognized within a text. As Wainwright explains, not only the voice of the dominant group within the community of reception, but also resistant voices which present a counter-story can be heard.[46] Within the Gospel of Luke, it may be possible to see the seeds of traditions of women's resistance and hear the resistant voices in the stories of women who take the initiative to speak outside a purely female realm – Elizabeth naming her son against convention (1.60); Anna who proclaims (2.38); Mary who speaks on behalf of herself and her husband (2.48); Martha who initiates speech with Jesus (10.40); the woman in the crowd who proclaims a blessing (11.27); the slave-woman who identifies Peter as a follower of Jesus (22.56); the women who proclaim the news of the resurrection (24.9). These women's actions resist the patriarchal ideal of public silence for women. As we have seen, various narrative strategies diminish the efficacy of these women's speech. While the resistant voices speak out, the dominant voice in the narrative seeks to curtail or control this speech. The strategies, however, cannot erase completely that some women characters resist the role of public silence.[47]

Perhaps it is in the world of the Lukan parables that the voice of women's resistance is most strongly heard within the narrative. As we have seen, within the Gospel of Luke, it is only in a parable that a woman can take the initiative to speak in the public world and 'win out' rather than 'lose' in some way. The widow who confronts the judge (18.1-8) continually seeks justice for herself against an oppressive system. She succeeds in her quest for justice and her agency and power are not compromised. A counter-story can be heard in this parable, a story which challenges the dominant voices heard through the Lukan Gospel and which refuses to be suppressed. Within the Gospel of Luke, therefore, it would seem that both the voice of women's resistance as well as the more dominant attempts to silence this voice of resistance are in evidence. It may be, however, 'that the dominant voices can be deconstructed by those who have ears to hear.'[48]

45. Schottroff, *Lydia's Imapatient Sisters*, 108.
46. Wainwright, *Shall We Look?*, 36–37.
47. While my focus in this study is on the women of the Lukan Gospel, the resistance of two women in Acts can be noted here. Lydia urges and prevails upon Paul and his companions to stay at her home (Acts 16.15) and Priscilla, together with her husband, explains the way of God to Apollos (Acts 18.24-27).
48. Mark G. Brett, *Genesis: Procreation and the Politics of Identity* (London: Routledge, 2000), 22. Brett is discussing Genesis here, but his words also have relevance to the Gospel of Luke.

6. *Power Inequities*

In the Parable of the Pounds, class differences produce the inequities in power which result in the third slave 'losing his pound.'[49] In the case of the Lukan women having their 'pound' taken away, gender difference is also involved in producing power inequity. Class and gender structures are not separate but are rather overlapping systems causing oppression. This raises the question of whether women of a particular class are more likely to have their 'pounds' compromised in the narrative.

The women in the Gospel of Luke come from a range of classes. Arlandson divides the Lukan women into the following classes – governing classes; retainers and religionists; rural peasants; urban landowners, merchants, artisans and crowds; slaves; unclean and degraded; and expendables.[50] He argues that it is important to consider the class of women when considering their characterization in the Lukan story and claims that the Lukan narrative demonstrates the elevation of women of the lowest classes at the expense of high-class men. Within the Lukan Gospel, he proposes four examples of this scenario – 7.36-50; 8.1-3 and 23.55–24.10; 13.10-17; and 21.1-4.[51]

Arlandson, however, fails to consider that, of the women in these examples whom he identifies as being elevated at the expense of privileged men, none is accorded direct speech. While the woman who anoints Jesus (7.36-50) is affirmed by Jesus for her faith, she remains silent as does the poor widow who is contrasted with the rich (21.1-4). The bent-over woman glorifies God when she is healed by Jesus but no speech is accredited to her (13.10-17). It is true that the direct speech of the privileged men, who are contrasted unfavorably with the women in these pericopes, highlights their lack of understanding of Jesus and, as such, leads to their loss of honor. As has been noted previously, however, there are many examples of men in the Gospel speaking and being affirmed by Jesus for their speech, so that silence as the appropriate state for men is not promoted in the Gospel. At the same time, these pericopes reinforce the silent presence of women, an image which is replicated through the narrative.

The remaining example contrasts Mary Magdalene with the twelve (8.1-3; 23.55–24.10). Arlandson categorizes Mary Magdalene as demonized (8.2) and therefore in the 'unclean and degraded' class. As one of the women who go to the tomb, receive the news of the resurrection and tell the eleven and the rest, she speaks to the apostles but the words are not

---

49. Furthermore, imperialist structures whereby one country has power over another country give the nobleman power over his fellow-citizens.

50. Arlandson, *Women, Class, and Society*, 124-26.

51. Arlandson, *Women, Class, and Society*, 151–85.

recorded. Furthermore, the apostles do not believe the women's words (24.1-11).

Noting the irony in the Lukan resurrection narrative in which the men are portrayed as ignorant and the women as perceptive and faithful, Arlandson labels Mary Magdalene and the other women 'the true heroines of the resurrection narrative.'[52] He also emphasizes, however, the 'institutionalized place of prominence' of the twelve in Luke-Acts and sees the women's role as helping to restore the twelve to this prominence:

> If women (and other men) are barred from this unique position of power, then Luke can make sure that it is Mary and other women who re-establish the eleven, later the twelve (Acts 1.15-26). Significantly, Luke does not use lesser men to restore them. If he had wanted to restrict and suppress women, then he could have overlooked them altogether or made passing reference to them . . .[53]

As we have seen, however, strategies of silencing may be more subtle than overlooking women altogether. Though Arlandson concentrates on the elevation of the women at the tomb, he overlooks the fact that this elevation is not sufficient to give the women a public voice in the story of the early Church in Acts, despite evidence in Paul's correspondence of women in leadership roles (see, for instance, Rom. 16.1-16).

Nevertheless, it is possible to see from Arlandson's work that gender division, rather than class division, is the main factor in the women's 'pound' being taken away from them. In the Lukan narrative, it is the collective voice of women characters in the public world which is diminished by the end of the Gospel. Women of both low and higher classes have their public voice diminished. The only woman in the Lukan Gospel who is accorded direct speech in a public setting, and is not denied, corrected or disbelieved, is the widow who challenges a judge in the parable of 18.1-8. As a widow she falls into Arlandson's 'expendables' category. This widow, however, is a character in a parable rather than a character in the narrative world itself. Furthermore, she is the only widow accorded direct speech in the Lukan Gospel. Of widows in the actual narrative world of the Lukan Gospel, Anna's words to those awaiting the redemption of Jerusalem are not recorded while Simeon's direct words are highlighted (2.25-38), and neither the widow of Nain nor the poor widow speaks (7.11-17; 21.1-4). Hence, giving direct speech without correction to widows is not a common practice of the Lukan narrator.

That the only woman in the Lukan Gospel to be given direct speech without being corrected is a widow suggests, on the one hand then, that the widow status may be significant in granting the woman more

---

52. Arlandson, *Women, Class, and Society*, 167.
53. Arlandson, *Women, Class, and Society*, 167.

autonomy and thus more freedom with regard to public speech. Given that no other widow in the Gospel is accorded direct speech suggests, on the other hand, however, that class is not the determining factor on the issue. Unlike the women, several men of the lowly classes are given direct public speech within the narrative world. Of Arlandson's 'unclean and degraded' category, lepers (5.12; 17.12-13), a demoniac (8.28, 30), and a blind man (18.38-39, 41) have their voices heard. In particular, the blind man's public voice is vindicated by Jesus against those demanding the man's silence (18.39-42). Unlike the blind man, however, women who are silenced by other characters or the narrator in the Lukan Gospel are not explicitly vindicated within the Lukan narrative.

7. *Release for the Oppressed?*

In the case of the third slave and the citizens in the Parable of the Pounds, John the Baptist and Jesus – characters who 'lose their pound' in the Lukan Gospel – the violence inflicted on these characters is overt. Such physical violence is not present in the women's stories, yet we have seen that there *is* a violence evidenced in the text nonetheless, a violence connected with the silencing of women's public voice and the marginalization of their agency. There is a tragic sense in which 'the pound' of the women characters is taken away though the theology of the Gospel would suggest condemnation of such a result.

As we have seen earlier, Jesus is portrayed in the Lukan Gospel as proclaiming and embodying release (ἄφεσις). This liberation is at the heart of this Gospel, yet the extent of the liberation for women characters needs further consideration. By the end of the Gospel of Luke the women's 'pound' is taken away, resulting in the loss of their public voice. Furthermore, a range of narrative techniques reduces the impact of many of the women on the reader. Therefore, it must be asked whether the women do indeed experience liberation, or does all of this reflect that the women are still subject to oppressive structures? Jesus describes the healing of the woman with a spirit of infirmity (13.10-17) as a freeing from bondage (13.16). But from what kind of bondage are this woman and the other women of the Lukan Gospel freed?

It would seem that the women do not experience release from all the structures which serve to oppress them. As we have seen, while there are areas in which women 'gain' through their characterizations in the Gospel of Luke, there are also examples where the women 'lose.' Women lose their public voice by the end of the Gospel and this has consequences for the roles in which women are portrayed as well as reinforcing a silent model for women.

The life-giving potential of God's radical love, which Jesus embodies, is central to the theology of the Lukan Gospel. We have seen that the women characters are drawn into a knowledge of the forgiveness of their sins and their inclusion in the community of God, as well as benefiting from Jesus' healing. In the Gospel of Luke, however, women characters (and women readers) are also drawn into the knowledge that if they initiate public speech they risk suffering the consequences of not being believed, having their words dismissed as idle chatter or of being rebuked or denied. In Acts, women are brought to the knowledge that they are ineligible to be considered apostles despite satisfying the requirements.

If the generous salvation which lies at the core of the Gospel of Luke stops being generous at this point then the Lukan portrayal of women is limiting the potential of the hospitality of God. The theology of the Lukan Gospel, however, can be used to critique the taking away of the women's 'pound.' In other words, Lukan theology can critique Lukan portrayal of women whereby women 'lose their pound.' The radical love, the expansive hospitality which Jesus embodies, offers more than the Lukan women are portrayed as receiving.

Some scholars excuse the Lukan author for the portrayal of Lukan women. According to Talbert, for instance, it is the social context of the Greco-Roman world, rather than the evangelist, which is responsible for the limited roles for women in this Gospel: 'It would appear that the third evangelist is as positive toward the ministry of women in the church as his social structure would allow.'[54] This argument is undermined, however, by the fact that in some other parts of the New Testament the roles of women are not restricted in the same way. In the Gospel of Luke there is no Canaanite woman who refuses to be silenced by rebuke and who demands to be heard in the public world, claiming for herself and her daughter the fruits of the βασιλεία of God (Mt. 15.21-28; cf. Mk 7.24-30).[55] Neither is there a Samaritan woman who engages in a theological dialogue with Jesus before witnessing to the people of her city (Jn 4.7-42). Pauline letters show women in leadership roles within the early Church, but the women of the Lukan Gospel are not portrayed as public witnesses.

Given that other New Testament texts can display women speaking publicly and in apostolic roles, it would seem that the marginalization of women in the Lukan Gospel cannot be attributed solely to the Greco-Roman context. Choices of the Lukan author impact significantly on the women's portrayal. The women in the Lukan Gospel share some of the fruits of the hospitality of God but they are not released from all the structures which oppress them. Jesus' words to the women as he is led to

---

54. Talbert, *Reading Luke*, 93.
55. As previously noted, the Lukan widow who demands justice for herself is a character in a parable (18.1-8). The public voice which she is given is not given to any woman character in the narrative.

his crucifixion – 'Daughters of Jerusalem, do not weep for me, but weep
for yourselves ...' (23.28) – can, ironically, be considered an appropriate
response to the taking away of the women's 'pound' in the Gospel of
Luke. Women can weep for themselves and mourn the taking away of
their 'pound.'

8. *Acclamation*

Perhaps, however, the Lukan narrative can be read in a way which finally
acclaims the women who speak out in public. The theme of reversal in the
Gospel of Luke has its supreme expression in God's raising of Jesus. God
vindicates and acclaims Jesus' ministry and the salvation that he has
embodied. The one who challenges oppressive practices triumphs against
those who impose violence on others. John the Baptist and the third slave
and citizens in the Parable of the Pounds, who also 'lose their pounds,' are
thus likewise acclaimed against the powerful oppressors whom they
challenge. If the women characters who have their 'pound,' their efficacy,
their ministry, their voice compromised can be said to stand in line with
the other characters who 'lose their pound' when they resist oppressive
practices, then there is a sense in which the text can be seen ultimately to
acclaim the actions of the women while providing a critique of the
structures which take away the women's 'pound.' As the Lukan Gospel
narrative shows, those who challenge oppressive practices stand with
Jesus and God vindicates them against their opponents.

Ironically, while the Lukan Gospel operates, on the one hand, to take
away the women's 'pound,' it also can provide a critique of the violence
done to women in taking their 'pound' away. In a way, the text subverts
itself.[56] As such, there is a sense in which the silencing and marginalization
of the Lukan women is deconstructed and the women implicitly stand
finally acclaimed for challenging oppressive structures despite 'losing their
pound.' Hence, it can be argued that the dominant voices in the Gospel of
Luke which appear to take away the women's efficacy when they initiate
speech are not only challenged by the resistant voices within the narrative,
but they are also challenged by the dynamism of the Gospel narrative
itself.

It can be seen, then, that the Parable of the Pounds is a very effective
lens through which to view the characterization of the women of the
Lukan Gospel, focusing the material in its own way. Not only is the
parable particularly apt in explaining the different characterizations of the
women – sometimes 'gaining,' sometimes 'losing' – but it also opens up a

---

56. For a different explanation and interpretation of how the Lukan text can deconstruct
itself, see Kahl, 'Reading Luke Against Luke,' 70–88.

deconstructive reading of the Gospel of Luke in which the women are finally acclaimed for challenging patriarchal structures and ideals that serve to suppress them.

CONCLUSION

1. *Summary of Findings*

Different lenses affect light in different ways. Some lenses converge light to a point, while others diffuse the light. Some prisms disperse the light into a spectrum, producing a rainbow of colors. The glasses we wear, the lenses we employ to view our world or a particular text impact greatly on our vision. A new lens can produce new possibilities for sight and insight. In this study, I have used the lens of the Parable of the Pounds (Lk. 19.11-28) to view the characterizations of the women in the Gospel of Luke.

In particular, I have explored the power dynamics operating in sections of the Lukan Gospel as a result of differences in class, imperial status and gender, arguing that the power dynamic operating in the Parable of the Pounds can give insight into the power dynamics operating in the stories of women in the Lukan Gospel. The 'pound' is used as a metaphor for what one has that can be taken away by a more powerful other.

The reading of the Parable of the Pounds employed in this study is not the majority reading of the parable. Instead of identifying the third slave as a failure, this slave is identified in this reading as one who resists the oppressive practices of his master. The nobleman/king is revealed to be an oppressor and likened in his actions to Antiochus whose tyrannical actions featured prominently in the minds of the Jewish people.

Those who offer resistance to the nobleman/king's oppressive practices are seen to pay a price for their actions. The third slave has his pound taken away from him, as well as the opportunity to have a position of influence himself. He loses the possibility of power, status and future manumission, reinforcing his powerlessness and vulnerability. Moreover, the third slave is portrayed as knowing the nature of his master, implying that this slave would expect that his resistance would have adverse consequences for himself. The citizens who oppose the nobleman lose their lives.

An important feature of the parable for its use as a lens for focusing the women's characterizations is that not all slaves receive the same treatment from their master. While the master is in a position of power over all the slaves, some of the slaves benefit from their dealings with the master. Two are granted power over cities. These slaves are not portrayed as opposing the master in any way; rather they have furthered the master's oppressive practices, thus 'perpetuating the system.' The key to determining how the slaves fare in the parable is whether or not they resist the oppression which the master controls. Those who resist suffer the consequences while those who do not resist reap the benefits.

In this study, I have argued that the pattern of challengers to oppressive practices paying the penalty for their actions is also evidenced in the Lukan Gospel in the cases of John the Baptist and Jesus. Both challenge those in positions of power and both pay with their lives. Thus the third slave, the citizens of the Parable of the Pounds and John the Baptist can be said to stand with Jesus in challenging oppressive structures and suffering the consequences for so doing. Ultimately, however, in the great reversal, the resurrection triumphs over evil and oppression. In a sense then, the third slave and citizens, along with John the Baptist, are ultimately acclaimed just as Jesus is acclaimed and vindicated.

Using the Parable of the Pounds as a lens provides insight into the characterizations of the women in the Lukan Gospel. In particular, it helps account for the different ways in which women characters can be seen to fare in this Gospel. Those women who take the initiative to speak out in the presence of males can be shown to 'lose their pounds' whereas those who remain silent or who speak in female-only company 'gain.'

The patriarchal ideal of attributing silence to women has persisted from the ancient world to recent times. The women characters in the Gospel of Luke who initiate public speech can, therefore, be seen to be challenging an oppressive patriarchal ideal. Since women who take the initiative with their actions rather than their words in the presence of males do not explicitly 'lose their pounds' in this Gospel, it would seem that women's public actions do not present as much of a challenge to the 'system' portrayed in the Lukan Gospel as women's public speech.

There are a number of ways in which women can be said to 'lose their pounds' in this Gospel. Some women are not believed or are denied though they speak the truth. Here it is other characters who take away the efficacy of the women's words and diminish their role in the ensuing narrative. Some women are rebuked or corrected when they speak in the presence of men. Again, it is other characters who operate here to marginalize women's speech. In particular, the Lukan Jesus rebukes or corrects every woman who is accorded direct speech and who speaks to him in this Gospel. At times, the words of women who do speak are not recorded though the narrative presents an expectation of direct speech. Here it is the narrator who diminishes the impact of the women's words on the reader and thus marginalizes for the reader the significance of the women's speech. The mimetic development of the women characters is compromised. Several women are portrayed as demon-possessed which serves to vilify the women and marginalize their διακονία. It is possible that demon-possession is being used to stereotype women healers. Since commissions to heal and to proclaim are linked, women's public voice is compromised as well by this stereotype.

Hence, some of the women characters are vilified and silenced in this Gospel. As such the characters are subjected to a form of violence, not a physical violence but nonetheless debilitating. This leads to a margin-alization of their characterizations. The rhetorical effect of these narrative strategies is to reinforce that public speech for women is inappropriate or to be diminished in significance, and the roles in which the women are engaged are marginalized.

This is not the only story of women's characterizations in this Gospel, however. Women who speak in female-only company or who remain silent have many 'positive' features within their characterizations. These include, in various cases, prophetic speech, paradigmatic faith, independ-ent action, taking initiative, offering hospitality, being a beneficiary of Jesus' healing and affirmation, and modeling characteristics of disciple-ship. Thus, many features of women's characterizations in this Gospel serve to promote the women as faithful to God's purposes. Like the first two slaves in the Parable of the Pounds, some women characters' stories end on an affirming note. It is only those who are a threat to the oppressive system who have their 'pound' explicitly taken away.

We have also seen, however, that there is a sense in which the silent women *do* 'lose their pound.' Women who are portrayed as faithfully modeling openness to the word of God but who do not progress to the stage of proclamation can also be considered to have their roles marginalized. The silent women characters of the Lukan Gospel may not explicitly 'lose their pound' in the Gospel narrative but they do lose it in the ongoing story of the Church as portrayed in Acts.

One woman character in a parable (a character in a story within a story) is portrayed as initiating speech in a public setting and maintaining her efficacy and power. The widow who continually confronts the unjust judge (18.1-8) achieves justice for herself and does not 'lose her pound.' It is significant that this widow is not a character in the Gospel narrative itself. The efficacy of this widow's direct public speech is not granted to any woman character in the actual narrative. That none of the other widows in the Gospel is accorded direct public speech, suggests that it is not so much that the woman is a widow but that she is a character in a parable which may influence her portrayal. While women of different classes in the ancient Mediterranean world had access to different levels of power, the public voice of *all* women characters in the Lukan Gospel narrative is marginalized. Hence, the narrative strategies in regard to public speech in this Gospel reflect differences in gender more than differences in class.

Perhaps in the parable we hear a different voice from that in the dominant narrative. Whereas the dominant voice reinforces the public silence of women, this widow's voice reflects the voice of resistance to women's public silence and marginalization. Further resistance and subversion of the public silencing of women can be exercised by aligning the women characters who challenge this oppressive practice, by taking the initiative to speak in public, with the other characters in the Gospel who also 'lose their pound' when they challenge oppressive structures. Like Jesus, they are ultimately acclaimed through the triumph of the resurrection over evil and injustice, and the structures that produce this oppression are condemned. Such a counter-reading subverts the dominant rhetoric of the Lukan Gospel narrative, enabling the women characters who take the initiative for public speech to be perceived as acting honorably, like the third slave in the Parable of the Pounds. They refuse to be bound by oppressive practices and do not perpetuate the system of oppression.

It is impossible to know with certainty the intentions of the author of the Gospel of Luke. The only resource we have for determining this is the text itself. Given that Jesus is the hero of the Gospel narrative, his rebuke or correction of all women characters who initiate speech with him highlights that the dominant rhetoric of the narrative functions to silence or marginalize women's public speech. As such, the dominant rhetoric brings the Gospel of Luke in line with first-century laws and literature that sought to limit the public voice and power of women. Even so, the seeds of resistant voices can also be found in the Gospel narrative, enabling a counter-reading which ultimately acclaims the women who do speak out in public. It must be said, however, that the resistant voice is heard only by those who have ears to hear. The resistance is seen only by those who use lenses that allow them to focus the light in a variety of ways.

2. *Implications for the Twenty-first Century*

The marginalization of women's voices is not just an ancient phenomenon but something which has continued in various forms across the centuries. This study, therefore, speaks to the contemporary experience of women who are silenced and marginalized, those women who 'lose their pound' when they claim justice for themselves and others.

The twenty-first-century reader of the Gospel of Luke who has ears to hear the voice of women's resistance to oppressive structures, and who uses the lens of the Parable of the Pounds to acclaim those women characters who *do* resist being silenced and marginalized, is able to challenge the dominant voices of this Gospel and strive so that the silence of women characters in the Gospel of Luke is not used to reinforce a silent or marginalized role for women in contemporary times. Such a reader, therefore, ensures that the women characters of the Gospel of Luke are brought into focus and 'heard.'

This study, however, speaks not only to the contemporary experience of women who are silenced, but to the experience of all people who have had their 'pound' taken away by those in a position of power over them. The study encourages exposing those practices which are oppressive and identifying those actions which perpetuate the system of oppression. It also calls us to acclaim and honor those who resist oppressive practices and suffer adverse consequences for their resistance.

The citizens in the Parable of the Pounds hate the nobleman and do not want him to rule over them, but he obtains power over them from a distant ruling country and takes the βασιλεία for himself. The citizens have no power to stop him assuming this role. The experience of the citizens is the experience of all indigenous peoples colonized by a foreign power, peoples who have 'lost their pound,' their land, their culture, their families and even their lives when they resist this colonization.

Remembering that it is not only humans who are the victims of abusive power, the Parable of the Pounds also speaks to the experience of our environment which is mastered and exploited by human domination. 'The pound' which our environment has had compromised by humanity is its beauty, its fertility, its sustainability, its resources, its variety of life forms.

The reading of the Parable of the Pounds presented in this study can shape the world in front of the text in regard to the contemporary experience of all who are oppressed. The possibilities of resistance, opened up by the use of the Parable of the Pounds as a lens, not only challenge oppressive practices and acclaim those who refuse to perpetuate them, but also give hope that the contemporary struggles can lead to resurrection. The contemporary reader can stand with all the Lukan Gospel characters who embody release rather than oppression.

Given that the dominant rhetoric of the Gospel of Luke marginalizes the public voice of women, particular care needs to be taken in reading this Gospel today. In contemporary times, the text cannot be read in a way that contributes to the marginalization of women. Rather, contemporary interpretations need to subvert such rhetoric.

Developments in the interpretation of the characterization of the Jews in New Testament texts can provide insight into the way the Gospel of Luke must be approached. In a 2001 document entitled *The Jewish People and Their Sacred Scriptures in the Christian Bible*, the Pontifical Biblical Commission recognizes that New Testament texts have been used in the past to foster anti-Jewish sentiment. Furthermore, the Commission highlights that it is essential to understand that historical contexts have influenced the writing of these texts:

> ... it must be admitted that many of these passages are capable of providing a pretext for anti-Jewish sentiment and have in fact been used in this way. To avoid mistakes of this kind, it must be kept in mind that the New Testament polemical texts, even those expressed in general terms, have to do with concrete historical contexts and are never meant to be applied to Jews of all times and places merely because they are Jews.[1]

Thus the Pontifical Biblical Commission rightly speaks out against anti-Jewish interpretations and reinforces that polemical texts are not normative for today. This same concern must be given to New Testament texts and interpretations which marginalize women. Such texts cannot be considered normative for today. Rhetoric which marginalizes women must be identified and critiqued.

Though the Lukan text commends silence for women, contemporary readers can subvert such a message, promoting and honoring the public voice of both women and men. The *Magnificat*, which speaks of bringing down the powerful and raising up the lowly, is the perfect example of subversion of oppressive practices. Moreover, within the Gospel of Luke, the *Magnificat* is proclaimed by a woman in the private space of women but the words become public in the reading. The *Magnificat* is part of the common language of worship. By proclaiming the canticle, contemporary readers can ensure that a Lukan woman's voice is heard in the public world.

Readers of the Gospel of Luke who view the text through the lens of the Parable of the Pounds can pay attention to difference and strive to ensure that their interpretations of the text do not reinforce an oppressive rhetoric. New lenses produce new possibilities for sight. Such lenses reflect the richness of the text and are a gift to those with the eyes to see.

---

1. Pontifical Biblical Commission, *The Jewish People and their Sacred Scriptures in the Christian Bible* (May 24, 2001), n. 87; http://www.vatican.va/roman_curia/congregations/cfaith/pcb_documents/rc_con_cfaith_doc_20020212_popolo-ebraico_en.html Accessed June 4th, 2006.

BIBLIOGRAPHY

1. *Ancient Texts and Translations*

'The Acts of Paul and Thecla.' In *The New Testament and Other Early Christian Writings: A Reader*. Edited by Bart D. Ehrman, 177–82. New York, NY: Oxford University Press, 1998.

Aristotle. *Generation of Animals*. Translated by A. L. Peck. LCL 366. London: Heinemann, 1942.

—*Politics*. Translated by H. Rackham. LCL 264. London: Heinemann, 1959.

—*Poetics*. Translated by Stephen Halliwell. 2nd edn. LCL 199. Cambridge, MA: Harvard University Press, 1995.

The Babylonian Talmud. Translated and edited by I. Epstein. 35 vols. London: Soncino Press, 1935–48.

Biblia Hebraica Stuttgartensia. Bible Windows. [CD-ROM; Cedar Hill, TX: Silver Mountain Software, 2001].

Demosthenes. *Works*. Translated by J. H. Vince, et al. 7 vols. LCL. Cambridge, MA: Harvard University Press, 1926–49.

Didascalia Apostolorum in English. Translated by Margaret Dunlop Gibson. London: Clay and Sons, 1903.

Euripides. *Trojan Women; Iphigenia Among the Taurions; Ion*. Translated by David Kovacs. LCL 10. Cambridge, MA: Harvard University Press, 1999.

The Greek New Testament. Edited by B. Aland, et al. 4th revised edn. Stuttgart: Deutsche Bibelgesellschaft, 1994.

Hippolytus. 'ΕΙΣ ΤΟ ΑΣΜΑ.' In *Hippolytus Werke: Exegetische und Homiletische Schriften*. Edited by G. N. Bonwetsch and H. Achelis, 341–74. GCS 1. Leipzig: J. C. Hinrichs'sche Buchhandlung, 1897.

Jenkins, Claude. 'Documents: Origen on 1 Corinthians. IV.' *JTS* 10 (1909): 29–51.

Josephus. *Works*. Translated by H. St. J. Thackeray, et al. 10 vols. LCL. Cambridge, MA: Harvard University Press, 1926–65.

Klostermann, Erich, (ed.), *Apocrypha*. 3rd edn. Vol. 2. Berlin: De Gruyter, 1929.

Lectionary. 3 vols. London: Collins Liturgical Publications, 1983.

New Revised Standard Version Bible. Catholic Edition. Nashville, TN: Catholic Bible Press, 1993.

Origen. *Commentary on the Gospel according to John*. Translated by Ronald E. Heine. 2 vols. The Fathers of the Church 80, 89. Washington, DC: Catholic University of America Press, 1989–93.

Philo. *Works*. Translated by F. H. Colson, et al. 12 vols. LCL. London: Heinemann, 1929–62.

Schneemelcher, Wilhelm, and R. McL. Wilson, (eds.), *New Testament Apocrypha Vol One: Gospels and Related Writings*. Revised edn. Cambridge: James Clarke and Co, 1991.

The Septuagint. Bible Windows. [CD-ROM; Cedar Hill, TX: Silver Mountain Software, 2001].

Sophocles. *Works*. Translated by Hugh Lloyd-Jones. 3 vols. LCL. Cambridge, MA: Harvard University Press, 1994–96.

Stroker, William D. *Extracanonical Sayings of Jesus*. Atlanta, GA: Scholars Press, 1989.

Xenophon. *Works*. Translated by E. C. Marchant, et al. 7 vols. LCL. London: Heinemann, 1968–79.

2. *Grammatical Tools*

Bauer, Walter, William F. Arndt, F. Wilbur Gingrich, and Frederick W. Danker. *A Greek-English Lexicon of the New Testament and Other Early Christian Literature*. 2nd edn. Chicago, IL: University of Chicago Press, 1979.

Blass, F., and A. Debrunner. *A Greek Grammar of the New Testament and Other Early Christian Literature*. Translated by Robert Funk. Chicago, IL: University of Chicago Press, 1961.

Brown, Francis, S. R. Driver, and Charles A. Briggs. *A Hebrew and English Lexicon of the Old Testament*. Oxford: Clarendon Press, 1907.

Collins English Dictionary. 4th Australian edn. Glasgow: HarperCollins, 1998.

Friberg, Timothy, Barbara Friberg, and Neva F. Miller. *Analytical Lexicon of the Greek New Testament*. Grand Rapids, MI: Baker Books, 2000.

Kittel, Gerhard, and G. Friedrich, (eds.), *Theological Dictionary of the New Testament*. Translated by Geoffrey W. Bromiley. 10 vols. Grand Rapids, MI: Eerdmans, 1964–76.

Metzger, Bruce M. *A Textual Commentary on the Greek New Testament*. 2nd edn. Stuttgart: Deutsche Bibelgesellschaft, 1994.

Moulton, James Hope, and George Milligan. *The Vocabulary of the Greek*

Testament: Illustrated from the Papyri and Other Non-Literary Sources. London: Hodder and Stoughton, 1930.

Spicq, Ceslas. *Theological Lexicon of the New Testament*. Translated by James D. Ernest. 3 vols. Peabody, MA: Hendrickson Publishers, 1994.

3. *General*

Aletti, Jean-Nöel. 'Parabole des Mines et/ou Parabole du Roi. Lc 19, 11–28: Remarques sur l'Écriture Parabolique de Luc.' In *Les Paraboles Évangéliques: Pespectives Nouvelles*. Edited by J. Delorme, 309–32. LD 135. Paris: Éditions du Cerf, 1989.

Alter, Robert. *The Art of Biblical Narrative*. New York, NY: Basic Books, 1981.

Anderson, Janice Capel. 'Mary's Difference: Gender and Patriarchy in the Birth Narratives.' *JR* 67 (1987): 183–202.

Applegate, Judith K. ' "And She Wet His Feet With Her Tears": A Feminist Interpretation of Luke 7.36–50.' In *Escaping Eden: New Feminist Perspectives on the Bible*. Edited by Harold C. Washington, Susan Lochrie Graham, and Pamela Thimmes, 69–90. Sheffield: Sheffield Academic Press, 1998.

Arlandson, James Malcolm. *Women, Class, and Society in Early Christianity: Models from Luke-Acts*. Peabody, MA: Hendrickson, 1997.

Ashton, Gail. *The Generation of Identity in Late Medieval Hagiography: Speaking the Saint*. London: Routledge, 2000.

Bakhtin, M. M. *The Dialogic Imagination: Four Essays*. Translated by Caryl Emerson and Michael Holquist. Edited by Michael Holquist. Austin, TX: University of Texas Press, 1981.

Balch, David L. 'Luke.' In *Eerdman's Commentary on the Bible*. Edited by James D. G. Dunn and John W. Rogerson, 1104–60. Grand Rapids, MI: Eerdmans, 2003.

Bauckham, Richard. *Gospel Women: Studies of the Named Women in the Gospels*. Grand Rapids, MI: Eerdmans, 2002.

Beal, Timothy K. 'Ideology and Intertextuality: Surplus of Meaning and Controlling the Means of Production.' In *Reading Between Texts: Intertextuality and the Hebrew Bible*. Edited by Danna Nolan Fewell, 27–39. Louisville, KY: Westminster/John Knox Press, 1992.

Beavis, Mary Ann. 'Ancient Slavery as an Interpretive Context for the New Testament Servant Parables with Special Reference to the Unjust Steward (Luke 16:1-8).' *JBL* 111 (1992): 37–54.

Bemile, Paul. *The Magnificat Within the Context and Framework of Lukan Theology*. Frankfurt am Main: Verlag Peter Lang, 1986.

Black, Matthew. *Romans*. London: Marshall, Morgan & Scott, 1973.

Boatwright, Mary Taliaferro. 'Plancia Magna of Perge: Women's Roles and Status in Roman Asia Minor.' In *Women's History and Ancient History*. Edited by Sarah B. Pomeroy, 249–72. Chapel Hill, NC: University of North Carolina Press, 1991.

Bock, Darrell L. *Luke*. Downers Grove, IL: InterVarsity Press, 1994.

Bovon, François. *Das Evangelium nach Lukas*. 3 vols. Zürich; Neukirchen-Vluyn: Benziger; Neukirchener Verlag, 1989–2001.

Bradley, K. R. *Slaves and Masters in the Roman Empire: A Study in Social Control*. Bruxelles: Latomus, 1984.

Brett, Mark G. *Genesis: Procreation and the Politics of Identity*. London: Routledge, 2000.

Briggs, Sheila. 'Slavery and Gender.' In *On the Cutting Edge: The Study of Women in Biblical Worlds*. Edited by Jane Schaberg, Alice Bach, and Esther Fuchs, 171–92. New York, NY: Continuum, 2003.

Brock, Ann Graham. *Mary Magdalene, The First Apostle: The Struggle For Authority*. Cambridge, MA: Harvard University Press, 2003.

Brooten, Bernadette J. ' "Junia ... Outstanding Among the Apostles" (Romans 16:7).' In *Women Priests: A Catholic Commentary on the Vatican Declaration*. Edited by Leonard Swidler and Arlene Swidler, 141–44. New York, NY: Paulist Press, 1977.

—*Women Leaders in the Ancient Synagogues: Inscriptional Evidence and Background Issues*. BJS 36. Chico, CA: Scholars Press, 1982.

Brown, Cheryl Anne. *No Longer Be Silent: First Century Jewish Portraits of Biblical Women*. Louisville, KY: Westminster/John Knox Press, 1992.

Brown, Raymond E. *The Birth of the Messiah: A Commentary on the Infancy Narratives of Matthew and Luke*. New York, NY: Doubleday, 1979.

Byrne, Brendan. 'Forceful Stewardship and Neglectful Wealth: A Contemporary Reading of Luke 16.' *Pacifica* 1 (1988): 1–14.

—*Romans*. Sacra Pagina 6. Collegeville, MN: Liturgical Press, 1996.

—*The Hospitality of God: A Reading of Luke's Gospel*. Collegeville, MN: Liturgical Press, 2000.

Cameron, Deborah. 'Introduction: Why is Language a Feminist Issue?' In *The Feminist Critique of Language*. Edited by Deborah Cameron, 1–28. London: Routledge, 1990.

Cardman, Francine. 'Women, Ministry, and Church Order in Early Christianity.' In *Women and Christian Origins*. Edited by Ross Shepard Kraemer and Mary Rose D'Angelo, 300–29. New York, NY: Oxford University Press, 1999.

Carter, Warren. *Matthew and the Margins: A Socio-Political and Religious Reading*. JSNTSup 204. Sheffield: Sheffield Academic Press, 2000.

—'Getting Martha Out of the Kitchen: Luke 10:38-42 Again.' In *A*

Feminist Companion to Luke. Edited by Amy-Jill Levine and Marianne Blickenstaff, 214–31. London: Sheffield Academic Press, 2002.

Cixous, Hélène. 'Castration or Decapitation.' *Signs: Journal of Women in Culture and Society* 7 (1981): 41–55.

Cohen, David. 'Seclusion, Separation, and the Status of Women in Classical Athens.' *Greece and Rome* 36 (1989): 3–15.

Coleridge, Mark. *The Birth of the Lukan Narrative: Narrative as Christology in Luke 1–2*. JSNTSup 88. Sheffield: JSOT Press, 1993.

Collins, John N. *Diakonia: Re-interpreting the Ancient Sources*. New York, NY: Oxford University Press, 1990.

—'Did Luke Intend a Disservice to Women in the Martha and Mary Story?' *BTB* 28 (1998): 104–11.

Collins, Raymond F. *Letters That Paul Did Not Write: The Epistle to the Hebrews and the Pauline Pseudepigrapha*. Wilmington, DE: Michael Glazier, 1988.

Conzelmann, Hans. *The Theology of St. Luke*. Translated by Geoffrey Buswell. London: Faber & Faber, 1960.

Corley, Kathleeen E. *Private Women, Public Meals: Social Conflict in the Synoptic Tradition*. Peabody, MA: Hendrickson, 1993.

—*Women and the Historical Jesus: Feminist Myths of Christian Origins*. Santa Rosa, CA: Polebridge Press, 2002.

Council of Christians and Jews (Victoria). *Rightly Explaining the Word of Truth: Guidelines for Christian Clergy and Teachers in their Use of the New Testament with Reference to the New Testament's Presentation of Jews and Judaism*. Kew, Vic: Council of Christians and Jews (Victoria) Inc., 1994.

Craig, Kerry M., and Margret A. Kristjansson. 'Women Reading as Men/ Women Reading as Women: A Structural Analysis for the Historical Project.' *Semeia* 51 (1990): 119–36.

Crossan, John Dominic. *The Dark Interval: Towards Theology of Story*. Niles, IL: Argus Communications, 1975.

—*In Parables: The Challenge of the Historical Jesus*. Sonoma, CA: Polebridge Press, 1992.

—'The Parables of Jesus.' *Int* 56 (2002): 247–59.

Culpepper, R. Alan. *Anatomy of the Fourth Gospel: A Study in Literary Design*. Philadelphia, PA: Fortress Press, 1983.

Cummings, Mary Lou. *Surviving Without Romance: African Women Tell Their Stories*. Scottdale, PA: Herald Press, 1991.

Curkpatrick, Stephen. 'Dissonance in Luke 18:1-8.' *JBL* 121 (2002): 107–21.

—'A Parable Frame-Up and Its Audacious Reframing.' *NTS* 49 (2003): 22–38.

D'Angelo, Mary Rose. 'Women in Luke-Acts: A Redactional View.' *JBL* 109 (1990): 441–61.

—'(Re)Presentations of Women in the Gospel of Matthew and Luke-Acts.' In *Women and Christian Origins*. Edited by Ross Shepard Kraemer and Mary Rose D'Angelo, 171–95. New York, NY: Oxford University Press, 1999.

—'The ANHP Question in Luke-Acts: Imperial Masculinity and the Deployment of Women in the Early Second Century.' In *A Feminist Companion to Luke*. Edited by Amy-Jill Levine and Marianne Blickenstaff, 44–69. London: Sheffield Academic Press, 2002.

Danker, Frederick W. *Jesus and the New Age: A Commentary on St Luke's Gospel*. Completely revised and expanded edn. Philadelphia, PA: Fortress Press, 1988.

Darr, John A. *On Character Building: The Reader and the Rhetoric of Characterization in Luke-Acts*. Louisville, KY: Westminster/John Knox Press, 1992.

Davies, Stevan. 'Women in the Third Gospel and the New Testament Apocrypha.' In *'Women Like This': New Perspectives on Jewish Women in the Greco-Roman World*. Edited by Amy-Jill Levine, 185–97. Atlanta, GA: Scholars Press, 1991.

Dawsey, James M. *The Lukan Voice: Confusion and Irony in the Gospel of Luke*. Macon, GA: Mercer University Press, 1986.

de Beauvoir, Simone. *The Second Sex*. Translated by H. M. Parshley. London: Jonathan Cape, 1953.

de Boer, Esther A. *Mary Magdalene: Beyond the Myth*. Translated by John Bowden. Harrisburg, PA: Trinity Press International, 1997.

—'The Lukan Mary Magdalene and the Other Women Following Jesus.' In *A Feminist Companion to Luke*. Edited by Amy-Jill Levine and Marianne Blickenstaff, 140–60. London: Sheffield Academic Press, 2002.

de la Potterie, Ignace. 'La Parabole du Prétendant à la Royauté.' In *À Cause de l' Évangile: Études sur les Synoptiques et les Actes*. Edited by François Refoulé, 163–93. Paris: Publications de Saint-André, 1985.

Delling, Gerhard. 'πλήρης.' *TDNT* 6.283–86.

Derrett, J. D. M. 'Law in the New Testament: The Parable of the Unjust Judge.' *NTS* 18 (1971–72): 178–91.

—'A Horrid Passage in Luke Explained.' *ExpTim* 97 (1986): 136–38.

Dewey, Joanna. 'Jesus' Healings of Women: Conformity and Non-Conformity to Dominant Cultural Values as Clues for Historical Reconstruction.' *BTB* 24 (1994): 122–31.

—'Women in the Synoptic Gospels: Seen but not Heard?' *BTB* 27 (1997): 53–60.

—'1 Timothy.' In *The Women's Bible Commentary*. Expanded edn. Edited by Carol A. Newsom and Sharon H. Ringe, 444–49. Louisville, KY: Westminster John Knox Press, 1998.

Doble, Peter. *The Paradox of Salvation: Luke's Theology of the Cross*. SNTSMS 87. Cambridge: Cambridge University Press, 1996.

Dodd, C. H. *The Parables of the Kingdom*. Revised edn. London: Collins, 1961.

Donahue, John R. *The Gospel in Parable: Metaphor, Narrative and Theology in the Synoptic Gospels*. Philadelphia, PA: Fortress Press, 1988.

Dornisch, Loretta. *A Woman Reads the Gospel of Luke*. Collegeville, MN: Liturgical Press, 1996.

Dowling, Elizabeth. 'Rise and Fall: The Changing Status of Peter and Women Disciples in John 21.' *AusBR* 52 (2004): 48–63.

Dube, Musa W. 'Toward A Post-Colonial Feminist Interpretation of the Bible.' *Semeia* 78 (1997): 11–26.

—'Fifty Years of Bleeding: A Storytelling Feminist Reading of Mark 5:24-43.' In *Other Ways of Reading: African Women and the Bible*. Edited by Musa W. Dube, 50–60. Atlanta, GA: SBL, 2001.

duBois, Page. *Centaurs and Amazons: Women and the Pre-History of the Great Chain of Being*. Ann Arbor, MI: University of Michigan Press, 1991.

Durber, Susan. 'The Female Reader of the Parables of the Lost.' *JSNT* 45 (1992): 59–78.

Eagleton, Terry. *Criticism and Ideology: A Study in Marxist Literary Theory*. London: NLB, 1976.

Eilberg-Schwartz, Howard. 'Introduction: The Spectacle of the Female Head.' In *Off With Her Head!: The Denial of Women's Identity in Myth, Religion, and Culture*. Edited by Howard Eilberg-Schwartz and Wendy Doniger, 1–13. Berkeley, CA: University of California Press, 1995.

—'The Nakedness of a Woman's Voice, the Pleasure in a Man's Mouth: An Oral History of Ancient Judaism.' In *Off With Her Head!: The Denial of Women's Identity in Myth, Religion, and Culture*. Edited by Howard Eilberg-Schwartz and Wendy Doniger, 165–84. Berkeley, CA: University of California Press, 1995.

Eisen, Ute. *Women Officeholders in Early Christianity: Epigraphical and Literary Studies*. Translated by Linda M. Maloney. Collegeville, MN: Liturgical Press, 2000.

Elliott, J. K. 'Anna's Age (Luke 2:36-37).' *NovT* 30 (1988): 100–2.

Elvey, Anne. 'The Birth of the Mother: A Reading of Luke 2:1-20 in Conversation with Some Recent Feminist Theory on Pregnancy and Birth.' *Pacifica* 15, no. 1 (2002): 1–15.

—'Storing Up Death, Storing Up Life: An Earth Story in Luke 12.13-34.' In *The Earth Story in the New Testament*. Edited by Norman C.

Habel and Vicky Balabanski, 95–107. London: Sheffield Academic Press, 2002.

Esler, Philip Francis. *Community and Gospel in Luke-Acts: The Social and Political Motivations of Lucan Theology*. Cambridge: Cambridge University Press, 1987.

Evans, C. F. *Saint Luke*. London/Philadelphia, PA: SCM Press/Trinity Press International, 1990.

Farmer, William R. 'Modern Developments of Griesbach's Hypothesis.' *NTS* 23 (1976–77): 275–95.

Fee, Gordon D. *The First Epistle to the Corinthians*. Grand Rapids, MI: Eerdmans, 1987.

Finley, M. I. *Ancient Slavery and Modern Ideology*. London: Chatto and Windus, 1980.

Fitzmyer, Joseph A. *The Gospel According to Luke*. 2 vols. AB 28, 28a. New York, NY: Doubleday, 1981–85.

—*Luke the Theologian: Aspects of his Teaching*. New York, NY: Paulist Press, 1989.

—*Romans: A New Translation with Introduction and Commentary*. New York, NY: Doubleday, 1993.

Flender, Helmut. *St. Luke: Theologian of Redemptive History*. Translated by Ilse and Reginald Fuller. Philadelphia, PA: Fortress Press, 1967.

Flusser, David. 'Aesop's Miser and the Parable of the Talents.' In *Parable and Story in Judaism and Christianity*. Edited by Clemens Thoma and Michael Wyschogrod, 9–25. Mahwah, NJ: Paulist Press, 1989.

Ford, Richard Q. *The Parables of Jesus: Recovering the Art of Listening*. Minneapolis, MN: Fortress Press, 1997.

—'Body Language: Jesus' Parables of the Woman With the Yeast, the Woman With the Jar, and the Man With the Sword.' *Int* 56 (2002): 295–306.

Fortna, Robert T. 'Reading Jesus' Parable of the Talents Through Underclass Eyes: Matt 25:14-30.' *Forum (Foundations and Facets)* 8 (1992): 211–28.

Foster, George M. 'Peasant Society and the Image of Limited Good.' *American Anthropologist* 67 (1965): 293–315.

Frye, Marilyn. *The Politics of Reality: Essays in Feminist Theory*. New York, NY: Crossing Press, 1983.

Frymer-Kensky, Tikva. *In the Wake of the Goddesses: Women, Culture, and the Biblical Transformation of Pagan Myth*. New York, NY: Free Press, 1992.

Funk, Robert W. *Parables and Presence: Forms of the New Testament Tradition*. Philadelphia, PA: Fortress Press, 1982.

Gardner, Jane F. *Women in Roman Law and Society*. Bloomington, IN: Indiana University Press, 1991.

Gillman, Florence M. *Women Who Knew Paul*. Collegeville, MN: Liturgical Press, 1992.

Glancy, Jennifer A. *Slavery in Early Christianity*. Oxford: Oxford University Press, 2002.

Gooding, David. *According to Luke: A New Exposition of the Third Gospel*. Leicester: Inter-Varsity Press, 1987.

Goulder, Michael. *Luke: A New Paradigm*. 2 vols. Sheffield: JSOT Press, 1989.

Green, Joel B. *The Theology of the Gospel of Luke*. Cambridge: Cambridge University Press, 1995.

—*The Gospel of Luke*. Grand Rapids, MI: Eerdmans, 1997.

Gregory, James R. 'Image of Limited Good, or Expectation of Reciprocity?' *Current Anthropology* 16 (1975): 73–92.

Guy, Laurie. 'The Interplay of the Present and Future in the Kingdom of God (Luke 19:11-44).' *TynBul* 48 (1997): 119–37.

Harrington, Daniel J. *The Gospel of Matthew*. Collegeville, MN: Liturgical Press, 1991.

Heine, Susanne. *Women and Early Christianity: Are the Feminist Scholars Right?* Translated by John Bowden. London: SCM Press, 1987.

Hengel, Martin. *Property and Riches in the Early Church: Aspects of a Social History of Early Christianity*. London: SCM Press, 1974.

Herndl, Diane Price. 'The Dilemmas of a Feminine Dialogic.' In *Feminism, Bakhtin, and the Dialogic*. Edited by Dale M. Bauer and Susan Jaret McKinstry, 7–24. Albany, NY: State University of New York Press, 1991.

Herzog, William R. *Parables as Subversive Speech: Jesus as Pedagogue of the Oppressed*. Louisville, KY: Westminster/John Knox Press, 1994.

Hooker, Morna D. 'Authority on her Head: An Examination of 1 Cor. XI. 10.' *NTS* 10 (1964): 410–16.

Hornsby, Teresa J. 'Why is She Crying? A Feminist Interpretation of Luke 7.36–50.' In *Escaping Eden: New Perspectives on the Bible*. Edited by Harold C. Washington, Susan Lochrie Graham, and Pamela Thimmes, 91–103. Sheffield: Sheffield Academic Press, 1998.

—'The Woman is a Sinner/The Sinner is a Woman.' In *A Feminist Companion to Luke*. Edited by Amy-Jill Levine and Marianne Blickenstaff, 121–32. London: Sheffield Academic Press, 2002.

Horsley, Richard A. 'Subverting Disciplines: The Possibilities and Limitations of Postcolonial Theory for New Testament Studies.' In *Toward a New Heaven and a New Earth: Essays in Honor of Elisabeth Schüssler Fiorenza*. Edited by Fernando F. Segovia, 90–105. Maryknoll, NY: Orbis Books, 2003.

Hultgren, Arland J. *The Parables of Jesus: A Commentary*. Grand Rapids, MI: Eerdmans, 2000.

Ilan, Tal. *Jewish Women in Greco-Roman Palestine: An Inquiry into Image and Status*. Tübingen: J. C. B. Mohr, 1995.

—'In the Footsteps of Jesus: Jewish Women in a Jewish Movement.' In *Transformative Encounters: Jesus and Women Re-viewed*. Edited by Ingrid Rosa Kitzberger, 115–36. Leiden: Brill, 2000.

James, Deborah, and Janice Drakich. 'Understanding Gender Differences in Amount of Talk: A Critical Review of Research.' In *Gender and Conversational Interaction*. Edited by Deborah Tannen, 281–312. New York, NY: Oxford University Press, 1993.

Jeremias, Joachim. *The Parables of Jesus*. 3rd revised edn. London: SCM Press, 1972.

Johnson, Luke Timothy. 'The Lukan Kingship Parable (Lk. 19:11-27).' *NovT* 24 (1982): 139–59.

—*The Gospel of Luke*. Sacra Pagina 3. Collegeville, MN: Liturgical Press, 1991.

Joshel, Sandra R., and Sheila Murnaghan. 'Introduction: Differential Equations.' In *Women and Slaves in Greco-Roman Culture: Differential Equations*. Edited by Sandra R. Joshel and Sheila Murnaghan, 1–21. London: Routledge, 1998.

Kahl, Brigitte. 'Reading Luke Against Luke: Non-Uniformity of Text, Hermeneutics of Conspiracy and the "Scriptural Principle" of Luke 1.' In *A Feminist Companion to Luke*. Edited by Amy-Jill Levine and Marianne Blickenstaff, 70–88. London: Sheffield Academic Press, 2002.

Kahler, Christoph. *Jesu Gleichnisse als Poesie und Therapie: Versuch eines integrativen Zugangs zum kommunikativen Aspekt von Gleichnissen Jesu*. Tübingen: J. C. B. Mohr, 1995.

Kampen, Natalie Boymel. 'Between Public and Private: Women as Historical Subjects in Roman Art.' In *Women's History and Ancient History*. Edited by Sarah B. Pomeroy, 218–48. Chapel Hill, NC: University of North Carolina Press, 1991.

Karris, Robert J. *Luke: Artist and Theologian*. New York, NY: Paulist, 1985.

—'Women and Discipleship in Luke.' *CBQ* 56 (1994): 1–20.

Käsemann, Ernst. *Commentary on Romans*. Translated by Geoffrey W. Bromiley. Grand Rapids, MI: Eerdmans, 1980.

Kehde, Suzanne. 'Voices from the Margin: Bag Ladies and Others.' In *Feminism, Bakhtin, and the Dialogic*. Edited by Dale M. Bauer and Susan Jaret McKinstry, 25–38. Albany, NY: State University of New York Press, 1991.

Kiley, Bernadette. 'Silence as Repression and Denial: Insights from Mark's Stories of Women.' Paper presented at the Women Scholars of Religion and Theology Conference, Melbourne, 2004.

Kilgallen, John J. 'A Proposal for Interpreting Luke 7, 36–50.' *Bib* 72 (1991): 305–30.

Kim, Kyoung-Jin. *Stewardship and Almsgiving in Luke's Theology.* JSNTSup 155. Sheffield: Sheffield Academic Press, 1998.

Kingsbury, Jack Dean. *Conflict in Luke: Jesus, Authorities, Disciples.* Minneapolis, MN: Fortress Press, 1991.

Kitchen, Merrill. 'The Parable of the Pounds.' Unpublished TheolM Thesis. Melbourne College of Divinity, Melbourne, 1993.

—'Rereading the Parable of the Pounds: A Social and Narrative Analysis of Luke 19:11-28.' In *Prophecy and Passion: Essays in Honour of Athol Gill.* Edited by David Neville, 227–46. Adelaide: Australian Theological Forum, 2002.

Kopas, Jane. 'Jesus and Women: Luke's Gospel.' *TTod* 43 (1986): 192–202.

Kozar, Joseph Vlcek. 'Reading the Opening Chapter of Luke from a Feminist Perspective.' In *Escaping Eden: New Feminist Perspectives on the Bible.* Edited by Harold C. Washington, Susan Lochrie Graham, and Pamela Thimmes, 53–68. Sheffield: Sheffield Academic Press, 1998.

Kraemer, Ross S. 'Jewish Women and Christian Origins: Some Caveats.' In *Women and Christian Origins.* Edited by Ross Shepard Kraemer and Mary Rose D'Angelo, 35–49. New York, NY: Oxford University Press, 1999.

—'Jewish Women and Women's Judaism(s) at the Beginning of Christianity.' In *Women and Christian Origins.* Edited by Ross Shepard Kraemer and Mary Rose D'Angelo, 50–79. New York, NY: Oxford University Press, 1999.

Kramer, Cheris. 'Perceptions of Female and Male Speech.' *Language and Speech* 20 (1977): 151–61.

Kurz, William S. *Reading Luke-Acts: Dynamics of Biblical Narrative.* Louisville, KY: Westminster/John Knox Press, 1993.

La Hurd, Carol Schersten. 'Rediscovering the Lost Women in Luke 15.' *BTB* 24 (1994): 66–76.

Lambrecht, Jan. *Once More Astonished: The Parables of Jesus.* New York, NY: Crossroad, 1983.

—'The Parable of the Throne Claimant (Luke 19,11–27).' In *Understanding What One Reads: New Testament Essays*, 112–24. Leuven: Peeters, 2003.

Laurentin, René. *The Truth of Christmas: Beyond the Myths: The Gospels of the Infancy of Christ.* Translated by Michael J. Wren and associates. Petersham, MA: St. Bede's Publications, 1986.

La Verdiere, Eugene. *Luke.* Dublin: Veritas, 1980.

Lawson, Veronica Mary. 'Gender and Genre: The Construction of

Female Gender in the Acts of the Apostles.' Unpublished PhD Thesis. Trinity College, Dublin, 1997.

Leaney, A. R. C. *A Commentary on the Gospel According to St. Luke.* 2nd edn. London: Adam & Charles Black, 1966.

Lee, Dorothy. *Flesh and Glory: Symbolism, Gender and Theology in the Gospel of John.* New York, NY: Crossroad, 2002.

Lefkowitz, Mary R., and Maureen B. Fant. *Women's Life in Greece and Rome: A Source Book in Translation.* 2nd edn. Baltimore, MD: Johns Hopkins University Press, 1992.

Lerner, Gerder. *The Creation of Patriarchy.* New York, NY: Oxford University Press, 1986.

—*Why History Matters: Life and Thought.* New York, NY: Oxford University Press, 1997.

Levine, Amy-Jill. 'Discharging Responsibility: Matthean Jesus, Biblical Law, and Hemorrhaging Woman.' In *Treasures New and Old: Recent Contributions to Matthean Studies.* Edited by David R. Bauer and Mark Allen Powell, 379–97. Atlanta, GA: Scholars Press, 1996.

—'Second Temple Judaism, Jesus and Women: *Yeast of Eden.*' In *A Feminist Companion to the Hebrew Bible in the New Testament.* Edited by Athalya Brenner, 302–31. FCB 10. Sheffield: Sheffield Academic Press, 1996.

—'Lilies of the Field and Wandering Jews: Biblical Scholarship, Women's Roles, and Social Location.' In *Transformative Encounters: Jesus and Women Re-viewed.* Edited by Ingrid Rosa Kitzberger, 329–52. Leiden: Brill, 2000.

—'Gender, Judaism, and Literature: Unwelcome Guests in Household Configurations.' *BibInt* 11 (2003): 239–46.

Levine, Amy-Jill, and Marianne Blickenstaff, (eds.), *A Feminist Companion to Luke.* FCNT 3. London: Sheffield Academic Press, 2002.

Lieu, Judith M. *The Gospel of Luke.* London: Epworth Press, 1997.

—'The "Attraction of Women" in/to Early Judaism and Christianity: Gender and the Politics of Conversion.' *JSNT* 72 (1998): 5–22.

Longman, Tremper. *Literary Approaches to Biblical Interpretation.* Grand Rapids, MI/ Leicester: Academie Books/Apollos, 1987.

McBride, Denis. *The Parables of Jesus.* Hampshire: Redemptorist Publications, 1999.

McClure, Laura. 'Introduction.' In *Making Silence Speak: Women's Voices in Greek Literature and Society.* Edited by André Lardinois and Laura McClure, 3–16. Princeton, NJ: Princeton University Press, 2001.

MacDonald, Margaret Y. 'Reading Real Women Through the Undisputed Letters of Paul.' In *Women and Christian Origins.*

Edited by Ross Shepard Kraemer and Mary Rose D'Angelo, 199–220. New York, NY: Oxford University Press, 1999.

—'Rereading Paul: Early Interpreters of Paul on Women and Gender.' In *Women and Christian Origins*. Edited by Ross Shepard Kraemer and Mary Rose D'Angelo, 236–53. New York, NY: Oxford University Press, 1999.

—'Was Celsus Right? The Role of Women in the Expansion of Early Christianity.' In *Early Christian Families in Context: An Interdisciplinary Dialogue*. Edited by David L. Balch and Carolyn Osiek, 157–84. Grand Rapids, MI: Eerdmans, 2003.

Macherey, Pierre. *A Theory of Literary Production*. Translated by Geoffrey Wall. London: Routledge & Kegan Paul, 1978.

McPhillips, Kathleen. 'Post-modern Sainthood: "Hearing the Voice of the Saint" and the Uses of Feminist Hagiography.' *Seachanges* 3 (2003): 1–20. http://www.wsrt.com.au/seachanges/volume3/doc/mcphillips. doc. Accessed June 4th, 2006.

Malbon, Elizabeth Struthers, and Janice Capel Anderson. 'Literary-Critical Methods.' In *Searching the Scriptures. Volume One: A Feminist Introduction*. Edited by Elisabeth Schüssler Fiorenza, 241–54. North Blackburn, Vic: Collins-Dove, 1993.

Malina, Bruce J. 'Wealth and Poverty in the New Testament and its World.' *Int* 41 (1987): 354–67.

—*The New Testament World: Insights from Cultural Anthropology*. 3rd, revised and expanded edn. Louisville, KY: Westminster John Knox Press, 2001.

Malina, Bruce J., and Jerome H. Neyrey. *Calling Jesus Names: The Social Value of Names in Matthew*. Sonoma, CA: Polebridge, 1988.

—'Honor and Shame in Luke-Acts: Pivotal Values of the Mediterranean World.' In *The Social World of Luke-Acts: Models for Interpretation*. Edited by Jerome H. Neyrey, 25–65. Peabody, MA: Hendrickson, 1991.

Malina, Bruce J., and Richard L. Rohrbaugh. *Social-Science Commentary on the Synoptic Gospels*. 2nd edn. Minneapolis, MN: Fortress Press, 2003.

Maloney, Linda. '"Swept Under the Rug": Feminist Homiletical Reflections on the Parable of the Lost Coin (Lk. 15.8–9).' In *The Lost Coin: Parables of Women, Work and Wisdom*. Edited by Mary Ann Beavis, 34–38. London: Sheffield Academic Press, 2002.

Maly, Eugene H. 'Women and the Gospel of Luke.' *BTB* 10 (1980): 99–104.

Manns, Frédéric. 'La Parabole des Talents Wirkungsgeschichte et Racines Juives.' *RevScRel* 65 (1991): 343–62.

Marshall, I. Howard. *The Gospel of Luke: A Commentary on the Greek Text*. Exeter: The Paternoster Press, 1978.

Melzer-Keller, Helga. *Jesus und die Frauen: Eine Verhältnisbestimmung nach den synoptischen Überlieferungen.* Freiburg: Herder, 1997.

Meyers, Eric M. 'The Problems of Gendered Space in Syro-Palestinian Domestic Architecture: The Case of Roman-Period Galilee.' In *Early Christian Families in Context: An Interdisciplinary Dialogue.* Edited by David L. Balch and Carolyn Osiek, 44–69. Grand Rapids, MI: Eerdmans, 2003.

Meynet, Roland. *L'Évangile Selon Saint Luc: Analyse Rhétorique Commentaire.* Paris: Les Éditions du Cerf, 1988.

Michel, Otto. 'σφάζω.' *TDNT* 7.925-38.

Moloney, Francis J. *Woman in the New Testament.* Homebush, NSW: St Paul Publications, 1981.

Moore, Stephen D. *Literary Criticism and the Gospels: The Theoretical Challenge.* New Haven, CT: Yale University Press, 1989.

Morris, Ian. 'Remaining Invisible: The Archaeology of the Excluded in Classical Athens.' In *Women and Slaves in Greco-Roman Culture: Differential Equations.* Edited by Sandra R. Joshel and Sheila Murnaghan, 193–220. London: Routledge, 1998.

Moxnes, Halvor. *The Economy of the Kingdom: Social Conflict and Economic Relations in Luke's Gospel.* Philadelphia, PA: Fortress Press, 1988.

Myers, Ched. 'Jesus' New Economy of Grace.' *Sojourners* 27, no. 4 (1998): 36–39.

Neyrey, Jerome H. 'What's Wrong With This Picture? John 4, Cultural Stereotypes of Women, and Public and Private Space.' *BTB* 24 (1994): 77–91.

Nolland, John. *Luke.* 3 vols. Dallas, TX: Word Books, 1989–93.

Oduyoye, Mercy Amba. 'Violence Against Women: Window on Africa.' *Voices from the Third World* 18, no. 1 (1995): 168–76.

Okure, Teresa. ' "I Will Open My Mouth in Parables" (Matt 13.35): A Case for a Gospel-Based Biblical Hermeneutics.' *NTS* 46 (2000): 445–63.

Osiek, Carolyn. 'Slavery in the Second Testament World.' *BTB* 22 (1992): 174–79.

—'The Women at the Tomb: What are They Doing There?' *Ex Auditu* 9 (1993): 97–107.

—'Female Slaves, *Porneia*, and the Limits of Obedience.' In *Early Christian Families in Context: An Interdisciplinary Dialogue.* Edited by David L. Balch and Carolyn Osiek, 255–74. Grand Rapids, MI: Eerdmans, 2003.

O'Toole, Robert F. *The Unity of Luke's Theology: An Analysis of Luke-Acts.* Wilmington, DE: Michael Glazier, 1984.

Panier, Louis. 'La Parabole des Mines: Lecture Sémiotique (Lc 19, 11–

27).' In *Les Paraboles Évangéliques*. Edited by J. Delorme, 333–47. Paris: Éditions du Cerf, 1989.

Parvey, Constance F. 'The Theology and Leadership of Women in the New Testament.' In *Religion and Sexism: Images of Woman in the Jewish and Christian Traditions*. Edited by Rosemary Radford Ruether, 117–49. New York, NY: Simon & Schuster, 1974.

Pattel-Gray, Anne. 'Not Yet Tiddas: An Aboriginal Womanist Critique of Australian Church Feminism.' In *Freedom and Entrapment: Women Thinking Theology*. Edited by Maryanne Confoy, Dorothy A. Lee and Joan Nowotny, 165–92. Blackburn, Vic: Dove, 1995.

Phillips, Gary A. ' "What is Written? How Are You Reading?" Gospel, Intertextuality and Doing Lukewise: A Writerly Reading of Lk 10:25-37 (and 38–42).' In *SBL 1992 Seminar Papers*. Edited by Eugene H. Lovering Jr., 266–301. SBLSP 31. Atlanta, GA: Scholars Press, 1992.

Pilch, John J. 'Sickness and Healing in Luke-Acts.' In *The Social World of Luke-Acts: Models for Interpretation*. Edited by Jerome H. Neyrey, 181–209. Peabody, MA: Hendrickson, 1991.

Plaatjie, Gloria Kehilwe. 'Toward a Post-apartheid Black Feminist Reading of the Bible: A Case of Luke 2:36-38.' In *Other Ways of Reading: African Women and the Bible*. Edited by Musa W. Dube, 114–42. Atlanta, GA: SBL, 2001.

Plummer, Alfred. *The Gospel According to S. Luke*. 5th edn. Edinburgh: T & T Clark, 1922.

Pomeroy, Sarah B. *Goddesses, Whores, Wives, and Slaves: Women in Classical Antiquity*. New York, NY: Schocken, 1975.

Pontifical Biblical Commission. *The Jewish People and their Sacred Scriptures in the Christian Bible*. May 24, 2001. http://www.vatican.va/roman_curia/congregations/cfaith/pcb_documents/rc_con_cfaith_doc_20020212_ popolo-ebraico_en.html. Accessed June 4th, 2006.

Portefaix, Lilian. *Sisters Rejoice: Paul's Letter to the Philippians and Luke-Acts as Received by First-Century Philippian Women*. Stockholm: Almqvist & Wiksell International, 1988.

Powell, Mark Allan. *What are they Saying About Luke?* Mahwah, NJ: Paulist Press, 1989.

Price, Robert M. *The Widow Traditions in Luke-Acts: A Feminist-Critical Scrutiny*. SBLDS 155. Atlanta, GA: Scholars Press, 1997.

Puig i Tàrrech, Armand. 'La Parabole des Talents (Mt 25, 14-30) ou des Mines (Lc 19, 11-28).' In *À Cause de l' Évangile: Études sur les Synoptiques et les Actes*. Edited by François Refoulé. Paris: Publications de Saint-André, 1985.

Quesnell, Quentin. 'The Women at Luke's Supper.' In *Political Issues in*

Luke-Acts. Edited by Richard J. Cassidy and Philip J. Scharper, 59–79. Maryknoll, NY: Orbis, 1983.

Rebera, Ranjini. 'Polarity or Partnership? Retelling the Story of Martha and Mary from Asian Women's Perspective.' *Semeia* 78 (1997): 93–107.

—'Power and Equality.' *Voices from the Third World* 21, no. 2 (1998): 85–101.

Reid, Barbara E. *Choosing the Better Part? Women in the Gospel of Luke*. Collegeville, MN: Liturgical Press, 1996.

—*Parables for Preachers: The Gospel of Luke Year C*. Collegeville, MN: Liturgical Press, 2000.

— 'Beyond Petty Pursuits and Wearisome Widows: Three Lukan Parables.' *Int* 56 (2002): 284–94.

—' "Do You See This Woman?" A Liberative Look at Luke 7.36-50 and Strategies for Reading Other Lukan Stories Against the Grain.' In *A Feminist Companion to Luke*. Edited by Amy-Jill Levine and Marianne Blickenstaff, 106–20. London: Sheffield Academic Press, 2002.

Reimer, Ivoni Richter. *Women in the Acts of the Apostles: A Feminist Liberation Perspective*. Translated by Linda M. Maloney. Minneapolis, MN: Fortress Press, 1995.

Reinhartz, Adele. 'From Narrative to History: The Resurrection of Mary and Martha.' In *A Feminist Companion to the Hebrew Bible in the New Testament*. Edited by Athalya Brenner, 197–224. FCB 10. London: Sheffield Academic Press, 1996.

Rengstorf, K. H. 'δοῦλος.' *TDNT* 2.261-80.

—'δώδεκα.' *TDNT* 2.321–28.

—'ἑπτά.' *TDNT* 2.627–35.

Resenhöfft, Wilhelm. 'Jesu Gleichnis von den Talenten, ergänzt durch die Lukas-Fassung.' *NTS* 26 (1980): 318–31.

Ricci, C. *Mary Magdalene and Many Others: Women Who Followed Jesus*. Translated by Paul Burns. Minneapolis, MN: Fortress, 1994.

Richard, Earl. 'Pentecost as a Recurrent Theme in Luke-Acts.' In *New Views on Luke and Acts*. Edited by Earl Richard, 133–49. Collegeville, MN: Liturgical Press, 1990.

Ricoeur, Paul. 'Biblical Hermeneutics.' *Semeia* 4 (1975): 27–148.

Rigato, Maria-Luisa. ' "Remember" … Then They Remembered: Luke 24:6-8.' In *Luke and Acts*. Edited by Gerald O'Collins and Gilberto Marconi, 93–102. Mahwah, NJ: Paulist Press, 1991.

Ringe, Sharon H. *Luke*. Louisville, KY: Westminster John Knox Press, 1995.

Robbins, Vernon K. 'The Woman Who Touched Jesus' Garment: Socio-Rhetorical Analysis of the Synoptic Accounts.' *NTS* 33 (1987): 502–15.

—'Socio-Rhetorical Criticism: Mary, Elizabeth and the Magnificat as a Test Case.' In *The New Literary Criticism and the New Testament*. Edited by Edgar V. McKnight and Elizabeth Struthers Malbon, 164–209. Valley Forge, PA: Trinity Press International, 1994.

Rohrbaugh, Richard L. 'A Peasant Reading of the Parable of the Talents/Pounds: A Text of Terror?' *BTB* 23 (1993): 32–39.

Rosenblatt, Marie-Eloise. 'Gender, Ethnicity, and Legal Considerations in the Haemorrhaging Woman's Story Mark 5:25-34.' In *Transformative Encounters: Jesus and Women Re-viewed*. Edited by Ingrid Rosa Kitzberger, 137–61. Leiden: Brill, 2000.

Ryan, Rosalie. 'The Women from Galilee and Discipleship in Luke.' *BTB* 15 (1985): 56–59.

Sawicki, Marianne. 'Magdalenes and Tiberiennes: City Women in the Entourage of Jesus.' In *Transformative Encounters: Jesus and Women Re-viewed*. Edited by Ingrid Rosa Kitzberger, 181–202. Leiden: Brill, 2000.

Schaberg, Jane. *The Illegitimacy of Jesus: A Feminist Theological Interpretation of the Infancy Narratives*. Sheffield: Sheffield Academic Press, 1995.

—'Luke.' In *Women's Bible Commentary*. Expanded edn. Edited by Carol A. Newsom and Sharon H. Ringe, 363–80. Louisville, KY: Westminster/John Knox Press, 1998.

—'Magdalene Christianity.' In *On the Cutting Edge: The Study of Women in Biblical Worlds*. Edited by Jane Schaberg, Alice Bach, and Esther Fuchs, 193–220. New York, NY: Continuum, 2003.

Schneiders, Sandra M. *The Revelatory Text: Interpreting the New Testament as Sacred Scripture*. San Francisco, CA: Harper, 1991.

Schottroff, Luise. *Let the Oppressed Go Free: Feminist Perspectives on the New Testament*. Translated by Annemarie S. Kidder. Louisville, KY: Westminster/John Knox Press, 1993.

—*Lydia's Impatient Sisters: A Feminist Social History of Early Christianity*. Translated by Barbara and Martin Rumscheidt. London: SCM Press, 1995.

—'Through German and Feminist Eyes: A Liberationist Reading of Luke 7.36–50.' In *A Feminist Companion to the Hebrew Bible in the New Testament*. Edited by Athalya Brenner, 332–41. FCB 10. Sheffield: Sheffield Academic Press, 1996.

Schüssler Fiorenza, Elisabeth. 'A Feminist Critical Interpretation for Liberation: Martha and Mary: Luke 10:38-42.' *Religion and Intellectual Life* 3, no. 2 (1986): 21–36.

—*But She Said: Feminist Practices of Biblical Interpretation*. Boston, MA: Beacon Press, 1992.

—*Bread Not Stone: The Challenge of Feminist Biblical Interpretation (With a New Afterword)*. Boston, MA: Beacon Press, 1995.

—*In Memory of Her: A Feminist Theological Reconstruction of Christian Origins*. 2nd edn. London: SCM Press, 1995.

—*Sharing Her Word: Feminist Biblical Intepretation in Context*. Boston, MA: Beacon Press, 1998.

—*Wisdom Ways: Introducing Feminist Biblical Interpretation*. Maryknoll, NY: Orbis, 2001.

Schweizer, Eduard. *The Good News According to Luke*. Translated by David E. Green. London: SPCK, 1984.

—*The Good News According to Matthew*. Translated by David E. Green. London: SPCK, 1975.

Scott, Bernard B. *Hear Then the Parable: A Commentary on the Parables of Jesus*. Minneapolis, MN: Fortress, 1989.

Sealey, Raphael. *Women and Law in Classical Greece*. Chapel Hill, NC: University of North Carolina Press, 1990.

Segovia, Fernando F. ' "And They Began to Speak in Other Tongues": Competing Modes of Discourse in Contemporary Biblical Criticism.' In *Reading from This Place: Volume 1, Social Location and Biblical Interpretation in the United States*. Edited by Fernando F. Segovia and Mary Ann Tolbert, 1–32. Minneapolis, MN: Fortress Press, 1995.

Seim, Turid Karlsen. *The Double Message: Patterns of Gender in Luke-Acts*. Edinburgh: T & T Clark, 1994.

—'The Gospel of Luke.' In *Searching the Scriptures: A Feminist Commentary*. Edited by Elisabeth Schüssler Fiorenza, 728–62. New York, NY: Crossroad, 1994.

Senack, Christine M. 'Aristotle on the Woman's Soul.' In *Engendering Origins: Critical Feminist Readings in Plato and Aristotle*. Edited by Bat-Ami Bar On, 223–36. Albany, NY: State University of New York Press, 1994.

Senior, Donald. *Matthew*. Nashville, TN: Abingdon Press, 1998.

Setel, Drorah O'Donnel. 'Exodus.' In *Women's Bible Commentary*. Expanded edn. Edited by Carol A. Newsom and Sharon H. Ringe, 30–39. Louisville, KY: Westminster John Knox Press, 1998.

Shelley, Carter. 'A Widow Without Wiles.' In *The Lost Coin: Parables of Women, Work and Wisdom*. Edited by Mary Ann Beavis, 53–61. London: Sheffield Academic Press, 2002.

Sim, David C. 'The Women Followers of Jesus: The Implications of Luke 8.1-3.' *HeyJ* 30 (1989): 51–62.

Sly, Dorothy. *Philo's Perception of Women*. Atlanta, GA: Scholars Press, 1990.

Smith, Dennis E. 'Table Fellowship as a Literary Motif in the Gospel of Luke.' *JBL* 106 (1987): 613–38.

Soskice, Janet Martin. *Metaphor and Religious Language*. Oxford: Clarendon Press, 1985.

Spelman, Elizabeth V. 'Who's Who in the Polis.' In *Engendering Origins: Critical Feminist Readings in Plato and Aristotle*. Edited by Bat-Ami Bar On, 99–125. Albany, NY: State University of New York Press, 1994.

Spencer, F. Scott. 'Out of Mind, Out of Voice: Slave-girls and Prophetic Daughters in Luke-Acts.' *BibInt* 7 (1999): 133–55.

Spender, Dale. *Man Made Language*. 2nd edn. London: Routledge & Kegan Paul, 1985.

Squires, John T. *The Plan of God in Luke-Acts*. Cambridge: Cambridge University Press, 1993.

Strathmann, Hermann. 'πόλις.' *TDNT* 6.516–35.

Sweetland, Dennis M. 'Luke the Christian.' In *New Views on Luke and Acts*. Edited by Earl Richard, 48–63. Collegeville, MN: Liturgical Press, 1990.

Swidler, Leonard. *Biblical Affirmations of Women*. Philadelphia, PA: Westminster Press, 1979.

Talbert, Charles H. *Reading Luke: A Literary and Theological Commentary on the Third Gospel*. New York, NY: Crossroad, 1982.

—*Reading Luke-Acts in its Mediterranean Milieu*. Leiden: Brill, 2003.

Tannehill, Robert C. *The Narrative Unity of Luke-Acts: A Literary Interpretation. Volume 1: The Gospel According to Luke*. Philadelphia, PA: Fortress Press, 1986.

—*Luke*. Nashville, TN: Abingdon Press, 1996.

Taylor, Joan E. 'The Women "Priests" of Philo's *De Vita Contemplativa*: Reconstructing the Therapeutae.' In *On the Cutting Edge: The Study of Women in Biblical Worlds*. Edited by Jane Schaberg, Alice Bach, and Esther Fuchs, 102–22. New York, NY: Continuum, 2003.

Tetlow, Elisabeth M. *Women and Ministry in the New Testament*. New York, NY: Paulist, 1980.

Thibeaux, Evelyn R. ' "Known to be a Sinner": The Narrative Rhetoric of Luke 7:36-50.' *BTB* 23 (1993): 151–60.

Thimmes, Pamela. 'The Language of Community: A Cautionary Tale (Luke 10.38–42).' In *A Feminist Companion to Luke*. Edited by Amy-Jill Levine and Marianne Blickenstaff, 232–45. London: Sheffield Academic Press, 2002.

Thiong'o, Ngugi wa. *Devil on the Cross*. Oxford: Heinemann, 1987.

Thompson, Marianne Meye. *The Promise of the Father: Jesus and God in the New Testament*. Louisville, KY: Westminster John Knox Press, 2000.

Thurston, Bonnie Bowman. *The Widows: A Women's Ministry in the Early Church*. Minneapolis, MN: Fortress Press, 1989.

—*Women in the New Testament: Questions and Commentary*. New York, NY: Crossroad, 1998.

Tiede, David L. *Luke*. Minneapolis, MN: Augsburg, 1988.

Tolbert, Mary Ann. *Perspectives on the Parables: An Approach to Multiple Interpretations*. Philadelphia, PA: Fortress Press, 1979.

—*Sowing the Gospel: Mark's World in Literary-Historical Perspective*. Minneapolis, MN: Fortress Press, 1989.

—'Social, Sociological, and Anthropological Methods.' In *Searching the Scriptures: A Feminist Introduction*. Edited by Elisabeth Schüssler Fiorenza, 255–71. North Blackburn, Vic: Collins Dove, 1993.

—'The Politics and Poetics of Location.' In *Reading from this Place: Volume 1, Social Location and Biblical Interpretation in the United States*. Edited by Fernando F. Segovia and Mary Ann Tolbert, 305–17. Minneapolis, MN: Fortress Press, 1995.

Torjesen, Karen Jo. 'Reconstruction of Women's Early Christian History.' In *Searching the Scriptures: A Feminist Introduction*. Edited by Elisabeth Schüssler Fiorenza, 290–310. North Blackburn, Vic: Collins Dove, 1993.

—*When Women Were Priests: Women's Leadership in the Early Church and the Scandal of Their Subordination in the Rise of Christianity*. San Francisco, CA: Harper, 1993.

Trainor, Michael. '"And on Earth, Peace..." (Luke 2.14): Luke's Perspective on the Earth.' In *Readings from the Perspective of Earth*. Edited by Norman C. Habel, 174–92. Sheffield: Sheffield Academic Press, 2000.

Trible, Phyllis. 'Miriam 1.' In *Women in Scripture: A Dictionary of Named and Unnamed Women in the Hebrew Bible, the Apocryphal/ Deuterocanonical Books, and the New Testament*. Edited by Carol Meyers, 127–29. Boston, MA: Houghton Mifflin Company, 2000.

—*Texts of Terror: Literary-Feminist Readings of Biblical Narrative*. London: SCM Press, 2002.

Troost, Arie. 'Elizabeth and Mary – Naomi and Ruth: Gender-Response Criticism in Luke 1–2.' In *A Feminist Companion to the Hebrew Bible in the New Testament*. Edited by Athalya Brenner, 159–96. FCB 10. Sheffield: Sheffield Academic Press, 1996.

Vander Stichele, Caroline. 'Gender and Genre: Acts in/of Interpretation.' In *Contextualizing Acts: Lukan Narrative and Greco-Roman Discourse*. Edited by Todd Penner and Caroline Vander Stichele, 311–29. Atlanta, GA: SBL, 2003.

Varela, Alfredo T. 'Luke 2.36–37: Is Anna's Age What is Really in Focus?' *BT* 27 (1976): 446.

Vernant, Jean-Pierre. *The Origins of Greek Thought*. London: Methuen, 1982.

Via, E. Jane. 'Women in the Gospel of Luke.' In *Women in the World's Religions, Past and Present*. Edited by Ursula King, 38–55. New York, NY: Paragon House, 1987.

Wainwright, Elaine. *Shall We Look For Another? A Feminist Rereading of the Matthean Jesus*. Maryknoll, NY: Orbis, 1998.

—' "Your Faith Has Made You Well." Jesus, Women and Healing in the Gospel of Matthew.' In *Transformative Encounters: Jesus and Women Re-viewed*. Edited by Ingrid Rosa Kitzberger, 224–44. Leiden: Brill, 2000.

—'The Lucan Demon Possessed Women – Were They Healers?' Paper presented at the Catholic Biblical Association of America's Annual Meeting, Cleveland, OH, 2002.

—'The Pouring Out of Healing Ointment: Rereading Mark 14:3-9.' In *Toward a New Heaven and a New Earth: Essays in Honor of Elisabeth Schüssler Fiorenza*. Edited by Fernando F. Segovia, 157–78. Maryknoll, NY: Orbis Books, 2003.

Walker, Michelle Boulous. *Philosophy and the Maternal Body: Reading Silence*. London: Routledge, 1998.

Warhol, Robyn R. 'Reading.' In *Feminisms: An Anthology of Literary Theory and Criticism*. Edited by Robyn R. Warhol and Diane Price Herndl, 489–91. New Brunswick, NJ: Rutgers University Press, 1991.

Webster, Roger. *Studying Literary Theory: An Introduction*. 2nd edn. London: Arnold, 1996.

Wegner, Judith Romney. *Chattel or Person? The Status of Women in the Mishnah*. New York, NY: Oxford University Press, 1988.

Weinert, Francis. D. 'The Parable of the Throne Claimant (Luke 19:12, 14–15a, 27) Reconsidered.' *CBQ* 39 (1977): 505–14.

Weissenrieder, Annette. 'The Plague of Uncleanness? The Ancient Illness Construct "Issue of Blood" in Luke 8:43-48.' In *The Social Setting of Jesus and the Gospels*. Edited by Wolfgang Stegemann, Bruce J. Malina and Gerd Theissen, 207–22. Minneapolis, MN: Fortress Press, 2002.

Witherington, Ben. 'On the Road with Mary Magdalene, Joanna, Susanna, and Other Disciples – Luke 8.1-3.' *ZNW* 70 (1979): 243–48.

—*Women in the Ministry of Jesus: A Study of Jesus' Attitudes to Women and their Roles as Reflected in His Earthly Life*. Cambridge: Cambridge University Press, 1984.

—*Women in the Earliest Churches*. Cambridge: Cambridge University Press, 1988.

—*Women and the Genesis of Christianity*. Cambridge: Cambridge University Press, 1990.

Wohlgemut, Joel R. 'Entrusted Money (Matthew 25:14-28).' In *Jesus and his Parables: Interpreting the Parable of Jesus Today*. Edited by V. George Shillington, 103–20. Edinburgh: T & T Clark, 1997.

Yamaguchi, Satoko. *Mary and Martha: Women in the World of Jesus*. Maryknoll, NY: Orbis Books, 2002.

Yee, Gale A. 'The Author/Text/Reader and Power: Suggestions for a

Critical Framework for Biblical Studies.' In *Reading from this Place: Volume 1, Social Location and Biblical Interpretation in the United States*. Edited by Fernando F. Segovia and Mary Ann Tolbert, 109–18. Minneapolis, MN: Fortress Press, 1995.

York, John O. *The Last Shall Be First: The Rhetoric of Reversal in Luke*. JSNTSup 46. Sheffield: JSOT Press, 1991.

Young, Frances. 'Allegory and the Ethics of Reading.' In *The Open Text: New Directions for Biblical Studies*. Edited by Frances Watson, 103–20. London: SCM Press, 1993.

Young, Iris Marion. *Justice and the Politics of Difference*. Princeton, NJ: Princeton University Press, 1990.

Zerwick, M. 'Die Parabel vom Thronanwärter.' *Bib* 40 (1959): 654–74.

INDEX OF REFERENCES

INDEX OF AUTHORS

Taking Away the Pound